Creating Internet Entertainment

JEANNIE NOVAK
PETE MARKIEWICZ

WILEY COMPUTER PUBLISHING

JOHN WILEY & SONS, INC.
New York • Chichester • Brisbane • Toronto • Singapore • Weinheim

Executive Publisher: Katherine Schowalter
Editor: Philip Sutherland
Managing Editor: Mark Hayden
Electronic Products, Associate Editor: Mike Green
Text Design & Composition: Pronto Design & Production, Inc.

This text is printed on acid-free paper.

Published by John Wiley & Sons, Inc.

Library of Congress Cataloging-in-Publication Data:

Printed in the United States of America ISBN 0-471-16073-3

10 9 8 7 6 5 4 3 2 1

Contents

Introduction

Intertainment—or entertainment created and produced for the Internet and the ever-expanding World Wide Web—is the focus of this book. While the Internet has become the dominant medium for interactive communication in business and education, its development as a new entertainment medium is only just beginning. Since most existing literature does not address the entertainment industry's particular interests, we have created a guide specifically for those of you who are interested in creating Web-based entertainment — whether you're an independent artist or musician, game designer, industry executive, Web developer, Internet consultant, stage performer, film director, agent, media buff, or even nonentertainment company executives who want to make their Internet sites more entertaining.

The book grew out of our longtime involvement (in Internet terms) with Web-based entertainment. Since 1994, the Kaleidospace® Web site (http://kspace.com) has provided multimedia-based samples, reviews, interviews, biographical information, and product ordering for hundreds of independent artists, musicians, filmmakers, writers, performers, and software developers. Since Kspace was launched, Internet-based entertainment has grown from a novelty to the cutting edge of Internet design and audience participation. More than any other place, Intertainment sites are venues for experimenting with true interactiviy between content providers and audience, real-time sound and video delivery, and even connections to real-world events. Despite this, most books on the subject have addressed getting connected to the Internet or have provided a travelogue of *cool sites*. In contrast, this book specifically addresses *Intertainment* as a new entertainment medium and provides both practical and theoretical guidelines for creating, maintaining, and enjoying Web-based entertainment content. The text assumes some basic knowledge of the Internet and the World Wide Web; if you are completely new to the medium, you may want to check out Paul Gilster's *The New Internet Navigator*.

Outline of the Book

The overall text has been divided into five main sections, each containing three chapters. Part I covers how the Internet has become a new entertainment medium. Chapter 1 presents the features of the Internet that make it the hottest area of interactive entertainment, by illustrating selected cutting-edge entertainment sites, demonstrating how Intertainment sites differ from traditional entertainment, and showing why individuals at all levels of the entertainment industry can benefit from getting involved. In Chapter 2 the nature of Internet-based entertainment as it is currently experienced by the millions of people exploring the Web is described. Their hunter-gatherer approach to content is compared with audience behavior in more traditional media and the concept of consumers (*prosumers*) who produce entertainment as well as consume it is introduced. Chapter 3 presents content providers—ranging from individual artists and musicians to large media organizations—as pioneers of a new Renaissance of entertainment. The chapter illustrates the great diversity of entertainment that has steadily developed since the emergence of the World Wide Web in 1993 and discusses the features that have contributed to a startling array of new content providers running over half a million Web sites.

Part II is structured as a handbook for constructing entertainment-oriented Web sites. Chapter 4 is a guide to the development of appropriate concepts and strategies for entertainment Web sites. Its main purpose is to help content providers design the type of Web site that is appropriate to their project. Chapter 5 concentrates on the specific software, hardware, and human resources needed to create effective Web sites, and shows how to develop an Internet production studio and put together a Web development team. In Chapter 6 the actual development—of the site—including media, content, navigation, and artistic nuances essential to creating a popular site is discussed.

The focus of Part III is on long-term solutions to maintaining successful Internet entertainment sites and creating a steady following for them. Chapter 7 contains details on how to increase awareness of a newly-created Intertainment site by identifying its audience and using online and offline promotion methods to reach them. In Chapter 8 the radically different methods used to achieve brand loyalty on the Internet are presented. Since the Internet allows the audience to interact with itself as well as with the content provider, it is necessary to go beyond the traditional definition of an audience and build a community. Both site maintenance and interactive enhancements enabling virtual community-building are considered. Chapter 9 deals with the diverse ways in which Intertainment can make money for its providers. The current tension between user subscriptions versus paid advertising is explored and the possible impact of micro-payments on entertainment-oriented Web sites is discussed.

Part IV presents an overview of the enormous array of entertainment and entertainment-related resources already available on the Internet. In Chapter 10 the rising participation of traditional entertainment on the

Internet is illustrated. Also discussed is how artist representatives such as agents, managers, and publicists are using the medium to further their own work. Chapter 11 is a consideration of the Web's tranformation of recreational activities, such as sports and games, into entertainment media in their own right. The Internet has increased the visibility for many kinds of recreational entertainment and is expanding their audience in new and often interesting ways. Chapter 12 focuses on the exciting, new Internet-specific forms of entertainment under development. While still at an early stage, new Intertainment such as virtual worlds, online chat, episodic Web "soaps", and sites combining advertising with entertainment promise to be a major force on the Web.

Part V is concerned with how to prepare for long-term changes the Internet may bring to entertainment due to its decentralized structure, unique two-way interaction, and vast global reach. Chapter 13 concentrates on legal issues such as intellectual property, censorship, and privacy. Chapter 14 discusses how Intertainment fits into the current culture of the Internet: its main purpose is to show that the Internet is not only a delivery medium, but also a true, interactive community. Chapter 15 concentrates on the hardware, software, and media content changes which will have decisive effects on the future of Intertainment. Attention is paid to the increasing use of real-time audio and video, the long-term integration of information and entertainment on the Internet, and the enabling effect of media convergence on new content providers.

How to Use This Book

The topic of Internet-based entertainment is already so large that certain readers may benefit from initially concentrating on particular sections of the text. If you're an individual artist or entertainer, or a representative from an entertainment company that will be providing original content, it is probably best to read all the sections in this book—since it is likely you will be directly involved in designing and programming your own presence on the web. Part II and Part III are both practical guides for initial creation and subsequent maintenance of entertainment sites. If your primarly interest is in the mechanics of setting up Web-based entertainment sites on the Internet for others, be sure to read Part II carefully. Individuals who will manage, but not directly create Web sites should pay particular attention to Part III. Part IV has more of a *general interest* focus, since it concentrates on what's happening on the Internet with regard to traditional, recreational, and completely new Intertainment. Media buffs and curious readers will want to check out this area first; its many illustrations will provide a quick peek at what's happening online. Part I and Part V are more theoretical sections. Researchers interested in the general features of Intertainment and in audience and content provider demographics may want to pay particular attention to Part I; those interested in future trends may want to start with Part V.

Since discussing the Internet often requires the use of technical terms, words in italic throughout the text are defined in the Glossary. A complete list of software included on the accompanying CD-ROM is also listed at the end of this book. Due to the rapid pace of change for all things Internet, updates to the book's information (particularly links to relevant Web sites) will also be available through our Web site at the following URL:

http://kspace.com/intertainment

We hope this book will inspire you to build your own "Intertainment empire." Just as in the 1890s and 1940s, respectively,—the film and television industries were in their infancy, we are standing on the threshold of a new revolution in entertainment today!

Jeannie Novak
jeannie@kspace.com

Pete Markiewicz
pete@kspace.com

PART I

THE INTERTAINMENT REVOLUTION

http://kspace.com/intertainment

CHAPTER 1

WHAT IS ENTERTAINMENT?

Sometimes the world is stood on its head. Such was the case of the touted *Information Superhighway* announced with much fanfare by the Clinton administration. After the original announcement in early 1994, numerous articles and discussions centered on who would build the broadband network and how soon set-top boxes enabling interactive TV could reach American households. Debates ranged over the relative roles of cable and telephone companies, who could best create interactive content, and the technical problems with implementing large-scale, video-on-demand networks.

> ***"Cute," as said by an angry marketing representative at an Internet convention, upon hearing of the Internet's low-cost distribution potential (June 1994).***

But somehow, the future happened differently. Instead of the superhighway, we have the Internet—the proverbial "dark horse" of the interactive age. Contrary to almost everyone's expectations, the Internet *is* the first generation of the anticipated superhighway. While one media giant after another scales back its plans for broadband service, the Internet continues to add millions of new users every few months while steadily acquiring more sophisticated audio and video components. As the Internet's growth continues, it has become clear that part of its future—in addition to science, education, and business—lies in true, interactive entertainment.

The computer and telecommunications industries weren't the only ones that were caught by surprise. Interestingly, the traditional entertainment industry was not involved in creating the initial burst of Internet-based entertainment, beginning in 1994 (see Figure 1.1). Instead, smaller independents such as our own company (Kaleidospace), used the Internet to

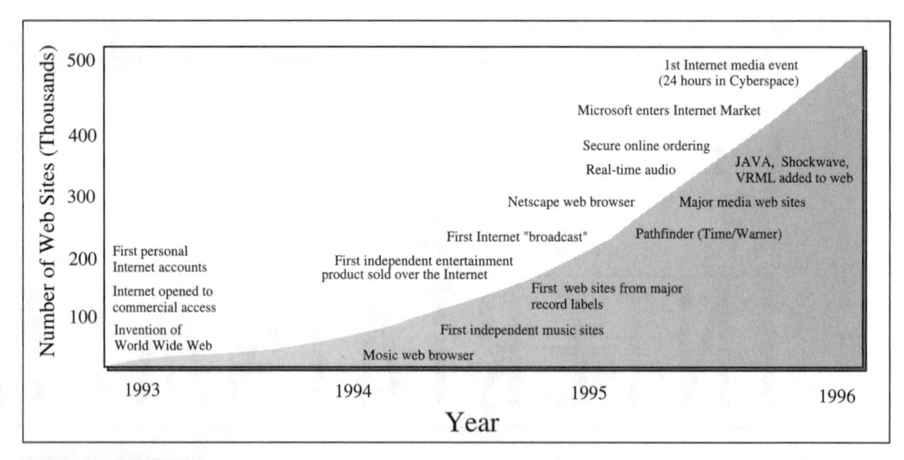

FIGURE 1.1 Phases in development of Intertainment and general Internet growth, 1993-1996.

define new modes of entertainment as well as to create novel channels for distribution of existing entertainment. Many of these *pioneering* companies did not have a pre-existing entertainment presence in the offline—or physical—world. They were often created specifically as virtual corporations. Although many larger media companies began to provide entertainment on the Internet during the second phase of Intertainment development (beginning late in 1995), the atmosphere remains firmly independent. Unlike the offline world—where a small group of media giants deliver their content to a largely passive audience—millions of *surfers*, from individuals and small companies to larger media organizations, *actively* explore the Internet's 500,000 Web sites. Frequently, the hottest entertainment on the Internet is produced by companies outside the traditional industry. Unlike any other medium today, the Internet offers individuals and companies at all levels the chance to create the next great entertainment medium.

> ***It seems that the Internet is at this time where television was perhaps in the early 1950s—and hopefully the Internet can avoid the errors that television and radio made as access to airplay/creative work in those fields was quickly corrupted.***
>
> —ROB DAME, JAZZ GUITARIST
> http://kspace.com/dame

This book is designed for everyone who would like to join the emerging Internet entertainment industry. You should be able to benefit from it whether you are a performer, agent, production company, non-entertainment company seeking to make yourself entertaining, talent scout, publicist, songwriter, technician, author, CD-ROM developer, marketer, animator, unsigned band, art gallery, talk show host, or large media company executive. The book is not a travelogue or list of *cool sites* to visit and is not designed as a general introduction to the whole of the Internet. Your local bookstore will carry *plenty* of books on these subjects. The purpose of this book is fundamentally different, since it focuses on the emergence of a new form of entertainment. It is a practical guide to creating, maintaining, expanding, and promoting your own Intertainment. It also contains an analysis of the impact of this new medium on other forms of entertainment and on sociopolitical, legal, and technological developments.

As a new medium, the Internet poses both opportunity and challenge to everyone who lists *entertainment* as a profession. Opportunity exists because the Internet is inexpensive, global, decentralized, and has low entry costs. These features allow virtually anyone—whether an individual or a major corporation—to create new and exciting forms of entertainment and promote this entertainment content online. The two-way interactivity—a basic feature of all Internet communication—allows development of novel entertainment combining the best of current media with the control and intimacy of a phone conversation.

These very same features will lead to dramatic changes in current entertainment. Since the rise of mass media in the late 1800s, entertainers have become accustomed to delivering a heavily produced, packaged, and finished product to millions of unseen consumers. The Internet is changing this. In a medium where every member of the audience can easily become an entertainment provider, the current entertainment industry must find new ways to create, promote, and distribute its products as it makes the transition to the world of Intertainment. Certain cherished features of entertainment today—such as superstars, megaconcerts, and even ad-supported programming—may cease to exist in their present form. On the other hand, small-scale entertainment venues such as music clubs, theater, coffeehouses, and retail stores hosting in-store appearances will be sustained and acquire a global importance through the virtual world of the Internet. The change will extend to areas not currently concerned with entertainment. As work, education, and play begin to run through the same network, they will increasingly become one and the same—a sort of *info-edutainment* experience.

> ***Within the area of commerce through the Internet, there is a*** **special** ***case—those professions that cannot only*** **talk about** ***their product on the Internet but can also offer the casual browser an*** **actual sample** ***of their product. This allows for instant gratification of anything desirable that you happen to sample!***
>
> IASOS, NEW AGE MUSICIAN
> http://kspace.com/iasos

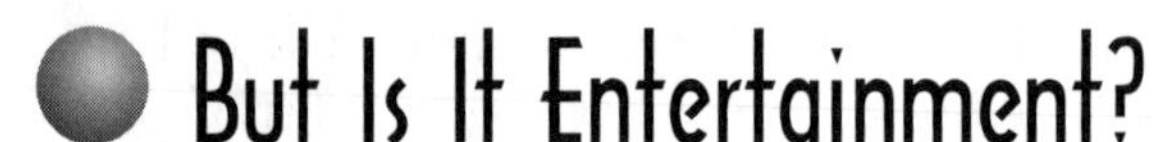

But Is It Entertainment?

Of course, anyone who has struggled with a modem and PC may question the Internet's entertainment value. (The Internet doesn't seem like entertainment to everyone.) Connecting to the Internet is still a daunting task and the majority of people in the United States have never used it. At the beginning of 1996, only about one third of households with personal computers were online—less than 15 percent of the total population. In contrast to radio, 30 seconds of Internet music may require up to 10 minutes of *download* time before it can be heard. A single color picture may take several seconds to be drawn onscreen. There are no top shows or favored time slots. There are no Internet-specific stars that are identified by the public at large. Magazines covering the Internet, despite their snazzy graphics and attitude, bear little resemblance to *Entertainment Weekly* or *People*. But in 1995, the number of new users on the Internet's World Wide Web jumped from a few hundred thousand to 10 million.

> ***Once people are educated on the Internet, how to use it, and participate in it as a community, entertainment becomes a natural application.***
>
> SKY DAYTON, FOUNDER AND CHAIRMAN, EARTHLINK NETWORK, INC.
> http://www.earthlink.net

Of course, many of these new users got online for business or educational reasons. However, in a 1995 poll of these Internet users conducted as part of a survey by Neilsen and CommerceNet, over 60 percent listed entertainment as their primary online pastime. Despite the delays in

Type of Site	Development	Yearly Budget
Individual Home Page	>$100	$500
Small Site (e.g., professional service ad)	$ 1,000	$ 1,000
Small Independent Entertainment Site	$ 5,000	$ 50,000
Site with extensive user input/interactivity	$ 20,000	$ 50,000
Large Independent Site	$150,000	$200,000
Major In-house site	$500,000	$1-2 million
Large Media Site (multiple departments)	$10 million	$20 million

FIGURE 1.2 Cost of creating entertainment on the Web.

downloading information over the Web and the difficulty of setting up an Internet-ready computer, the majority of respondents indicated they were already spending over five hours online every week—even with competition from television, books, and radio. In online households, equal time is devoted to video rentals and the Internet. A small but significant fraction of users already indicate that they have ceased to watch television entirely and use the Internet as the *sole source* of their entertainment. The costs for creating entertainment on the Web are shown in Figure 1.2.

> ***The rapid growth of the Net has produced such a concentration of intense activity, in such a brief time span, that Internet 'dog years' aren't even funny anymore. Being in the Net zone actually distorts our time sense (and I'm not sure whether that's going to end up being for good or for ill), but stuff that happened less than a year ago* feels *like the distant past.***
>
> —Jeannine Parker, Director, National Information Infrastructure Awards; Principal, Magnitude Associates; Executive Board, International Interactive Communications Society (IICS); Board of Directors, Internet Developers Association (IDA)
> http://www.gii-awards.com

Despite its tremendous growth, the Internet is still sometimes written off as a fad comparable to the CB radio craze of the 1970s. After all, sound quality is low and video is small and jerky. To understand why Internet-based entertainment is here to stay, it is essential to realize that its appeal does not depend on its ability to duplicate radio, television, or the intimate feel of a live performance. The strength of the Internet lies in two main areas: its ability to combine existing media into new forms and to replace the one-to-many model of current mass media with an interactive many-to-many system.

Early in 1995, executives of a major radio station in the Los Angeles area became interested in establishing an Internet presence. When presenting their concepts for *virtual radio*, they specificially indicated that they wanted no feedback via email from users. Little interest was shown in the graphical features of the Web; instead, the focus was on broadcasting the station's existing content without modification. The radio station personnel saw the Internet solely in terms of its ability to act like a radio and were uninterested in exploring the new possibilities open to them. Needless to say, their Internet site was small, poorly visited, and far less successful than other virtual radio stations utilizing the Internet's unique features.

How the Web Delivers Entertainment

Figure 1.3 illustrates the unique features of Internet-based entertainment through a Web site displayed by the standard Internet Web *browser*, Netscape. A row of buttons are visible across the top of the screen. These mouse-clickable buttons provide the ability to *page* back and forth through a Web site as if it were an electronic book, as well as saving or printing onscreen content. This is an immediate departure from current media; the complete content of any Web site can be viewed 24 hours a day in any order and at any time. Web sites do not compete for "time slots," and as a consequence each has the same potential chance for attracting an audience.

Immediately beneath the buttons, a text field displays the Internet address of the current Web site, referred to as the *URL (Uniform Resource*

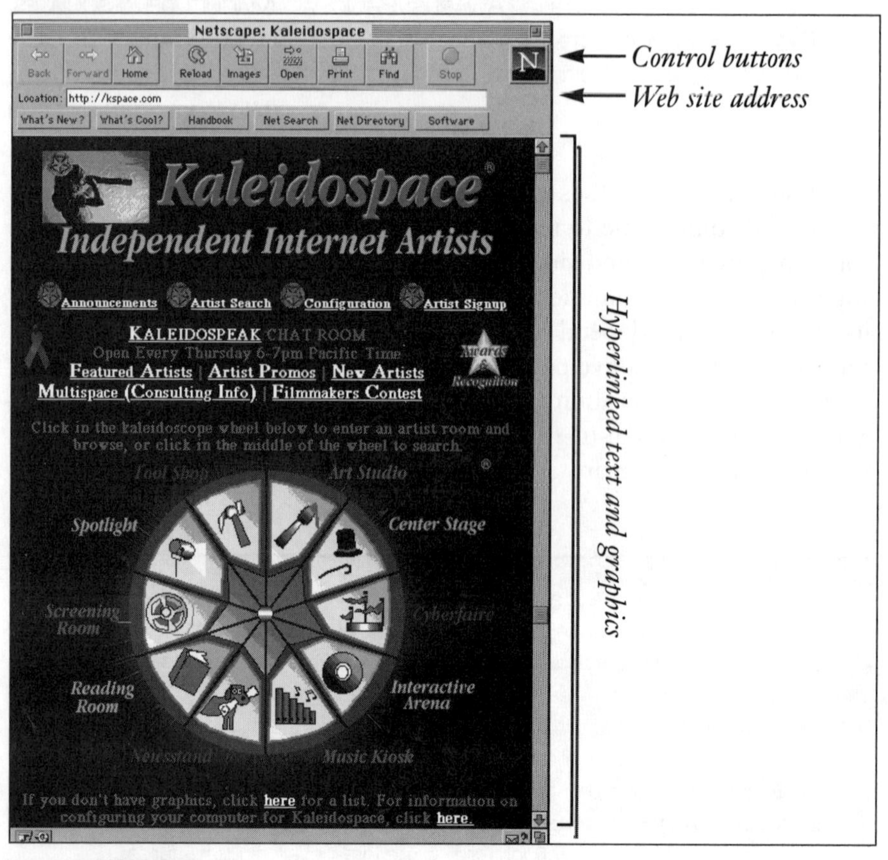

FIGURE 1.3 Netscape browser window.

Locator). If one thinks of URLs as rough equivalents of channels, the Internet has as many channels as there are Web sites—which was over *half a million* in June 1996. Remember the 500-channel promises of a few years ago? On the Internet, *every single computer* is potentially a URL-type channel. A significant percentage of the *entire* population of the Internet already has its own *home pages* on the Web, each of which can be accessed by unique URLs.

Underneath the row of buttons and URL reference, Netscape displays the Web page that has been accessed by the user. In Figure 1.3, Netscape is displaying the home page of Kaleidospace (http://kspace.com). Web pages contain text, graphics, audio clips, video clips, and downloadable programs. These multimedia components are all integrated into what might be described as a "living" desktop publishing document. (Although the desktop publishing analogy does not reflect the open system and interactivity of the Internet, it might be easier for you to initially understand how the software works by comparing it to software you might currently use on your home PC.)

Hyperlinks and User Control

While the content of a Web page bears similarities to other interactive media such as CD-ROMs, the *hyperlinks* indicated in Figure 1.3 form an additional and extremely powerful feature. By design, the Web is inherently "open"; the multimedia content is not confined to a single disk or computer, but instead is scattered throughout the Internet. Each content element is connected by a hyperlink which appears as a highlighted text or outlined graphical element onscreen. Each hyperlink is actually a connection to another Web page or file (such as an audio or video clip). By clicking on the hyperlink, you will either navigate through the local Web site (by accessing new pages) or cause some other action to occur while remaining on the page (such as downloading audio or video clips). The act of clicking on different areas becomes a form of travel or navigation or personal choice (e.g., having control over which audio clip you want to hear). Not only can you navigate through the site, but you can also travel through the whole Web (known as *surfing*) by clicking on hyperlinks. Due to the nonlocal nature of Internet communication, a Web page on a particular site easily links to *any other page on any other site* using this mechanism of clicking on hyperlinks, which sometimes gives the feeling of jumping or hopping. To illustrate the power this provides, consider that each page from a given Web site could be stored on different computers in different countries—with *no effect* on the user's experience.

Hyperlinks also provide the extreme interactivity characteristic of the Internet; selecting one may link the visitor to an online *chat* session, a form for sending email, or one of the many contests and opinion polls common to Web sites. While the audience may "talk back" to newspapers, radio, television, and other media, the Web is the first medium where they also talk to each other and contribute to the entertainment content on the site itself.

Examples of Intertainment

The hottest sites on the Internet fuse the Web's features into new, unique entertainment packages unequaled in any other medium. The following examples provide an overview of the varied forms of entertainment already available on the Internet. The sites and the categories of entertainment they represent are discussed in greater detail in Part IV.

The Spot

At The Spot (Figure 1.4), an ongoing narrative soap opera is supplemented by glimpses into the personalities of the characters at many lev-

FIGURE 1.4 The Spot (http://www.thespot.com).

els, including subjective diaries, third-person biographies, and commentaries from the other characters' points-of-view. Visitors don't watch a "show;" instead, they explore the results of each day at The Spot at their own speed, selecting items of interest to build their understanding. The Spot has attracted an enormous audience, as a result, dozens of other "episodic" Web sites are in the works. The core Web site is already surrounded by a host of related sites offering additional fan discussions, a place for comments that were rejected by The Spot itself, fan sites for individual characters, and a behind-the-scenes site.

TV Net

At TV Net (Figure 1.5), the main attraction is not a TV show. Visitors use this Web site to read the latest TV listings from all over the world and—more importantly—talk to each other. Through a series of chat rooms, opinion polls, contests, and bulletin boards, they demonstrate that talking to each other about TV is just as entertaining as TV itself. TV Net is more of a TV community than a show or resource and it's bound together in a way that television itself could never duplicate. An

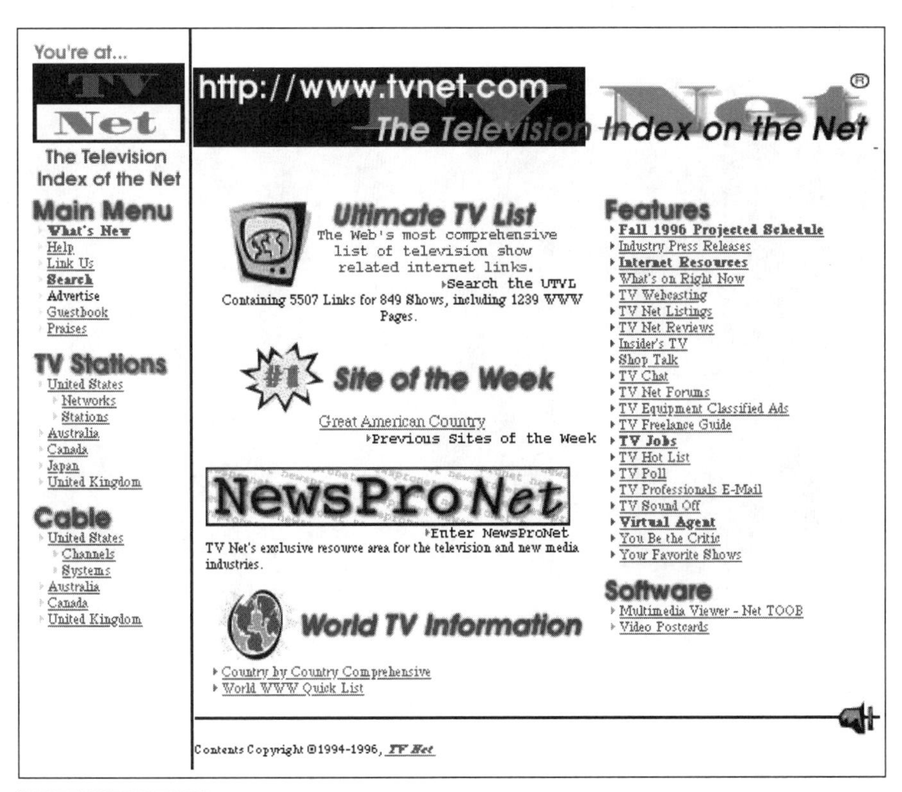

FIGURE 1.5 TV Net (http://tvnet.com).

independent startup, TV Net has enormous traffic compared to many established media sites.

Radio HK

Radio HK (Figure 1.6), provides a point of departure for a broadcast medium like radio to expand into a many-to-many paradigm. Radio HK draws its playlist from hundreds of independent musicians from around the world and allows their music to play in the background while the visitor explores other Web sites. But the key feature of Radio HK is a user-generated playlist which draws from a larger pool of bands. Instead of deciding which bands the users will like, Radio HK allows them to choose their own from a large list. In this single innovation, Radio HK has challenged the primacy of playlists and increased the exposure of independent music.

Waxweb

Waxweb (Figure 1.7), is a ground-breaking site which converts David Blair's independent film feature, *WAX or the discovery of television among the bees*, into interactive hypermedia. According to Blair, it provides a "...scalable 'virtual movie theater,' where the 30 hour version of the film can be

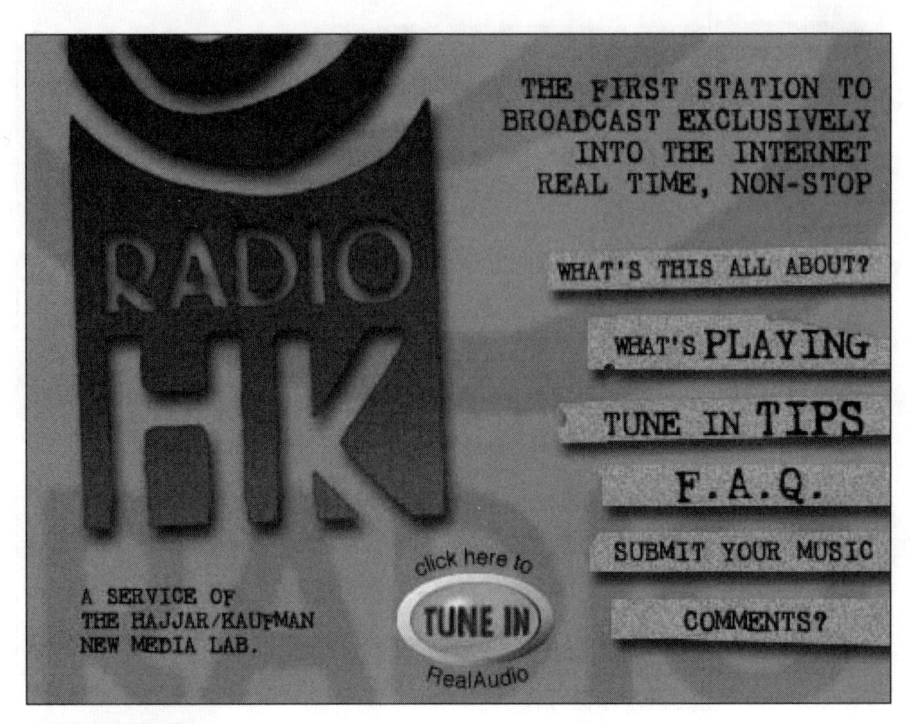

FIGURE 1.6 Radio HK (http://radiohk.com/radio).

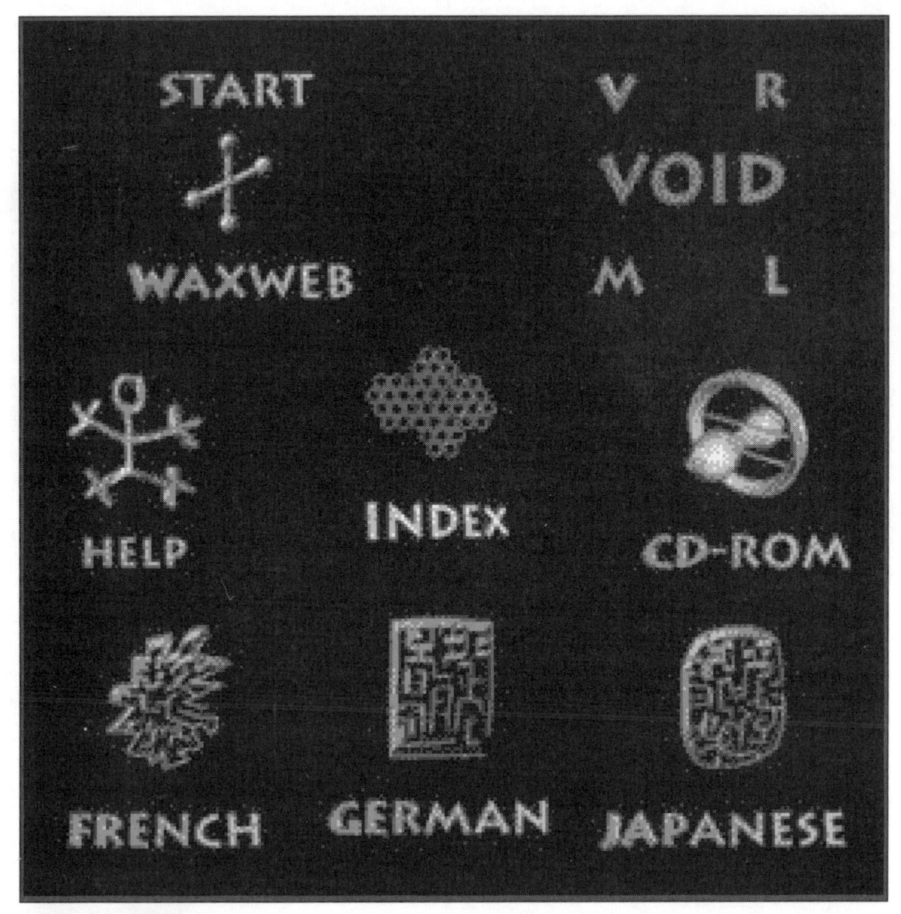

FIGURE 1.7 Waxweb (http://bug.village.virginia.edu).

browsed or roared through, while people meet at the same time, maybe remake the movie a bit, or work on their own movie." Waxweb is distingushed by its enormous size and an *authoring interface* that allows Waxweb visitors to collaboratively add to the story. It showcases the transformation of film from a linear narrative to a user-controlled adventure.

Web-a-Sketch

Web-a-Sketch (Figure 1.8), combines the interactive features of the Web with the notion of showcasing art never seen outside of the Internet. Anyone can make an original Web-a-Sketch at this site and have the work displayed in the site's gallery. The site also runs a weekly contest and displays the current winner on the home page. It converts a medium most people expect to view passively into fun, interactive entertainment.

FIGURE 1.8 Web-a-Sketch (http://digitalstuff.com/web-a-sketch).

Mission: Impossible

The site for Paramount's film, *Mission: Impossible* (Figure 1.9), is an example of a popular form of Intertainment which expands a promotion for a movie into an interactive game. Besides the usual information on the plot, actors, and production, visitors are invited to join in a series of interactive games running across multiple Web Sites. The integration of the games into the film promotion converts simple advertising into interactive entertainment in its own right and points the way to a future where the theater release of a film is only part of the total entertainment experience.

JetPack

JetPack (Figure 1.10), is one of the top virtual magazines on the Web and has consistently provided a cutting-edge source of music, book and other reviews, articles, and a general style geared to an audience of sophisticated Net surfers. Much more than a conventional magazine copied to the Web, JetPack has successfully defined a niche for electronic publishing.

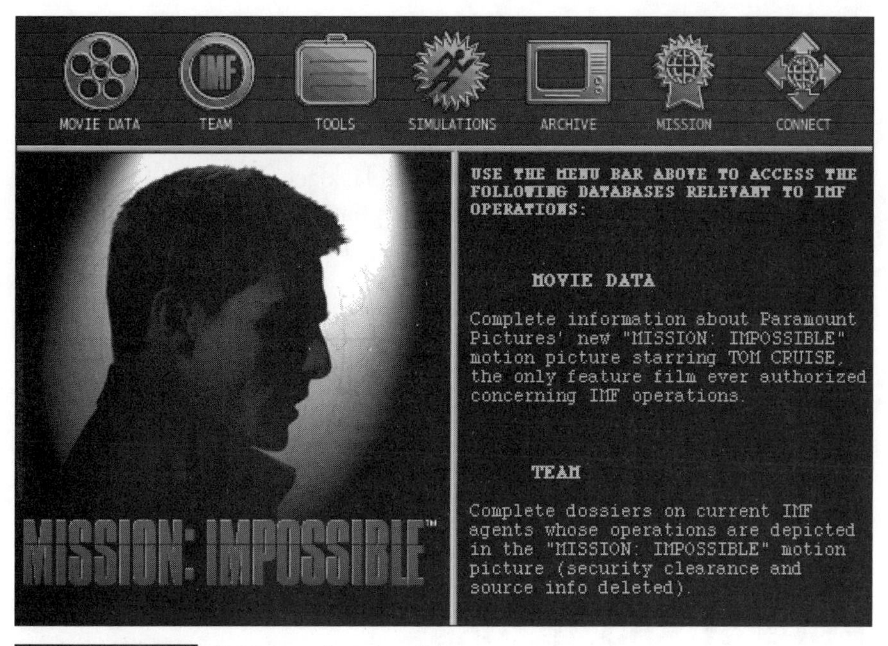

FIGURE 1.9 *Mission: Impossible* (http://www.missionimpossible.com).

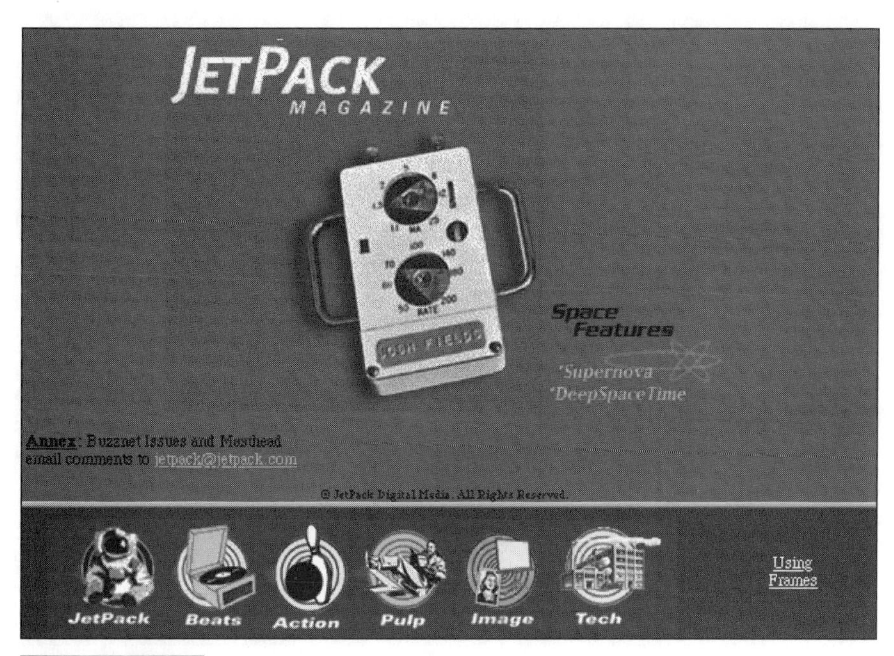

FIGURE 1.10 JetPack (http://jetpack.com).

Virtual Vegas

Virtual Vegas (Figure 1.11), has "raised the stakes" for Internet entertainment by creating a Web site devoted to gambling. While lounge lizards may prefer hanging out in the chat rooms, the real action is offered by various games: roulette, poker, slots, and blackjack. For now, Virtual Vegas issues equally virtual money, but it points to a future where worldwide, online betting will challenge industry and government.

The Troubadour

The Troubadour site (Figure 1.12) demonstrates the many-to-many features of Internet-based entertainment. A popular club in Los Angeles, The Troubadour has created a Web site where visitors can tune into nightly broadcasts directly from its performance stage. Similar *venue* Web sites are springing up worldwide; in the near future, most performance spaces will have a virtual Internet audience in addition to the live one. Like the live audience, the virtual audience will be able to communicate with each other as well as the performer.

ESPNet SportsZone

ESPNet SportsZone (Figure 1.13), has already created a new way for sports fans to keep informed. It is a two-tiered Web site, which means that part of the site requires membership or advanced payment to enter.

FIGURE 1.11 Virtual Vegas (http://virtualvegas.com).

FIGURE 1.12 The Troubadour (http://troubadour).

Up-to-the-minute scores are available from the site, as well as news, editorials, contests, and opinion polls. For more sophisticated reports and results, visitors can have an initial free trial subscription to the *premium* part of the site. Rates are $4.95 per month or $39.95 per year after the free trial runs out. The enormous success of this site has demonstrated that Web sites can be profitable to run.

Preview Vacations Online

Preview Vacations Online (Figure 1.14), is a travel site offering virtually all the services of real-world travel agencies. Visitors can begin with extensive travel previews including pictures, sound bytes, and video clips. Should they decide to on a package tour, they can make reservations immediately (including plane tickets). There are also several contests that anyone can join by submitting photos or an essay on "I need a vacation." The site

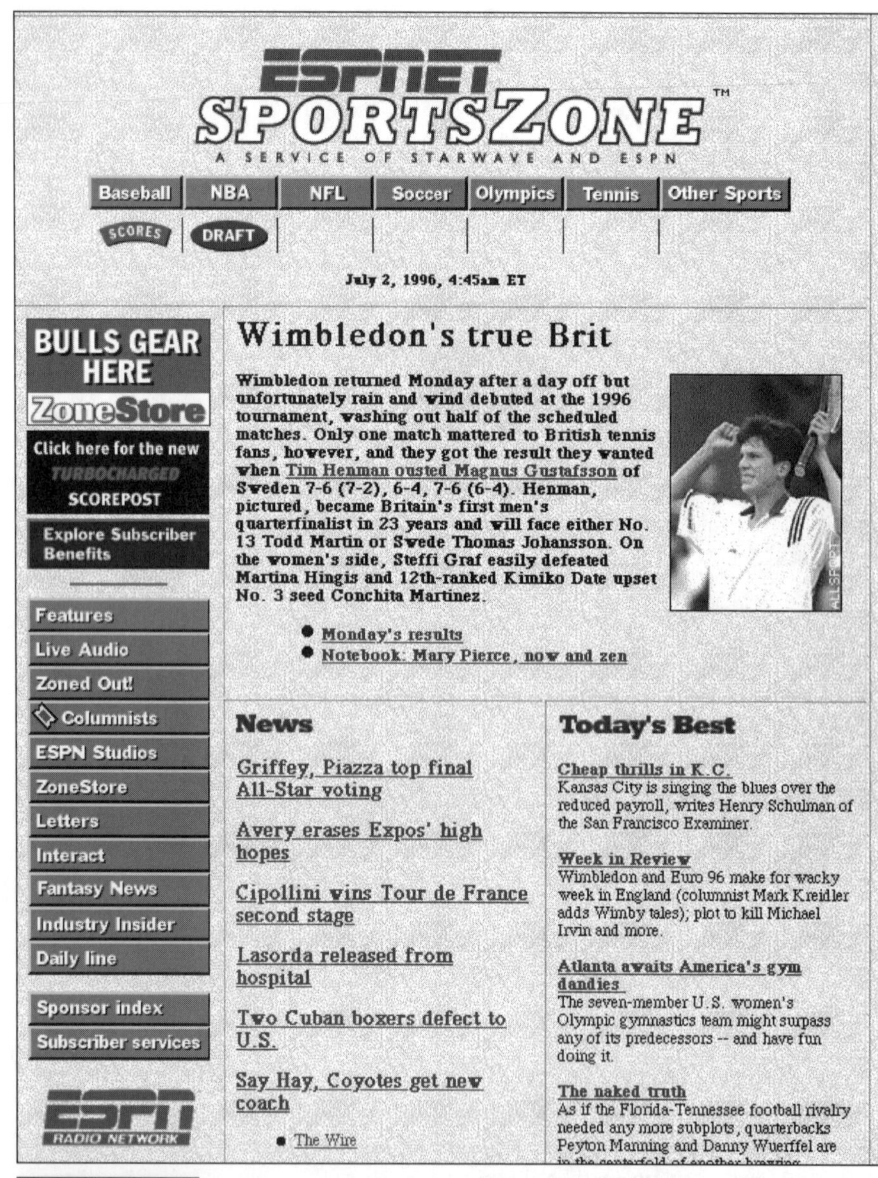

FIGURE 1.13 ESPNet SportsZone (http://espnet.sportszone.com).

holds the dual promise of scheduling real vacations and allowing less fortunate stay-at-homes to experience virtual travel to the same places.

Joe Boxer

The Joe Boxer site (Figure 1.15), has been a major success story in Internet-based entertainment. Despite the fact that the company is in the business of

FIGURE 1.14 Preview Vacations Online (http://vacations.com).

FIGURE 1.15 Joe Boxer site (http://www.joeboxer.com).

selling underwear, it has emerged as a major player in online entertainment. Unlike a simple advertisement, the Joe Boxer site converts its customers into "fans" with its entertainment-oriented content. Through innovative and modem-friendly graphics, humor, and features allowing extensive interactivity with its audience, it is helping to define a sophisticated fusion of business and entertainment than has been possible elsewhere.

Why Should You Get Involved?

You've probably seen the TV ads where a young high-metabolism nerd (who looks like he's in his own bedroom) is sputtering at such a rapid pace that only those familiar with Internet jargon can catch what he is saying—primarily that his company has "really fast T1s and 45-megabit connections." It might appear that the reason to get involved in the Internet is to join a "technological wonderland," not a world of art and entertainment. Given this image, why would anyone in entertainment want to get involved? The ad—or rather, the ad agency that created the TV spot—is misrepresenting the true situation. The reasons to get involved in the Internet have nothing to do with its technology per se, but with the creative potential this technology unleashes. Here are a few reasons which may help you decide to "take the plunge."

> ***The Internet is already well on its way to becoming a mass medium, but it will never support "mass media" in the sense most people attach to that phrase. However, in the aggregate, the myriad micro-audiences online will, in effect, create massive opportunities in both business and entertainment.***
>
> ***In fact, the net is already a major entertainment medium for a large proportion of its current users. Network TV share stats are down across the boards I understand. Where do you suppose these folks went?***

—Christopher Locke, Chairman and Chief Executive Officer, Entropy Gradient Reversals
http://www.panix.com/~clocke/EGR/index.html
and Program Director, Online Community Development, IBM
http://www.panix.com/~clocke/

Anticipating the Future

Even if the Internet does not become the "next television," so many of its features are certain to appear in future entertainment that it is the

While advertising for Internet service has begun to appear in the traditional mass media, many ad agencies have had trouble adjusting to the Internet. In a discussion hosted by Mecklermedia's *WebWeek Magazine* (January 1996), representatives of traditional ad agencies indicated that they were frequently the only people in their entire company who had seen the Internet. This bias may explain the unrealistic, skewed portrayal of the Internet in radio and TV ads supposedly designed to promote it. Currently, the best promotions come from independent agencies who have created their business alongside the Web.

proving ground of choice for new media projects. The Internet represents the endpoint for trends in other media including 500-channel systems, electronic commerce, phone and computer integration, and more. Working in the Internet will give any group a head start in new media.

Low Cost to Get Involved

"Rock-bottom" presences on the World Wide Web are available for as little as $50 per month. This means that it is practical for individual artists, musicians, and performers to showcase their words, pictures, audio, and video online. Typical entertainment sites created by independent production companies cost $10,000 to $100,000 to produce and maintain. In short, creating cutting-edge Internet entertainment costs a tiny fraction of that found in mass media. While production values for Internet entertainment will continue to rise, the financial entry level is likely to remain far below other media.

> ***When I first started doing TV Net a good friend thought I was crazy and said 'The Internet? Three words . . . 8-Track Tapes.***
>
> DAVID CRONSHAW, CREATOR TV NET
> http://tvnet.com

Large and Small Groups on Equal Ground

Low entry costs make it harder for companies to compete on the Internet simply by outspending their rivals. Once online, bandwidth and software limitations set an upper limit to the production values that can be attained through large budgets. The consequence of this is not surprising; the quality of the site frequently bears little connection to how much money was spent. Once again, the Internet tends to favor independent and "unsigned" entertainers. Consider that the number of music sites on the Internet run in the tens of thousands—most created by unsigned bands and songwriters. Many of these sites are very popular and a large number allow direct sales from the musician to the public without benefit of a major label.

Full Multimedia

As late as 1993, the Internet was a cryptic *text-only world* and multimedia comparable to CD-ROMs was unknown. But by early 1996, sophisticated Web *browsers* like Netscape were rapidly erasing the differences between CD-ROMs and network-based multimedia. With the appearance of hot programming languages like Java, it is now possible to provide sophisticated animation and interactivity through tiny programs downloaded over the Internet. Improvements in software promise to deliver real-time audio and video over existing consumer modems. While new media will continue to come through both channels, people cannot say they are working in interactive media and confine themselves to CD-ROMs alone. It is also important to understand that the software needed to create Web sites is completely different from CD-ROM development platforms. Knowledge of one does not prepare you for the other.

Open System

Web sites also differ from CD-ROMs in that they can be updated, enlarged, and modified at any time—and the changes will be visible to the entire audience. This means that the Web can support projects requiring frequent dynamic changes in content, including ongoing travelogues, magazine issues, and reports on the progress of film and TV productions. Because the Internet is an open system, it also allows the audience to witness and participate in live online events such as con-

> When we developed Kaleidospace as a Web site for independent art and music in early 1994, it was very difficult to describe what we were doing. At the time, interactivity was a synonym for CD-ROM—and the Web pages we displayed at the 1994 New Media Expo in Los Angeles were almost invariably interpreted as a CD-ROM system. The irony was further compounded by the reaction of the CD-ROM community. Early on, we worried that the Kspace Web site would be overrun with CD-ROMs and that it would be difficult to interest traditional artists and musicians. The exact opposite has occurred; while hundreds of musicians use Kspace, only a handful of CD-ROM developers promote their product through it. In the case of CD-ROM and the Web, the similarity of the media has blinded one to the potential of the other.

certs, where the audience can communicate with the performers and with the rest of the crowd.

Niche Marketing

To get a feel for the difference between the Internet and current mass entertainment, consider the following: The total number of cable and network television channels available in the United States is in the low hundreds. Since the total TV viewing audience is in the range of 150 million, there are approximately one million viewers per channel, if viewing were divided evenly. The huge potential audience per channel strictly enforces mass-marketing principles. Now consider the Internet. At the beginning of 1996, there were about 10 million active Web surfers worldwide moving between at least 100,000 distinct sites. In this case, the ratio of entertainment sites to their audience is a mere 100 to 1. The *narrowcasting* possible through the Internet has no counterpart in other media.

> ***The reward [of the Internet] has been to touch people that I would have never had the opportunity to reach.***
>
> —ANTHONY RAIN STAREZ, INTROSPECTIVE DARKISH POP MUSICIAN
> http://kspace.com/starez

Professional-to-professional Contacts

The two-way nature of the Internet makes it perfect for supporting a network of professional contacts. Organizations can easily support a global membership without creating an expensive proprietary network or paying for long-distance charges. Unsigned artists can create an online "portfolio" in their Web site for agencies, film producers, *A&R* representatives, managers, and other industry personnel to visit. The industry professional's life is also made easier by this arrangement. Artists avoid the time and expense of mailing hundreds of copies of their work and professionals can examine all the portfolios anonymously. As the Internet grows, it is certain that the mail-room syndrome of hundreds of tapes, videos, and portfolios will become a thing of the past.

> ***The Net has definitely served as a bridge between me and my fans. . . . However, I do not plan to use the Internet much for entertainment. It is a work tool.***
>
> —DAVID BRIN, AUTHOR OF *EARTH* AND OTHER SCIENCE FICTION NOVELS
> http://www-leland.stanford.edu/~blandon/brin. html and http://kspace.com/brin

Global Reach

By early 1996, the Web was available from approximately 140 countries; one-third of these have significant populations of users outside technical departments at universities. Any site on the Web affords the potential for immediate international promotion and distribution. As an example, it is possible for independent musicians to get radio play, foreign retail and wholesale distribution, and even arrange tours in other countries through the Internet. Entertainment providers everywhere can take advantage of low startup costs on the Web to develop an instant worldwide audience for their content. The global reach of the Internet also has the potential to make entertainment truly multicultural.

The Entertainment of Choice

The Internet entertainment industry is already the fastest-growing entertainment medium in history. Its ability to combine and enhance other media makes it the entertainment of choice for the next century. Its rapid expansion has already taken everyone by surprise—and there's no sign of any slowdown. One of the major features of its expansion is probably its most unique—the active role the audience or consumer has taken in the formation of entertainment content. The following chapter discusses the unique features of this active audience.

CHAPTER 2

SURFERS AND VISITORS:

The New *Active* Audience

As said by an anonymous audience member at a convention of entertainment industry professionals, "I don't know about that Internet. It would work a whole lot better if they had more people on it than Web sites."

Once the exclusive domain of programmers and researchers, the Internet today boasts a large diversified audience whose primary interest is entertainment. Understanding the features of this audience is critical to anyone planning to create Internet-based entertainment. This chapter focuses on Internet entertainment audience demographics; the differences between the Internet entertainment audience and its traditional media counterparts; and the unique blurring between producer and consumer which is characteristic of the Internet. Examining the features of this audience will enable you to understand the ways in which content providers create and distribute Internet-based entertainment in Chapter 3.

Due to the unique nature of the Internet, it is necessary to define the terms "surfer" and "visitor" used in the chapter title. *Surfers* refer to Internet users exploring a large number of Web sites and rapidly jumping from place to place after brief stops. *Visitors* comprise a subset of the Internet audience who carefully examine and experience the content of a particular Web site.

Internet Hunter-gatherers

One key to understanding the Internet audience is through analogy to cultural types. Though audience behavior on the Internet bears little resemblance to *watching* conventional entertainment, it is similar to the first phase of human culture—the *hunter-gatherer*. In the real world, hunter-gatherers are opportunistic explorers who wander through their environment collecting food and other materials as they travel through an extended *home range*. The architecture of the Internet allows virtual hunter-gatherers to "forage" for entertainment in a virtual environment. The lack of property in hunter-gatherer societies echoes to the Internet; as a whole, it is not owned or controlled by anyone. Traditional mass media entertainment, on the other hand, shows a division of labor in which small numbers of individuals produce entertainment for the many—which seems closer by analogy to agricultural or industrial societies.

If this description of Internet users seems too far-fetched, consider an era closer to home at the beginning of this century. During this time, the piano was the cornerstone of the home entertainment center. Entertainment involved participation of the family in sing-alongs and discussions often proceeded through lengthy letters penned to distant friends and relatives. The interactive environment of the Internet has more in common with this world than the recent mass entertainment culture.

Size and Growth of Audience

Statistics about the Internet continue their astonishing advance: The Internet has doubled in size approximately every seven months for the last several years. Of many summaries, the MIDS (Matrix Information and Directory Services, Inc.) Internet Demographic Survey, created by John S. Quarterman, provides some of the clearest information on recent growth. Located at http://www.mids.org, the MIDS divided the Internet on October 1995 into the following three categories—core Internet, consumer Internet, and matrix—which nest inside each other like puzzle boxes (see Figure 2.1).

Core Internet

This group of 17 million people is defined by its ability to send *and* receive information. Core Internet users have access to all Internet services, including the World Wide Web. They also may share information by creating their own Web sites or through other Internet-specific systems like FTP

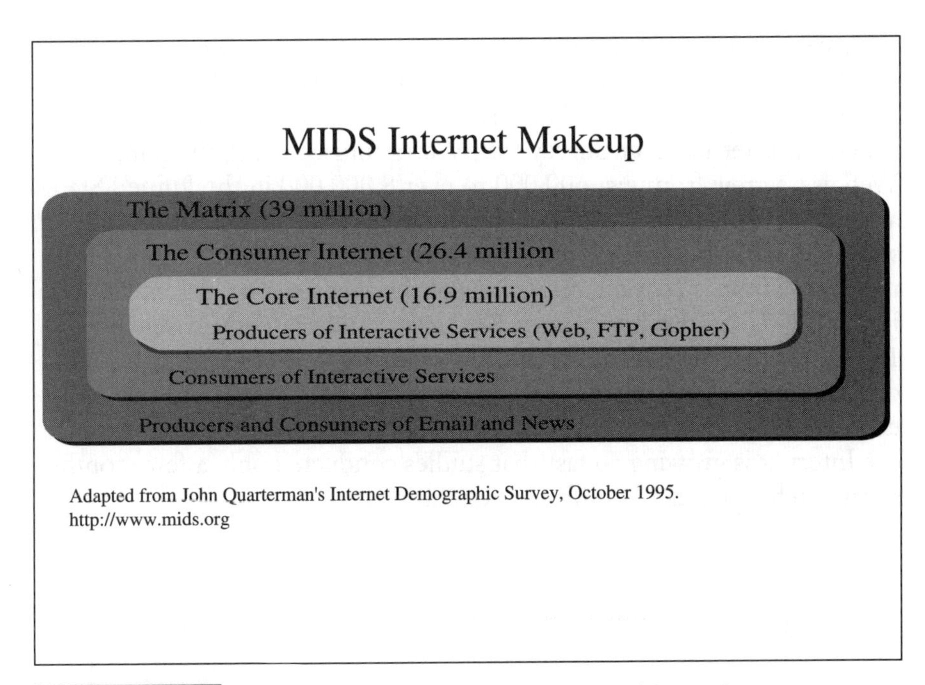

FIGURE 2.1 MIDS categories (http://www.mids.org).

and gopher. With the power to view, create, and distribute content, they form the *Internet elite*.

Consumer Internet

The core Internet overlaps with a larger group (26 million) that can access the total Internet (including the Web), but cannot *provide* information beyond exchange of email or *posting* to Web sites and discussion groups. The largest component of this group is members of online services such as America Online and CompuServe. While able to view entertainment content such as Web sites, they cannot create their own entertainment.

Matrix

Outside the familiar Internet, there is an outer ring that cannot access new services like the Web, but can send and receive email. These individuals (39 million) are normally connected through older non-Internet services like UUCP (UNIX To UNIX Copy Protocol) or through a local BBS (Bulletin Board System). While this audience has the ability to communicate over the Internet, it is largely restricted to *text-only* messages—excluding relatively newer features such as the Web.

Access to the Web portion of the Internet has increased at rates that put the Internet itself to shame. According to Network Wizards Internet Domain Survey, created by Mark Lottor (see Figure 2.2) and Find/SVP's American Internet User Survey (http://etrg.findsvp.com), the number of Web users grew from just 600,000 to over 8,000,000 in the United States alone in 1996. Other studies—including the Nielsen-CommerceNet study shown in Figure 2.3 (http://www.nielsenmedia.com), Donna Hoffman and Thomas Novak's re-analysis of the Nielsen data in Internet Use in the United States (http://www2000ogsm.vanderbilt.edu/baseline/1995.Internet.estimates.html), and the O'Reilly-Trish study (http://www.ora.com/survey/)—have indicated comparable figures for the Web audience. Often, differences between the studies are simply a matter of time; the Internet is growing so fast that studies conducted only a few months apart reach significantly different conclusions.

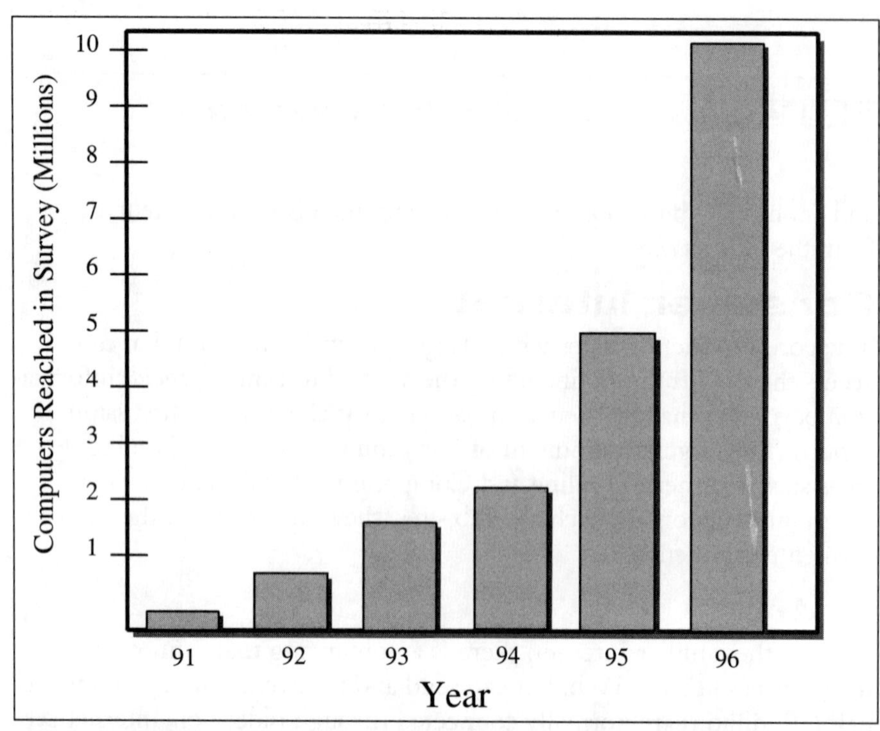

FIGURE 2.2 Net host growth (Network Wizards/Mark Lottor): *Internet World* (June 1996): 74—stats available at http://nw.com/zone/WWW/top.html. Produced by Network Wizards; data available on the Internet at http://www.nw.com/.

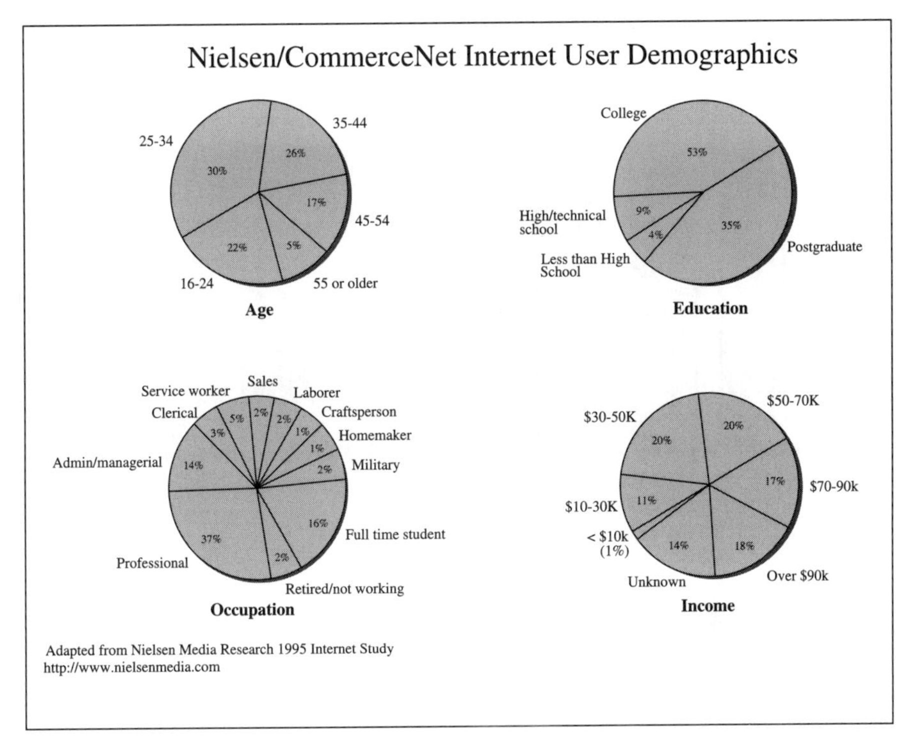

FIGURE 2.3 Nielsen-CommerceNet study.

Since the Internet is expected to grow at its current rate for the next 3 to 4 years, its audience may soon rival its mass-media counterparts. Access—hovering around 10 percent of the American population in 1996—may reach 30 percent by 1998 and up to 50 percent by 2000. The 50 percent figure is also supported by a study conducted through Carnegie-Mellon University, which distributed free Internet access to hundreds of randomly selected families in the Pittsburgh area. Even after six months, approximately 50 percent were still using the accounts. The results are significant since the test families frequently had never used computers prior to the study. Currently, the study is collecting long-term statistics on the subjects' preferences and behavior patterns on the Web.

 Methods of Access

The previous studies also indicated that almost 80 percent of all Internet users in 1995 were restricted to relatively slow 14.4 and 28.8 modem connections. (The majority of these connections come through online services, with America Online providing access to almost 30 percent of all

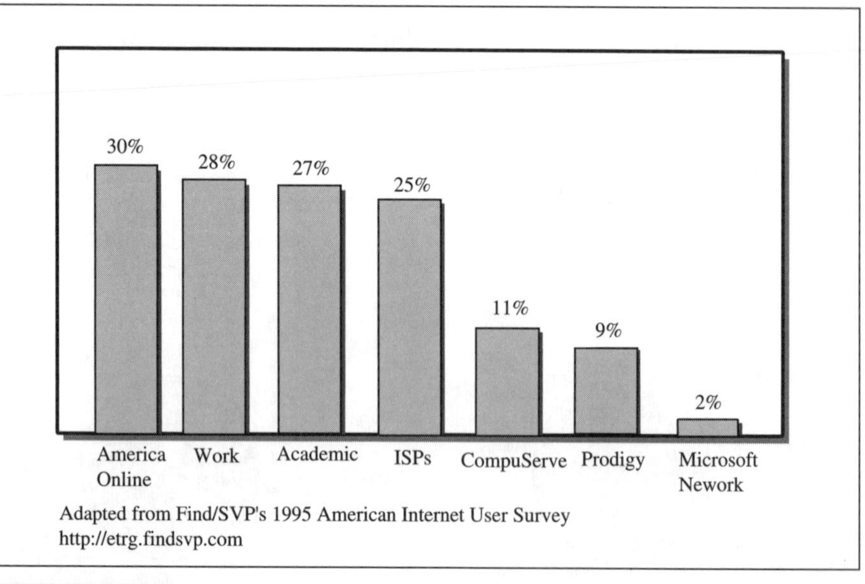

FIGURE 2.4 Services used to access the Internet (Find/SVP); (http://www.findsvp.com).

Web users.) At these speeds, a typical home page takes 20 to 30 seconds to appear onscreen and a 10-second, CD-quality uncompressed sound clip takes several minutes to download. Such constraints put great pressure on content providers to make highly efficient use of multimedia on their Web sites. Despite the slow rates, a study by the Software Publishers Association (http://www.spa.org) indicated that almost 80 percent of the total Internet audience was using the Web in preference to less media-intensive systems such as email. About 20 percent of the total audience has faster connections, typically 20 to 50 times as fast as modem users; this group is concentrated in business and university environments. The vast majority of slower speed connections has given rise to Web-specific, real-time audio and video software operating at low data transfer rates (Chapters 5 and 6) and technologies for delivering high-speed access (Chapter 15). Figure 2.4 shows some major services used to access the Internet.

 Demographics

Internet growth rates are normally determined by automatic programs which tabulate the number of computers connected to the system. To get more specific results—such as personality profiles—questionnaires taken through email and regular phone trials have been used by a variety of studies including the Find/SVP, MIDS, and Nielsen studies previously introduced. An excellent summary of these studies may be found at the CyberAtlas Web site (http://www.cyberatlas.com). Differing significantly from the general population, Internet users divide themselves into several well-defined groups.

> ***My Internet Space Ship is open to all kinds of people. On my Web voyage, the audience that is with me ranges from students to musicians, women and families, sci-fi fans and the techno-driven culture to new age and avant-garde followers, national and international. That's the real beauty of the Internet! Cosmic connection directly to the world.***
>
> —DR. FIORELLA TERENZI, ASTROPHYSICIST, MUSICIAN, AND AUTHOR
> http://www.fiorella.com and http://kspace.com/terenzi

Technically Sophisticated

Getting an Internet connection is not as simple as turning on a television set. Companies providing Internet links—Internet Service Providers (ISPs)—only provide software and do not make house calls to set up personal connections. As a result, the bulk of the Internet audience is made up of technically sophisticated individuals, sometimes referred to as Technologically Advanced First-Adopters (TAFs). TAFs comprise about 15 percent of the U.S. population, and have relatively high incomes averaging $65,000 per year. Compared to the entire population of personal computer users (of which they form less than half), TAFs are more likely to have systems incorporating the latest multimedia enhancements needed to effectively use the Web. According to a recent study by the Yankee Group (http://www.yankeegroup.com), fully two-thirds of TAFs are already online. TAFs are overwhelmingly professionals and typically access the Internet both at home and from work. While only a minority have purchased goods and/or services online, they have an interest in entertainment products, especially music.

Stanford Research Institute's VALS 2 (Values and Lifestyles) study (http://future.sri.com/VALS/ovalshome.html) of trends on the Web indicates that many Internet users fall into the *Actualizer* category. As a group, Actualizers largely overlap with TAFs. Actualizers are typically highly motivated people in positions of authority who are at the forefront of social innovation and accomplishment. The study indicates that the Internet as a medium is mixing the restlessness of the young with the sophistication of older and well-off individuals. Interestingly, the Internet is *not* for information junkies: The VALS *Fulfilled* category—characterized by people who value information and are generally comfortable with

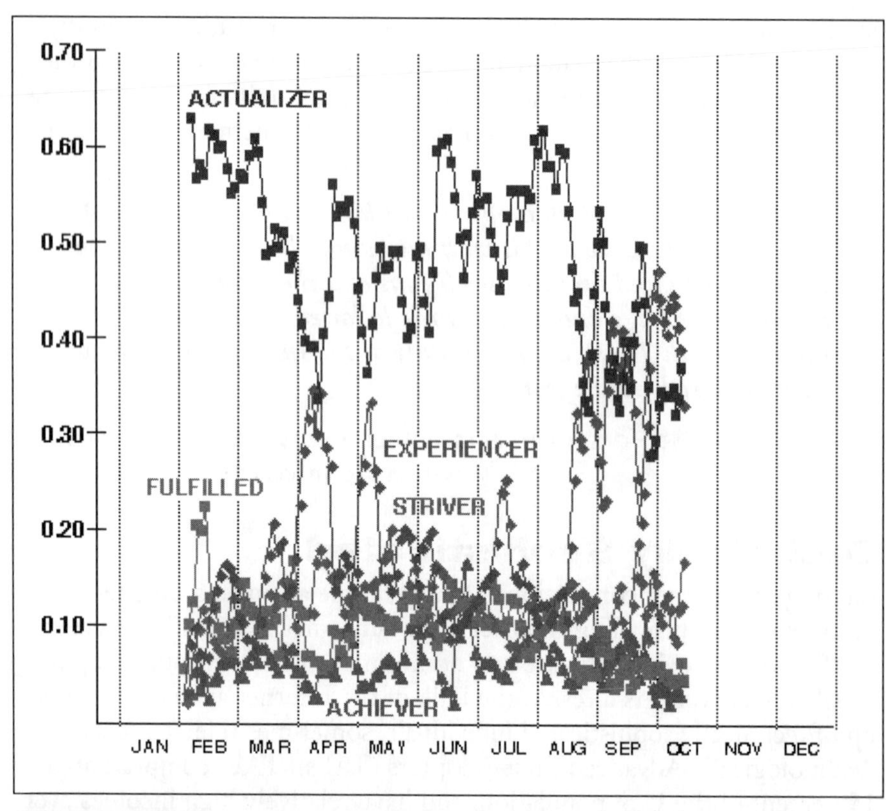

FIGURE 2.5 VALS psychotypes (http://future.sri.com/VALS/ovalshome.html).

their current position in society—has been steadily declining in importance on the Internet as the audience shifts its tastes from data to entertainment. Currently, Stanford Research Institute is developing a new group of Internet-specific psychotypes (iVALS); questionnaire results of this study are expected to be available later in 1996 (see Figure 2.5).

> ***[The Internet] is an alternative to any other form of media, and the bonus is that* you *control the show.***
>
> —Jon Steele of the post-punk band Furniture
> http://kspace.com/furniture

Students

Students are distinguished by an even higher awareness of the Internet than TAFs and usually have free or low-cost Internet access. Students form a substantial proportion of the VALS *Experiencer* category, characterized by a desire for variety, excitement, and nonconformity. This group often has high-speed Internet connectivity, with access at speeds 20 to 1,000 times faster than that of home users. This allows students easier access to sophisticated multimedia presentations that may take too long to download through a home-based computer.

Corporate Employees

With many businesses connecting their corporate networks to the Internet, large numbers of individuals now have Web access on their desktops. While some corporations have tried to minimize Internet use from work, most have found it has a positive effect. The end result is that a significant fraction of the Internet audience consists of employees at work, frequently with the same high-speed access to Web sites enjoyed by students.

Entertainment Industry Professionals

A small but extremely important subset of the total audience for entertainment on the Internet includes those people—such as agents, managers, publicists, A&R personnel, gallery and club owners, and film producers—who are searching for talent on the Web. Currently, their numbers are difficult to estimate, but it is not unreasonable to assume that the percentage online with at least email capabilities is approximately 10 percent (the same percentage of the U.S. population as a whole that is online). How many of them are actually using the Web for their professional work remains to be seen. Figure 2.6 shows the Speakers, Consultants, and Entertainment Directory, an example of a Web site aimed at a professional audience.

Women

One of the biggest myths of the Internet is that it is a "boys club." National advertising tends to show male characters using the Internet who frequently display classic "nerd" behavior and sometimes are laughed at by a woman, who obviously isn't interested in using the Internet herself! The reality of the Internet is far different. Virtually all studies showed that during 1995 women comprised at least 35 percent of the total Internet audience. In certain progressive regions, such as the San Francisco Bay area, women comprise as high as 47 percent of the total. Figure 2.7, Women's Wire, shows an example of a site aimed at women. Virtually all studies indicate that the gender gap will be nonexistent by the end of 1996.

Women's behavior on the Internet is similar to the general audience, except that a greater proportion of women use the Internet from work instead of home and typically spend about 20 percent less time online than men. While women and men tend to be interested in similar con-

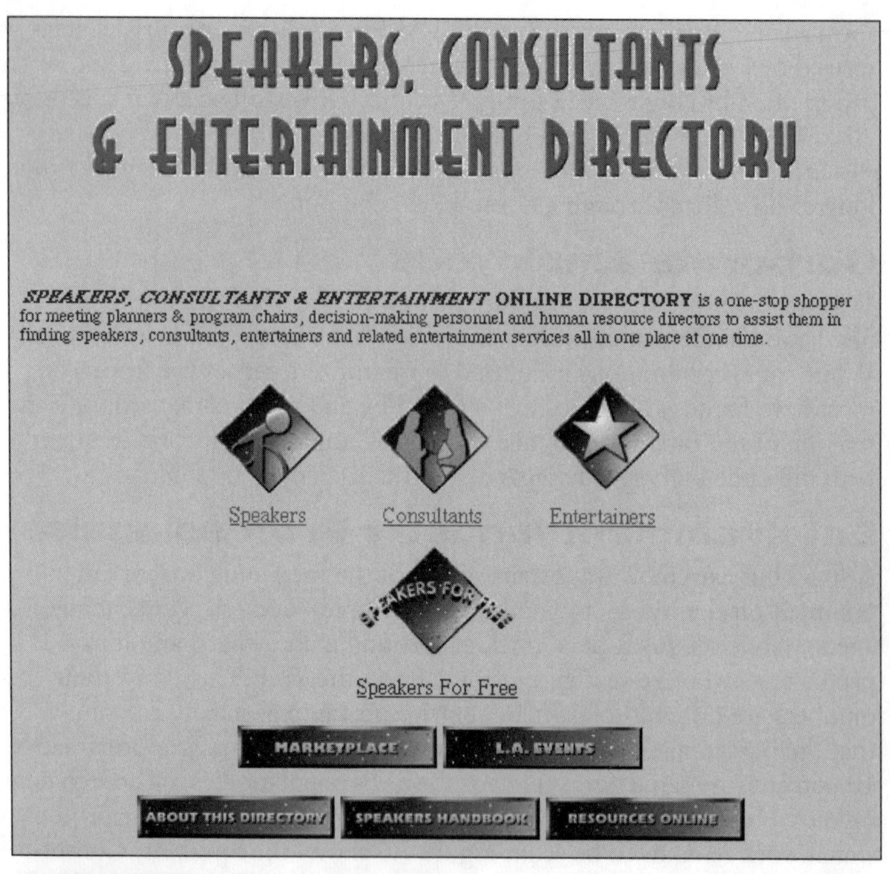

FIGURE 2.6 Speakers, Consultants, and Entertainment Directory (http://www.a2zpros.com).

tent, fewer women have actually purchased products through the Internet. This stunning reversal of real-world purchasing patterns offers a significant opportunity for Web sites specifically providing entertainment for women (and should also alert the advertising industry to start portraying women as part of the Internet audience)!

Children

While children currently form a minority of the Internet audience, their numbers are rapidly increasing. According to Find/SVP, nearly 1.1 million children under 18 were using the Internet from home or school as of early 1996. Frequently, families decide to connect to the Internet in order to further the education of their children. The Internet holds multiple appeal for kids as a place to find friends, search out information on their favorite subjects, and even as a place to impersonate adults! Figure

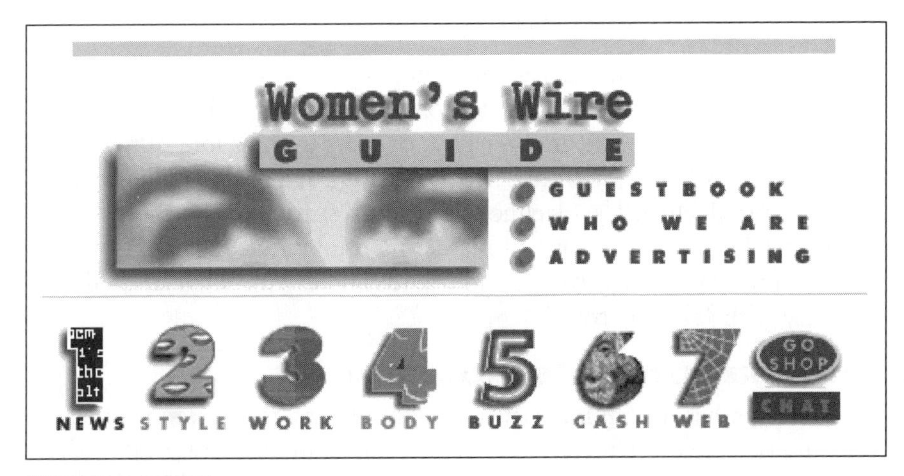

FIGURE 2.7 Women's Wire (http://www.womenswire.com).

2.8, Kids Com, shows a Web site for kids. Use of the general Internet by children for entertainment raises many questions, some of which are further addressed in Chapters 13 and 14 (legal and sociopolitical issues). Already, controversy has erupted over the use of brand-name personalities interacting with children to sell products online.

FIGURE 2.8 Kids Com (http://www.kidscom.com).

Age Demographics

The median age for the Internet audience is widely quoted as 30 to 35. Students in the 15 to 24 age bracket form a significant subgroup and heavy use by TAFs causes another peak of users in their mid-30s. Some studies, such as VALS, indicate that the average age of the audience is beginning to decline. Use declines significantly after age 45, though there have been many reports of increasing use by retired persons who see the Internet as a way to find old friends and expand their limited mobility with "virtual" travel.

International Demographics

The Internet has had an international component almost from its inception; use outside the United States is growing at an even faster rate than within the United States. According to the international statistics from Mark Lottor's Network Wizards Internet Domain Survey (see Figure 2.9), at least 130 countries have direct connectivity—indicating that at least

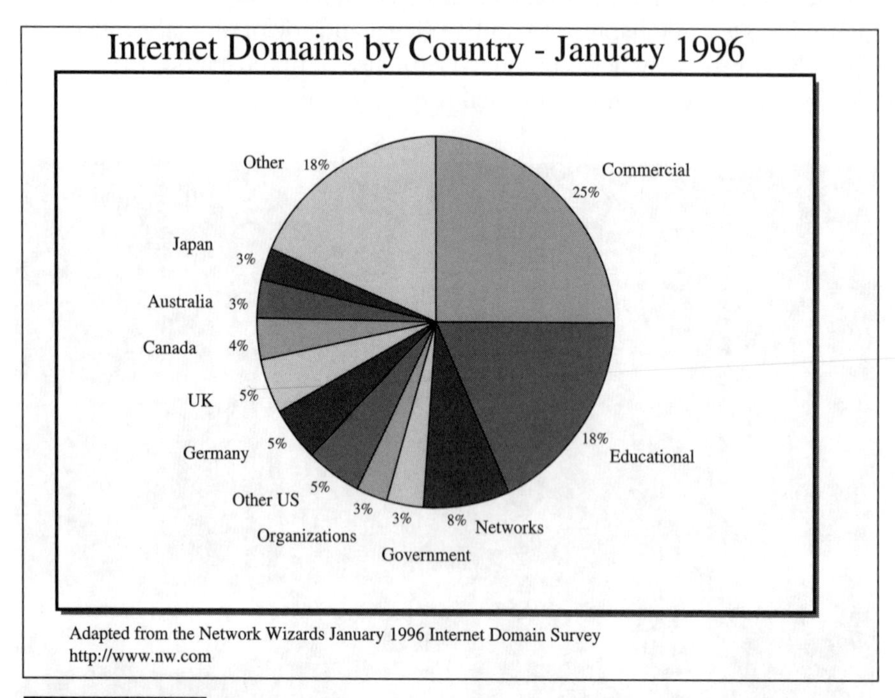

FIGURE 2.9 Domain breakdown (Network Wizards/Mark Lottor): *Internet World* (June 1996): 70—stats available at http://nw.com/zone/WWW/top.html. Produced by Network Wizards; data is available on the Internet at http://www.nw.com/.

some of the local population can access the Internet and provide information via the Web. Lottor's statistics indicate that about 40 percent of total Internet traffic originates from outside the United States. Note that the total number of computers does not necessarily indicate how "Internet-literate" a country is (e.g., Norway has equal or greater percentages of people using the Web than the United States). In 1996 both France and Germany were making major strides in Internet access. The large numbers of non-U.S. users is already changing the nature of the Internet; many Web sites are creating language-specific versions of their Web sites, most commonly in Japanese and Western European languages. According to a study by Digital Media (http://www.digmedia.com), rapidly growing linguistic groups include Arabic, Chinese, Italian, Portuguese, Spanish, and Dutch.

Time Spent Online

Estimates of time on the Internet vary considerably among the studies. Find/SVP reported that the average Internet user in 1995 spent 6.6 hours per week on the Internet, compared to Nielsen's estimate of 2.5 hours. The lower figure is comparable to time spent watching video rentals. Internet use is frequent; Nielsen found that 72 percent of those with Internet access had used the Web in the last 24 hours. Despite increasingly efficient use of the Internet by its audience, the total amount of time spent online is rising. Families with children form a special group: These households (usually of the TAF variety) spend considerably more time online, approaching 20 hours in many cases. These rates are comparable to the amount of television viewing in the same households and demonstrate that the Internet can provide serious competition to other media, particularly in higher-income households.

Search Engines and Audience Interests

While demographics for overall use illustrate the rapid rise of the Internet audience, they do little to illuminate the audience interests online. During the short "early" Web (1993-1994), determining audience interest was nearly impossible, due to the difficulties of following the users' convoluted path through a maze of Web sites. During 1995 and 1996, this situation changed with the introduction of *search engines*, complex programs such as Lycos (http://www.lycos.com), Yahoo (http://www.yahoo.com), and Alta Vista (http://www.altavista.com). Lycos and Alta Vista focus on automatically building indices of the millions of documents scattered throughout the Internet, allowing visitors to search by topic and keywords. These search engines are known as spiders. Yahoo!, arguably the most popular search engine in existence, depends primarily on manual postings by visitors to the site. More information and details of search engine use may be found in Chapter 7, but their main interest here is what they reveal about the Internet audience. During the short time that search engines have existed, they have recorded millions of visitor searches (actual topics and keywords entered by the user into the engine). Recently, the search engines have begun to compile this information to show audience interests. These results are astonishing for anyone who assumes that computers are the only topic of interest in a computer-driven medium.

Entertainment Is Number One

An April 29, 1996 article in *Web Week* by Whit Andrews illustrates that entertainment is the primary interest of Internet users. On the InfoSeek (http://www.infoseek.com) and Magellan (http://www.mckinley.com) search engines, almost 20 percent of all queries route the visitor to the Arts and Entertainment section. An additional 3 of the top 10 search topics (Travel & Leisure, Sports) also fall into entertainment-related categories. Similar results have been reported for Yahoo! and Lycos. Search engine results have been corroborated in a recent survey by Georgia Tech GUV4 (http://www.cc.gatech.edu/gvu/user_surveys/survey-10-1995/), in which nearly 60 percent of all users gave entertainment as their primary reason for using the Internet. When individual keywords are examined, "music" is the number one query, followed closely by "games" as the number three query, as shown in Figure 2.10.

Top Search Engine Query Statements

Most Common Topics	Keywords	Phrases	Names
Arts & Entertainment	Music	Chat rooms	Pamela Anderson
Travel & Leisure	Software	USA Today	Anna Nicole Smith
Computer & Internet	Games	Star Trek	Jenny McCarthy
Living/Consumer	Windows	Stock quotes	Cindy Crawford
Business & Finance	College	Las Vegas	Brad Pitt
Sports	News	Real Estate	Sharon Stone
Education	Free	Hewlett-Packard	Demi Moore
News	Jobs	Star Wars	Jennifer Aniston
Science & Technology	—	New York Times	Teri Hatcher
Government & Politics	—	Sports Illustrated	Alyssa Milano
—	—	Grateful Dead	—

Data adapted from Infoseek report, April 1996

FIGURE 2.10 Queries by search engine users, breakdown by topic searched, keywords, phrases, and names (*Web Week* article).

Interest in Both Traditional and Internet-specific Entertainment

When common phrases used to search the Internet are grouped, well-known media names including "Star Wars," "Pearl Jam," and "Grateful Dead" appear in the top 15. Popular names in search queries include "Pamela Anderson," "Cindy Crawford," "Brad Pitt," and "Demi Moore." However, these titles are easily beaten by *chat rooms*—a uniquely Internet-online form of entertainment. Clearly, while the Web audience is searching for more information on existing entertainment, they are actively embracing new forms as well.

Diversity of Interest

Most individuals listen to a single radio station and move between a few carefully selected channels on cable TV. By contrast, the Internet audience can keep track of a much larger variety of favorite entertainment-related Web sites through personal lists (often referred to as *hotlists* or *bookmarks*). A study by Find/SVP revealed that most Internet users visit 10 to 20 sites of their bookmarked sites on a periodic basis. These studies show that a small portion of the audience is extremely active; approximately 20 percent of the Internet audience has visited more than 100 sites.

Support for Niche Interest

The tremendous power of search engines, combined with individual control, allows the Internet audience to explore areas of entertainment impossible to find in mass media. Since Web sites make all their content available 24 hours a day, there is no pressure to create a "program" of content available in a specific time and order. Once the material is online, the audience may easily find it through search engines, even if the material is buried on the site like a "needle in a haystack." This increased availability gives the Internet audience a wider range of entertainment options.

Audience Behavior on the Web

While demographics may give a comforting illusion of understanding the Internet, in reality much more is needed to correctly interpret the current push toward Internet-based entertainment. Radio and TV can count on their listeners and viewers accepting a continuous flow of information, but Internet-based entertainment providers must take into account the highly interactive, exploratory nature of Internet use. Names such as *surfers* and *visitors* reflect the fact that the audience does not wait for entertainment to be delivered, but actively seeks it out.

To further understand the relationship between Internet audience behavior and Internet entertainment content, consider a movie fan who learns that a favorite film is finally scheduled to come out on video. Since short, 10 to 30-second clips of many movies are available online, the fan decides to search for a short video clip, previewing the movie over the Internet. However, the fan won't simply "dial up" the movie and watch it. Internet-based entertainment requires active exploration by the fan and combines most of the behavior, which happens prior to watching a movie in a real theater: reading a review, checking for exhibition venues and showtimes, and even prepaying admission for the movie. In addition to actually viewing a clip, the fan will often carry out all of these operations, and consider them part of the entertainment experience.

Surfing

Virtually all Web sites contain links to other sites (known as *outlinks*). "Surfing the Net" is nothing more than following a trail of these links between Web sites. Web surfing goes far beyond "channel surfing"—the act of pushing a button on a remote control to change channels. If a television, complete with cable, contains a few dozen channels to flip through, the Web has literally millions of "channels" to explore. Despite this, our movie fan will have an easier time surfing the Net for information on the video through related hyperlinks. The two adjacent television channels accessed through the remote typically have no relation to each other, whereas adjacent (or *linked*) Web sites often share similar or complementary content. Furthermore, the act of surfing itself is a form of Internet-based entertainment: the freedom of jumping anywhere in the world and discovering something new.

> ***I do [see the Internet rivaling mass media], mainly because the Internet is more controlled by the user. Active, not passive. Internet users direct their own entertainment. As the Internet becomes more accessible, I think more and more people will be drawn to its interactive nature.***
>
> —SIDNEY HILLMAN,ACOUSTIC ROCK MUSICIAN
> http://kspace.com/hillman

Searching

When Internet users have more specific ideas in mind, they visit the search engines previously described. The growth of the Internet has provided content for virtually any interest and searches for popular topics easily produce links to thousands of appropriate Web sites. In the example, our movie fan might provide a list of query words like the film's title, year, director, cast members, and even the studio's name to the search engine. After the search is complete, the fan can immediately select from a list of relevant Web sites by clicking on their names. Some of these sites may actually contain information about the film itself; others may mention it or discuss related topics.

Visiting

Upon arriving at the desired Web site, the fan selects various graphic and multimedia navigation tools, directories, and graphical *road maps* provided by the site's developer. One of the keys to developing an effective entertainment site is to organize the content so it can be effectively explored by the visitor. In general, this site visitor behavior is a mini version of surfing, confined in the bounds of the Web site. Unlike general surfing, the visitor's movements are automatically recorded in logs available to the site administrator. This information can be invaluable for publicity, maintenance, and expansion of the site's content.

Downloading and Copying

Once the fan finds a Web site containing information on the film, the fan will most likely download the various media available on the site—such as text, graphics, audio, and video. Text and graphics often download automatically within seconds for the visitor to view. Once the material is visible, the audience member may decide to make a copy of it and store it on his own computer. Standard Web browsers allow text and graphics to be copied by merely clicking on them with a mouse button. By contrast, high-quality audio and video may take several minutes to download. This greater time investment results in more "choosy" behavior from the visitor; it also reflects the power the audience has over what it experiences, compared to other media. Faced with a long wait, our film fan will likely start multiple *sessions* with the Web software while the preferred video clip is downloading to allow continued site exploration. Once the downloading is complete, copying audio and video is fairly straightforward since most multimedia players have automatic save options.

Discussion and Commentary

After exploring the content and viewing a clip of the movie, the fan may participate in one of many types of discussion groups maintained by the Web site for its audience. Internet discussions may be *synchronous* (such as a live telephone conversation), but are more often *asynchronous*: (such as a "phone tag" conversation through answering machines or voicemail).

Mailing Lists

Visitors may join an email-based discussion group, known as a *mailing list* or *listserv*. List members send in questions or comments to all other list members in a *broadcast email* format. Since email is available to everyone in the Matrix (as opposed to the core Internet), a listserv allows non-Web users to participate in entertainment-related discussions. Sometimes mailing lists are configured so that only the list owner can send out communications to the rest of the list. Although this is antithetical to a real discussion, these broadcast lists are extremely useful for newsletters, calendars of events, and site announcements.

Threaded Postings

A site emphasizing more user interactivity will often contain *threaded discussion groups* or *postings*. While Usenet consists of thousands of discussions of this type, threaded mini-discussions are becoming increasingly popular on many Web sites. Instead of individual email messages, these discussions are listed on the Web pages themselves. Threaded discussion groups are more open than mailing lists; anyone accessing a Web page displaying a list of postings can add a message to the list. Threaded discussions allow one to follow the history of an extended conversation—sometimes through hundreds of individual postings, which may also guide the fan to even more Web sites with information about a favorite topic.

Live Chat

More interactivity is provided by *chat sessions*, which differ from the other two modes of discussion because they are more "live" or synchronous; they are often held in *chat rooms*, an analogy to location that further emphasizes the immediacy of the discussions. Note that this time-dependence presents a unique contrast to most of the Web, since the very asynchronous and "non-live" nature of the Web lends itself to emphasis on user control. During an *open* or *unmoderated* chat session, fans discuss their interest among themselves. *Moderated* chats usually involve a featured speaker (such as a film actor or director), who may field live questions from the fans and be interviewed by a chat moderator. Within the moderated chat, some open discussion among fans may take place in parallel conversations, creating a cocktail party atmosphere. A chat room may have a simple text-only interface or may show a three-dimensional scene with characters called *avatars* representing the chatters.

Feedback

Virtually all Web sites have hyperlinks which allow their visitors to comment on the site and suggest additions or improvements. For example, the film fan may decide to send a message to the site administrator about the quality of the downloaded video clip or suggest corrections to the text describing the film. If the site visitor turns out to have been directly involved in the making of the film—such as the film editor—this feedback may be particularly valuable! In this case, the visitor—in effect, one of the content providers for the site—switches rapidly back and forth from audience member to content provider while submitting comments. This blurring of producer and consumer—discussed in greater detail later—is a fundamental distinguishing feature of the Internet audience.

Shopping

If the Web site in question sells products, the visitor can order the product using an online order form. Such a system allows the filmfan to order a selected video directly over the Internet—often outside of established distribution channels. Most Web sites support *secure* transactions, in which sensitive information such as credit card numbers is transmitted over the Internet as unbreakable code. The behavior of shoppers varies widely from those who immediately buy a product without even sampling it beforehand to those who commit only after lengthy email conversations with the content providers. Since online shopping is still somewhat intimidating for the majority of the Internet audience, many visitors will see a product online, but order it through more traditional methods such as snail mail, fax, or telephone.

Types of Audience Interactivity

The Internet provides many modes of interactivity between the audience and content providers. Unlike other media, the Internet enables communication ranging from intimate conversation to global communities involving thousands of individuals.

One-to-one

The most common form of Internet communication is an email message sent between two members of the audience or a member of the audience and a content provider. The ease and ubiquity of email makes it the primary interactive component of any Web site. More recently, Internet telephone software such as Quarterdeck's WebTalk (http://www.qdeck.com) has allowed one-to-one voice conversations in real time.

One-to-few (Narrowcasting)

Perhaps the most unique feature of the Internet is that it is practical to reach small, widely scattered audiences effectively for very low cost. A personal Web page for a niche-oriented musician such as an upright bass player is a perfect example of narrowcasting. With careful use of netpublicity (Chapter 7), a single individual can create a mini Web site containing a complete portfolio and attract a small but loyal following—regardless of the audience members' geographical separation. Broadcast mailing lists, previously discussed, are also good examples of narrowcasting. Since list membership is voluntary, the audience forms a small, targeted group highly interested in the list's topic.

> ***The most important aspect of Internet-delivered entertainment is that it can be customized (for an audience of one). Thus the experience of each user can be tailored. This is very hard to achieve through noninteractive media.***
>
> —ARIEL POLER, CHAIRMAN AND FOUNDER, I/PRO
> http://www.ipro.com

Few-to-few

Small group communication is the most common form of discussion on the Web. In fact, all three of the discussion and commentary methods previously described (mailing lists, threaded postings, and live chat) consist primarily of few-to-few interactions. (Note that, in addition to few-to-few communication, chat rooms also allow for one-to-one conversations—which are usually witnessed by the other chatters, but are sometimes hidden from view.) Few-to-few discussions form the basis of larger online communities, such as The Well (http://www.well.com) and America Online (http://www.aol.com). Most few-to-few discussions originally ran in text-only worlds like *IRC (Internet Relay Chat)* and *MUDs (Multiuser Domains* - or Dungeons), but more sophisticated programming is integrating them into the Web's environment.

One-to-many (Broadcasting)

Although a one-to-many broadcasting mode often defeats the purpose of the Web's exploratory nature, it is sometimes useful for online promotional events. This type of Internet *broadcasting*, usually consisting of audio or video *streaming*, is the closest thing to radio or television available to the Internet audience. Examples of this include live concerts and interviews. Due to the nature of the Internet, broadcasts are limited to several thousand people at once. (See Chapter 10 for a detailed discussion of audio and video streaming.) Theoretically, a single individual or organization can send information to *everyone* on the Internet. Another type of broadcast is less welcome—*spamming* through email (Chapter 7). Certain individuals have used email accounts to send unsolicited messages to large numbers of people on mailing lists and Usenet groups touting anything from drug tests to multilevel marketing. Despite its similarities to direct mail, spamming is very unprofessional—and it's a great way to ruin your reputation on the Internet. More than one *Internet Service Provider* has been literally shut down by tens of thousands of angry mail messages sent in response to a spam.

Many-to-many

These large-scale interactions can occur through *crosstalk* between fans of entertainment on the Web, collaborative entertainment within virtual "worlds," and larger virtual communities. Unlike the real world, the Internet can connect communities widely scattered in geographic location, interests, and culture. One way to initiate many-to-many interaction is to allow the audience of a large-scale Internet broadcast to communicate with each other during the broadcast.

 The Internet Audience as Prosumers

As defined by futurist Alvin Toffler, *prosumers* are individuals who produce as much information as they consume. While other interactive media such as CD-ROMs rigidly separate content creators and consumers, the Internet is rapidly realizing Toffler's vision by blurring these boundaries. The Internet and the Web are especially powerful at enabling prosumers due in part to the following features relating to content production and distribution.

Low Barriers to Entry

Similar to desktop publishing, first-rate Web-based content may be created easily by individuals. This is partially due to the power of personal computers and the Web's current limitations in delivering conventional broadcast audio and video.

Low Cost Distribution

Information placed on a single Web site is accessible to the entire Internet 24 hours a day, for costs as little as $20 per month for maintenance. While Web sites may compete for an audience, they do *not* compete for the resources needed to display their content to the audience.

No Regulation

Despite increasing efforts to regulate Internet content (see Chapter 13), it is unlikely that the medium will ever be censored to the extent of broadcast radio or television. The Internet has no licensing fees beyond name registration ($100 per domain; see Chapter 4). The global, decentralized nature of the Internet inherently frustrates comprehensive censorship.

Home Grown Acceptable

Internet audiences have clearly shown that, while they enjoy advanced entertainment sites created for their favorite mass-media entertainment, they are also highly interested in personal home pages and entertainment from independent artists, musicians, and companies.

The prosumer aspect of the Internet is consistent with the earlier analogy to hunter-gatherers. When people lived in a scattered, decentralized culture of small groups, they depended largely upon themselves for most of their entertainment. Modes of interactivity unique to the Internet promote the creation of virtual communities unknown in mass entertainment culture. The shift previously described that occurs in an audience member who is also a content creator is a shift to a more intimate relation with content. In the case of the film editor involved in the making of the original film, encountering the film clip brings back a sense of control present when originally creating the content. This intimacy is a result of the ability to control and modify content in a way impossible for broadcast media. Since site visitors who had nothing to do with the film's creation are also given the same power as the editor who stumbles upon the clip, they, too, experience the producer aspects of Internet entertainment. In all cases, the sense of intimacy has the potential to make the overall entertainment more meaningful to the audience than passively consumed entertainment, resulting in increasing acceptance of the Internet as a standard medium for delivery of entertainment.

 Future Audience Trends

Despite the dangers in predicting the future of fast-changing media like the Internet, certain trends in the audience for Internet entertainment are likely to hold through the next few years. These predictions should be taken as conservative; the reality may be far different. After all, who would have predicted in 1991 that the Internet would be: (1) 20 times larger; (2) multimedia-based rather than text-based; (3) commercial rather than academic; and (4) the replacement for well-funded concepts like set-top boxes and interactive TV on the Information Superhighway?

Normalization Relative to General Population

As the Internet becomes more widespread and easier to use, more of the less technically sophisticated audience will become connected and cost barriers will continue to decrease. Currently, a computer capable of showing the Web costs several thousand dollars, but falling prices may lower the cost of a multimedia-capable system to under $1,000 by mid-1996. In addition, the introduction of diskless network computers designed specifically for the Internet may lower costs to less than $500. For people who can't afford these, the increasing number of Internet connections available in public places like restaurants and coffeehouses (Chapter 11) will allow essentially free access for all.

Increasing Global Growth

The number of international users will continue to rise relative to the United States Internet audience; in a few short years, the majority of the Internet audience may not use English as their primary language. This will result in consequences ranging from multilingual Web sites to increasing amounts of locally produced content.

Fast Connections

Within a few years, conventional modems will become obsolete as new technologies such as *ISDN (Integrated Services Digital Network)*, *ADSL (Asymmetric Digital Subscriber Line)*, and cable modems allow consumers to connect to the Internet at speeds hundreds of times faster than today. Increased speeds will greatly increase the use of the Web. In a trial by Cogeco—a Canadian cable company which provides *high-speed* Internet access to its customers—it was found that online hours skyrocketed, and many individuals surfed the Web to the exclusion of TV.

Increasing Interest in Interactivity

As more people grow up with computers and the Internet, they will accept interactivity as the norm—ultimately integrating it into their entertainment experience alongside the current reigning mass media. The prosumer characteristic of the Internet audience has an effect on the ways in which content providers create Internet entertainment. The next chapter considers the producer-consumer phenomenon in greater detail, shifting emphasis toward the content provider's point-of-view.

CHAPTER 3

THE NEW MEDIA PIONEERS:

Intertainment Content Providers

The audience producer-consumer phenomenon discussed in the previous chapter also affects the nature of Internet content providers. The prosumer role has an impact on the types of Internet entertainment content available on the Web, the way in which this content is presented, the motivation behind this new content creation, and the characteristics of the individuals and companies creating entertainment Web sites. Most of these Intertainment content providers come from outside the traditional industry or are involved in their own content production and distribution in nontraditional ways. These are the new media pioneers—going into uncharted territory and creating a unique form of entertainment which often goes against the grain of traditional media.

> ***This medium gives the little guy an opportunity—maybe the* only *opportunity—to level the playing field a bit.***
>
> —John Hager of Pure White Dove, Country Rock Vocalist
> http://kspace.com/dove

Characteristics of Content Providers

The new media pioneers explore a frontier containing no accepted boundaries for type and presentation of entertainment content. This "wild west" atmosphere is resulting in astonishing diversity of experimentation where none existed only a few years ago. Since the interests and tastes of the Internet audience are not well-defined, content which works well in one medium may utterly fail on the Internet. Given this uncertain environment, the ultimate form that Internet-based entertainment will take is unknown—but the new media pioneers are convinced that their payoff for creating successful content will be enormous. Unlike any other era in entertainment, a diverse group of people from all areas of society have a chance to become Internet entertainers, provided that they have a unique set of personality characteristics.

- *Risk-taking*—willing to gamble on an untried medium.
- *Flexibility*—willing to constantly experiment and change their course of action at a moment's notice; wear many hats ranging from artistic design to hardware installation.
- *Open to dialogue*—willing to listen and respond to the audience.
- *Self-educating*—willing to take the initiative and learn new ways of creating Internet content; maintain awareness about new Internet features and business developments appearing on a daily basis.
- *Ability to synthesize information*—willing to put diverse facts together to form new concepts and ideas from the confusing array of facts, announcements, and general hype surrounding the Internet to predict its future course.

These features fit into Stanford Research Institute's VALS 2, Values and Lifestyles (http://future.sri.com/vals/trends/intro.html) categories of Actualizers and Experiencers, who in the previous chapter were seen to be the fastest growing audience on the Web. Compared to the general population, these groups are most likely to have the creative daring necessary to jump into the largely untested waters of Internet content development. Due to these risks, it is likely that Experiencers are behind many of the actual startups. Typically, at earlier positions in their career, they have less to lose and are likely to be attracted to unconventional media.

We've always believed we weren't alone.
On July 4, we'll wish we were.
INDEPENDENCE DAY
LAUNCH PAD
CONTACT
AREA 51
RESTRICTED AREA
Launch Pad | Contact | Area 51
What's New | Help | Release Dates | Credits

FIGURE 3.1 Example of a promotional site for *Independence Day* (http://www.id4.com).

Motivations for Becoming a Content Provider

There are a large number of reasons to become part of the Internet "revolution." However, the majority of content providers involved in entertainment are developing Web sites for four basic reasons.

Promotion

The primary reason for establishing an entertainment Web site is to promote existing entertainment. In most cases, these Web sites repurpose entertainment content which originally appeared in other media. Due to the multimedia capabilities of the Web, promotions are not restricted to "billboard" advertising but can contain actual excerpts of text, images, audio, and video which serve as *teasers* to the main entertainment. Since sales are not a primary objective, the Web site is not expected to pay for itself directly. Promotional sites may result in developing a *fan base* for artists and entertainers, indirectly increasing sales of entertainment products through worldwide exposure and enhancing the image of media companies.

One of the first promotion-only sites created for release of a major motion picture was MGM's *Stargate* site online in mid-1995, which was said to have indirectly increased ticket sales through the advanced publicity the site generated. (The official site is no longer online, but several fan sites remain.) Other more recent promotional film sites—20th Century Fox's *Independence Day* (see Figure 3.1) and Paramount's *Mission: Impossible* (http://missionimpossible.com)—use advanced multimedia technologies (see Chapters 5 and 6) and provide games as part of their entertainment. The sophistication and interactivity of these sites make

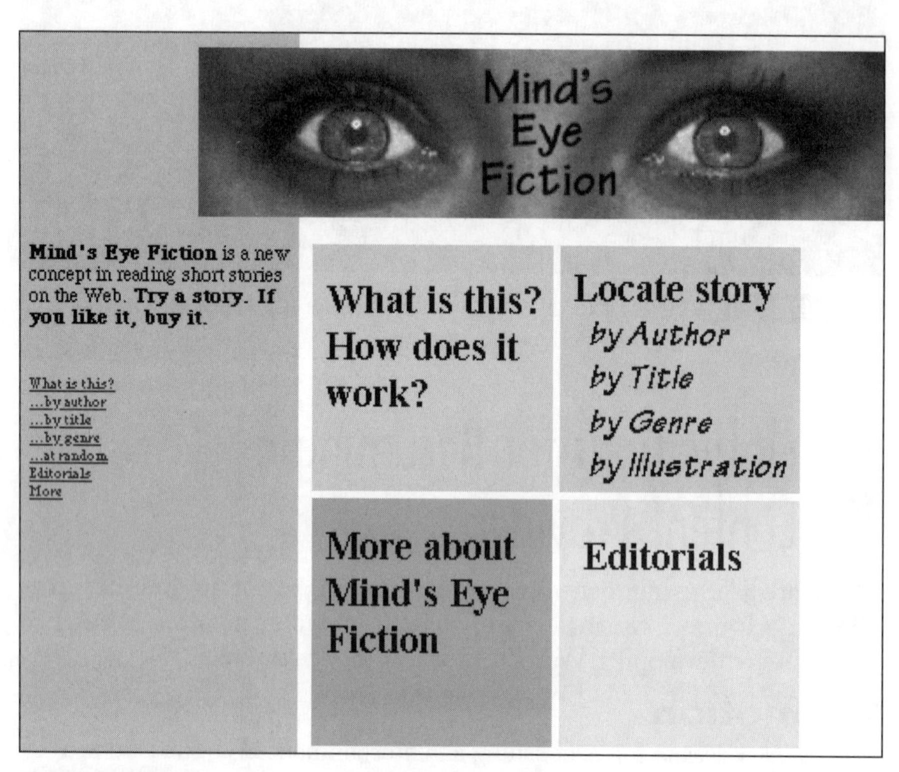

FIGURE 3.2 Example of online distribution site—Mind's Eye Fiction (http://www.ghgcorp.com/mindseye).

them more than just promotions for their respective movies; they are entertainment experiences in their own right. Many promotional sites are not permanent and are taken offline after the promotional item (e.g., film, album, festival, tour) is no longer in current release.

Sales and Distribution

Another common reason for developing Intertainment sites is to directly sell products to the global Internet audience, outside traditional distribution systems. Currently, most Web sites are selling physical products such as CDs and CD-ROMs, videos, books, software, works of art, and other merchandise. Examples include large online music malls such as CDNow! (http://www.cdnow.com) or the independent Ann Arbor, MI store, Schoolkids' Records (http://www.schoolkids.com). A small but increasing number of sites offer purely digital products that are directly downloadable (e.g., electronic books, digital art, multimedia software) as shown in Figure 3.2, Mind's Eye Fiction is a great example of a true electronic bookstore or services (e.g., script coaching, songwriting consulting, psychic counseling). While Songwriters Consultants http://websites.earthlink.net/~songmd is a good example of a service. Finally, some sites have begun to charge for access to entertainment located on the site itself (e.g., sports, games, and concerts; see ESPNet SportsZone at http://espnet.sportszone.com). In this case, the audience is often charged for access to specific areas of the site, either on a per-visit basis or through paid subscriptions.

> ***For may years the 'standard deal' where the artist loses control and ownership of* their work *has been one of the greatest crimes ever. That's why I like pushing my CD this way; at least I know it's still mine and I have an influence over what happens to it.***
>
> —Brett McEntire, New Age Keyboardist
> http://kspace.com/mcentire

Placement and Industry Contacts

A rapidly growing use for Web sites is to provide a contact point for entertainers and industry professionals. Instead of a general audience, many musicians, writers, and filmmakers have created personal Web sites primarily to get the attention of booking agents, managers, record labels, and talent agencies. Unlike a business card, there are no reproduction costs to distribute an *online portfolio*. A great example of such a site was created by screenwriter Gary Apple (http://www.verbaljudo.com/apple); a page from his site, "hard pitch," shown in Figure 3.3, speaks for itself. At the other end, sites created by industry professionals provide A&R,

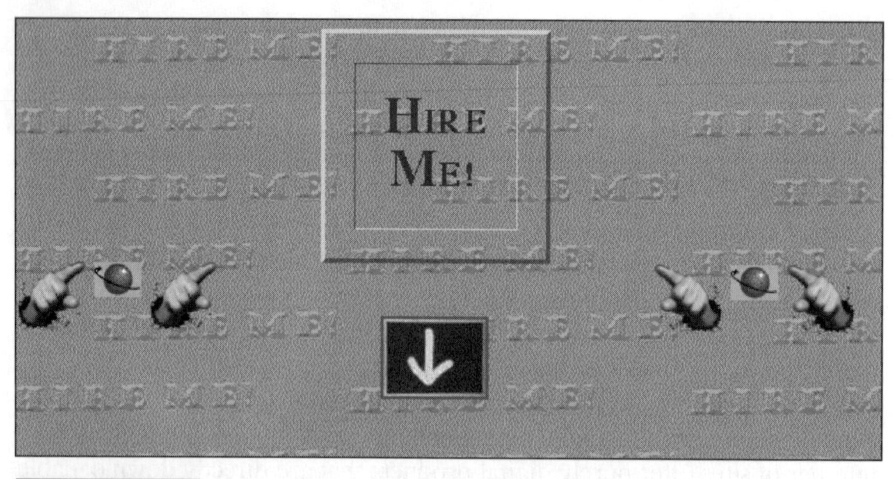

FIGURE 3.3 Gary Apple "Hire Me!" page (http://www.verbaljudo.com/apple).

agenting, casting, and other services to the online audience. Taxi (http://www.taxi.com) exemplifies this trend. Specifically designed to help independent musicians get their material in front of industry scouts, it has an impressive lineup of A&R personnel. As the Web improves, services such as Taxi will likely evolve to support real-time contacts in the form of "virtual pitch sessions." Another feature of placement sites involves peer-to-peer contacts, such as musicians looking for band members and artists looking for models. While most collaboration presently occurs offline, it is likely that the interactive, multiuser features of the Internet will be used to create art and music.

Exploration

Exploration is most often carried out by large media companies whose primary interest is to establish an "I am here" presence to match their competition. These Web sites primarily serve as place holders for the company while it explores creating a "virtual production" studio (see Chapter 5) and learns enough about the Web to find a concept worth large expenditures of time and money. For obvious reasons, we're not providing examples — but you should have no trouble finding them yourself!

 Demographics

Traditional entertainment media professionals might be stunned to discover just how many individuals and groups are creating entertainment for the Internet. Currently, statistics on content providers are not as readily available as those for the Internet audience (Chapter 2), but there are some obvious trends. As of May 1996, the registry for U.S. Internet *domain names* at the InterNIC (http://www.internic.net) listed about 325,000 names—with a growth rate of 15 percent *per month*. Almost 90 percent of new domain names designate commercial sites (as opposed to educational, non-profit, or government). Based on these figures, the Web is already light-years beyond the 500-channel universe predicted only a few years ago.

Every week, over 1,000 new Web sites appear on the Internet—created by individuals, companies, foundations, educational institutions, and the government. The Network Wizards Internet Domain Name Survey (created by Mark Lottor; http://nw.com/zone/WWW/top.html) indicates that 58 percent (approximately 190,000) of the computers used by the core Internet audience—the true prosumers—(see Chapter 2) contain "www" in their names. This prefix is normally applied only to *server* computers that host Web sites. Since each computer typically runs *several* sites, the actual total of distinct Web sites is closer to 500,000. Based on estimates of user interests described in Chapter 2, it is possible that as much as *one-third* of this total is entertainment-related.

> ***Like other corporations, traditional media companies are typically scanning the horizon for competitors*** **their own size.** ***Thus, they miss the ants eating away at their feet! One little Web outfit may take away only a fraction of a percent of any established company's market. But thousands of them can erode an existing market overnight. I believe a lot of companies—and not just in radio and television—will wake up one day soon to find their audiences and markets have evaporated.***
>
> —CHRISTOPHER LOCKE, CHAIRMAN AND CHIEF EXECUTIVE OFFICER, ENTROPY GRADIENT REVERSALS
> http://www.panix.com/~clocke/EGR/index.html and
> PROGRAM DIRECTOR, ONLINE COMMUNITY DEVELOPMENT, IBM
> http://www.panix.com/~clocke/

With such huge numbers of sites, it is obvious that Internet-based entertainment differs drastically from traditional media in which a few content providers get their material to the public through an even smaller number of distributors. Since prosumer behavior is enabled on the Internet, everyone has the ability to become a content distributor—and may have access to *the same* audience regardless of size and resources. Since there is a Web site for every 50 to 100 Internet users, it is obvious that the Internet audience takes prosumer behavior to heart! With the enormous diversity of Web sites available, the potential exists for content providers to exhibit extreme niche material and still find an audience.

Who's Creating the Content

Examining the entertainment areas of the major *search engines* such as Yahoo! (http://www.yahoo.com) shows that tens of thousands of Web sites are devoted to entertainment of all types. Despite this diversity, content providers can be divided into two major groups. The largest group consists of individuals who are Internet audience prosumers. Smaller, but equally significant, are groups such as traditional media companies and new media startups.

Individuals

A large group of people are creating little islands of entertainment on the Web. Similar to home movies and photo albums, individual sites (or *personal home pages*) illustrate the interests, recommendations, and personal lives of their creators. Graphic design and layout are frequently first-rate and comparable to larger Web sites. Personal home pages are ends in

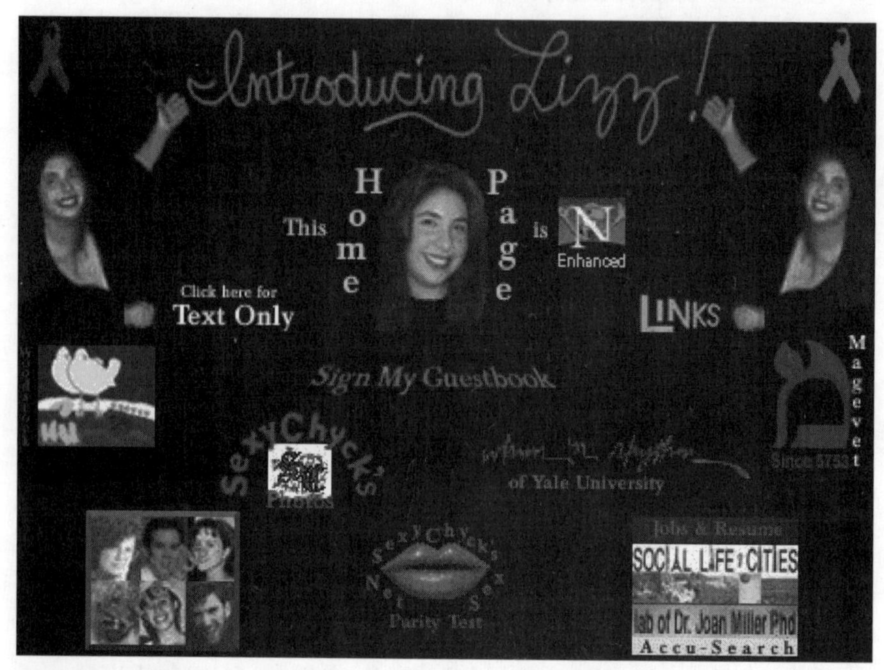

FIGURE 3.4 Example of individual site—Lizz's Better Than Sex page (http://pantheon.cis.yale.edu/~lizzz).

themselves, usually designed for audience enjoyment rather than career promotion or industry contacts. Many have a strong secondary purpose to promote the creator as an interesting person—and potential friend. A good example of a highly entertaining personal site of this sort can be found at Lizz's Better Than Sex Page (Figure 3.4), which introduces the Internet audience to the life of a Yale college student and even contains an original NetSex Purity Test! A few personal sites, like the Tabatha Holtz - Hutchison Media Software site (http://tabatha.hasc.com), have become high-traffic entertainment sites with a fan base while retaining their individualistic flavor. Tabatha's page has won several *cool site* awards, and it is well-known for its fake press releases mixed with graphics showing herself among famous personalities. Personal sites of this type may signal the beginning of Internet-specific entertainment stars.

Due to the enormous number of individual pages on sites like the Netizens listing at GNN (http://bin-1.gnn.com/gnn/netizens/alphabet.html), it is sometimes difficult to find quality entertainment-related sites. The best starting points for exploring individual pages are *cool lists* created specifically for personal home pages, such as There's No Page Like Home (http://www.soton.ac.uk/~agt/popular.html). Larger home page archives like Housernet (http://www.housernet.com) and The Meeting Place (http://www.nis.net) are searchable by age, interests, and even appearance; these are likely to evolve into pen-pal and matchmaking services discussed in Chapter 11.

Independent Entertainers

The second major group providing Internet-based entertainment are independent artists, musicians, performers, writers, filmmakers, animators, and artisans. Unlike sites created by individuals, independent entertainers create sites with specific promotion or distribution goals in mind. As a group, these individuals frequently have problems getting their work seen by the public and the Internet—with its low-cost, universal promotion and distribution—is an ideal medium for them. Independents have led the way in Intertainment; many were providing entertainment on the Web late in 1993, a full year before most media companies began creating their Web sites. For example, the Violet Arcana site (http://www.teleport.com/~arcana/arcana_g2/h_main.html) began providing samples of this group's ethereal, ambient musical style early in 1994. Through the years, Violet Arcana has operated a variety of sites on the Web; its current offerings now include advanced multimedia as well as text, audio, and graphics. The band's long Web experience allowed it to create an audience-friendly site, which allows visitors to adjust their experience to the capabilities of their computer. In com-

FIGURE 3.5 Example of independent entertainer site—Rodney Dangerfield (http://www.rodney.com).

mon with other independents who create their own Web sites, Violet Arcana has offered freelance Web development services as well. Other independents have outsourced their Web development—either to freelance designers, or meta-sites providing space for a large number of artists (such as the authors' own Kaleidospace).

> ***I do like the idea of using the Internet as a main delivery point for my recordings. It's a direct channel and you do not have to depend on others like distributor and retail outlets to get your recordings to the people who want it. Hopefully in the near future it will be practical to deliver real-time CD-quality audio over the Internet.***
>
> —David Duddleston, Violet Arcana
> http://www.teleport.com/~arcana

Independent entertainer sites are not restricted to the "unsigned;" many well-known entertainers have also developed Web sites on their own. One prominent example is comedian Rodney Dangerfield. His site (see Figure 3.5) bears a clear personal stamp and features anything fans could want—including home movies, the joke of the day, reviews, and, most surprisingly, the results of a recent tabloid lawsuit. Albums and other merchandise are sold directly to fans through the site and links to other Web sites show the surprising amount of "respect" Mr. Dangerfield has acquired on the Internet. A series of contests, including Dangerfield look-alikes, keep the fans coming back. The site showcases the best in independent entertainment on the Web — providing quality material while actively supporting its audience of fans. Another group that has been very active in creating its own Intertainment sites includes X-rated film stars; they are usually motivated to allow direct correspondence with their audience. These examples show individual entertainers can use the Web to entertain their existing audience and expand to a new community.

Fans

Prior to the introduction of the Web, fan resources were the only sites on the Internet that might be properly called entertainment. As Web-based entertainment has grown, fan sites have remained a major force. Fundamentally grassroots efforts, these sites are normally produced by one individual or a very small group. In contrast to personal home pages, the majority of fan sites are created and maintained by students. In addition to media stars, sites exist for virtually every major filmmaker, musician, author, and performer—including models, athletes, and magicians. The number of fan sites is enormous; many media stars have in excess of 100 sites in addition to the *official* one created for them. Fan sites range far beyond the stars of the hour; with the arrival of the Internet, no celebrity may ever fear disappearing from view.

The tone of fan pages ranges from biographical (Elizabeth Montgomery at http://sebastian.physics.lehigh.edu/~grumbine/em.shtml) to passionate worship (Brad Pitt at http://www.csclub.uwaterloo.ca/~cbnorman/

FIGURE 3.6 Example of fan site—Gillian Anderson Testosterone Brigade (http://www.bchs.uh.edu/~ecantu/GATB/gatb.html).

WWWbrad) to parody (The Kevin Bacon Game at http://www. mind-spring.com/~mab/kevin/kevin.html). One of the largest Internet fan groups has formed around Fox's *The X Files*—evident in popular sites such as the David Duchovny Estrogen Brigade (http://www.exit109.com/~fazia/DDEB.html) and Gillian Anderson Testosterone Brigade (see Figure 3.6). These are just two of several hundred fan sites devoted to the show. Many of these sites are particularly interesting because they also link to *X-Files*-related, email-based lists and Usenet discussion groups available to the Internet audience outside the Web.

Fan sites and personal home pages are too numerous to examine thoroughly; the best course is to look for a personality in a search engine or consult one of the many indices of fan sites. An excellent list for fan sites of all kinds can be found at The Unknown Psychic's Celebrity Address list (http://www2.islandnet.com/~luree/fanmail.html). A more unusual list, Pan Galactica's Celebs on the Net (http://home.earthlink.net/~grumpus/celebs1.html), provides direct links to celebrities' own home pages.

Students and Educators

While this group is represented in most of the other content-developer categories, it deserves special mention because of its contribution to advancing the technology of Intertainment. Students are responsible for many individual home pages and fan sites, and continue to create much of the free software available for Web sites. After graduating, students form the bulk of Web developers and frequently are involved in new Web-based entertainment startups. Educators in computer science work with their students in developing new features for the Web; they also frequently curate specialized entertainment archives and create online courses for public use.

Since their work is not commercial, students and educators are also able to explore long-range concepts, such as connecting robotic hardware to the Web. The Mercury Project at USC, completed in April 1995 by co-directors Ken Goldberg and Michael Mascha, used an industrial robot to allow remote excavation of a sand-filled archaeological site. In 1996, some members of the same team completed The Tele-Garden (see Figure 3.7). The project allows Internet audience members to view and interact with a remote garden filled with living plants. Members can plant, water, and monitor the progress of seedlings via the movements of an industrial robot arm. Both projects illustrate the hunter-gatherer behavior of the Internet audience as discussed in Chapter 2. According to the USC team, the purpose of The Tele-Garden is to "consider the 'post-nomadic' community, where survival favors those who collaborate." The position of students and educators allows them to consider the

FIGURE 3.7 Example of academic site—USC's Tele-Garden (http://cwis.usc.edu/dept/garden/index.html).

philosophical, as well as commercial, aspects of Internet-based entertainment and leisure.

Web-specific Developers

As the Web acquired more audio-video and multimedia features throughout 1995, many new developers entered the business of creating Web sites. Many of the most sophisticated developers have specialized in creating the advanced interface and media characteristic of entertainment-based Web sites. Web developers frequently come from outside the CD-ROM and game industries and many did their first Web development while they were students. Since developers need to advertise their services, they usually lavish special care on their own Web sites, which frequently become entertainment works in their own right. Internet Outfitters (see Figure 3.8), for example, specializes in developing sites for the entertainment industry. Clients include Davis Entertainment, Pressman Films, and Hotz Virtual Music Studio (and specific projects such as *The Crow: City of Angels* and *War of the Worlds*). Digital Planet (http://digiplanet.com) began as a Web developer specializing in building sites for large media companies such as MCA/Universal. Following a trend that may become common among Web developers, it has expanded into providing original entertainment content—such as Madeleine's Mind (http://www.madmind.com), an interactive exploration using advanced *Shockwave* animation.

Interestingly, only a tiny fraction (under 10!) of the several thousand developers listed in Yahoo! mentioned entertainment in their descrip-

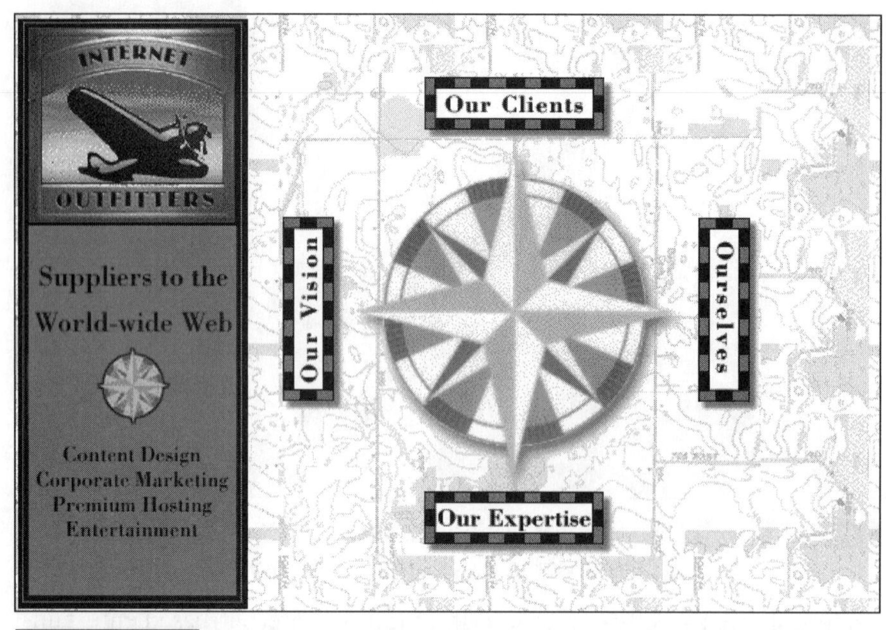

FIGURE 3.8 Example of Web-specific developer site—Internet Outfitters (http://www.netoutfit.com).

tions. We expect that this will change dramatically by the time you are reading this book.

Established Media Companies

With low entry costs the norm, it is possible for traditional entertainment producers to experiment with repurposing their material for the Internet. In some cases, content is developed by existing "new media" departments; in others, the marketing and publicity departments have taken the lead. Established media companies frequently outsource part or all of the development to Web-specific developers. Record labels have been particularly aggressive in establishing an Internet presence, followed closely by media companies specializing in broadcast radio and television. With the advent of *real-time* audio on the Internet, many radio stations have begun to put their signals into cyberspace.

A good example of an established media company on the Web can be found at Paramount (Figure 3.9), which refers to its cyberspace content development group as Paramount Digital Entertainment (PDE). A business unit of the Paramount Television Group, PDE contains three areas of content development. The first of these develops interactive entertainment using existing Paramount film and television property. PDE has also developed a second kind of site for advertisers, such as Women's Link (http://www.womenslink.com), described as an "entertaining" Web

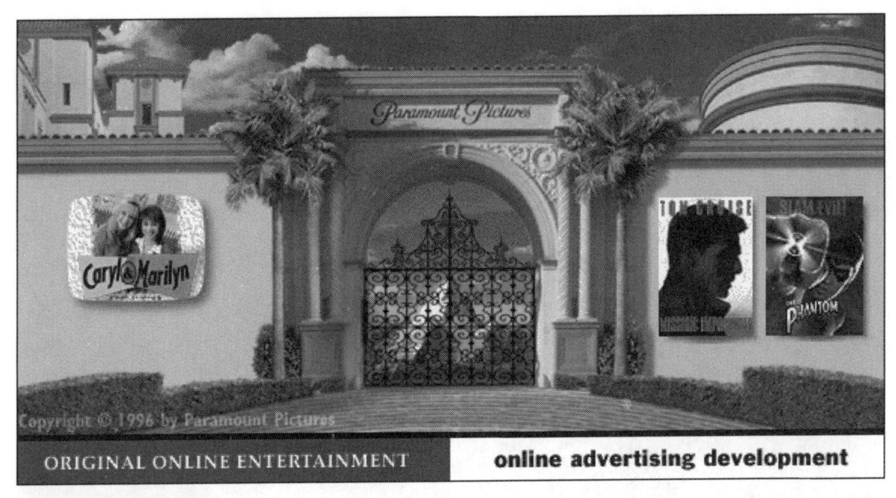

FIGURE 3.9 Example of established media company site—Paramount Pictures Online Studio (http://paramount.com).

site promoting non-entertainment products. (Sites of this sort are discussed further in Chapter 11.) Currently, the phrase "Original Online Entertainment" on the Paramount home page is linked to a page about PDE, which promises a third area of original online "programming" for the Web and the Microsoft Network.

New Media Startups

The Internet is providing a starting point for many new companies outside the traditional industry. The first, and most common, of these deals is with existing entertainment. In this case, the company creates an umbrella *meta-site* affording a novel means of promotion and distribution for independent artists and musicians. Examples include sites containing independently produced art and entertainment of all types such as the authors' own Kaleidospace (http://kspace.com) and New York City-based Visual Radio (Figure 3.10), and sites devoted to independent music such as Virtual Radio (http://www.vradio.com) and the Internet Underground Music Archive (http://www.iuma.com). Examples of sites containing new forms of entertainment (see Chapter 12 for an in-depth discussion on this topic) include episodic storytelling sites like The Spot (http://www.thespot.com) and virtual reality worlds like Virtual Vegas (http://www.virtualvegas.com).

Publishers

Lured by the prospect of paperless, worldwide distribution of newspapers and magazines, publishers are jumping onto the Internet. Experience with

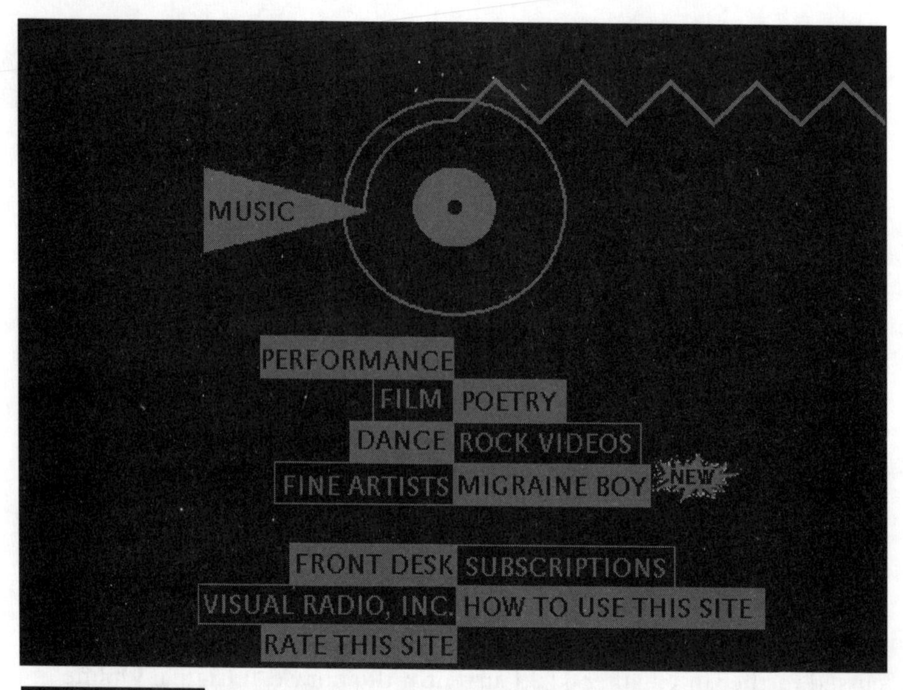

FIGURE 3.10 Example of new media startup site—Visual Radio (http://www.visualradio.com).

managing large volumes of frequently updated information gives these companies a distinct advantage in developing content for the Web. Many online publications have taken the lead in constructing advanced sites providing visitor-specific content and real-time newsfeeds. Publishers are also leaders in bringing a professional and editorial legacy to the Web. Spurred by the rise of entertainment on the Web, major consumer magazines including *Entertainment Weekly* (http://www.timeinc.com/ew) and industry trades such as *The Hollywood Reporter* (Figure 3.11) have created Web sites. The pioneering Electronic Newsstand (http://www.enews.com) provides links to several thousand magazines on the Internet and has created *Off the Rack*, a publication devoted to media of all types.

Venues and Events

Music clubs, theaters, and coffeehouses are increasingly creating sites, as well as providing Internet access from their location for surfing or event broadcasts. Since local and regional broadcasts appear to be major components of the future of Internet entertainment (see Chapter 15), venue owners are positing themselves to become content providers. Having frequently had to master the hardware and software for Internet access from

THE Hollywood REPORTER
a BPI publication
Your Prime Site for Entertainment News and Information
Welcome to The Hollywood Reporter's web site! The Reporter was the first daily trade paper for the entertainment industry, and now it's the first on the World Wide Web.

THE REPORTER
Boxoffice at record pace
For a word from our publisher, check out the Welcome from Bob Dowling. To get delivery of The Reporter, complete our Subscription Form.

FIGURE 3.11 Example of publisher site—*The Hollywood Reporter* (http://www.hollywoodreporter.com).

their location, it is not surprising that many venues develop their own sites. In the larger leisure category, many amusement parks, fairs, and festivals create Web sites—usually by outsourcing to independent developers. One of the first venues to go online was The Troubadour (http://troubadour.com; see Chapter 1), which distinguished itself by broadcasting portions of its shows live on the site. Coffeehouses, known as "cybercafes," are starting to define themselves as a new type of entertainment venue. CyberJava (http://www.cyberjava.com) in Venice, CA and the thematic niche-oriented Fiddler's Dream Coffeehouse (see Figure 3.12) in the Phoenix, AZ area are great examples. (See Chapter 11 for further discussion of cybercafes.)

> ***The possibilities on the Internet are only limited by our own imagination. This factor alone allows an enterprising original-thinking independent artist to compete with anything else on the Net. All the tools are available to everyone, and for once money plays almost no role in their function.***

—Alan Naggar, President, Alan Naggar Productions/New Music Scene
http://nms.org and http://kspace.com/nms

FIGURE 3.12 Example of venue site—Fiddler's Dream Coffeehouse (http://www.primenet.com/~fiddler).

Entertainment Professional Organizations

As more entertainment professionals have become content providers, they have appreciated the Web's potential for facilitating the business of entertainment, as well as entertainment itself. Many are promoting the goals of their organization, helping their members get online, and creating completely new services aimed at the Internet audience as well as fellow entertainment professionals. Currently, the most prevalent organizations include performance rights societies—such as BMI (http://www.bmi.com) and ASCAP (http://www.ascap.com)—and arts and entertainment organizations' awards sites such as The National Academy of Recording Arts & Sciences Grammy site (http://www.grammy.com), The Academy of Television Arts & Sciences Emmys site (http://www.emmys.org), The Tony Awards Online (see Figure 3.13), and The Envelope Please: The Official Interactive Guide to the Academy Awards (http://oscars.guide.com).

FIGURE 3.13 Example of professional organization site—Tony Awards (http://www.tonys.org).

Who's Not There Yet

While virtually everyone in the arts and entertainment industry has heard of the Internet, they are not necessarily using it to further their work. Currently, the following types of entertainment providers are underrepresented on the Internet.

Traditional Publicists, Agents, and Managers

Despite the enormous potential for increasing contacts online, these groups have only begun to explore the Internet. Many do so at the request of their clients, who are already online. One early entry was publicist Bobbi Cowan & Associates (http://www.i-site.com/~bobbi).

Independent Filmmakers

Although they have a tradition of experimentation and adaptation, filmmakers are only beginning to use the Internet as a way to promote and distribute their films outside the conventional industry. One of the few sites created by an independent filmmaker to promote her own material is Jayne Loader's site (http://www.publicshelter.com).

Game Developers

For years, the game industry largely dismissed the Internet. The main reasoning was that the communication lags inherent in the Internet prevented the tenth-of-a-second response times necessary to support "twitch" games. Now that the Internet has become the dominant online network, some companies are taking a fresh look at enabling games over the Internet. However, a surprising number of game companies such as Dwango (http://www.dwango.com) are concentrating on proprietary, non-Internet systems and major game companies such as Sega (http://www.sega.com) provide information-only Web sites. Moving in the opposite direction, the ImagiNation Network, originally a non-Internet online service, has expanded into Internet-based games through its CyberPark site (http://www.inngames.com). While many entertainment Web sites have provided online games, they have yet to become a major feature of Intertainment.

CD-ROM Developers and Desktop Publishers

While some multimedia groups have seized on the Web, others have continued to avoid it. As with game developers, concerns about the Internet's slow data transfer (a 28.8k modem delivers data at less than a tenth of the speed of a CD-ROM) have caused many developers to dismiss it as incapable of supporting full multimedia. An exception is The Voyager Company (http://www.voyagerco.com), which not only established an early presence on the Web, but has also developed software—CDLink—allowing visitors on Web sites to control CD-ROMs and audio CDs in their local computer. As new Internet technologies have allowed multimedia delivery at Web speeds, CD-ROM developers are beginning to see the Internet as a way to expand their interactive environments.

Writers

Text transmits faster than anything else over the Internet, yet professional writers are barely exploring this medium. While most publishing houses have created Web sites for their authors (see Random House's The Lost World site for Michael Crichton at http://www.randomhouse.com/site/lostworld), concerns about unauthorized copying of work and the difficulties of reading text from the computer screen may have discouraged established writers from creating their own Web-based fiction. In contrast, many unpublished writers have been experimenting in this medium; there are several hundred works of hypertext fiction by new authors available on the Web.

Future Content Provider Trends

As the Internet grows, the type and character of content providers will change rapidly. In this last section, some possible future trends in content providers are considered in light of their impact on Internet-based entertainment.

Internet Service Providers Move into Content

Internet Service Providers (ISPs) have traditionally provided access to the Web without creating content of their own. However, the entry of giant telecommunications companies like AT&T into the ISP market has sent smaller regional access providers scrambling for ways to add value to their service. Increasingly, ISPs are tapping their user base to provide original content and it is likely that many will attempt to become exclusive content distributors.

Online Services Move Their Content to the Web

Online services such as CompuServe have always tied their content to proprietary access software. However, the overwhelming success of the Web is causing these companies to "unbundle" their content for Internet distribution. As a step in this direction, America Online has already signed a deal with AT&T to offer its proprietary content through the latter's Worldnet Internet access program. This trend will continue as the online services convert to Internet and Web-based services by the end of 1996.

Increase in Web-specific Entertainment

As the Internet audience becomes larger and the potential of the medium is increasingly explored, many promotional sites for entertainment outside the Web will become entertainment in their own right. This trend can already be seen in the more sophisticated promotional sites for major film releases—where games, user interaction, and sophisticated multimedia already make the Web site worth visiting long after its object has disappeared from the (silver) screen. The push to Web-specific entertainment will also increase once reliable methods of collecting revenue from a Web site (such as the micro-payments discussed in Chapter 9) are available.

Rise in Production Values

As recently as early 1995, most Web sites consisted of text sprinkled with simple pictures. Even on more sophisticated sites, it was common to make an incomplete version of the content available to the public and wait for visitors to the site to catch programming mistakes. By mid-1996, the "under construction" symbol was decreasing in popularity; support for advanced audio, video, and multimedia was routine; and widespread use of 3-D virtual worlds was just around the corner. As software advancement increases the potential of the Web, the production values necessary to create compelling entertainment will continue to rise. However, until modems are replaced by much faster Internet connections, a bandwidth-defined ceiling will exist for production values—limiting the entertainment advantage of large media companies relative to smaller groups.

Small Sites Hold Their Own

Collectively, individual sites are the primary content created for (and visited by) the Internet audience. Despite the entry of traditional entertainment companies, it appears that independently produced Web entertainment is here to stay—causing an array of long-range effects discussed more fully in Part V. As Internet access becomes more common, a substantial majority of the audience may maintain a personal information and entertainment resource—a full, multimedia-based *front end* far surpassing an amusing message on an answering machine—and closer to a virtual agent. Barring major changes in the underlying structure of the Internet, the prosumer-hunter-gatherer nature of content production, consumption, and distribution are likely to continue for the foreseeable future. With these encouraging thoughts, the next section of the book considers the process of creating, launching, administering, and publicizing your own Web-based entertainment.

PART II

BUILDING AN INTERNET ENTERTAINMENT SITE

http://kspace.com/intertainment

CHAPTER 4

THE FOUNDATION: Concept Development and Planning

The first and most important goal of building an Internet entertainment site takes place almost entirely in the mind of the site developer: the creation of a clear concept. While this may seem obvious, keep in mind that many of the entertainment-related Web sites created in 1995 through 1996 showed evidence of haphazard planning, resulting in inferior Web sites that ultimately required additional development time and expense to correct their problems. Often, the sites were nothing more than worried reactions to the challenge of the Internet and to competitors who got online early. In other cases, site concepts have shifted back and forth as the content providers learned the nature of the industry—with some larger organizations passing responsibility for Web site development from department to department until a final development team was formed. The following discussion provides an exposition of the main points needed to develop a Web site concept and examples of well-conceived sites already online. Assembling a development team and the actual development process are considered in Chapters 5 and 6.

 Should You Build a Site?

Before committing to create an entertainment-related Web site, ask yourself if it is really worth doing. You will need to determine whether you should invest the time, effort, and training to develop for the Internet. While anyone connected with entertainment needs a personal Internet connection to explore the new medium, there is little point in developing a site if it "isn't time" for your brand of entertainment. To decide if it is worth doing, both individuals and organizations will need to ask themselves the same questions.

Have You Explored the Internet Enough to Use It Effectively?

Consider the chances for promoting an act you have never seen or producing a film without ever watching one! The Internet is a unique medium, distinct enough from other media that it has features which do not exist elsewhere. Web sites designed blindly from the outside have little chance of success. It is not sufficient to get the "resident nerd" online; anyone responsible for content should have at least a *personal* Internet connection or ready access to one. Successful development requires that everyone involved in the project understand how the Internet differs from other entertainment media. Misunderstandings of topics like appropriate "netiquette" for promoting Web sites, the role of audience feedback, or even the average speed of a home user's connection can lead to serious problems. By making sure your Web site fits with the "Internet way" you will avoid some of the missteps taken by even the largest media companies.

Consider the stages in the evolution of a Web site put up by a major entertainment company. As is typical for the industry, initially a small group of "believers" within the company secured a small amount of funding to create the site, largely responding to pressure from other competitor entertainment corporations already on the Web. The first incarnation of the site, developed in isolation, contained some interesting visual concepts, but only began to scratch the total range of entertainment available. Its main effect after going online was as a catalyst for "war" within the company, involving employees who felt that they, too, should have control over the content of the site. As a result, the group involved in the site became much larger and less able to reach a consensus. The end result of this stage was a radical redesign of the site into a generic form in order to please the lowest common denominator. Instead of the initial quirky graphics, a sterile wall with plastic buttons greeted visitors. This state of affairs continued for some time until finally a team was formed consisting of new employees and several existing staff from the marketing and graphics departments. Once again abandoning the current concept, they imposed a new design which essentially repackaged the graphics and promotional material found in the company's magazine advertising. Clearly, a well-developed concept planned from the very beginning for expansion—rather than repeatedly reworked and replaced—would have saved a great deal of energy and expense.

Is Your Industry Online?

Adoption of the Web has proceeded much more rapidly in some areas than others. With current trends, anyone involved in the creation, promotion, and distribution of music should get involved. Other hot areas are visual art, electronic magazine publishing, and entertainment venues such as clubs and coffeehouses. Up-and-coming areas include live performance and virtual meeting places. Paradoxically, other *new media* such as games and CD-ROMs have moved more slowly and sites devoted to this area must be planned carefully to be useful. Despite the hype about Internet-based broadcasting, this area is furthest away from practical use.

Is a Low-cost Alternative to a Full Web Site a Better Starting Point?

It is possible to post simple classified ads and phonebook-style listings on hundreds of Web sites, usually for free. Typically, all that is required to put information into a directory is to log onto the site and type information into a fill-out form. Certain sites, such as Planet Tripod (http://www.tripod.com/planet) provide *free home pages* which are very similar to classifieds. More sophisticated listings, frequently catering to a specific area of the industry cost between $10 and $200 to create and maintain. These options are most useful for providing contact information like phone numbers and addresses for virtually nothing, and their impact is similar to a yellow pages listing in the offline world.

A much more sophisticated option which still falls short of an independent Web site is to buy a place in a meta-site such as Kaleidospace (http://kspace.com). These sites typically showcase the content of dozens to thousands of arts and entertainment professionals, including individuals and companies. Meta-sites are often very low in cost (ranging within a few hundred dollars) and allow individuals and companies to have a sophisticated presence without having to actually develop the Web pages. If you are an individual or group associated with a larger entertainment corporation (such as a musician signed to a label), you might be able to avoid development costs altogether if the entertainment corporation has already built a site and is offering free space to its artists. However, if the corporation has not yet gotten online, you may want to build an independent site or encourage the corporation to get some sort of Web presence. Since meta-sites usually have large numbers of visitors, they are effective in getting unknown individuals and companies in the arts and entertainment industry noticed.

On the other hand, the artist's site is usually accessed through the meta-site's Internet address rather than one of their own. For example, New Age musician Steven Halpern on Kaleidospace is accessed by typing http://kspace.com/halpern. In contrast, the URL linking to the custom "home page" developed specifically for Halpern is http://www.innerpeacemusic.com. The tradeoff here is between the branding the meta-site provides and the value of a unique site name. Kaleidospace and some other meta-sites also provide custom domain names for an additional fee in order to give their clients more autonomy. For example, URL http://halpern.com could be linked to the same page accessed by typing http://kspace.com/halpern.

Is the Concept Practical?

Despite its rapid growth and increasing sophistication, the Web is not an appropriate medium for all concept applications. For example, allowing visitors to the Web site to download entire movies isn't practical; *a single second* of full-screen, full-motion video could take *hours* to download through the average home Internet connection. Another problem is that the typical Web server can only handle a few hundred people simultaneously connected to the same online chat or audio broadcast. (In practice, several times this number may be using the site for looking at Web pages, but since they click their mouse buttons at slightly different times, the load is distributed.) Other concerns include underestimating the effort required to update content on the Web site or the time needed to bring the site online. For example, if you were planning to manually update the listings in MovieLink (http://www.777film.com)—which contains thousands of daily entries—you might as well hire a small army! Due to the frequent gap between concept and implementation, it is always helpful to have a proposal reviewed by someone who has experience building and maintaining Web sites.

A medium-sized record label had operated a basic Web site for over a year; the site served up pictures, sound clips, and "inside" information. Because of its simplicity, the site was able to serve thousands of individuals daily from a single computer without slowdowns. Pleased with this success, the company made plans to run a virtual "concert" which would allow up to 30,000 people to enjoy a live broadcast feed digitized on-the-fly and sent over the Internet. They confidently assumed that they could use their existing Web site for this purpose, until they were informed that they would need close to 50 high-speed computers to handle the concert! Needless to say, the budget for the project wasn't approved and more than a few individuals were embarrassed.

Is the Concept Affordable?

Chapter 1 discussed how launching a basic site on the Web is relatively inexpensive. However, larger sites require significant amounts of money to complete. The figure is only a guide, but costs for entertainment-related Web sites will be near the higher end. This is due to their extensive use of audio and video multimedia, as well as frequent application of advanced programming techniques. When the content on the site is *repurposed* from other media, such as movies and books, additional licensing and administrative charges may apply. After the Web site is created, there will be additional (often monthly) charges to simply keep it connected to the Internet. Monthly charges for smaller sites are comparable to maintaining an individual Internet account, while large sites requiring dedicated computer hardware may cost several thousand dollars per month simply to remain online. The latter cost can be lowered if the larger site is initially maintained on a rented computer on a remote server rental service, instead of being in-house.

Who Will Create the Site?

Once the decision has been made to build an entertainment-oriented Web site, the next step is deciding who will build it. More detail on using the following options is provided in Chapter 5.

Do It Yourself

For an individual with artistic and technical leanings, it is perfectly possible to learn the basics of creating a Web page in only a few hours of study. This option is ideal for individual entertainers or professionals who must build their site as economically as possible.

Outsource to a Consultant or Design Group

This is the best decision for those who don't have the time for Web programming themselves, at the expense of some loss of control over the *look and feel* of the final site. Often, the most repetitive work of a larger site is outsourced, while the key creative work is done by the in-house team.

Develop an In-House Design Team

This is the preferred choice for larger companies already planning to connect their employees to the Internet or those with existing design-marketing-publicity groups that want to expand their work to the Internet.

What Is the Source of the Site's Content?

A key decision point in creating Internet-based entertainment is the source of the content on the site. Three main sources are available: repurposed, original, and user-generated—though most sites will contain some of each.

FIGURE 4.1 Sony online (http://www.sony.com).

Repurposed

This is content which existed in another medium prior to being put on the Internet. Examples of repurposed sites include those running trailers from current movies, displaying book excerpts from bestsellers, and rebroadcasting radio or TV news spots. A specific example is Sony, as shown in Figure 4.1.

Original

These sites cannot rest on their reputation in other media—everything they do is on the Internet. The first form of this site is content which has been specifically developed for the Web and does not have a counterpart elsewhere. Examples include Web-based dramas and games, original art and music developed for the Web, and technologies such as virtual reality. An excellent example is The Spot, http://www.thespot.com (see

Chapter 1). The other type of original site contains material created outside the Web, which, because of a lack of promotion or distribution, is unavailable elsewhere. A good example of a site with material not found elsewhere is our own site for "unsigned" artists and musicians, Kaleidospace at http://kspace.com (see Chapter 1).

User-Generated

This form of content is virtually unique to the Internet and could be seen as part of the *original* category, yet it needs special attention during the concept development stage. Content within user-generated sites is literally created by the user or site visitor as opposed to the content provider. In this case, the provider must pay more attention to implementing interactive technologies such as tools which enable site visitors to contribute to content on the site. The audience both contributes to and is entertained by the site's content. More examples include collaborative art and fiction projects, dating and personals sites, industry question-and-answer forums, and user opinion polls. TV Net at http://tvnet.com (see Chapter 1) is an excellent example of a site with a large amount of user-generated input.

Each kind of site puts different demands on the development plant. If the content from other media is being repurposed, the main concerns will include securing the right to put it on the Internet, converting it into Internet-accessible form, and organizing it for effective use by fans. Since repurposed entertainment has a counterpart outside the Web, the goal of the site will naturally steer more towards promotion and sales of the product in the other medium. For original content, make the site compelling enough so that the audience will explore it and become involved. Also, focus attention on how to make original content sites pay for themselves, an issue which is less important for repurposed content sites. User-driven content shares the concern of making money and adds the requirement for advanced programming and design to collect and organize visitor input into a coherent whole. The site developer must allow visitors to post comments, share opinions through voting programs, and interact with each other through chat rooms—instead of digitizing existing material or managing arts and entertainment clients.

Will the Content Require Frequent Updates?

Web sites occupy an intermediate position between *static* products such as books and CDs, and *dynamic* content such as television programming. For this reason, any concept developed for a Web site must include provisions for modifying material on a regular basis. Updates include changes to the content itself, the format, and the *look and feel* of the graphic links used to navigate through the Web site. For most sites, the overall look and feel changes over a period of months or years, while content changes every few days. Certain sites may not require continual updates, such as those created for time-specific events (e.g., annual concerts and conventions). Normally, these sites are updated before and during the event, and become static archives thereafter. On the other extreme, sites providing time-sensitive information such as sports scores need to change literally by the minute; this requires specialized Web programming (see Chapter 6) to constantly digitize information and feed it into the Web site.

An important feature of Web-based updates is that the old material doesn't have to be discarded. In fact, most visitors will expect to find an *archive* of older material. For example, a site listing current events may simply store its old pages in an archive area of the site. This is a tremendous boon for electronic publishing, since archiving back issues creates an instant library of material. If archives will be created, it is necessary to provide for the additional storage space—which can be considerable for audio and video clips. In general, costs for updating are roughly equivalent to developing the same amount of material for the very first time. On small-scale Web sites, it is practical to rewrite Web pages directly. Large sites will require custom programs which can regenerate large numbers of pages on-the-fly to reflect updates.

User-driven input is a special case. New content is continually supplied without any work by the developer. Because of this, adding user-driven input can help make a relatively static site more dynamic and interesting, as well as lowering update costs. For example, a small Web site might run an opinion poll ranking favorite entertainment personalities or a simple chat room for its fan club. (This could be made easier with programming techniques mentioned in Chapter 6 which allow the site to update itself automatically and ensures that the user-driven content is well-organized.)

Who Is the Audience for the Site?

Now that Internet demographics (see Chapter 2) have become widely available, it is possible to look at the goals of an Internet-based entertainment site and compare them to the interests of a real audience. Forget market trends which identify the Internet user as a nerd; the demographics speak otherwise! Since time slots do not exist on the Web, a site does not have to appeal to the largest audience to be successful. In fact, the best strategy may be to identify a smaller, extremely specific audience and build the site to provide *micro-entertainment* specifically for them.

One of the most interesting features of this chart is that categories of music popular on the radio show lower sales relative to extremely *niche* artists. If the site had been created based on radio trends, sales would have suffered significantly. Because of the Internet's strength in micro-marketing to niche groups, define the *intended* audience very carefully (e.g., art collectors, sound therapists, actors' agents, comedy club owners) and develop a Web site that speaks specifically to it.

If a site contains "adults only" material, it will be necessary to develop a system to restrict access to the content. First, get a "rating" for material using PICS (Platform for Internet Content Selection) or another system, then contact companies providing lists of "adult" sites to Internet users. (See Chapter 13 on Cyberlaw for additional discussion.)

Is the Site Isolated or Does It Fit within an Existing "Community" of Web Sites?

The hyperlink allows Internet users to seamlessly jump between dozens of Web sites in a short period of time. For some sites, creating a network of relationships with other complimentary or related sites will be the key to their success. Examples would be movie archives with extensive hyper-linking to personal Web pages of actors and directors, or country folk art and ragtime music album pages linking to relevant history and travel sites. Contrary to what one might expect, reciprocal links between com-petitors (usually exchanged without charge) are standard on the Internet and are almost essential to ensure high visitor traffic. If a large number of *outlinks* are needed, the development concept should include a plan for contacting other Web sites to arrange reciprocal connections. (Note that most individuals trying to *sell* links—especially through mass email—are attempting to raise their own traffic rather than benefit yours!)

What Result Do You Expect from the Web Site?

If you decide to create an entertainment presence on the Web, the next step is to specify what you expect it to do for you or your group. Your intended results must be clearly defined and understood by the content provider and the development group.

Promotion

Even the most basic Web sites can provide effective promotion for enter-tainment found offline. Promotional sites are simple to construct, but their success may be harder to gauge (see Chapter 8). Measure the value of the site by a combination of the quantity of overall visitor traffic and

FIGURE 4.2 *Batman Forever* (http://batmanforever.com).

the subset of visitors who respond to the promotion. Of course, a more specific indication of the site's effectiveness comes from qualitative feedback from the audience through survey forms and email. The inclusion of these types of feedback forms turns the site from a billboard to a promotional screening complete with audience surveys—a two-way interface. Figure 4.2 is an example of a site containing promotion-only material—*Batman Forever* (http://batmanforever.com).

Sales and Distribution

Advancements in programming and *secure* Web software allow virtual shopping on a global basis; total product sales over the Internet exceeded $140 million in 1995. Average sales, while still relatively small compared to other media, should be especially appealing to artists and entertainers who currently do not have distribution for their products. Online sales also offer the opportunity to sell tickets to shows and entertainment on the Web itself. Many companies will also want to provide entertainment to sell non-entertainment products. By creating Web sites which are branded with their product while simultaneously providing entertaining sites, they have expanded the definition of advertising. For an example of a site which concentrates on selling existing products, see Figure 4.3 on CDnow.

Placement

Web sites may also function as placement centers where individual artists and entertainers can communicate with industry professionals, and where

FIGURE 4.3 CDnow (http://cdnow.com).

professional-to-professional relationships can be mediated. Individuals can display portfolios and participate in online music or script *pitch sessions* without the time and expense of mass mailings. Other sites of this type can provide a bulletin board or classified ad service for industry pro-

FIGURE 4.4 TalentCast (http://www.talentcast.com).

FIGURE 4.5 Hollywood Network (http://hollywoodnetwork.com).

fessionals to communicate with each other and with entertainers. Examples of sites of this type include talent agencies displaying actor *head shots* such as TalentCast (Figure 4.4) or the industry posting board on the Hollywood Network (Figure 4.5).

Pure Intertainment

Some ambitious Web sites are designed as entertainment in themselves, instead of promoting or distributing existing entertainment. Providing Internet-based entertainment requires compelling content and extensive interactivity with site visitors to be successful. This online entertainment could also have a counterpart in the offline world (e.g., services such as online concerts, art auctions, and script pitch sessions). Creating new entertainment that is Internet-specific is challenging but can lead to immense popularity. Not surprisingly, these site developers must use the most advanced design and programming to be effective. For an example of an online entertainment site, check out the Internet-wide game site, Riddler (Figure 4.6).

Will Access to the Site Be Unlimited or "Members-Only?"

When the first graphical Web sites appeared in 1993, they were "wide-open"—anyone from the general Internet could log onto them and remain anonymous. If the site's content consists of promotions found in other media, a completely open site will be the system of choice. However, if the site contains pay-per-view material or content of an explicit or

FIGURE 4.6 Riddler (http://www.riddler.com).

adult nature, a subscription model with restricted access is more appropriate. Even if overall access is restricted, it is a good idea to allow unlimited, "free" access to an area of the site. This *foyer* of what is referred to as a two-tiered (or multi-tiered) site can introduce the audience to the nature and purpose of the site, give a limited guided tour of the site, provide examples of the subscription area in order to attract a subscription audience, and provide signup forms and other means of registering for membership. Totally closed sites tend to irritate casual visitors who often

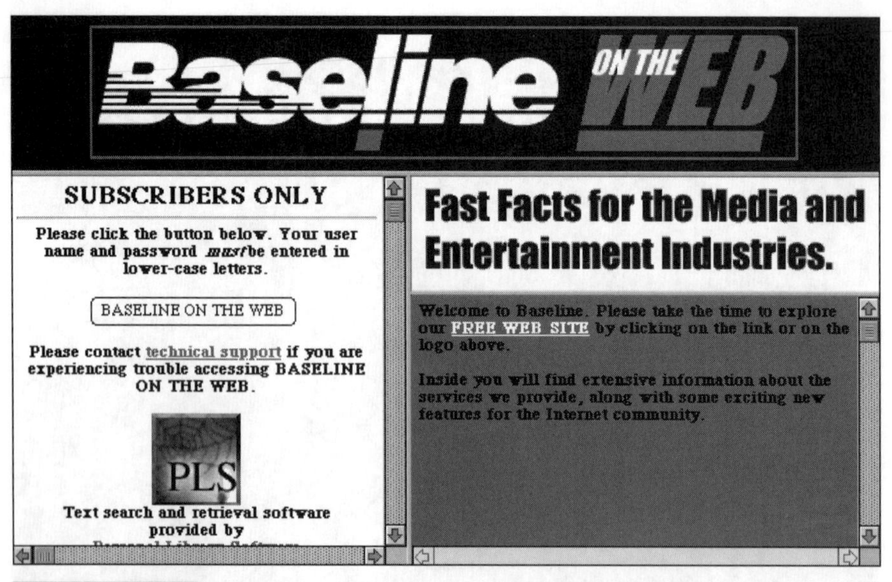

FIGURE 4.7 BaseLine (http://www.pkbaseline.com).

become frustrated when they are unable to find out what the site is all about. An example of a two-tiered site is Paul Kagan's BaseLine (Figure 4.7), a subscription-based entertainment and media resource that offers a free preview of the site as an option to its site visitors.

 Steps in Concept Development

Your content, no matter how entertaining, will be difficult to appreciate if it is not organized into a larger vision. Developing this vision, or concept, is the key step leading to a viable Intertainment site.

Choosing a Name for the Site

The first thing any prospective site visitor needs to know is the Internet URL address of your Web site. In order to obtain a URL, you need to register a domain name. These names are administrated by an organization known as the InterNIC (http://internic.net)—one of the few points of central control on the Internet. To reserve a name for your site, contact the InterNIC and request the name. The InterNIC also maintains a database of names already in use. (Yes, most of the obvious ones are taken!)

Domain names have a very specific basic structure. The domain name for the Kaleidospace site is kspace.com (with "kspace" representing the name of the company that created the site and the name of the site itself).

"Kspace" is merely short for "Kaleidospace" and was chosen so that site visitors would not have trouble spelling the site's domain. The ".com" which ends the address is especially significant, since it distinguishes the site as commercial—as opposed to another type of site such as government or educational—in nature. This ending in many cases also indicates the country of origin (e.g, .ru = Russia; .uk = Great Britain) The complete URL (as introduced in Chapter 1) is in the following format: http://kspace.com (with email usually illustrated as: name@kspace.com). Note that the "www" prefix found on many sites (e.g., www.kspace.com) is *not* essential. Both versions of the name should work on a properly configured Web site. The only exceptions are sites connected to certain brands of security *firewall* software (see chapter 5) that insist on the "www" prefix.

There are several things you should consider when choosing an Internet domain name for the Web site. Remember that it is more than a label; it is a shorthand that visitors will have to type in order to reach the site. Thus, brevity should win out over being specific. Just as kspace.com is a better choice than kaleidospace.com, bigthing.com is a *much* better domain name than hollywoodsbiggestthing.com (even if the latter is the actual site name). It is also important to use a name that is unlikely to be misspelled because it resembles another word. For example, if your last name is "Chacken" and you own an agency called Chacken Artist Management Inc., the domain chacken.com might not be the greatest choice because it may often be mis-typed to reflect a more common English word (e.g., chicken.com). In this case, it may be better to reserve an acronym (cam.com or cami.com) if available.

In addition to misspellings, general awkwardness should be avoided. For example, if your company is called A & B Films, you might want to avoid a domain name such as aandbfilms.com or aandb.com. (Ampersands [&] cannot be used in domain names.) It not only looks a bit awkward, but it will be easy for your prospective audience to omit the first "a" and have general trouble remembering the name. In the case of A & B Films, a better choice would be abfilms.com or the name of the actual site, if different (e.g., filmspace.com).

If you're absolutely set on a particular name that is owned by someone else, it still may be possible to buy the name. While the rampant "name speculation" of 1994 and early 1995 is for the most part over, many individuals and groups own names which they intend to sell to the highest bidder rather than use directly. The cost for a name is likely to be several thousand dollars and may be considerably higher for a *golden* name like movies.com. Due to the demand for names, several Web sites specializing as *name brokers* are available on the Internet. At one of these sites, BrokerAgent.Com (http://brokeragent.com), it is possible to bid on domain names and even complete Web sites.

Choosing the General Class of Site

The next step in concept development is to identify the type of site you want to create. In the short history of Internet-based entertainment, a variety of distinct Web sites have been developed. While some of these may seem familiar, many of them are new services unique to the Internet. For example, your needs will be vastly different if you are running a site devoted to a single album release as opposed to an entire label. In the first case, you will have more of a micro-level concentration on the album concept and the artists and production team behind it; in the latter case, you may present more of a macro-level overview of the label's image. Refer to Chapter 3 for detailed descriptions of site classes. If you need more ideas after choosing the class, refer to Part IV. Don't feel restricted to standard entertainment forms. The Internet will undoubtedly help to create entertainment that no one has thought of yet!

Choosing a Literal or Metaphorical Web Site

Once the basic concept is in place, it is necessary to define the general interface it will present to visitors. Many Web sites solve this by organizing their entertainment around familiar place metaphors such as malls, towns, and studios. This has the advantage of providing an immediate

FIGURE 4.8 Southwest Airlines (http:/iflyswa.com).

FIGURE 4.9 Warner Bros. (http://warnerbros.com).

mental image to visitors navigating through the site, as well as suggesting a layout for the Web pages. Metaphorical concepts are likely to become more common as software enabling virtual reality and 3-D worlds are integrated into the Web. Following are some examples of site concepts.

Spatial

This category refers to Web sites built on macro spaces, such as cities or solar systems, and micro spaces, such as a room or a backyard. An example of a micro space home page is Southwest Airlines' home gate (Figure 4.8), and an example of a macro space is Warner Bros.' film studio lot home page (Figure 4.9).

Representational Object

Much less common than spatial sites are object-oriented sites, which tie different aspects of entertainment content to parts of a single object. For example, different areas of a travel site might be accessed by selecting parts of a train, ship, or airplane. Examples of object sites include american recordings (Figure 4.10), which uses the record label's American flag logo as its object; Los Angeles radio station KSCA (Figure 4.11), which uses a tunable radio as its object; and Kaleidospace itself (Figure 4.12), which uses the "end" of a kaleidoscope—also one of its company logos—as its object.

Person or Entity

A Web site may be designed as the *home* of an entity or person who expects to receive visitors there. The site is organized around favorite things, services provided, products sold, and where the entity or person

FIGURE 4.10 American recordings (http://american.recordings.com).

"lives" in the virtual world. This concept is particularly suited to sites which dispense advice or facilitate person-to-person contacts. An example of this type of site is the distinctly non-entertainment-related (yet "entertaining") TaxWizard (Figure 4.13), which depicts the wizard in his room containing objects that aid him in performing his services for visitors.

Time or Event

The visitor to sites of this type experiences an event or progression. These sites range from those which change depending on the time of the

FIGURE 4.11 KSCA (http://ksca.com).

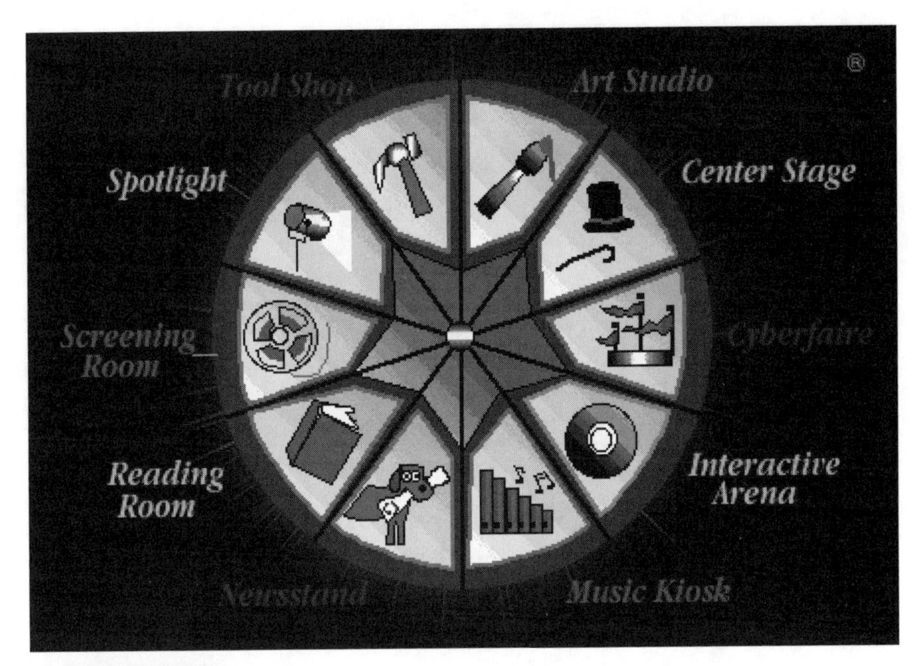

FIGURE 4.12 Kspace wheel logo (http://kspace.com).

day, those sites which consist of rapidly changing information like sports, or those presenting an ongoing story (episodic) or game. Unique to the Internet are sites which allow the audience to control remote devices like cameras or mechanical arms. On these sites, the action—rather than

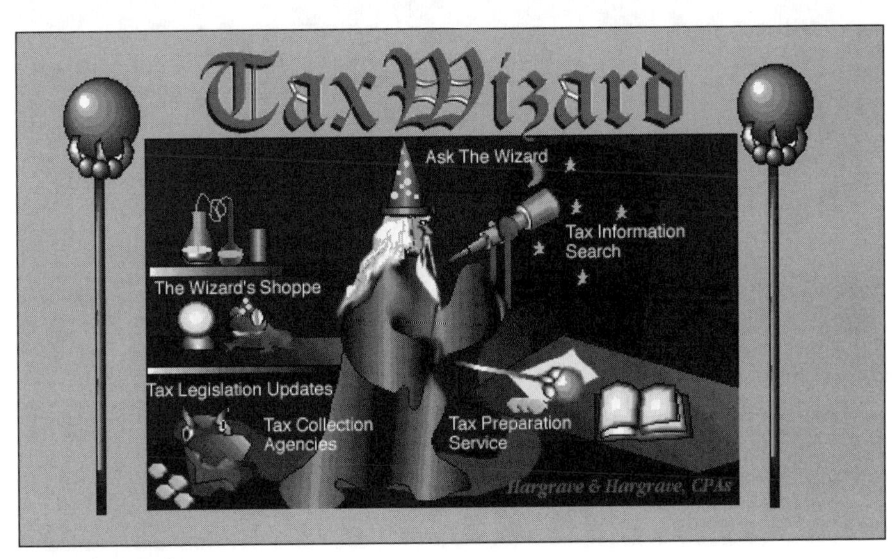

FIGURE 4.13 TaxWizard (http://taxwizard.com).

FIGURE 4.14 Fishcam (http://www.netscape.com/fishcam/fish_refresh.html).

places, objects, or people—is the main attraction. A fascinating example of this is the Fishcam (Figure 4.14), where an hour's worth of ongoing activities inside a saltwater aquarium is compressed into a short animation sequence which is refreshed every 15 seconds! At the "Hey! What's

FIGURE 4.15 Comedy Central (http://www.comcentral.com/CC/livetv.htm).

On Comedy Central Right Now?" page (Figure 4.15)—which is part of the Comedy Central Web site—the audience can see a screen shot of what is actually being broadcast on Comedy Central. By hitting the *reload* button on the browser, any site visitor can see a new "live" shot of what's happening on the cable channel.

Another aspect of Web metaphor concerns the entertainment itself. While *episodic* sites on the Internet bear little resemblance to television shows, their creators nevertheless refer to their product as *virtual television*. Until the Internet has become a well-established medium in its own right, it will sometimes be necessary to analogize its entertainment to existing media.

Literal

While metaphorical sites are very common, many sites forego this to provide more straightforward interfaces with purely functional controls and abstract graphics. *Literal* sites with straightforward, no-nonsense concepts are useful when the entertainment content is itself easily recognizable (e.g., video clips from popular movies) or for sites promoting professional-to-professional contacts. In this case, visitors already understand the content and don't need additional help from a graphic analogy. While literal sites may use graphics and even icons, these are created based on the structure of the site rather than the metaphor determining the structure of the site. Examples of literal sites include the Discovery Channel (Figure 4.16) and C|Net (Figure 4.17).

FIGURE 4.16 Discovery Channel (http://www.discovery.com).

join now
To access member-only services

departments
- CNET news
- CNET radio
- CNET television
- reviews
- features
- CD-ROM central
- best of the Web
- personalities
- product finder
- gamecenter

resources
- software central
- info source
- glossary
- tech central
- tech advisers

community
- feedback
- about CNET
- CNET audio tour
- live studio cam
- member services
- posting
- polling

search services
- SEARCH.COM improved!
- SHAREWARE.COM
- product finder

marketplace
- hot deals
- sponsors

upgrade central:
pump up your pixels
in features

The ultimate guide to ISDN
CNET puts 16 new ISDN adapters to the test. Plus: everything you need to know about getting connected.

200-MHz Pentiums
CNET reviews the fastest Pentiums yet.

Microsoft gets a jolt of Java
Battle of the beta browsers, continued: Internet Explorer 3.0 beta now supports Java.

Quake is here!
Let *gamecenter* show you where to get it and how to win.

10 color ink jets for less than $500
Color printouts have never been easier. Find out which printers deliver the best quality fastest--and cheapest.

Is the Net threatening your privacy?
Find out what information about you is on the Web.

The future of money
Digital cash promises to make paying for goods and services simpler than ever. When will it be ready for you?

30 new games to download!
Don't comb the Net for games: the power gamer's downloading guide can do it for you.

top news
Georgia trademark law challenged

CEO resigns as Borland expects loss

typo.com
What's in a (domain) name?

Happy birthday, CNET.COM!
Barr takes a look back at CNET's whirlwind first year

Mike Slade
Celebs and sports put Starwave on the virtual map

Find it with SEARCH.COM
The only complete search site on the Web

Supercharged Windows video
Number Nine pushes graphics boards to the max with Series 2

Longbow afterglow
Why Jane's new attack helicopter sim is a sure shot

Polling
Do you use Java?

join now
To access member-only services

FIGURE 4.17 ClNet (http://www.cnet.com).

Developing a Flowchart for the Web Site

Unlike broadcast media, the visitor's experience of a Web site does not proceed in a strict order from beginning to end; it often resembles a branching exploration of an unknown environment. Because of this, content on a Web site must be linked in complex, multidimensional patterns which let visitors find their own way to it. As an essential step in concept development, therefore, sketch a series of rough flowcharts for the site including individual Web pages, multimedia, and the hyperlinks connecting them. Figure 4.18 shows an example of such a flowchart representing the pages in two dimensions. Such a graphic is far easier to evaluate than a page-by-page description or worse, no design at all. (Once you have begun the actual site development process, you may want to make a more detailed storyboard for design and navigational purposes.) The chart should help you determine the following information:

- Average number of hyperlinks the visitor clicks on to find material
- Locations of *short-cuts* linking information back to the *home page*

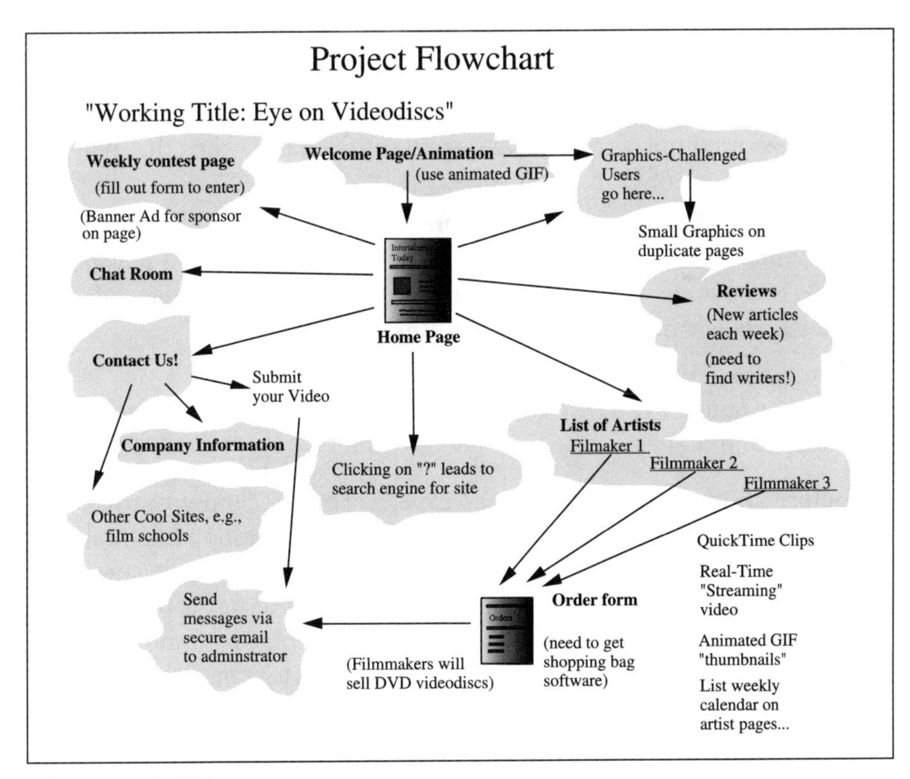

FIGURE 4.18 Initial flowchart for Web site concept.

- Potential *cul de sacs* where the visitor can get lost
- Locations of *help* information and visitor *feedback*
- Set of navigational elements that need to be designed in the display
- Location of order forms, ads, and special promotions
- Placement and format of *outlinks* that will link to other Web sites
- Structure of alternate paths for visitors with slow connections
- General type of concept for graphic design

Degree of User Control

Another element of Web navigation is the degree to which the audience has control of what it sees and hears. The basic structure of Web pages and hyperlinks allows for almost complete freedom, but recently some Web designers have integrated constraints into their sites. Consider the following features (discussed in more detail in Chapter 6):

- Auto-refresh: This HTML programming tag allows the Web site to update the visitor's page at periodic intervals. Some developers have used it to create an automatic "slide show" on the visitor's screen.
- Inline Animation: Animated sequences—whether simple image swaps or complex multimedia—present fixed programs that play independent of visitor control.
- Delivery of Content Tailored to the Visitor: Using the *cookie* technology (see Chapter 8) possible with Netscape and other advanced Web browsers, it is possible to restrict access based on the audience's behavior on earlier trips to the Web site.
- Audio and Video Broadcast: Programmers can present a fixed sequence of audio or video information by utilizing broadcast technologies.

Before controlling the audience's experiences, the content providers should take a very hard look at whether visitors will respond favorably. As discussed in Chapter 2, it is a mistake to think that this new audience prefers to let the Web site make its choices. The Internet is fundamentally a two-way, on-demand system; if visitors are *channeled* into predefined programming, they may resist and cease to visit the site altogether. For example, many sites have made themselves unpopular simply by forcing visitors to listen to a sound clip when they connect to the site's home page. Even if entertainment offered by the site consists solely of broadcast audio and video, protocols already exist or are being rapidly developed that allow visitors to control the broadcast just like a VCR tape player. The successful Web sites limit visitor choice only briefly and for maximum effect, such as short animation clips playing at key locations in the site.

Types of Interactivity

Adding interactive components to the site can enhance the audience's ability to interact with the content providers and each other. Although details for implementing interactive methods are described in Chapter 6, a general knowledge of their existence is necessary for planning the site.

Email

Virtually any Web page can contain email links. This is a good way to allow feedback to the site designers or developers, or for comments on particular aspects of the site. With email links mixed into the content pages, visitors can respond while they are being entertained.

Fill-Out Forms

By adding text fields, buttons, and menus to a page, the audience can order products and provide demographic information.

Bulletin Board Postings

Posting software allows users to respond to messages left by other visitors to the site, allowing *threaded* discussions to take place.

Polls

Polling allows visitors to record their opinions by voting and see the results displayed online.

Online Chat

Chat rooms serve a dual function: the audiences can meet their favorite entertainer or talk with each other in real time.

Multilanguage and Multi-browser Support

Newer Web servers can detect the national origin of the visitor and deliver Web pages in the default language. Similar systems allow users to configure access to the site depending on the display capabilities of their Web browser.

How Will You Determine If the Site Is Fulfilling Its Purpose?

A final issue which must be addressed during concept development is how to monitor the success of the project. Depending on the purpose it could be number of visits, number of sales, or successful execution of programming. One general indication of a site's success is how many links on the Internet point to it after several months online; this topic is discussed as part of netpublicity in Chapter 7. Email from visitors can greatly help in determining if a site is working. In addition to compliments, email frequently helps developers spot errors such as *broken links* and graphics that don't display properly on all monitors.

From Concept to Plan

After the concept has been developed, you may want to put together a plan for the site. The plan could be two to three pages long for a personal Web site or several times that length for a large site. If you are developing a site for another company, it is generally necessary to create a proposal for the site—complete with estimated costs and time to completion. Sometimes, including demographic data such as that discussed in Chapters 2 and 3 bolsters the case for the Web site. The final result should be succinct and clear. The following is a suggested format for the proposal:

- Short summary of proposal. This should be a compact, one-to-two-page version of the proposal, following the "executive summary" format.
- Description of site purpose. This should describe why the site is being created and what effect it will have on promotion, sales, marketing, and distribution.
- Concept for the site. This section describes the type of site, size, the general method of implementation, graphics, method for navigation, and any special and/or unusual features.
- Features used to implement the concept. Description of any advanced programming methods like CGI, Java, or Shockwave (Chapter 6) necessary for the site appears here.
- Cost summary. This should include estimated costs for hardware, software, personnel, and site hosting on an ISP or IPP (Chapter 5)—broken down into development and maintenance categories.
- Estimated timetable for completion of project. The breakdown includes research, creating the production studio, site development, and preparations for site launch.
- Maintenance and upgrades. This should list the work that will be necessary once the site is online, including personnel, hardware, and software.

- Future expansions options. Provisions for adding to the site as it grows, including additional programming, hardware and software upgrades, and changes in administration and updates are given.
- Appendix. A graphical flowchart shows navigational structure of site, Candidate graphics, navigational tools for the site, a mock-up of one or more pages, and any demographics and marketing information relevant to the site.
- Formal business plan. In some cases, particularly if you are seeking funding for development, it will be necessary to create a full business and marketing plan as well. While a comprehensive discussion of Web business plans is beyond the scope of this book, a good starting point for research has been written by Dennis Galletta (http://www.pitt.edu/~galletta/iplan.html) as part of his ongoing courses at the University of Pittsburgh.

With your underlying concept firmly in place, the next step in realizing your vision for Internet-based entertainment is to create a virtual production studio for Web development. The next chapter describes the tools and other resources needed to build a virtual production studio for Web sites of all sizes.

CHAPTER 5

THE FRAMEWORK:

Tools, Parts, Labor, and the Virtual Production Studio

After reading the last chapter, you should have a clear concept in mind for your Web site. Before beginning actual development, assemble the hardware, software, and personnel needed to carry the project to its completion. If you have decided to put your material on a meta-site such as Kaleidospace, you only need to supply your material to the site owners—in effect, outsourcing all the Web development work. However, if you are creating a custom Web site of your own, you will be doing a significant amount of production work. First, in order to turn your concept into reality, create a *virtual production studio* using the following components:

- Hardware and software for content development
- A Web server computer which stores the Web site content and automatically provides it to Internet visitors
- A physical connection between the Web server and the Internet
- Personnel to develop the content and maintain the Web site once it is online

This chapter focuses on each of these components in turn to show how each can be used to turn an entertainment concept into a functioning Web site. The chapter assumes some knowledge of computers and the use of HTML (Hypertext Markup Language), known as the "language of the Web."

Types of Production Studios

Figure 5.1 shows the main components used to develop Web sites of different sizes. Despite costs ranging between a few hundred to a million dollars, essentially the same components are necessary in all cases. A *development system* is used to create and digitize the text, graphics, audio, and video content for the Web site. Completed content is sent to a *Web server* which automatically responds to content requests from the general Internet. Two connections run between the development system and Web server. The first allows content to be sent from the development system to the server and the second connects the server to the general Internet. Depending on the concept, budget, and existing resources, you can assemble a production studio with these components at several levels:

- Studio A: Individual Site Development. If you are putting up a basic site for your band, consulting service, or art gallery, you can build a small but complete studio starting with a single personal computer. Standard text and graphic processing programs can be used to create individual Web pages—though additional hardware will be necessary to convert photos, sound, and video material into digital form. Once complete, the site will be *hosted* on server computers maintained by an *Internet Service Provider (ISP)*, who also provides the connection between the development system and the Internet. If you lack the time and resources to develop the whole site yourself, outsource part of the work to a freelance Web developer.
- Studio B: Adapting an Existing In-house Multimedia Studio for Web Development. If you already have several computers at your

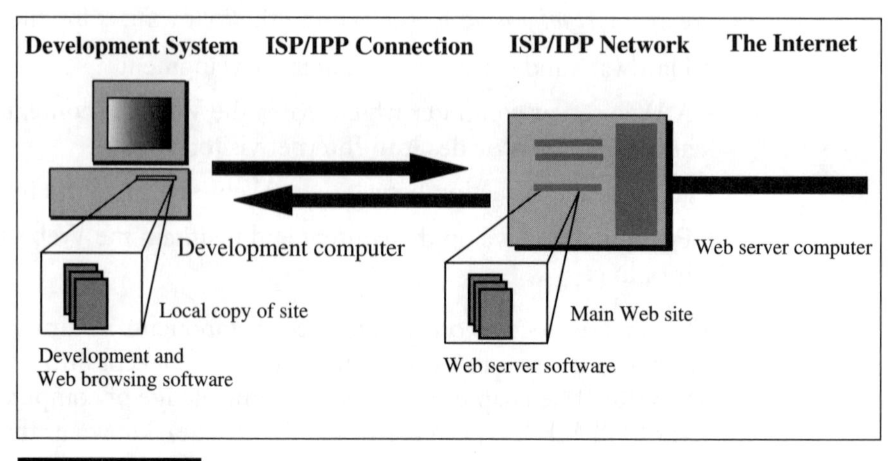

FIGURE 5.1 Generalized Web production studio.

disposal or your company is involved in computer-related development—such as desktop publishing or CD-ROM authoring— you can adapt the existing systems for Web production. You also need to establish a connection between the development computers and an ISP capable of hosting the Web site.

- Studio C: Running the Web Server on an In-house Network. For companies investing heavily in Internet-based entertainment and supporting a large development staff, serving content directly to the Internet through the studio's own network is the method of choice. In this case, a very fast link is established between the Internet and the company and the Web server is placed directly on the development network. In addition to developing the site's content, the studio will be responsible for administering the Web server and installing specialized hardware.

In the remainder of the chapter, each type of studio is considered in turn, detailing differing requirements for hardware, software, and personnel. Based on the complexity of your original concept, you should already have some idea of which studio is appropriate for your production.

Studio A: Individual Site Development

One of the remarkable features of the Web is that, unlike other media, it is possible for a single individual with the right concept and content to create a cutting-edge, popular site. A personal computer and a low-cost connection to the Internet through a phone line to the nearest ISP provide the starting point. Figure 5.2 shows the requirements for creating a studio using a personal computer. A typical consumer multimedia PC using Pentium (http://www.intel.com) or Macintosh PowerPC (http://www.apple.com) hardware works fine for most Internet systems. If you're on a budget, an older Macintosh Quadra 660A/V with built-in audio and video is an ideal all-around Web development system. Older systems (such as black-and-white Macintoshes and 386 PCs) can be adapted for the Internet, but they are incapable of delivering or processing the sophisticated graphics, audio, and video so characteristic of the Web. Despite their sophisticated multimedia support, Amiga-based systems are difficult to connect to the Internet and should be considered only if other systems are unavailable.

Whatever hardware is used, the most critical component will be the RAM memory. In particular, most consumer systems are sold without adequate RAM; to upgrade to Studio A, you should install at least 8 megabytes—but 32 to 64 mb is not excessive for a system which will be manipulating audio and video.

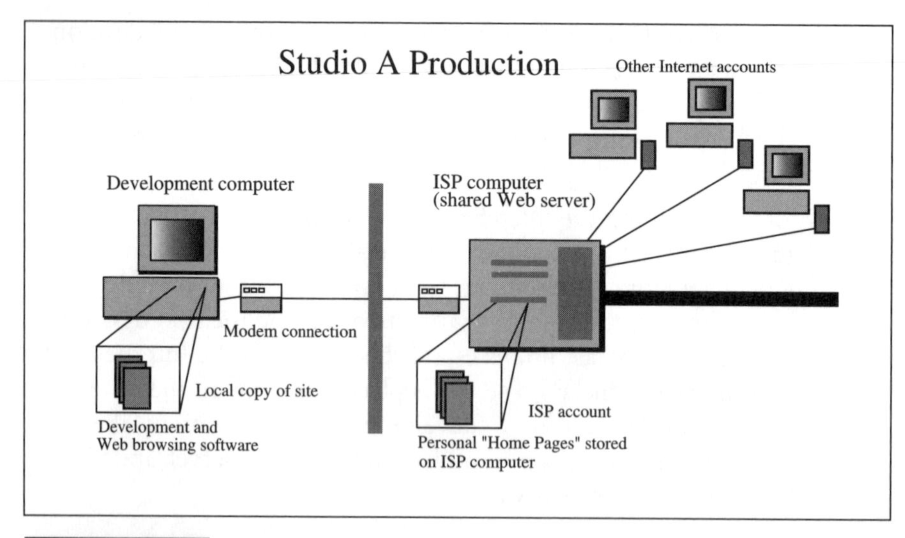

FIGURE 5.2 Studio A diagram.

To connect a Studio A system to the Internet, you will also need a *modem* and phone line. Developers should always insist on a 28.8 modem, preferably a premium model like the U.S. Robotics Sportster. Many hardware dealers continue to package the slower 14.4 systems, so make sure a 28.8 system is specified. If you can afford spending about $1,000, consider getting an *ISDN (Integrated Services Digital Network)* line also. ISDN connections are four to five times faster than 28.8 modems and they form an attractive option for full-time Web developers. Available in most large cities, ISDN lines must be specially installed by the phone company.

The Internet is a subscription-based system. Users log onto the Internet through their chosen ISP and pay hourly or flat monthly charges for their connection. While it is possible to get basic Internet service through one of the large online services (such as CompuServe or America Online), the full features of the Web are best experienced through *direct* Internet connections provided by an ISP. In choosing an ISP, remember that big is not necessarily better; smaller ISPs may have better service and fewer busy signals than larger ones. Long-distance companies such as AT&T and MCI have begun to offer Internet access, but their service, to date, is essentially the same as the independent ISPs.

When choosing an ISP, it is important to make sure it supports the full set of features needed to support Studio A. Many low-price ISPs offer only *shell* or *telnet* access, which is text-based and strictly for hackers. Make sure your connection uses a protocol like SLIP (Serial In-line Protocol) or PPP (Point-to-Point). If you need help configuring your computer's hardware and software, find an ISP that will provide technical support. Compile a short list of questions like those that follow to ask the ISP during the initial call.

Does the ISP Provide Web Server Rental?

This is the number one question for anyone developing a site in Studio A. You can configure your own computer as a Web server, but a *single* visitor will easily overload your modem connection. In order to effectively share your entertainment content with the rest of the Internet, you will need to *upload* the Web pages to a Web server provided by the ISP, whose connections run 20 to 1,000 times faster than modems or ISDN lines. Web development then becomes the ultimate in telecommuting; the Web site developer logs into the ISP's network from Studio A and remotely administers the Web site. (An ISP or other entity that provides Web server rental is referred to as *Internet Presence Provider* or *IPP*.) Some ISPs and IPPs refer to a low-cost server rental arrangement suitable for Studio A development as a *personal home page* rental. Keep in mind that these services are adequate for Web sites with relatively low traffic only (100 to 1,000 visitors per day). Examples include a site providing sound clips and promotional material for a single entertainer or a page advertising professional training or management services.

Does the ISP Support a Custom Domain Name?

As part of the concept development described in Chapter 4, you should have selected a custom Internet name for your site (in the format http://mysite.com). Any competent ISP will be able to register your chosen name and connect it to your Web site for a relatively modest fee (beyond the $100 required by the InterNIC for name registration).

Does the ISP Have a "One-step" Software Installation Package?

The ISP should provide software which automatically installs the connectivity software and dialer (which establishes the Internet link) and Internet programs including a Web *browser* such as Netscape Navigator or Microsoft's Internet Explorer. Despite aggressive competition from Microsoft, Netscape currently continues to define the cutting edge of Web software and is used by the majority of the Web. The ISP should provide the browser directly to you on floppies or other media. Recently, many ISPs have begun to offer software packages aiding the construction of Web sites, using their own service, of course! These packages are appropriate for a small-to-medium-sized company able to afford monthly rentals of approximately $100 for their sites. An example of such a package is *The Web Site Startup Kit* by Forman Interactive (http://www.forman.com). Forman's kit provides configuration information and a large selection of *prefab* Web pages.

Is the ISP's Modem to User Ratio 10:1 or Less?

This arcane question is the key to effective service. All ISPs have more customers than phone lines, since only a fraction of their customers use the service at any one time. A typical *overbooking* ratio of 10:1 indicates that the ISP has 10 times as many customers as phone lines. With normal use, a 10:1 ratio results in only occasional "busy signals." Higher ratios will prevent you from connecting at peak midday hours; the 30:1 ratios found with some small providers result in permanent overload, making it difficult to connect at any time. The lower the cost for your service, the less money the ISP is spending on your connection—so don't choose an ISP on price alone. If you are willing to spend two to five times as much, you can sometimes get a *dedicated* account which reserves an open line 24 hours a day. This may be the best solution for an industry professional who frequently logs onto the Internet; it is especially useful if you need to put large audio and video files on your site. Note that overbooking happens on all networks. For example, the major long-distance carriers overload if more than 5 percent of their customers pick up the phone at any one time.

Studio B: Adapting an Existing In-house Multimedia Studio for Web Development

Many entertainment companies interested in creating larger Web sites are already using computers for desktop publishing and multimedia development. In this case, instead of connecting a single computer to the Internet, the goal is to link the local company network to the Internet so that one or more of the development computers has Web access. A typical Studio B system is shown in Figure 5.3.

Computer Hardware

Like Studio A, B utilizes personal computers equipped to handle multimedia. Since more content is normally involved, it is usually necessary to provide for more storage—particularly on hard disks. A system with a 2 to 8 gigabyte drive and 32 or more megabytes of RAM is not unreasonable. These requirements compare to computers used in CD-ROM development. Current industry standards include PowerMac/AV systems, Windows NT (http://www.microsoft.com), and UNIX workstations from Sun Microsystems (http://www.sun.com) and Silicon Graphics (http://www.sgi.com). Though Macintosh systems are generally superior

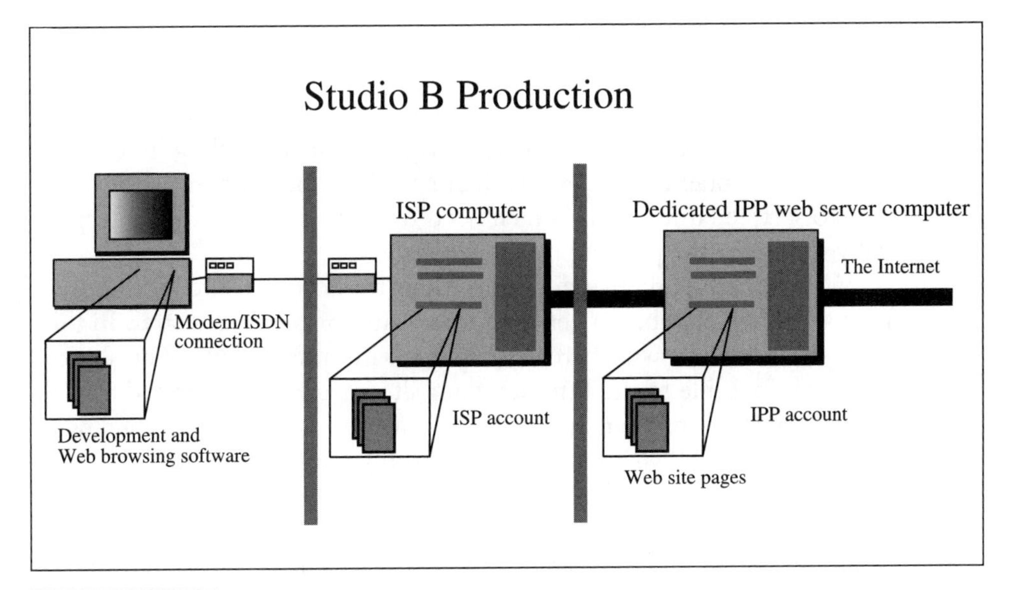

FIGURE 5.3 Studio B diagram.

for multimedia development, many of the most recent software enhancements to the Web, such as virtual worlds and real-time video, were initially created for Windows—due to the overwhelming numbers of these systems in the consumer market. For this reason, development involving these enhancements may require access to a system running Windows 95 or Windows NT. Larger production houses with UNIX *workstations* can adapt their systems for Web development, but the cost of development software is generally much higher than with personal computers.

Local Network

The existing company network is likely to be incompatible with Internet-style TCP/IP (Transmission Communication Protocol/Internet Protocol) communications and run a proprietary system such as Novell Netware. In order to run Web browsers and other Internet programs on the development computers, install additional software on each computer enabling TCP/IP communication.

Internet Connection

With several people working on the Web site at one time, Studio B requires faster connections than ordinary modems can provide. For smaller groups, ISDN lines provide sufficient speeds and are an economical alternative to more costly connections.

Hosting the Web Server

For the larger and more advanced Web sites developed in Studio B, the personal home page accounts discussed for Studio A are inadequate. Since the computers serving the Web pages are also handling hundreds of end-user modem connections, their speed and performance are too slow to service larger sites—which need to be hosted on computers specially set up for the purpose by the ISP/IPP.

Most IPPs provide two distinct options for hosting a site. For small Web sites, it is possible to get very cheap rates on a *virtual* server. In this case, your Web site will share a computer with other clients. The shared hosting is invisible to the Internet; your site appears unconnected to other tenants. Virtual servers work best for sites getting low to medium traffic (1,000-2,000 visitors per day), monthly rates run in the $200 to 300 range. They are well-suited for small record labels, sites offering travel information, and virtual art galleries.

If the site has higher traffic (> 3,000 visitors a day), rent an entire computer whose sole purpose is to host your Web site. Large record companies, movie studios, and sites providing real-time audio and/or video need this *dedicated* service. Rates are generally much higher for this service and setup costs include the price of a mid-range server (about $5,000). Kaleidospace's server rental service (part of its Multispace Internet Services division at http://multispace.com) offers a *bandwidth* rental option in addition to the virtual and dedicated servers. This bandwidth option allows clients to store their own systems at the Kaleidospace location for a lower setup fee (about $1,000).

Currently, hundreds of IPP services are advertised both on and off the Web, ranging from large national services like Navisoft (http://www.navisoft.com), Internet Direct (http://www.gosite.com), and BBN Planet (http://www.bbnplanet.com) to local ISPs. When shopping for IPP service, it is important to ask the right questions, a few of which follow.

Does the IPP Offer Dedicated, Bandwidth, and Virtual Server Options? Smaller ISPs frequently don't have the resources to offer the dedicated or bandwidth option. Make sure that the bandwidth available is sufficient to support your expected level of traffic. As a rule of thumb, you can estimate the number of visitors that can connect to you by dividing the ISP's bandwidth size (measured in kilobits per second) by a factor of 20. In addition, make sure that the servers used in the dedicated option are not also providing dialup modem access.

Do Clients Get a Custom Domain Name (http://mysite.com)? *All* options (including virtual server rental) should provide full domain-name support.

How Many Web Sites Per Machine Does the IPP Network Support? The answer will reveal as much about the honesty of the service provider as its speed does.

Does the IPP Provide Technical Support for Your Site? The IPP should provide support as part of the rental contract and through hourly consulting. A sign of a good IPP is a certain amount of free technical support and thoughtful attention to your project—especially on virtual and dedicated servers, which should be maintained daily by the IPP. If you have paid for dedicated or bandwidth service, the IPP should give your technical personnel administrator-level access to the server.

Can the IPP Provide Support for "Secure" Product Ordering? This should be a relatively low-cost service, usually consisting of a setup fee and nominal monthly charges. Since a variety of rapidly changing standards for secure transactions exists, make sure the IPP provides the ones you need.

Can the IPP Provide Access Statistics for Visitors to the Web Site? Discussed more fully in Chapters 7 and 8, this information will give you an idea of how many people are actually visiting your Web site, as well as some other demographics.

What Security Precautions Does the IPP Take? The IPP should be able to explain the steps they undertake to block access to your programming code and other privileged information stored on its network. Security precautions should include internal programs detecting "unwelcome visitors" on your Web server, as well as *firewall* services (discussed in greater detail for Studio C).

Does the IPP Support Real-time Audio and/or Video? If you require this support, it is essential that the ISP have an extremely fast ("10 megabit or T3") connection. One very important responsibility of a Web entertainment developer is to make sure that the Web site will really be accessible at the claimed speeds. IPPs (especially if they also offer ISP service) are notorious for overloading their systems with hundreds of Web sites, causing access to slow to a crawl. As with ISPs, going to the largest IPP provider provides no assurance of fast connections. To assure fast access, ask the IPP to provide names of Web sites they already host; then have at least two people access them at different times of the day from different locations. Some delay during peak hours is understandable; long delays late at night or on weekends are inexcusable.

Studio C: Running the Web Server on an In-house Network

If the Web site will be supporting several thousand visitors daily and require frequent updates by a large staff, it may be best to become your own ISP/IPP and install the Web server *in-house* within the company's own network. Studio C embodies this option, as illustrated in Figure 5.4. It costs significantly more to set up and maintain an in-house network than to store the Web site remotely, but there are many advantages.

Rapid Media Transfer

Since entertainment Web sites typically work with very large audio and video files, uploading them to a remote IPP via modems or ISDN can waste huge amounts of time. By contrast, if the Web site is on the local network, data transfers from the development computers run at speeds hundreds of times faster than a modem. This arrangement gives the development team guaranteed fast access to the Web server.

Control of Server Features

Having the Web server in-house makes it easier to upgrade to new features as they become available. For example, if a large Web site decides to provide real-time audio, the new service can be installed by the company's *MIS (Management Information Systems)* department—instead of relying on an ISP/IPP, which may be on the other side of the country. Having a local server also allows Studio C to take advantage of existing backup systems, spare hardware, personnel, and support for the company's existing network.

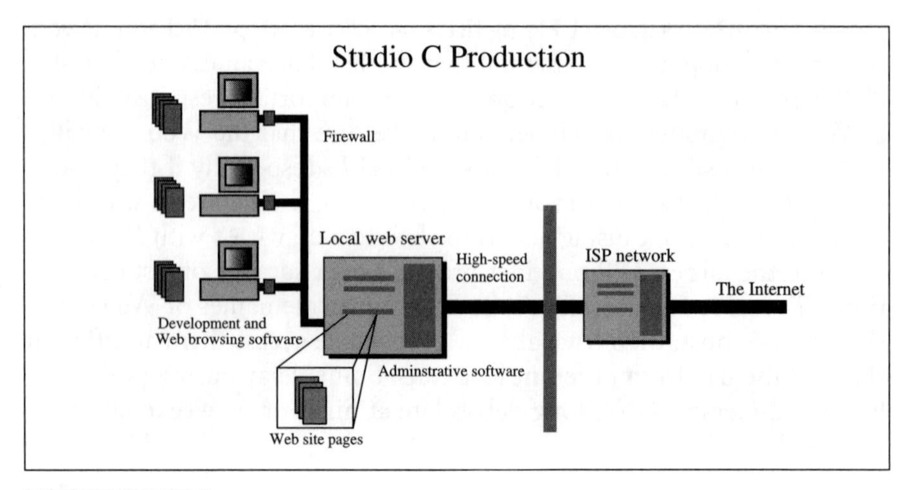

FIGURE 5.4 Studio C diagram.

Intranet

Widespread use of Web-based software allows a company to convert its *internal* communication to a Web-based system—referred to as an *Intranet*. Many companies are using the Web to organize their internal resources with the same simplicity and cost savings found on the general Internet. Netscape Communications (http://www.netscape.com) is the current leader in Intranet development.

Company-wide Access to the Web

An indirect but extremely important consequence of Studio C is that it potentially provides each individual in the organization a way to explore the Web at high speed. This is not an incidental point; designers and developers must be able to explore the Web in order to create cutting-edge, competitive work. A direct connection provides access to the enormous quantity of free software resources available on the Internet, as well as discussion groups on Usenet, invaluable to designers and programmers. Furthermore, an in-house connection will also increase the general awareness of the power of Web entertainment throughout the organization. The political impact of this can be extremely strong, especially if only a few people in the company initially understand the value of the Web.

Consider the experience of a major corporation that decided early in 1995 to create a Web site combining product information with entertainment of the type often found in company newsletters—jokes, puzzles, and "fun facts." Initially, the Web site was designed by outside contractors and hosted by an IPP, despite the fact that the company already installed a national network connecting its various offices. Neither the executive group nor the in-house MIS computer staff was connected to the Internet. As a result, the Web site remained underfunded and small throughout 1995—and no updates were made in its entertainment content. Near the end of 1995, the corporate network was connected to the Internet and near-universal Web access was granted to employees. The change was dramatic: Within a month, upper-level managers who had previously questioned the value of the Internet saw it as a valuable resource and they soon ordered a radical re-working of the Web site's structure and features.

Even if you have the luxury of doing Studio-C level production, it is useful to maintain some modem-based Web accounts to test the Web site as it develops. When the site development team relies exclusively on high-speed connections during development, it is tempted to include high-end graphics, audio, video, and advanced interactive features that look and sound great, but are impractical for the average site visitor to download. Cross-testing the site from a modem will ensure that it is practical to use from homes as well as university and corporate networks.

Maintaining a Studio-C level production requires additional hardware and software. Since the Web server is now part of the local network, it must be directly administered and protected. Your current network is unlikely to contain some of the following features and equipment, *all* of which are needed to run Studio C efficiently.

High-speed Internet Connection

In-house Web servers require specialized high-speed *leased lines* to provide fast, 24-hour service. These lines must be ordered from the phone company and normally take several weeks to install. An ISP may be able to order the line for you—and, in larger cities, the phone company may be an ISP itself. Most groups will normally start with *T1* connections, which run about 40 times faster than a modem. Connections of this speed are as fast as those run by smaller ISPs and are normally adequate for all but the largest Web sites. Monthly charges add up to approximately $1,000 to $3,000 per month in large cities. Once installed, the line connects to the local network through a *router* (providing traffic control between the Internet and your network) and a *CSU/DSU*, (equivalent of an extremely high-speed modem). The ISP or phone company will frequently offer to purchase this equipment as part of a package deal for the connection.

Firewall

Unlike Studios A and B, Studio C systems are completely two-way—potentially allowing anyone on the Internet to gain access to your network. To prevent unwelcome visits from hackers and curiosity-seekers, install a security screen which prevents them from reaching computers on your private network. These systems, referred to as *firewalls*, normally are high-speed UNIX-based workstations running specialized software which continually monitors Internet traffic for unauthorized requests. Properly constructed firewalls are virtually impenetrable, but it is essential that the company's MIS department maintain and support the firewalls. Dozens of firewalls are available, but the BorderWare product (http://borderware.com) is currently a favorite with many large sites.

Web Server

This computer will ultimately deliver your Web site to the Internet and its features will determine how many people can access your Web site. Excellent general-purpose systems can be created using Pentium computer hardware running UNIX software from Berkeley Systems Development (http://www.bsdi.com). Traditionally, system administrators have assembled the server from several vendors, but companies like Pacific Internet (http://www.bbnplanet.com) offer plug-and-play systems in the

$5,000 range. These systems are economical to set up, but hardware limitations may make them less efficient at high-bandwidth applications like audio and video delivery. They also require familiarity with UNIX, which is frequently lacking in corporate MIS departments. Web servers may also be constructed using Windows NT systems. While not as fast or as well-developed as UNIX solutions, it may be easier for the MIS department to maintain these systems if NT is an internal standard and there are a greater range of low-cost programs (e.g., databases) available for the system. The fastest Web servers use proprietary hardware created by Sun Microsystems or Silicon Graphics; these systems are necessary for operating the largest entertainment sites which receive millions of visitors per week.

Recently, many entertainment companies in particular have found that high-end Macintosh systems combine ease of administration with adequate performance. Apple's new Open Transport software (replacing MacTCP) allows Macs to handle large numbers of users at efficiencies comparable to UNIX workstations. Since a large number of entertainment companies are Mac-based, using an Apple Web server to host your site deserves a close look. Examples of Mac-based Web servers include record labels under Warner Brothers (http://www.music.warnerbros.com). More examples can be found through Apple (http://www.solutions.apple.com/HotSites/default.html).

In addition to the hardware, Web server software must be installed. There are several free UNIX-based software packages, such as Apache (http://www.apache.org) and NCSA httpd (http://www.ncsa.uiuc.edu)—both available for download from the Internet; these currently are used in the bulk of Web servers. Microsoft now builds a Web server into Windows, but at present it lacks the speed and features of other systems. Besides the basic software, many additions and modifications are necessary for the basic Web server to support advanced programming, control security, and allow for secure ordering. Details of these programs are beyond the scope of this book; additional references for server software can be found on the Apache and NCSA home pages.

If you install an in-house Web server, you must determine who will be responsible for purchasing and administering the hardware and system software. In the case of the Internet, the existing MIS department will frequently require outside help to install the Internet connection and Web server. Due to the relative simplicity of Web development, the publicity or marketing department may soon feel it knows more about the Web than MIS. This can lead to a conflict between the hardware administrators who feel their turf is being invaded and the content providers who insist on the right to create the site using their own computers and the latest techniques. In such cases, management must accommodate both groups in order to build a working coalition.

Additional Hardware for Repurposing Content

If your Web site will repurpose graphics, sound, and video from outside the Internet, additional hardware is needed to digitize information from these media. Depending on the level of studio you are creating, you may want some or all of the equipment in the following list and depicted in Figure 5.5. Examine your Web site concept and determine where most of your content will be coming from in order to select the needed peripherals. If, for example, you are planning to provide weekly video clips advertising upcoming theater releases, your studio should have its own video capture system. On the other hand, if you are providing a single video in an otherwise audio-based site, it may make more sense to outsource the digitization to an independent Web developer.

The following is a list of the most common types of equipment used to repurpose content for the Web:

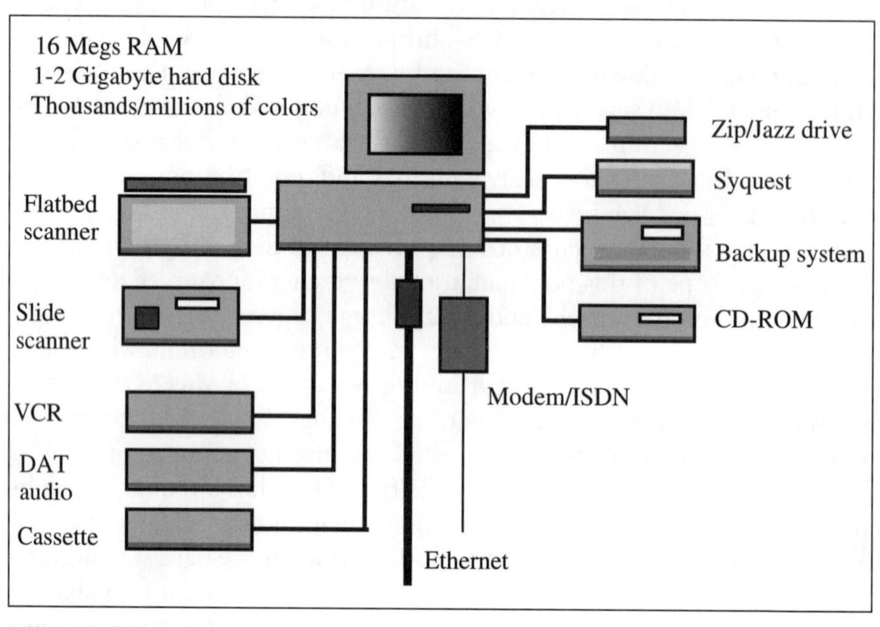

FIGURE 5.5 Diagram of peripherals used to repurpose content.

- *Scanner.* This should be a high-quality, color scanner with a potential scanning resolution of at least 300 dots per inch (dpi) and an adapter to scan transparencies.
- *Slide scanner.* Currently, the Nikon Coolscan (http://www.klt.co.jp/Nikon) is the system of choice.
- *Sound card/digitizer.* The system should support recording CD-quality stereo (44.1k sampling) directly to the computer's hard disk. Many Macintosh systems (carrying the "A/V" designation) have complete sound support built in, while PCs will usually require the purchase of an additional card.
- *Video input.* Video on the Internet is currently restricted to small windows taking up a fraction of the total screen. Because of this, it is unnecessary to purchase expensive video boards providing full-screen, full-motion video capture. Virtually all the studio's video requirements can be provided by an A/V Macintosh or Windows video cards in the $500 to $1,000 range. If you will be storing video, you should also buy the largest hard disk (2-9 gigabytes) you can afford.
- *MIDI support.* If you are producing music for the Web, you should definitely consider supporting MIDI. Since MIDI sends a code rather than an actual audio signal, it does not suffer from the distortion and low playback quality of Internet-based real-time audio. Both Netscape and Microsoft have announced support for MIDI in their Web browsers. MIDI music is likely to become more common as Web sites develop collaborative music, ambient music for individual Web pages, and *virtual mixing* systems running over the Internet.
- *CD-ROM drive.* CD-ROM drives allow access to large quantities of preexisting media on disc formats including Kodak's Photo CD, audio CDs, enhanced CDs, and CD-ROMs. Enhanced CDs and CD-ROMs frequently have compatibility problems on older Windows-based systems, so make sure that the computer's hardware and software supports the formats you need.

Web Software

Despite the great variation in hardware between Studios A through C, all of them will share essentially the same software for Web viewing, development, and administration. The central tool of all studios is the Web browser, which translates the contents of a Web site into multimedia.

Current browsers can display text in several sizes, color backgrounds, graphics, and simple animation. Features not widely supported on the Web include style sheets, custom fonts, and fine positioning of text and graphics (*kerning*).

It is important to remember during development that not all browsers can display advanced multimedia. A small but significant number of Web users will see your site with a text only browser like *Lynx*. Certain widely used formatting features such as tables are browser-specific and may not work properly for everyone. Make sure your studio has the most common browsers available so you can test your site with them during development.

Extensions for Web Browsers

The Web began as a form of electronic publishing; the HTML language used to create Web sites is restricted to passive displays of text and graphics. Most browsers support additional features which integrate non-HTML programming and multimedia into the Web—collectively referred to here as *extensions*. When combined with extensions, Web browsers can support advanced animation, CD-ROM-style multimedia, real-time audio and video, and even 3-D virtual worlds. Web extensions fall into three categories: helper apps, plug-ins, and applets. Each of these is discussed further in the following sections (and in more detail in Chapter 6).

Helper Apps

These are ordinary programs that the browser can call from the site visitor's hard disk when it detects information it can't handle itself. Common helper apps include sound and video players. Helper apps usually are configured by the site visitor to work with the Web browser—a disadvantage if your site is reaching a less technical audience. The *RealAudio* player provides an example of a sophisticated helper app in wide use.

Plug-ins

These allow the Web browser to display material provided from an external program within its own windows. For example, a movie player configured as a helper app will show the film in a separate window from the Web browser, while the comparable plug-in for movies displays the film directly in the Web page. Because of their advantages, plug-ins will likely replace helpers in the near future. A popular plug-in used for advanced Web programming is *Shockwave* by Macromedia (http://www.macromedia.com). The home page of the Lollapalooza site, (Figure 5.6) contains an example of extensive and effective use of the Shockwave plug-in.

FIGURE 5.6 Lollapalooza (http://www.lollapalooza.com).

Applets

These go beyond plug-ins and eliminate end-user installation entirely. Both *Java* from Sun Microsystems (http://www.sun.com) and *ActiveX* from Microsoft (http://www.microsoft.com) are applet languages allowing the Web browser to download mini-programs on demand and run them inside the browser window like a plug-in. There are many advantages to this system. Unlike other systems, Java programs need only be developed once; their operation is independent of the computer platform. Since the program is sent at the moment it is needed, the site visitor does not have to configure or update the local software. After the applet's work is done, it *evaporates* from memory. This download-and-execute structure allows a novel distribution strategy; Web sites may sell Java applets for single or multiple use directly over the Internet, bypassing traditional avenues of software distribution. An example of Java's potential can be seen with Jeff Orkin's Celebrity Painter program (Figure 5.7), which lets visitors create faces with famous eyes, ears, and mouths.

Text Processing and HTML Coding Software

The days of hand-coding your own Web pages are rapidly drawing to a close. With the arrival of commercial HTML editors, it is increasingly possible to create quality Web pages. Additional features such as page

CELEBRITY PAINTER V2.0 by Jeff Orkin

JARS
TOP 1%
WebApplet

As Reviewed in
MULTiMEDiA

MULTIMEDIA WORLD
ALL-STAR

JAVA
POWERED

Artists and non-artists alike can paint portraits using facial parts of celebrities. It's wacky! It's fun! It's easy! Here's how:
1. Choose a celebrity brush from the list box.
2. Hold down the left mouse button while slowly rubbing where the facial feature should appear.
3. If you make a mistake, click on the eraser and rub off unwanted areas, or click Clear to erase the whole image.
Example: Choose David Letterman, then rub the mouse on the blank face where the mouth should be to add Letterman's mouth, then choose Clinton and rub where the eyes should be to add Clinton's eyes.... you get the picture (pun intended). See the Gallery for more examples.
NOTE: This applet takes about 15 seconds to load with a 28.8. Changing brushes takes 5-8 seconds. Be patient, it's worth it!

FIGURE 5.7 Celebrity Painter (http://www.demonsys.com/jorkin/CelebrityPainter/).

templates, *drag-and-drop* linking, and spell checks make it much easier to manage large numbers of pages on major Web sites. An excellent resource for finding HTML editors is maintained at Canlink's Web design page (http://Web.canlink.com/Webdesign).

The current industry standard for page design is PageMill from Adobe Systems (http://www.adobe.com). PageMill allows drag-and-drop creation of HTML pages and integrates its own "preview" Web browser, eliminating the need for a separate Web browser. Connecting hyperlinks between page elements is easy: Dragging an image over text, automatically converts it to a hyperlink. PageMill also does automatic image file conversions.

Image Processing

Most of the software tools used to create graphics for other media can be used with the Web; the key is using them properly. A bitmap drawing program like Adobe Photoshop (http://www.adobe.com) can form the basis of graphic design for virtual production studios at all levels. The graphics program used should support conversion to common Web graphic formats. Drawing programs such as Adobe Illustrator or Corel Draw are less useful, since the Web does not support vector-based *draw* formats. The same can be said for desktop publishing programs like Quark Express (http://www.quark.com), since its page layout files are completely incompatible with the Web. The main reason for using programs such as Quark is repurposing. For example, a site processing promotional material from independent musicians will frequently receive desktop publishing files used to create their CD liners, flyers, and other material. It will be the job of the Web development team to "dissect" these files into individual text and graphic elements, and reassemble them into a comparable form using HTML coding.

Studio A developers who seek to avoid complex animation programs can use a special type of graphic which incorporates several images. This format, a variation of the standard GIF (Graphics Interchange Format) file, is referred to as an *animated GIF*. When this file is displayed on a Web browser supporting the protocol, the individual images within the GIF display in a simple *flip-book* style. The main advantage of this system is that virtually no special coding is required; the same HTML code used for static graphics will display animated GIFs. As such, animated GIFs are an ideal option for Studio A development. WebPainter from Totally-Hip Software (http://www.totallyhip.com) is a commercial, low-cost program specifically designed for assembling short cel-type animation sequences suitable for play as animated GIFs.

Audio Processing

Many individual developers will be able to make do with public domain sound capture programs available on the Internet at sites such as the Info-Mac Archive *mirror* (ftp://ftp.hawaii.edu). Useful tools in the sound and video archives include SoundEdit (an 8-bit AIFF editor) and Brian's Sound Tool (which converts between Mac and Windows sound formats). Commercial tools like SoundEdit 16 from Macromedia (http://www.macromedia.com) not only support capture and processing of 16-bit sound, but also allow the soundtrack from QuickTime videos to be separated for editing.

The severe limitations the Internet places on data transfer make it impossible to send uncompressed sound to site visitors in real time. New Web audio formats have been developed, the most notable of which is Progressive Network's RealAudio (http://www.realaudio.com). Existing sound formats can be changed to RealAudio format by using free converter programs available over the Internet. This makes it practical for smaller virtual production studios to create real-time audio. Developers working at Studio A and B levels will need to make sure that their ISP/IPP supports real-time audio; there are often additional charges for supplying audio "channels" on the Web site.

Video Processing

The vast majority of Web sites use the QuickTime Apple standard for video, primarily due to its extensive support for audio and video synchronization. The comparable Windows AVI format does not support audio and video synchronization; thus it is uncommon on the Web. MPEG video, common on CD-ROM systems, requires special hardware to encode and play back; it is also a relatively uncommon format. Editing and post-processing QuickTime video clips is easily accomplished with software tools like Adobe Premiere and Adobe AfterEffects.

While much attention has been focused on *streaming* technologies delivering video in real-time, standards are far from settled. Before beginning development, study major streaming sites such as VDOLive (http://www.vdolive.com) and the Net TOOB (http://www.duplexx.com). All these sites offer programs for converting standard video formats to streaming format. For a more detailed discussion of the prospects for video broadcast over the Internet, see Chapter 10.

Advanced Media Processing

The following programs provide content authoring within complete multimedia environments and conversion capabilities for Web-based delivery. They are distinguished by using the Web as a starting point for delivering their own brand of interactive content.

Director and Shockwave

Director movies (actually mixes of animation, user interactivity, and sound) provide user interfaces that are much more sophisticated than those possible with basic HTML—including animated controls with associated sounds, character animation, and simulations. Shockwave is simply a tool which compresses Director movies for transmission across the Web. In order to develop for Shockwave, purchase a Director development kit. While developers used to Director will feel comfortable with Shockwave, they must learn new ways of compressing their expertise into relatively tiny Web files.

Java

Virtually all entertainment sites will need to use Java, since it combines speed, power, and compatibility unmatched by any other multimedia environment. A full-featured programming language, Java is definitely not for the faint of heart. HTML experience is useless for Java; unless you are a professional developer with experience with programming languages like C++, you will find Java very difficult to learn. Large Web development projects at the level of Studio C should allocate resources strictly for Java programmers. Fortunately, Java has a simpler scripting language called *JavaScript*, which will be easier for developers to learn. Incorporated directly into Web documents, JavaScript allows interactive control of program applets written directly in the Java language. The object-oriented nature of JavaScript will let developers use it to integrate basic Java modules into complex applications. In practice, a simple JavaScript could call a set of standard modules from the Internet and combine them into programs with new functions.

Since development software for Java is still at an early stage, developers should check the main Java site (http://www.javasoft.com). Studio A and B productions should avoid development, at least until checking archives such as Gamelan (http://www.gamelan.com) for an existing applet that can be adapted to their needs. ActiveX is a Microsoft-specific language which duplicates many of Java's features. Needless to say, independent companies are already hard at work embedding Java in ActiveX and vice versa. While Microsoft will undoubtedly push its proprietary solution, it also has decided to incorporate Java support into its own Web browser.

Virtual Worlds/VRML

The most common virtual worlds on the Web are constructed using *VRML (Virtual Reality Markup Language)*, a specialized form of multimedia created specifically for the Web. This surprisingly simple language is text-based like HTML, but nevertheless it can convert navigation between *flat* Web pages to three-dimensional movement through a synthetic universe. VRML allows the site visitor to move in three dimensions and converts hyperlinks to *teleports* between locations in the virtual environment. An excellent starting point for VRML exploration may be found through WebFX (http://www.paperinc.com/wrls.html). Note that standard Web browsers cannot handle VRML unless it is installed as a plug-in or helper; a comprehensive list of VRML-enabled browsers is available through The Repository (http://www.sdsc.edu/vrml). Figure 5.8 shows Intel's Virtual Stonehenge, a site designed to illustrate the potential of virtual worlds in the Web environment.

Like Java, authoring systems for VRML are at an early stage; check out the current state of VRML at sites like the VRML Foundry (http://www.mcp.com/general/foundry). Individuals who are proficient with HTML or traditional programming languages should be able to develop the simple *walk-through* environments in the 1.0 version of VRML, even with the limited resources available for Studio A. The 2.0

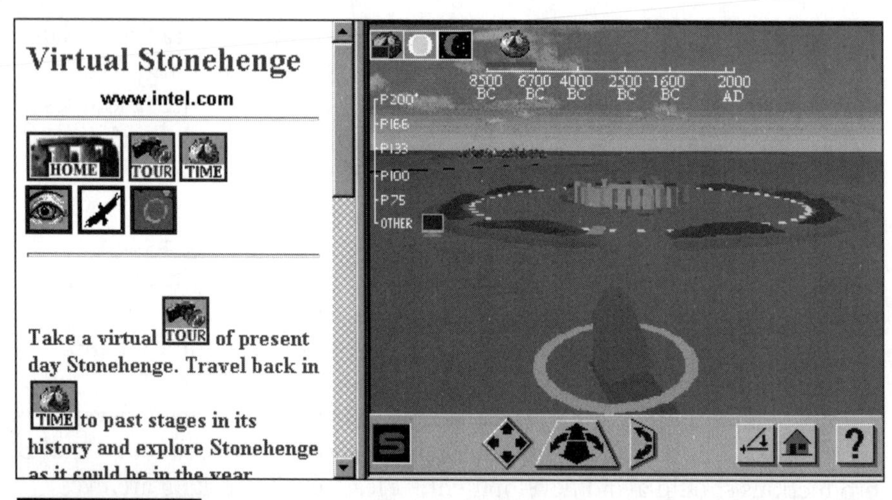

FIGURE 5.8 Intel's Virtual Stonhenge (http://www.intel.com).

standard for VRML adds the ability for site visitors to modify the virtual worlds; the resulting code required is considerably more sophisticated. As the 2.0 standard becomes widespread during 1997, it will be necessary to hire VRML specialists.

Advanced and Server-side Programming

Server-side programming, usually using *CGI (Common Gateway Interface)* lets the Web browser pass input from an HTML page—including user-supplied choices—to a second program running *behind the scenes* on the server. The latter program processes the input, carries out specified actions, and writes an HTML page that it delivers back to the Web server—which then returns the page to the site visitor. Typical applications of CGI include *interactive* enhancements such as user polls, order forms, user registration, and Web-based chat rooms. CGI is more difficult than HTML and requires the services of a professional programmer, as well as cooperation with the ISP/PPP or in-house department administering the Web server. At present, the vast majority of CGI is programmed in Perl (Practical Extraction and Report Language), a relatively straightforward and well-documented programming language. Extensive archives of free Perl-based CGI programs are available on the Internet at *numerous* sites within the Comprehensive Perl Archive Network (CPAN)—easily found via search engines such as Yahoo! (http://www.yahoo.com), Alta Vista (http://www.altavista.com), or Lycos (http://www.lycos.com). Adaptation of these programs for use is well within the reach of Studio A and B production.

Site Management Tools

As Web sites grow in sheer size and integrate various types of programming (e.g., CGI, Java, VRML), it will be increasingly necessary to develop management applications such as file tracking and error or broken-link reporting. Adobe SiteMill (http://www.adobe.com/Apps/Sitemill) is a good example of a management program useful for Studios A through C. It dynamically records information about documents creating Web pages. When individual pages are moved, SiteMill automatically updates internal links in the document; it also identifies "bad" HTML links and can fix them through drag-and-drop movement of files. Future releases of SiteMill will allow administering Web sites on remote servers; at that point, it will become an indispensable tool for everyone. Microsoft's FrontPage (http://www.microsoft.com/frontpage/productinfo/brochure) software offers outstanding Web site adminstration features for Windows platforms. Like SiteMill, it integrates a variety of editing and site management tools. FrontPage also lets site managers assign multiple team members to the Web site and allow them to work on the site simultaneously; its "to do" list simplifies the problems associated with continually updated content. Extensions to FrontPage allow all or part of the site to be transparently uploaded to a remote Web server.

For large sites with tens of thousands of pages, programs like FrontPage and SiteMill are no longer adequate. Many media groups that established Web sites in 1994 and 1995, such as C|Net (http://www.cnet.com) and Pathfinder (http://www.pathfinder.com), were forced to develop their own custom programming to automate site management. More recently, large-scale management systems have been developed—notably Netscape's LiveWire Pro (http://www.netscape.com/comprod/server_central/product/livewire), which integrates a wide variety of site management tools (including a graphical link-tracking manager, a JavaScript compiler, and database connectivity). The Windows NT version also includes tools for analyzing access statistics for your site (Chapter 8). Currently, similar products from a variety of vendors are under development.

Databases

Databases provide another feature not present in HTML: the ability to store formatted information and allow it to be searched. Since most databases have their own internal programming language, they can perform additional operations on information including calculations and sorting. In most current implementations of the Web, databases are called by the

Web server using CGI programming—though newer database tools include specialized connections with faster response. Database connection solutions exist for Oracle (http://www.oracle.com), Sybase (http://www.sybase.com), and Informix (http://www.informix.com) databases, as well as other *SQL (Structured Query Language)* systems. Database packages capable of handling Studio C development are available from ColdFusion (http://www.allaire.com) for Windows NT/Windows 95, Bluestone's Sapphire/Web (http://www.bluestone.com), and Spider Technologies' NetDynamics (http://www.w3spider.com) for Windows and UNIX. All these programs feature graphical development environments to simplify programming. With the ability to link into traditional development environments like C++, these packages can deliver several times the efficiency of CGI-only solutions. While it is possible to link Macintosh systems to 4th Dimension (http://www.4D-Center.com) and FileMaker (http://www.claris.com) databases, these systems presently run significantly slower than the UNIX and Windows NT software. FileMaker databases may be linked to Web sites using the ROFM CGI script (http://rowen.astro.washington.edu).

While detailed discussion of database-Web applications is beyond the subject of this book, one database of particular interest to entertainment sites delivering multimedia is Cumulus from Canto (http://www.canto-software.com). A Macintosh-based system designed to organize multimedia, it automatically creates catalogs of image files including color, resolution, size, "creator" program, age, overall color, and a thumbnail image. A new program called the Internet Image Server provides direct user access to the image database. Cumulus is already in use by companies like Atlantic Records (http://www.atlanticrecords.com).

Personnel for Web Development

Creating a Web site requires people as well as equipment. Since Web sites integrate the disciplines of computer programming, content development, and artist design, the developers should be familiar with a wide variety of disciplines. Indeed, on small Web sites the following job descriptions are normally filled by one person. Larger studios may elect to put Web-specific developers on payroll or outsource the work to freelance developers and design studios.

Content Assembler or Creator

Particularly important for entertainment sites, this person is responsible for developing or repurposing existing content. Depending on the type of content, this may include securing rights as well as adapting the material for use on the Web. This individual will also have design responsibility, in conjunction with the graphics and multimedia creator.

Digitizer

The digitizer must understand the confusing array of graphic, audio, and video formats, and use them to transfer content from the real world to the computer. The size and complexity of multimedia formats make this a full-time job for large Web sites.

Graphics and Multimedia Creator

This person is responsible for creating the graphical *look* and *feel* of a site. The graphics and multimedia creator works closely with the content assembler or creator.

HTML Coder

All sites will require people who provide basic page layout and formatting of digitized content. They will also have some knowledge of the Web server and frequently will operate site management tools. In some cases, large Studio C operations may outsource all or part of this work.

Programmer

The complexity of Java, CGI, and VRML makes it necessary to use specialists for their development. While programmers can easily learn HTML, it is generally not considered a good use of their time. Programmers should have experience with multiuser workstation environments. Some knowledge of the UNIX operating system is almost essential, even if a UNIX workstation is not actually used for the Web server. If use of advanced programming is limited, programming is a good candidate for outsourcing.

Computer and/or Network Administrator

The administrator is responsible for upkeep of the studio computers and Web server, and will also be involved in site management— possibly including analysis of visitor traffic. Care must be taken to find an administrator who understands the goals and purpose of the site, and can easily communicate with non-technical personnel in the development group.

Team Leader

The team leader oversees the others on the project and has primary responsibility for the Web site. Qualifications include familiarity with all the various aspects of Web development and the ability to provide the bridge between the Web development effort and the rest of the company. In common practice, the team leader is designated as a *webweaver*, *webmaster* or even a *spider*. Don't let that stop you from inventing your own name!

Hiring Developers and Outsourcing

In the likely event that you or your group does not already possess the required expertise for creating the site, tap the growing numbers of professional developers specializing in the Web—either freelance or full-time. To find developers easily, log onto a search engine such as Yahoo! (http://www.yahoo.com), whose "Internet Service" section lists literally hundreds of independent design studios. Other resources include CommerceNet's directory of consultants (http://www.commercenet.net), the International Directory of Women Web Designers (http://www. primenet .com/~shauna/women.html), and the Web Consultant's Showcase (http:// infotique.lm.com/cgi-bin/phpl.cgi?webcon.html). JobTrak (http:// www. jobtrak.com), which posts internship and employment opportunities at thousands of universities, is a source for student help. This site allows online submissions of employment and internship notifications, as well as paid advertising spots. The following questions may be useful to ask during the initial interview with a potential developer.

Is the Developer "Really" a Developer?

Many professed Web designers have technical knowledge but none of the artistic savvy necessary to create top-quality sites. It is currently a common practice for prospective Web designers to advertise their services before learning their trade. If the designer doesn't have a demonstration Web site of their own, don't bother. Programmers and administrators should be able to provide credentials showing they have some real knowledge of the work.

Does the Developer Have Sufficient Technical Knowledge?

If you are looking for someone to provide animation, Java programming, or other specialized features, make sure that the designer can actually do the work. Some designers only have a basic knowledge of HTML and are unable to create more sophisticated sites. Developers should have knowledge of cutting-edge Web sites and be able to apply their principles and innovations to their own projects. The best test is the designer's Web site; if it doesn't showcase the features you want, the designer probably can't provide them.

Is the Developer Charging Appropriately?

Assume reasonable times for creating text and graphics, and determine whether a freelance designer is charging enough to run a business. This is especially important for Web sites on a small budget that hire freelance developers based on cost. Many inexperienced designers desperate for work charge virtually nothing to secure clients. These clients later find themselves paying for the designer's training, as well as delays and mistakes caused by underestimating the work required. Good designers will charge between $50 and $150 per hour for their work. If the price seems too good to be true, it is.

Does the Developer Allow Viewing the Site as It Is Being Built?

Reputable designers will continue a dialogue with their client throughout the development process. If the site is being built remotely, the designer should provide a password-protected Web address so that you can view the pages as they are being created. In-house developers should be able to help people within the organization access the site through the internal network.

Is the Developer Familiar with Web Media Formats?

Developers must be familiar with the unique set of Web media formats (such GIFs and RealAudio), which are distinctly different from CD-ROM and game software. Be wary of developers who treat the Web as little more than a way to download existing multimedia products.

Can the Developer Work in Low Bandwidth?

Compared to CD-ROM-based multimedia, the Internet is very limited in the rate of data it can deliver. The fastest modem connections can only deliver data at a fraction of the speed of a CD-ROM and T1 connections commonly used to link a Studio C network to the Internet are comparable to a *single* 4x CD-ROM. Due to this, developers must be able to "make do" with small and/or reduced color graphics. On the Internet, developers need to say a lot with limited resources. As a test, try asking the developer what is the most probable technical constraint in developing the site. If the answer is something like "download speed," the developer understands the basics of Internet media delivery. If the concern is insufficient "disk space," the developer may be more familiar with CD-ROM development than the Web.

Can the Developer Maintain and Update the Site?

Unlike CD-ROMs or cartridge games, a Web site is never "finished." The ease of updating—coupled with the constant desire of the audience for something new—necessitates developers who can create a framework capable of undergoing constant modifications by others.

Can the Developer Provide for Cross-platform Compatibility?

On older computers common in universities and libraries, graphics may not be displayed at all—or users with slow modem connections may deliberately turn off graphic downloads. Beware of developers who appear to be new on the scene or appear to be specialists in only one type of computer software. For example, many new developers ignore the fact that not everyone uses Netscape—and they may suggest using HTML extensions that confuse or even "bomb" other browsers.

Becoming a Developer for Entertainment Clients

Individuals who have created their own personal Web sites frequently decide to go freelance and provide their services on a consulting basis. Web development is a new profession without formal schooling or accreditation; as such, developers must learn the trade on their own. While there is great demand for these services, the days where a few hours of study of an HTML manual were sufficient to create a "Web expert" are swiftly receding. Currently, the best strategy for budding developers is to check out the enormous training and tutorial resources online, and learn their trade by creating. There are many Web sites providing support to budding developers; Webreference (http://www.Webreference.com) is a good example.

If you have lasted through the many pages of this discussion, you have proven that you are ready for the actual development process. The next chapter focuses on how to apply your studio's resources to actually create your Web site.

CHAPTER 6

THE FORM, FACADE, AND FURNITURE:

Site Structure, Design, and Content

Now that you have set up your "virtual production studio," it's time to begin the actual site development process. This chapter illustrates the following three essential components of bringing an entertainment site online:

- *form*—organization of behind-the-scenes structure, including software, navigational structure, and use of *shorthand* aliases.
- *facade*—overview of external artistic features that will give the site a unique look and feel.
- *furniture*—development of content to fit within the site structure, including text, graphics, audio, and video.

These steps are discussed from the perspective of programmers and designers actually creating the individual pages. This chapter does not cover automated page production using a combination of programming and databases used by sites such as C|Net (http://www.cnet.com) and many online newspapers. To learn more about automated page production, consult the database vendors discussed in Chapter 5 and maintenance issues discussed in Chapter 8. While CGI-style programming (see Chapter 5) is briefly discussed, the details of programming CGI scripts are beyond the scope of the book; check articles such as Programming With HTML Forms (http://www.webreference.com/htmlform) for an introduction.

There are many sites devoted to the Web design process; the Webreference.com resource (http://www.webreference.com) provides a good starting point. Other comprehensive resources are available at Patrick Lynch's Web Style Manual (http://info.med.yale.edu/caim/StyleManual_Top.html) and Sun Microsystem's Guide to Web Style (http:// www.sun.com/styleguide). An excellent discussion of the aesthetics of page design is available in the Sept. 11, 1995 issue of Web Review by Ron Bohle (http://gnn.com/gnn/wr/design/talk/sept1/index.html). Also check out Webcraft (http://www.atdesign.com:80/~ake/cgi/reel/base/webcraft/index.html), an online book that compares Web-based and film-based media and shows how many design concepts from film can be effectively applied to the Web.

Form: Internal Organization

Before jumping into the actual project, it will be necessary to integrate the various components of hardware, software, content, and personnel into a coherent whole. Verifying that your development team has the correct organization and resources will reduce problems once actual development begins.

Development Timetable

Before beginning, it is strongly recommended that the individual developer or team construct a timetable listing major milestones along the way to opening day. This helps to refine the basic site concept into a work plan. Integrate other information with the timetable, such as phone numbers for designers and programmers, style sheets (discussed later), and general information that the site development team will need to need to know.

Functional Development Site

Since Web sites involve juggling multiple files and computers, verify that your virtual production studio can actually function as a Web development system. At the beginning, a simple test page should be the goal. Create two HTML files with a few lines of text and hyperlinks to each other and install them on your site. If you are creating a personal site through your ISP, they will sometimes set up a default page for you that you can replace with your own file. Make sure that the test page itself loads with your Web browser and that all graphics and links also work.

Once the test page is up, it is a good time to begin evaluating the ISP/IPP providing your link to the Internet. Keep track of times when server access is extremely slow (mid-afternoon and early evening are usually the hours of peak traffic) and contact the ISP/IPP if there are persistent problems. While providers frequently overload their systems, keep in mind that slow access is sometimes beyond their control. The most common reason for this occurs when maintenance is being done on the main "backbone" lines of the Internet. Since these outings or slowdowns are announced by email to ISPs and IPPs, you can request that they forward this information to you as well.

Accounts and Passwords

Whether your site is run in-house or on a remote server, you will need to create accounts for the developers to log onto. These accounts are used by the Web developers to copy text, graphics, and multimedia files to the Web server. Usually this access will be through FTP programs (Chapter 5). Programmers installing software or actively creating CGI programs (Chapter 5) will need an administrative-level or *root* level account providing complete access to all the server's resources. Use of the root or administrator account must be strictly controlled, since a single misstep could wipe the entire hard disk! While passwords are the responsibility of the individual providing system administration, the developer should check the accounts that are set up. In particular, plain English passwords should not be used under any circumstances. For example, the password, "entertain" is not acceptable, while "!enter#Tain%" is much better. Make sure that the password list is *not* printed or copied without authorization. Most security problems do not involve a supergenius hacker using exotic methods to break into your system, but are the result of a password given to someone who shouldn't have it. If you're overseeing a large development group, remember that security problems can originate within a company as easily as from the outside.

Many developers also password-protect access to the development site using the standard *.htaccess* system available on most Web servers. This controls who can actually see the site using a Web browser during development. To accomplish this, place the access file (containing a list of allowed users) in the desired directory. A second file elsewhere on the Web server contains the passwords. Note that these passwords may be completely different from those used for development and programming accounts.

Restricting Access

It is a good idea to prevent casual explorers on the Internet from viewing your half-completed site. Use the Web-based password system previously described to do this in the simplest way. If this isn't desirable for some reason, you can protect the site by changing the name of the default home page of your site. If you're creating an individual Web site, using a different name than the one required by your particular ISP (e.g., index.html) will automatically prevent access. Larger Web sites running in-house or on a remote ISP/IPP may be able to use a custom URL on a different *port* than standard Web traffic. For example,

```
http://company.com:2834/index.html
```

illustrates a URL running on port "2834," instead of the standard port "80" used by Web services. (You seldom see the "80" in a URL because it's a default port.) If the domain name you registered is already functional, it is appropriate to put up a "coming soon" Web page—regardless of which method you use to restrict access.

Configuration for Multimedia Delivery

Another common problem with Web server configuration concerns MIME (Multipurpose Internet Mail Extensions; see http://www.oac.uci.edu/indiv/ehood/MIME/MIME.html for a description) types. By default, Web browsers interpret everything as text, including the contents of audio and video files. Web servers recognize specific media types by consulting a file which maps MIME file types to their filename extension. For example, *.html* tells the browser to read text as HTML programming and *.wav* indicates a Windows-compatible audio file. If gibberish appears on your Web pages, an incorrect MIME type is often the cause. Make sure that your Web server is configured to support all the media types you plan to include in your Web site. Many newer formats, such as multimedia delivered by Macromedia's Shockwave (http://www.macromedia.com) and proprietary video formats like VDO (http://www.vdo.net) are not in the *default* MIME configuration supplied with commercial Web servers and need to be added directly to the server's configuration file.

When development begins, the initial flowchart in the concept proposal (see Chapter 4) needs to be expanded to show the actual pages on the site. In this process, the developer converts the symbolic description of how visitors navigate through the site into the actual directories and subdirectories in the Web server's *directory tree* needed to realize it (see Figure 6.1). Due to character and length restrictions imposed on filenames, you will not necessarily be able to recognize a file's contents. For example, a film clip of *Casablanca* may have to be called "casablan.mov" on the server. Large projects will need to correlate filenames and contents using a database.

The files on the site are never *above* the home page file (usually named "index.html"); they occupy either the same directory as the home

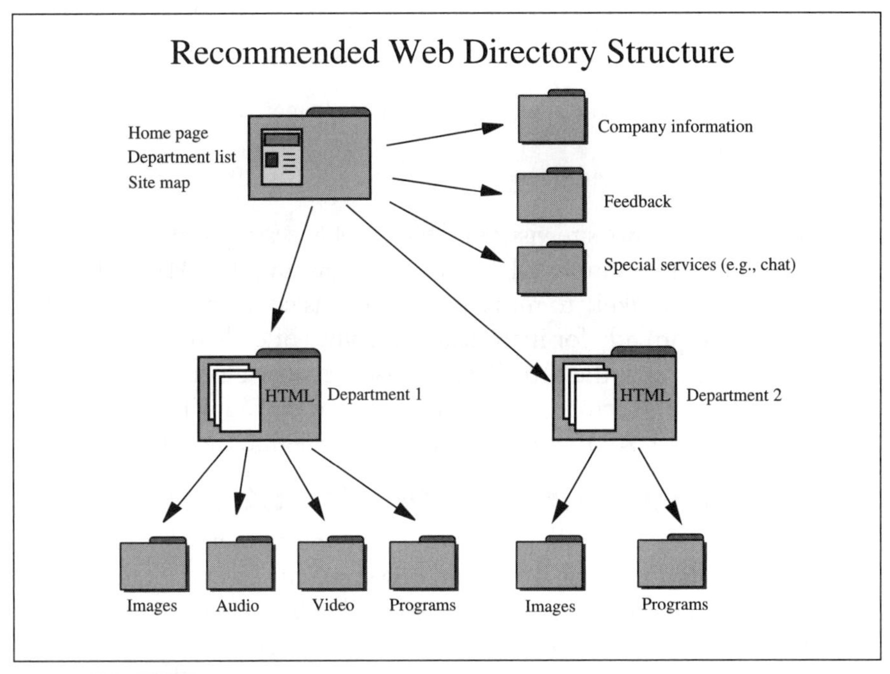

FIGURE 6.1 Recommended directory structure for a Web site.

page or a subdirectory within the directory. Files outside the home directory will be invisible, even though Web extensions like CGI programs may be able to call them during operation. This scheme has the advantage of security and also allows one computer to operate several distinct Web sites on a single computer, each with its own home directory and home page. Unless you want all your pages jumbled in a single directory, you will probably create subdirectories holding Web pages from different areas of the site. We recommend the following method, but feel free to experiment with some of your own:

- Create directories containing the names of your departments (one word summaries are best).
- Within each departmental directory, create subdirectories based on types of media files you will be using. (Some ideas are illustrated in Figure 6.1)

Aliases and Multiple Access Points

In many cases, you may want to provide access to the Web site through pages other than the home page URL. Since the path to a desired page may become quite long, create alternate names through aliases. An alias is simply a name which is shorthand for a longer file path. For example,

```
http://kspace.com/KM/kspace.sys/feedback/pages/mail/index.html
```
becomes:
```
http://kspace.com/feedback
```

Using aliases allows site visitors the ease of accessing different areas of your site by typing a simple URL. Aliases ensure that HTML coders and site visitors are less likely to mistype a short alias compared to a long file path. They also provide for increased portability of code during site updates. For example, the http://kspace.com/feedback alias may be used no matter where the actual pages it refers to are moved within the directory tree of the site. All that is necessary is to redefine the alias.

Hiding Your Directory Structure

After creating the "skeleton" of your Web site on the server, your first step is to hide it! The design of Web browsers and servers potentially allows any file or directory to be accessed individually instead of as part of a Web page. For example, if a visitor types the URL for the graphics directory in Figure 6.1, a list of individual graphics files will appear, instead of the pages they belong in. Prevent users from listing directories simply by creating a default file in each directory on the site. If the home page index.html file is present, any user trying to read the directory will get the index.html file instead. Password-protect individual directories by installing an .htaccess file in any directory. Administrators should realize that while these measures will protect the Web pages, separate security measures are necessary to protect the Web server software itself, as well as the operating system.

Creating Manuals and Style Sheets

Even if you are a lone developer creating small Web sites, constructing a manual for your Web development procedures is virtually a necessity. While many HTML editors allow saving style templates, you will need to record additional information (such as the procedure for graphics processing) to consistently reproduce the page style. A good manual will list the common login names and passwords, program versions and settings for sampling audio and video, standard sizes, foreground and background color combinations, and image sizes and resolutions. If you are developing a larger site, combine individual style templates into a larger manual. The manual should also list technical contacts, such as consultants, ISP/IPPs, and other people involved in the project. Taking time to develop a manual will pay off later by keeping the site easier to manage.

(Check the World Wide Web Consortium at http://www.w3.org/pub/WWW/Style for updates on the ongoing development of a universal style sheet standard based on a style sheet language such as *Cascading Style Sheets* by Håkon Lie.)

 The Facade: External Features

Design for the Web is distinct from other media. It differs significantly from CD-ROMs by having more of a "document" format with significant amounts of text on individual pages (screens). Due to the bottleneck imposed by the relatively slow speed of Internet connections, graphics are optimized to fit into the smallest file sizes possible; this requires specific color types, shading, and image complexity. Graphic designers used to 20-inch monitors and 2000 dpi printers will have to "unlearn" many design principles to function in the 640-x-480 world of the typical computer monitor. Because the Web extends quite literally through millions of computers, it has a different navigation architecture than the closed world of a CD-ROM. On the Web, your site is always a single mouse click away from losing its audience! Following are some basic principles used to create successful Web sites.

Fluff versus Content

As Robert Hertzberg of *WebWeek* (http://www.webweek.com) said in the magazine's June 3, 1996 issue: "Literature has its flowery turns of phrase. Music has its superfluous trills. And software has its bells and whistles." While content providers—particularly those providing entertainment—feel compelled to use the latest, flashiest techniques, remember that the purpose of the site is *not* to stun audience members on their initial visit. Rather, it is to provide real content and encourage repeat visits. After the initial excitement wears off, the real value of a site involves the extent to which it offers what it is supposed to. Make sure it isn't a chore to get at your content; the design should be elegant rather than feature-laden. During the design process, concentrate on content and add enhancements later—not the other way around. Otherwise, your work may end up on the Useless WWW Pages list (http://www.chaco.com/useless), which showcases pointless techie showboating.

Make It Fit

Where possible, size your pages to fit into the typical user's screen, which is about 480 pixels wide by 360 pixels high on a standard 15" monitor. Many designers use slightly smaller widths, such as 460 x 340, in plan-

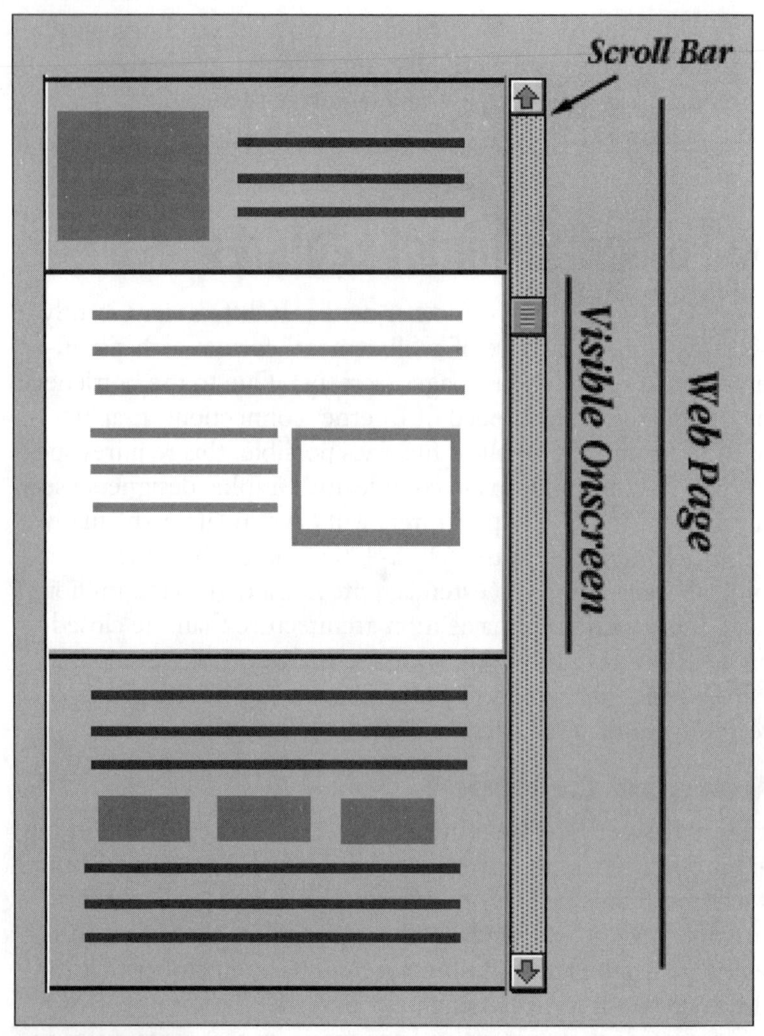

FIGURE 6.2 Visible screens and scrolling adapted from Patrick Lynch's Web Style Manual, (http://info.med.yale.edu/caim/StyleManual/M_II_3.HTML).

ning their pages. If it is absolutely necessary to make the page larger in the horizontal dimension, put a graphic showing the width that the Web browser window needs to be opened to. Vertical fit is also important. Since most visitors dislike scrolling through a long document, keep the length to no more than two typewritten pages (see Figure 6.2).

Include the Site Name on Each Page

The bookmarking feature discussed in Chapter 3 allows members of the Internet audience to save the location of arbitrary pages on your site. In addition, the majority of queries by the audience through search engines will list an individual page in your site, not the home page. As a result, a substantial fraction of site visitors will not see the home page at all. For this reason, it is necessary to indicate the name of the site on *every* page on the site and provide a link back to the main menus or navigation tools (discussed later) as well.

The original headers on the Kaleidospace Web site simply listed the associated department names (e.g., "Art Studio," "Screening Room," or "Music Kiosk"). During 1994, most visitors to the site came from *cool lists* compiled by other Web sites, which invariably linked to the home page. Due to this, visitors always saw information about the company before proceeding to individual departments. During 1995, when search engines appeared, many visitors started to find Kaleidospace based on the results of a query for a particular style of art, film, or music. The search results returned individual artists' pages, rather than the home page of the site, and first-time visitors often did not realize the main site existed. People that did check the header assumed the department name was the name of the site. After receiving numerous email queries about "Music Kiosk," we replaced the headers with ones containing the Kaleidospace name. After this change was made, traffic analysis showed many visitors eventually clicking on the header, proceeding to the appropriate departmental home page, and from there exploring other artists on Kaleidospace.

User Discretion

The Web site should provide a large number of options to visitors and avoid forcing them into a particular course of action unless absolutely necessary. Remember that the latest "cool thing" in Web multimedia may overload the average site visitor's computer system. If your site contains advanced multimedia, be sure to offer the site visitors the option of exploring a *lite* version of your site! If there are several aspects to the entertainment, make sure visitors can decide which ones they want to experience. Sites which force you to listen to a sound or watch long, involved animation sequences are simply obnoxious. If techniques like these are absolutely necessary, keep them as short as possible. For example, instead of a 30-second welcoming music clip, try a short 5 to 10-second version—or use a sound effect, such as the squeak of an opening door, if music isn't necessary. A comparable situation is a navigation control or navigation toolbar that makes sounds based on where it is selected.

A special case of automatic play is the provision for *ambient* audio supported by some Web browsers. Properly handled, background music can convey a much stronger "sense of place" to the site than visuals alone. The main problem is that the best real-time music on the Web sounds like a tiny transistor radio through a modem connection. Under these circumstances, extremely careful design will be necessary to make the music part of the experience rather than another annoyance detracting from the site's content.

Incremental Access to Content

Most entertainment sites want to provide precisely the type of data—audio, video, and multimedia—that takes most visitors several minutes to download. Due to this, the Web site should provide *incremental* access to the content of large media files. The most common way to do this is to provide a much shorter or lower-resolution preview of the text, audio, or video—usually referred to as a *thumbnail*. This should be used for any file which exceeds about 60k (which is about a 50-second download for visitors on a 14.4 modem).

Low- and High-bandwidth Pages

The majority of visitors to the site will be using relatively slow modem connections. In order to facilitate their surfing, create text-only versions of important pages on the site. More sophisticated sites may actually create two sets of graphics using the LOWSRC tag. This tag allows the Web server to quickly send a low-resolution *placeholder* graphic to visitors, over which the larger, high-resolution version loads.

When Disney introduced its new Web site early in 1996, it featured advanced graphics, unmatched content, and a highly sophisticated design. A major feature of the site was its full-screen, full-color graphics. Initially, the visitor saw black-and-white versions of the images which subsequently were *colorized* when the color graphics were loaded over them. Such a scheme has been a recipe for disaster on other sites. Two sets of full-screen graphics could take up to several minutes to appear over slow connections common with home users. Fortunately, the developers of the Disney site understood this and manipulated the images to decrease their size in memory without sacrificing onscreen appearance. The result was a set of images four times smaller than comparable graphics on other sites. The resulting graphics were still larger than the default window size for Netscape and other Web browsers. However, this was again anticipated and the Web site's Help section provided instructions for the "best view."

Put a Lid on Advanced Media

Good entertainment Web sites, while providing sophisticated features to those who can use them, should always contain a basic *core* of HTML that anyone on the Web can access. In practice, even those with the ability to run advanced multimedia will frequently prefer to conduct much of their Web exploration through simple hyperlinks. Beware of using too much advanced media as window dressing which does not enhance your content. Advanced media should only be used in large quantities when it is essential for presenting the content.

Design for Updatability

Even if you're coding your pages by hand, make sure that you follow a straightforward format that will be easy to change. For example, sites frequently change graphics, so don't assume that the same images will always be present on the site.

Support for Multiple Browsers

While Netscape is the dominant browser, a significant fraction of visitors will use Microsoft's Internet Explorer or another browser. While the difference between these two browsers has been narrowing, both companies support proprietary extensions to HTML which will make your site Netscape- or Microsoft-specific if used. While some sites may want to "brand" themselves with a particular Web browser, entertainment sites need to draw the maximum audience possible and cannot afford to play favorites.

Access to Required Software

It is important to create a page with links to sites carrying helpers, players, or plug-in software needed to experience your site's entertainment. Any page using specialized software should have links to the player download pages and supply some information on configuring the software as well.

Outlinks

Web sites do not exist in isolation; they are part of the larger Internet community. Visitors expect each site to provide links to other Web sites with similar content or which are simply rated as "cool" by the administrators. Links can also increase traffic, especially when each link on your site leads to a site that contains a link back to you! (See Chapter 7 for a discussion of *reciprocal links*.) In contrast, *cul de sac* sites tend to irritate serious surfers, who must manually enter a new site in order to find links related to their original interest.

Credits and Contact Information

Each site should credit the individuals involved in creating it. If you outsource development, a link to the developer's site should also be provided. Sites which do not list their origin tend to be regarded with suspicion and run against the general grain of openness which is a primary feature of the Internet.

FIGURE 6.3 Audionet (http://www.audionet.com).

Creating Navigation Tools

Most sites use an image—normally on the home page—to display the links to individual departments and provide a visual metaphor for them.

FIGURE 6.4 Ecospace (http://ecospace.com).

If the site concept mimics a real-world object, the navigation graphic will reflect its appearance. A good example of a site with this motif can be found at AudioNet, shown in Figure 6.3, where the navigation tool mimics the pushbuttons on a radio or tape player. More commonly, recognizable objects of symbols are grouped together as symbols for the departments of the site, as shown by our site, Ecospace (Figure 6.4), which uses the motif of a tree to connect a series of icons leading to the works of environmentally oriented artists and musicians. When designing graphic tools, make sure their purpose is easily understandable; visitors won't return to a site that requires them to memorize the meaning of clever, but obscure navigation graphics.

Road Maps

Extensions of the standard navigation graphic have become increasingly popular as the complexity of Web sites rises. An example of a road map is shown in the Cybertown Site Map, Figure 6.5. Unlike the main navigational tool, the road map lists more than the main departments and may contain hundreds of links. With the increasing use of *offline* browsers that automatically download part of a Web site for later viewing, home pages have provided road maps in the form of long lists—such as the Pathfinder home page in Figure 6.6.

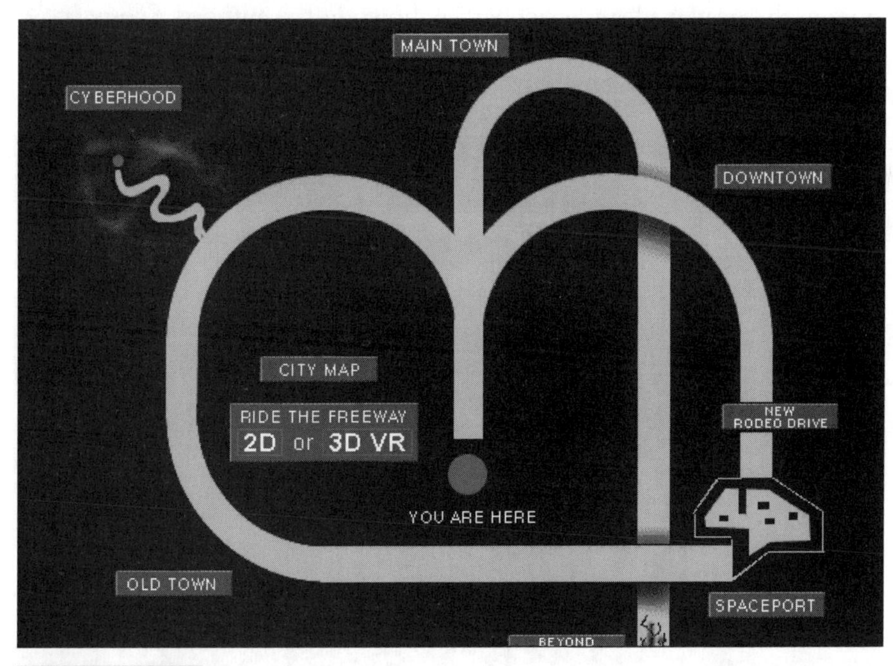

FIGURE 6.5 Cybertown site map (http://www.cybertown.com).

FIGURE 6.6 Pathfinder (http://www.pathfinder.com).

Headers and Footers

Most of the pages on a Web site contain a graphic at the top of the page which identifies the site itself, as well as the department the visitor is looking at. Examples of some headers from the authors' Kaleidospace are shown in Figure 6.7. Headers should extend the artistic design of the site and have navigational links back to home pages and road maps. A variation on the header idea is a sidebar, as shown in the authors' Ecospace (Figure 6.8). Footers are usually less elaborate. They may re-identify the site or contain links to email for the site administrators. Other informa-

FIGURE 6.7 Kaleidospace header and footer (http://kspace.com).

FIGURE 6.8 Ecospace sidebar (http://ecospace.com).

tion appropriate to footers includes credits, legal and copyright information, and the last revision date of the page.

Toolbars

The most common way to allow navigation within individual pages on a Web site is to provide a small *toolbar* listing the main departments.

FIGURE 6.9 Family.com toolbar (http://www.family.com).

FIGURE 6.10 Warner Bros. toolbar (http://warnerbros.com).

Examples of an effective toolbar are shown in Family.com, Figure 6.9 and Warner Bros., Figure 6.10. In general, toolbars should be simple in design, with an obvious function. Toolbars are normally horizontal, though HTML allows vertical toolbars to be placed to the left or right of the page's content.

Small Icons and Doodads

Small icons are most often used as direct links to audio and video content rather than other pages. For example, clicking on a microphone icon might cause a sound clip to download. A related use for icons on Web sites is as *bullet* replacements in the Bell Industries site (http://www.bellind.com). By default, Web lists have simple circles in front of each item in the list. A simple, though highly effective enhancement of the list bullet replaces it with a small graphic element. On some sites, such as Sega (http://www.sega.com), bullets have even been animated—though this would seem excessive for most content. Another common enhancement replaces the simple horizontal line provided by the <hr> HTML tag with a graphic line of one's own choosing.

Most sites also create small *New* and *Return* graphics, usually designed to fit in the same width as a line of text. New icons serve to draw the visitor's attention to updates in an otherwise vast array of choices. Return graphics are primarily useful hyperlinks within a longer page, where clicking on a Return icon can take the visitor back to the top of the page. Embedding a variety of graphic elements within text (used effectively in early entertainment sites like the now offline Megadeth Arizona site) has now been largely abandoned.

Furniture—Content Integration

Once the bare rooms of your basic Web site are up and running, add content to fill the space. The following section considers each of the major media types (text, graphics, audio, video, and multimedia) and ways to effectively adapt them to the Web.

Text Design and Formatting

Virtually all Web pages will contain some text, but effective use is just as important here as it is for graphics and multimedia programming. As with other content, make sure there is a strong reason for the visitor to read the text. Studies by the site designers for Sun Microsystems (http://www.sun.com/sun-on-net/uidesign) indicate that the average person reads text onscreen 25 percent slower than from a printed page. Since text is harder to read, include it only when necessary. Most visitors skip over superfluous material (e.g., extended welcome messages) and scan text for key terms and hyperlinks. A related discovery reported by the Sun designers and others is that visitors do not like to scroll through text. The following additional points are also useful in text formatting and HTML coding.

Use the ALT and NOEMBED tags

Any graphic you create allows for an alternative text description with the use of a companion ALT tag. The text within the ALT tag contains a description of the associated graphic so that site visitors with text-only browsers—or the 20 percent or so of visitors who have turned off their graphics due to a slow connection—don't miss anything. The NOEMBED command is used similarly with advanced media. Developed as a proprietary HTML tag by Netscape, it provides an alternate display for movies and multimedia running inside the browser window.

Don't Rely on Precise Text Alignment

The Web allows the site visitor to set the default font they will view your pages with. To make matters worse, the default font used by each browser varies, especially among those provided by online services.

Avoid Using Too Many Nested Tags

An example of this problem would occur with a construct like the following:

```
<a href="/filesys/file.html"><a name="one"><strong>Test of <font
size="+1">the</font> file</strong></a>
```

Many Web browsers will become confused by such complexity and fail to produce the desired format changes—or worse. If you must use a few nested tags, remember to use them in the following order: <tag a><tag b>text</tagb></tag a>.

Avoid the Use of Tabs

The implementation of tabs varies widely on different systems. If you have to create a columnar list, either use the table command, make an ordered-unordered list, or create a table by spacing text within the PRE tag.

Check Your Spelling

It is astonishing how many Web sites are riddled with spelling errors! Use a spell checker before importing your text into HTML, no matter how good you think your spelling skills are.

Index Long Stretches of Text

Long Web documents are more like an ancient scroll than a page from a book. If you have a long product description, press release or story, and put an index at the top—either by using the list (<UL></UL>) command or by making a horizontal index with separators such as pipes (|) between each header. (The latter is useful for short indices.) It is also a good idea to create a Return hyperlink from each section of the document back to the main index and mark it with a small icon. For extremely long documents (> 10 pages if printed), the document should be split into several HTML files to reduce download time.

Choose Compatible Colors

The same stylistic rules that apply to selecting compatible colors for text and background on the printed page are true on the Web, only more so due to the lower resolution of computer screens compared to paper. If the text and page background use very similar colors, some browsers will display these as one color—thereby rendering the text invisible. Strongly clashing colors, such as purple text on an orange page, should be avoided, since they greatly increase eyestrain (unless this is the effect you're trying to accomplish!).

Use of Nonstandard HTML Tags

With the complexity and sophistication of Web pages available on the Internet today, it is easy to forget that many of their best features are not defined in the current HTML standard. In the latter part of 1994, Netscape created its own HTML tags to overcome the limitations of the early Web. Some of these commands were sorely needed (e.g., the <center> command and text *flows* around graphics, which allowed reasonable formatting of pages), while others like the <blink> command were nearly useless. In 1995, additional tags allowed formatted tables, multiple columns of text, and *frames* which split up the Web page into individually addressable panels. Eager to compete with Netscape, Microsoft announced it would support all these tags and define more of its own. While both companies have endeavored to make their tags extensions of standard HTML, the ultimate fate of many proprietary tags is by no means certain.

Unfortunately for HTML purists, entertainment sites need the best presentation possible to achieve their effect and most will end up incor-

FIGURE 6.11 Atlantic Records (http://www.atlanticrecords.com).

porating a large number of nonstandard tags. Three particular extensions introduced by Netscape and adopted by Microsoft are of particular interest to entertainment sites which rely on presentation to achieve their effect.

Tables.
The table tag allows formatting long lists so that they can fit comfortably into the screen. In the Netscape implementation, a grid can be constructed around table entries, creating a spreadsheet appearance.

Frames.
Frames allow Web pages to work in a fashion closer to CD-ROM programs. Each frame has its own scrollable area that can hold the same information as a complete page. Frames are used to create a common array of selectable icons or text to aid navigation in the site and to define one frame to hold rapidly updated information such as news or sports, in an otherwise unchanging interface. Use frames sparingly; Web sites providing framed and unframed versions of their pages find that the audience usually takes the unframed option. Extensive frame use causes pages to load much slower on modem connections. Despite this, both the Atlantic Records (Figure 6.11) and the *Mission Impossible* sites (Figure 6.12) make intelligent use of frames.

Embedding.
The embed tag allows external players to display all or part of their windows within the browser window. For example, individual volume and forward and reverse controls from an audio or player can be embedded within the graphic design of a music or movie page.

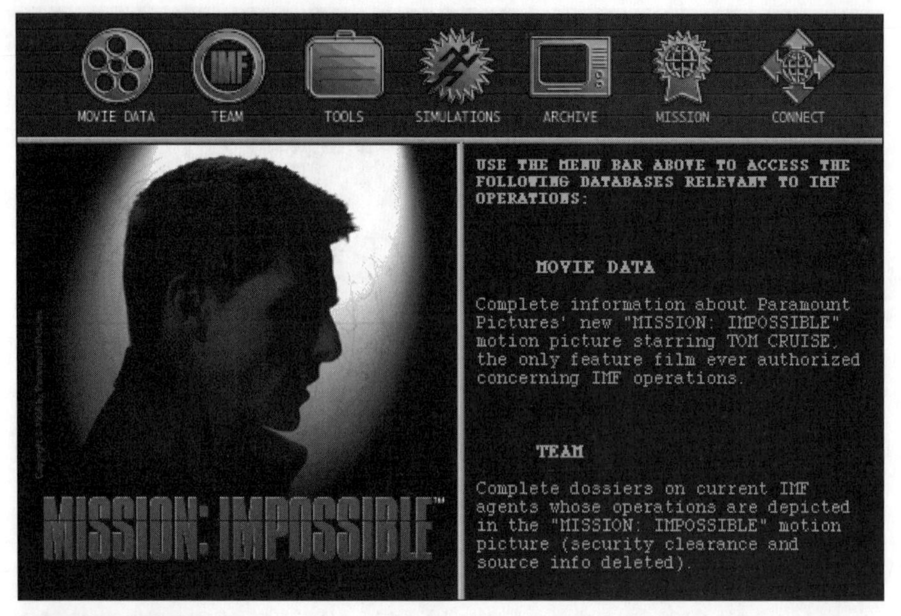

FIGURE 6.12 *Mission Impossible* (http://www.missionimpossible.com).

META Tag and Search Engine Support

The META tag, found at the top of HTML documents before the body of the text, can be used to support *smart* indexing by search engines. Compatible search engines adding a Web site to their database will read the information in the META tag and ignore the rest of the document. This way, when search engine users retrieve information, they read a well-formatted paragraph instead of a random block of information within the larger page.

Multilingual Sites

With rapid improvements in support for multiple languages on the Web, the biggest hurdle faced by the site developer is translation of the original Web pages. For small sites it may be sufficient to hire a translator for a few hours, while large sites can avail themselves of the translation services springing up on the Web. A good resource for finding translation services can be found at The Global Translation Alliance (http://www.aleph.com). Short of full translations, Web site developers can do several things to make their pages friendlier to non-English speakers. Check graphics for hidden cultural assumptions—remember that a particular color may mean something completely different to people in different countries. A good example of a multilingual site is the Cannes Film Festival, Figure 6.13,

FIGURE 6.13 Cannes Film Festival (http://www.festival-cannes.fr).

where visitors may enter their preferred language version of the site by clicking on a French or American flag.

Menus and Lists

Pop-up menus and scrolling-list HTML commands allow a large number of options to be compressed into a small area onscreen. As such, they are ideal for sites with dozens to hundreds of individual topics to choose from—such as archives, databases, or search engines. Since these selection tools are only available in the fill-out form syntax of HTML 2.0 and beyond, using this method requires that visitors click on a separate button to submit their menu or list selection. After submission. an external CGI-style program must be installed to process the visitor's selection.

Web Graphics Processing

Without processing, a single graphic filling the windows of a standard Web browser would be several hundred thousand bytes in size. One of the main goals of Web graphic design is to reduce these large files to a manageable size without reducing their value as content. Graphic size reduction is a major area in itself, and requires an artistic sensibility as well as technical knowledge. Numerous resources on the Web like Webreference.com (http://www.webreference.com) and Lynda Weinman's Homegurrl

Page (http://www.lynda.com) provide guidelines for creating Web-friendly graphics. Several steps that the graphic artist can use to create these graphics, are summarized below in the following section.

Color Reduction and Netscape's Color Cube

If you have created GIF-style graphics, you may have been occasionally surprised at how Netscape displays them. This is because Netscape uses its own color palette, which may not necessarily match the color palette you're using in your own graphics program. To complicate matters further, Netscape's palette has 256 colors on most monitors, but drops to 216 colors on SVGA monitors! When Netscape encounters an image whose palette does not match its own, it will attempt to reproduce it by *dithering*—frequently with significant reduction of image quality. The newest versions of Netscape partly compensate for these limitations by trying to match its preferred colors to those actually available on the system, but the result is not always perfect.

To match development colors with their final display by Netscape, install and use a custom color palette during graphic design. Using the same palette as Netscape when preparing the drawings in Photoshop or another program prevents dithering completely. For an even better solution, use HVS color reduction by Digital Frontiers (http://www.digfrontiers.com), which gives greater color reduction than the default algorithms in Photoshop without compromising image quality. Discussions of the Netscape color model and color reduction (including downloadable palettes) are available from Brian Cunningham's The 216 Colors of Netscape site (http://www.connect.hawaii.com/hc/webmasters/Netscape.colors.html) and Tom Venetianer's Webling's Cafe (http://mvassist.pair.com/Articles/NS2colors.html). BoxTop Software (http://www.aris.com/boxtop) provides an excellent tool for color reduction in both GIFs and JPEGs.

Transparent GIFs

The GIF89a format allows one of the 256 colors in a GIF to be specified as *transparent*, meaning that any underlying background will show through areas painted with the color. Use of transparent GIFs is essential if you are trying to place irregularly shaped images on top of your page background. BoxTop Software (http://www.aris.com/boxtop/PhotoGIF) provides a plug-in called PhotoGIF which is useful for creating transparent GIFs for the Macintosh. Windows users should check out WebImage (http://www.group42.com/webimage.htm). Note that there is no equivalent transparency format for JPEG images.

Drawing versus Scanning

Graphics drawn from scratch frequently have much smaller file sizes than the same graphic digitized using a scanner. This is primarily because the scanner may record a large white area as a set of almost identical colors, greatly increasing the file size of the image and, therefore, downloading time!

Removing Jagged Edges

Graphics created in a *draw* type of program like Adobe Illustrator will normally need to be smoothed when they are converted to a GIF or JPEG format. The simplest way to do this without introducing too many shades is to create the draw graphics several times larger than the final size. Copying them to a bitmap drawing program like Photoshop reduces them to their final size. Photoshop's built-in functions smooth sharp boundaries during the reduction.

Width and Height Information

By including the size (in pixels) of a graphic using WIDTH and HEIGHT in the HTML IMG tag, many Web browsers can instantly create a bounding box for the graphic without the need to examine the whole graphic to determine size information; for example,

```
<IMG SRC="picture.gif" WIDTH = 239 HEIGHT=88>
```

This will facilitate rapid page layout before the graphics actually complete downloading, making the page easier to understand.

Removing Unnecessary Shadings

A blue sky may contain hundreds of shades. If these colors are replaced by a small number of colors, the image will look less realistic, but the resulting "iconic" look is frequently acceptable for some images. As an example, graphics used as navigation tools may be dramatically simplified without changing their usefulness.

Image Consolidation

Since each picture on a page is loaded separately, designers can speed up the downloads for their Web pages by consolidating individual graphics into a larger image. This rule applies to file sizes no more than 50 to 60 kilobytes. Beyond this size, individuals with noisy Internet connections may not be able to download the graphic—which will *hang* after being partially drawn.

Background Design

Since most page backgrounds are built out of a large number of repeated images, take care so that the repetition enhances the foreground instead of calling attention to itself. Patterns which provide a texture such as wood grain or cloth are highly effective. Another successful kind of background is created from a low-contrast icon relevant to the foreground material, such as milk bottles for a page on cows. Some sites use the "torn paper" motif as a background. In this case, the pattern is formed from a thin band extended completely across the screen When repeated across the window, the background forms vertical lines or layers. Horizontal layering is also possible if the background image is very long and narrow, but most browsers draw these patterns more slowly than vertical backgrounds. Test background with low-end monitors. Frequently, backgrounds that are acceptable on a workstation monitor make the Web page illegible when displayed with 256 or 16 colors. A good place to look at some sample backgrounds is at the NCSA Web site (http://www.ncsa.uiuc.edu/SDG/Software/WinMosaic/Backgrnd/) and a useful archive can be found via the Design/Systems background page (http://www.design-sys.com/champ/background.html).

Web Animation

Until late 1995, Web pages tended to be static and resembled electronic desktop publishing documents. At that time, developments in Web browser technology began to support real-time animation on Web pages

FIGURE 6.14 Tony Awards site (http://www.tonys.org).

FIGURE 6.15 HBO site (http://hbo.com).

using a variety of techniques. The most frequent use for animation is to create movement in small onscreen objects, such as spinning or rotating logos. Certain entertainment sites have used larger images with only a few frames; The Tony Awards Online (http://www.tonys.org) and HBO (http://hbo.com) provide outstanding examples. The home page of the Tony Awards site, Figure 6.14, uses two frames of animation to simulate the flashing of a Broadway street sign. Since the animation is consistent with the object it represents, the effect is far more compelling than a jerky rendition of smooth movement (e.g., a flying plane). On the HBO site, Figure 6.15, several small animated sequences combine to give the effect of a city at night. One of the most sophisticated sites yet developed is Lollapalooza, Figure 6.16, which combines virtually every form of Web-based animation available.

On most entertainment sites small animated *doodads*, such as rotating logos, are more effective than large characters jerking clumsily around the screen. However, for certain entertainment sites, such as Lollapalooza, the popularity of a performer or animated character may overcome site visitors' resistance to extensive animation. The following sections list various animation techniques and effective ways in which they can be used.

Two-frame Animation

The Netscape LOWSRC tag used to preload low-resolution images allows a browser to load two images in succession. It was intended it to be used as a way to rapidly load a low-resolution image and reload a second, high-resolution image over it (see previous discussions of the

FIGURE 6.16 Lollapalooza site (http://www.lollapalooza.com).

Disney and HBO sites). When first introduced in late 1994, it was used as a way of creating simple animation in the then static Web. It is not currently recommended as an animation technique and is more appropriate for the uses previously discussed.

Server-push Animation

A method developed by Netscape for its browser allows *server push* and *client pull* animation. In this case, an HTML tag developed by Netscape allows the server to periodically refresh pages on the client's Web browser. The most common use to date has been for ad rotation on Web pages, where ads can cycle between several "billboards" every few minutes. A disadvantage of this method is that the entire Web page is redrawn during the refresh and images are re-downloaded each time a refresh occurs. A good example of a refresh that avoids redrawing the entire Web page can be found on the Happy Puppy Game Site (http://www.happypuppy.com), which uses frames to confine the refreshed area to a small portion of the screen.

CGI-based Animation

A more efficient animation method provides an HTML link to an image which is actually a CGI program. Using server push, the program sends a series of images to the Web browser. CGI scripts for server-push animation are very easy to write (see Matt's Script Archive at http://www.

worldwidemart.com/scripts). Since a single image is animated rather than the entire page, CGI-based animation is more efficient than general server push. A disadvantage of the method is that animation must be controlled by the Web server; this means it will be jerky as the number of visitors using the server computer's resources varies. An excellent example of scripted animation (which gives an "experimental video" feel) can be found at Parkbench (http://found.cs.nyu.edu/parkbench/parkbench.html).

Animated GIFs

Animation created with the same GIF89a format used for transparent GIFs is currently the method of choice for Web sites. Supported by major Web browsers, animated GIFs are simply strings of ordinary GIFs fused into a single file and called with the standard IMG tag used for ordinary graphics. By appropriate adjustment, animation can run one-time or loop repeatedly. Unlike server push, animated GIFs are only downloaded once and do not add an additional processing load to the Web server. Since Web browsers that don't support animation show the first frame of the animation sequence, it is safe to use animated GIFs for key graphics such as navigation icons.

When creating animated GIFs, it is important to use methods which decrease file size. Consider, for example, a 1k image of a spaceship passing over the 9k image of a planet (Figure 6.17). A single image with both objects will be 1+9=10k in size. If the entire image is redrawn for a 10-frame animated GIF sequence, the file will be 10 times the size of a single frame or 100k. However, if the spaceship alone is present in later frames, 9 of the files will be only 1k, and the total animation file size will

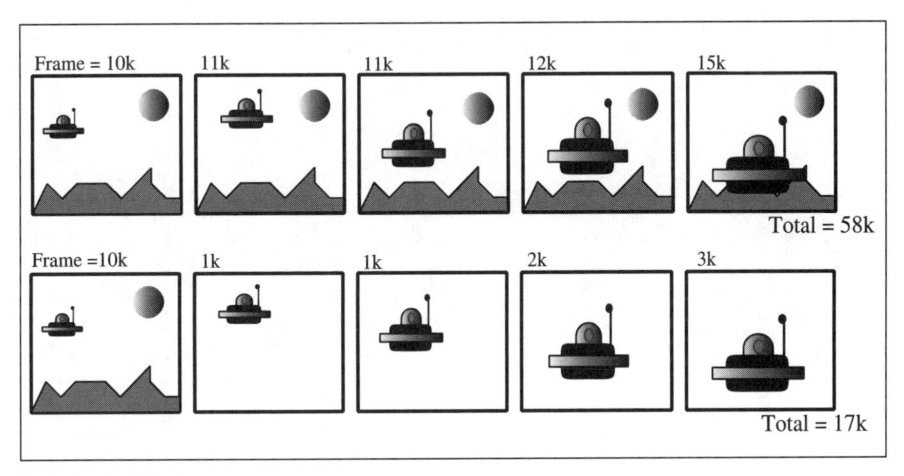

FIGURE 6.17 Reducing file sizes of animated GIFs.

be 19k. The appearance of animation created by the two methods is identical. By paying careful attention to development, download times for animated GIFs can be significantly reduced. A detailed discussion of this and other tricks to reduce file size can be found at GIF Animation on the WWW (http://members.aol.com/royalef/gifanim.htm).

Shockwave Animation

Developers already experienced with creating multimedia for CD-ROMs using Macromedia's *Director*, Authorware, and Freehand programs won't encounter much of a learning curve for *Shockwave*—which is primarily a conversion tool rather than a new authoring environment. Once a Director movie has been developed, Shockwave tools convert it into a Web-friendly form. Director provides an ideal medium for animation—particularly of small objects like *active* controls, logos, and ads. In these cases, Shockwave files actually have an advantage over other formats in file sizes. Unlike animated GIFs, Shockwave animated sequences can respond to user input. Examples include navigational tools which make a sound when selected and buttons which change shape when pressed. More sophisticated applications might be informational in content, such as explaining the process of film editing with an animated model. Good examples of Shockwave use in entertainment sites include Hollywood Online's (http://www.hollywood.com/

FIGURE 6.18 The Marc Canter Show (http://www.mediaband.com).

movies/shocked.html) interactive movie trailers and the The Marc Canter Show at Mediaband (Figure 6.18), which uses episodic Shockwave movies.

Unfortunately, most of the advantages of Shockwave disappear when longer Director movies are used. By default, most Director movies assume CD-ROM or faster access speeds, which translate to unacceptable delays on the Web. Director movies with file sizes > 100k will require substantial optimization for the Web. While individual changes are not difficult, the main hurdle may be for the developers to think at 14.4 modem speeds instead of much faster CD-ROMs. The following sections provide a few guidelines for effectively optimizing Director movies for data transfer over the Web.

Reduce Media Size.
Since Web browsers typically open to much smaller windows than full-screen, consider reducing the size of the Shockwave movie's stage to 400 x 300 pixels or less. Color should always be reduced to 8-bit and, in some cases (e.g., flashing controls), it may be possible to reduce down to 2-bit color. As with animated GIFs, make sure you erase any part of an animation sequence that doesn't change between successive frames. Shockwave movies should use the Web's approach to backgrounds and replace large background images with small, repeated ones. Examine how audio is being used by the movie; if it is not essential to have spoken words, consider substituting text. Currently, Shockwave does not support sound compression; therefore, audio would have to be sampled at 11kHz rather than the 22kHz or 44kHz common for CD-ROM.

Use Web-specific Commands.
The key to effectively creating Web-friendly Shockwave movies is to use commands added to the Lingo programming language. These commands allow Shockwave movies to link to Web pages via URLs (gotoNetPage), launch other Shockwave movies (gotoNetMovie), and preload external media elements into the Web browser's cache (preloadNetThing). Used together, these commands allow the developer to split a single large Director movie into several smaller Shockwave movies. This results in large time savings, since visitors will not have to download the entire presentation at once to begin using it.

Offload Calculations to CGI Programs.
Note that Shockwave movies can be used to execute CGI programs directly (getNetText) so that complex routines can be moved from the movie to a program on the Web server. In some cases, this will speed up execution and sometimes extend the interactivity of Shockwave movies. For example, a CGI-based chat room could be hooked to a Shockwave movie providing a rich graphical front-end.

Replace QuickTime Movies.

Currently, Shockwave does not support the inclusion of QuickTime movies. Until this feature is supported, each QuickTime movie must be broken down into individual image files then re-imported into Director as a film loop.

Thumbnails.

If it is absolutely necessary to use a large (e.g., > 100k) Shockwave file, consider providing a smaller thumbnail excerpt linking to it. The thumbnail can be a short Shockwave movie in the larger file which holds the visitor's attention as the larger movie loads.

Java-based Animation

Java programs can support virtually any form of animation. Like Shockwave, Java is an authoring environment for multimedia, allowing for full integration of sound with animated sequences. However, unlike Shockwave, Java is a general-purpose programming language. To understand the difference, consider that Shockwave itself could be implemented as a Java program (applet) instead of as a plug-in. If you or your group can master the difficult programming curve required for Java, animation can be created in a smaller space than Shockwave. An extraordinary example of this can be found at The Butterfly's Web (Figure 6.19) produced by the HuskyLabs developer group (http://www.butterfly.net/husky). In this case, selecting the butterfly or flowers changes the animation, which is also fully synchronized with ambient sound. It is also possible to implement real-time streamed animation, which can substantially improve performance. For an example of this, check the Dimension X site's Streaming Animation page (http://www.dimensionx.com/products/sa/index.html), which contains Duke, an animated character that dances across the screen. Even Macromedia has decided to hedge its bets and is developing Java-based multimedia tools (http://www-1.macromedia.com/Tools/Power Applets/Info/index.html).

Java's main drawback is that programming with it is much more difficult than it is in Shockwave, though simple animation like the *tickers* at the bottom of many Web pages can be created very easily using the simpler JavaScript. Java also has a slow startup on older Web browsers (e.g., Netscape 2.0), partially offsetting its smaller download size. For more information on Java and JavaScript, see the Live Software Resource Center (http://jrc.livesoftware.com).

Audio Development

Audio is fast becoming a necessity for entertainment sites. With the current proliferation of software, sound of virtually any type may be pro-

FIGURE 6.19 The Butterfly's Web (http://www.butterfly.net).

vided over the Internet. Most developers capture and edit sounds using the same hardware and software used for other multimedia applications, and use additional processing to make the sounds ready for the Web. Most Web sites continue to provide short clips, rather than complete songs. While lower-quality real-time streaming audio formats allow transmission of complete versions of songs or other audio works, such use raises issues of intellectual property and performance rights, discussed further in Chapter 13. The problem will be greatest for a Web site that uses music to enhance a customer's experience of other entertainment, rather than one which is selling the music directly. The following sections contain discussion of the incorporation of audio into entertainment Web sites in greater detail.

Download and Play Audio

Many Web sites currently supply sound in common Mac and Windows formats. Typically, sound quality is set at the quality of a good FM station, though quality may be as high as desired. Keep in mind that higher-quality formats require visitors to wait many minutes to hear the clips. An uncompressed, high-quality 8-bit/22k sampled sound takes about seven times longer to download over a 28.8 modem than to play. This means that for every minute of music you provide, most visitors to the site will be waiting for a significant amount of time for the sample. Increasing the quality to 16-bit and/or including stereo will increase download time even more.

RealAudio and Other Streaming Audio

During 1995, several companies introduced new Web-specific audio types designed to overcome the limitations of slow Internet connections and allow hearing speech and music in real-time. The current industry standard, RealAudio (http://www.realaudio.com) allows low-quality audio (equivalent to a small transistor radio) to be heard almost as soon as the site visitor selects it. By eliminating the several-minute download, RealAudio and other streaming audio formats make it practical to create music-based sites; they are becoming a virtual necessity for anyone who wants to provide sound of any type to their audience. An example of a site that uses RealAudio exclusively is The New Music Network, Figure 6.20.

The original RealAudio was optimized primarily for voice and could provide intelligible speech over 14.4 modem connections. The more recent 28.8 format is tolerable for music played through small speakers. Note that the actual sound of a RealAudio clip can vary widely; correct pre-processing of sound can make a tremendous difference in quality. The starting point for a RealAudio conversion should always be the highest-quality 16-bit sample to help the conversion run correctly.

If you are developing a small Web site within a standard ISP account, it may not be possible to use RealAudio at all. Contact your ISP to determine its policy; in some cases, you can buy a few channels for a monthly fee. Most ISP/IPPs will provide access to a RealAudio server for large Web sites and you can also negotiate installing a dedicated audio server computer on their network. If you are developing in-house, setting up RealAudio on your Web server is relatively simple. Remember that providing RealAudio requires your server to have the fastest Internet connections you can afford. As you serve dozens to hundreds of simultaneous visitors, your speed requirements will grow *tremendously*. A single T1-speed connection capable of supporting dozens of moderate-traffic Web sites will overload when about 20 users receiving RealAudio at one time. Large numbers of RealAudio channels require increasingly powerful Web-server hardware. Fortunately, at current Internet traffic levels even high-volume Web sites will normally need less than 50 channels.

During development with a RealAudio system, the Web server should be tested by running all the available sound channels at one time to

FIGURE 6.20 The New Music Network (http://www.newmusic.net).

ensure that the RealAudio server doesn't overload. This is especially important when the Web site is hosted by a remote ISP/IPP. Even those providers that appeared adequate when the Web server was installed may have problems with RealAudio.

Audio Thumbnails

A parallel type of *thumbnail* often used on music-related sites provides an excerpt of a longer audio clip or a RealAudio version of a higher-quality downloadable file. Supplying multiple resolution clips is an excellent idea which should be more widely used. In order to implement it, the developers need to provide the increased disk storage necessary to double or triple their existing number of audio files.

Automatic Audio Play

If you want sound to play automatically in the background when a page is loaded, the same mechanism used to enable server-push animation can make a sound clip play every time a given page is loaded. In practice, the server-push command is put into the <META> portion of the HTML file. A delay is normally added, allowing the page to load before the sound begins to play. For example, in the following HTML code, the server will wait 30 seconds after beginning to download the page before sending the sound:

```
<META HTTP-EQUIV=REFRESH CONTENT="30; URL=http://www.yoursite.
com/sound.au">
```

Unless your audience is restricted to individuals with high-speed connections, highly compressed audio formats like RealAudio are the only real alternatives. Choose appropriate clips that sound good at the low resolution RealAudio provides. It is also not a good idea to put automatic audio on pages that are accessed repeatedly, such as the home page or a navigational map. All but the most insensitive of users will be driven crazy by waiting for the same sound clip to load and play. More information can be found at Netscape's page on audio push at http://home.netscape.com/assist/net_sites/pushpull.html, and at Project Cool's page at http://www.projectcool.com/developer/alchemy/autosound.html.

Video Development

Video format is even more demanding than audio; 10 seconds of uncompressed color video in a tiny 2-x-2 (160 x 120 pixels)-inch window is already several times the size of a comparable audio file. Nevertheless, video use is on the rise on the Internet and will become a major part of most entertainment sites in the near future.

Even more than audio, video requires considerable processing to be useful in the small screen and slow frame rates possible on the Internet. In serving video to the Web, the restrictions placed by the speed of most Internet connections makes it essential that the clip's content is worth the download time. See Figure 6.21 for a comparison of media types.

While the capture window should stay small, try to sample the sound at the highest quality possible. In most cases, you will want to split the soundtrack from the video for separate enhancement with an audio processing program like Macromedia's SoundEdit (http://www.macromedia.com). High sound quality (double what would be possible otherwise) can be preserved by compressing the soundtrack using the IMA 4:1 option for QuickTime. After the video is captured, it will require editing with programs such as Adobe Premiere and AfterEffects (http://www.adobe.com).

Media Type	Average File Size (kilobytes)	Download Time, 28.8 modem (2500 bytes/second)
1 page text	5	2
Full-screen* bitmap	24	10
Full-screen 256-color* GIF	150	60
100 x 100 pixel 10-frame animated GIF	40	16
30 seconds of 8-bit mono audio	800	320
30 seconds of 16-bit stereo audio	3200	1280
30 seconds of RealAudio**	90	10
30 second QuickTime movie	2500	1000
20 second VDO-format movie**	600	10

* Full-Screen is VGA or 640 x 480 pixels.
** These *streaming* media formats begin a few seconds after downloads begin.

FIGURE 6.21 File size versus media format.

Download and Play Video

Since Macintosh remains the development system of choice, most Internet video is saved in QuickTime (http://www.quicktime.com) format. Currently, QuickTime has significant advantages over Windows AVI, especially with regard to its ability to synchronize a soundtrack with the images. Sampled video should be saved in either CinePak or Animation-8. CinePak (http://www.radius.com/cinepak), a good all-purpose compression system, is compatible with a wide variety of movie viewers on the Web. Animation-8 produces sharper but jerky motion and is most appropriate for animated sequences. QuickTime can be further optimized for the Internet by using a utility provided by Apple which adapts it for play using Apple's QuickTime plug-in (http://quicktime.apple.com/qt/dev/devweb.html). The plug-in allows the QuickTime movie to run in the Web browser's window and converts the download into a semi-streaming format.

Streaming Video

During 1995, dozens of companies promised real-time video delivered over modem lines. While some of these systems provide acceptable performance over ISDN or even 28.8 modem connections, their resulting video images are small and restricted to a few frames per second. Currently, a wide variety of video formats exist; real-time video is possible using Duplexx Software's NET TOOB (http://www.duplexx.com/ntlive.html), VDONet's VDOLive (http://www.vdolive.com), Xing Technology's Streamworks technology (http://www.streamworks.com), and at least a half dozen other formats. Vosaic (http://www.vosaic.com) offers a particularly interesting product; video can be delivered from Macintosh-based Web sites and moving objects within the video may be defined as hyperlinks to other locations on the

Web. For more detailed lists, consult the video portion of the Web Multimedia Tour (http://ftp.digital.com/webmm/fshop.html).

Unlike the audio scene, no clear standards "winner" has appeared for video. In general, streaming video should be used cautiously—and plenty of support should be provided so that visitors to your site may find,

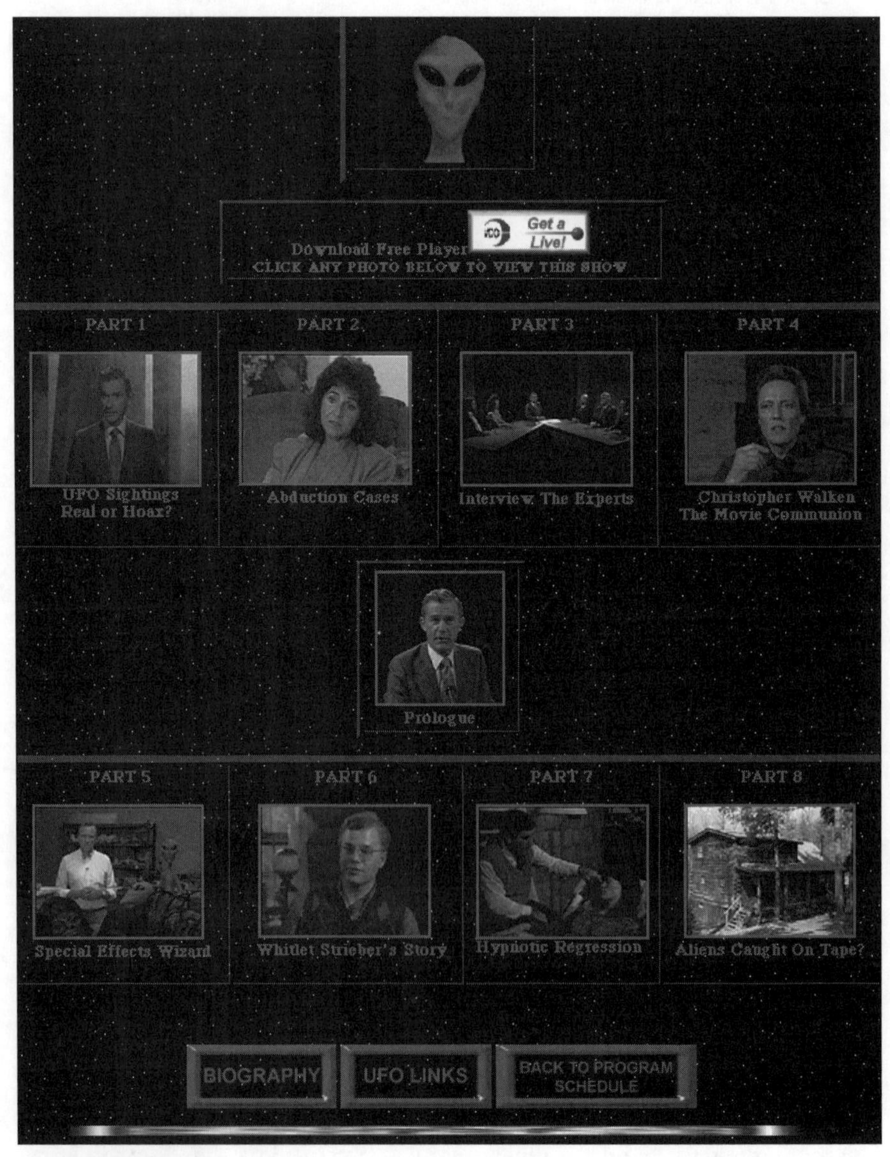

FIGURE 6.22 Cummings Multimedia Entertainment (http://www.cummingsvideo.com/home/preview.htm).

download, and configure the appropriate plug-in or player. A good example of an entertainment site providing streaming video is Cummings Multimedia Entertainment (http://www.cummingsvideo.com/home/preview.htm), shown in Figure 6.22.

Video Thumbnails

With video, there is no substitute for thumbnails. Instead of forcing an automatic download, visitors should be able to select a small image with a single frame from the movie. With the advent of animated GIFs, another possibility for thumbnails is shown on animator Phil Denslow's site (http://www.webcom.com/~kellyd/madcap/madcap.html). Denslow uses a simple two-frame animated thumbnail to suggest the content of the complete video clip.

Tips for Creating Effective Video Clips

Due to the extreme limitation of Internet video, it is a challenge to find clips which provide useful content while avoiding unacceptable download times. The following sections provide several suggestions for selecting video clips fitting this criteria.

Use Mid-range Shots.

Due to the small size of the video, distance shots (such as a pan over a concert audience) will not show enough detail to be interesting. In addition, be careful of using close-ups—particularly of faces talking or singing—since any sound-to-video synchronization problems will become more obvious.

Use Clips with Activity.

Nothing is more frustrating than downloading a long video clip which shows nothing more than someone standing nearly motionless onstage. A much better clip might jump between close-ups and full-body shots.

Look for Small, Complete Scenes.

The length restrictions imposed on video suggest that scenes should be selected the same way they are for movie previews. Study the short excerpts in previews to see how a complete thought can be suggested to the audience in a few seconds.

VRML Development

VRML worlds lend themselves naturally to extending a Web site's navigation tools into three dimensions. A simple example of this would be to take the "city" motif common on many Web sites and create a VRML version. Examples are found at NetBiz Town (http://www.stellar.co.jp/VRML/index-e.html) and Cybertown (Figure 6.23). Visitors to the sites navigate through the towns and visit specific buildings for content. VRML worlds based on 3-D objects are also possible; imagine navigating through the interior of a vir-

FIGURE 6.23 Cybertown (http://www.cybertown.com).

tual movie projector and finding clips inside it. A good tutorial on effective VRML use can be found at the Silicon Graphics VRML Tutorial (http://vrml.asu.edu). A third area with working virtual reality (currently non-VRML) is in interactive "chat" rooms, where programs such as The Palace (Figure 6.24) may provide a simpler introduction to virtual worlds.

Approach VRML development with caution. While virtual worlds are probably the future of the Web (see Chapters 12 and 15), take care not to

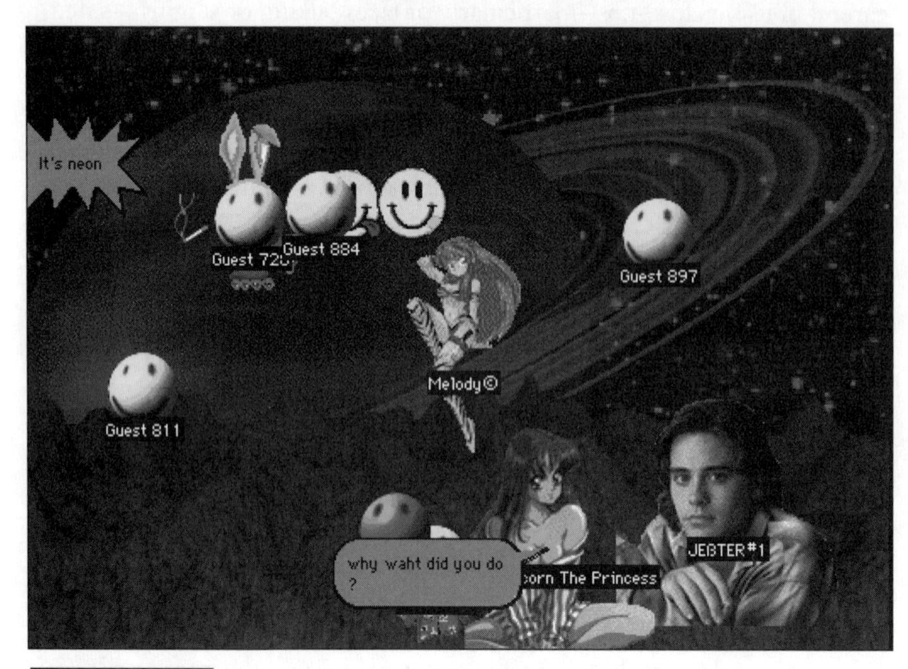

FIGURE 6.24 The Palace (http://www.thepalace.com).

alienate "VRML-challenged" site visitors. The following sections provide some guidelines for effectively including VRML into entertainment sites.

Control Time and Cost

Due to widespread interest in virtual reality, developers are constantly tempted to design sites that exceed the capabilities of Internet hardware and software. Development costs can be several times higher for virtual worlds than they are for two-dimensional graphic interfaces. Many entertainment Web sites were proposed that made extensive use of virtual worlds; in practice, nearly all of them had to be substantially scaled down when development actually began.

Provide HTML and VRML

Make sure there is always regular HTML counterparts to the VRML world. Currently, the general bugginess of VRML software makes it unsuitable as the primary interface for a Web site.

Keep It Simple

Simple VRML worlds created with geometric shapes can be much smaller than comparable 3-D video or Shockwave environments. Used in this way, VRML is actually a better solution for visitors on slow modem connections. In addition, the speed with which most personal computers can display VRML worlds drops rapidly with increasing complexity. For this reason, VRML worlds—particularly those which are used for navigation—should be kept as simple as possible.

Monitor New Technologies

A technology to watch is Netscape's Live 3D (http://home.netscape.com/comprod/products/navigator/live3d), which offers the potential for authoring VRML worlds in a Java environment. If Live 3D becomes a standard, the requirement for supporting a variety of helper and plug-in VRML applications will be greatly reduced. Also, check out the new VRML 2.0 standard (available near the end of 1996; check http://www.besoft.com/bef for a description of the proposal), which provides support for many new features such as directional sound and the ability for visitors to modify the VRML world (e.g., pick up objects).

Finishing and Testing the Site

At some point, the Web site—while not complete in every detail—will be ready for testing and debugging. During the early history of the

Web, site managers frequently opened up their nearly completed sites to the general Internet and allowed their audience to do the debugging. While users are a reliable source of bug reports, most entertainment sites will probably want to do professional-style debugging (similar to that done for software) before opening. Several steps common to the debugging process follows.

Check Consistency of Graphics and Multimedia

If several artists have prepared content, the results are likely to be uneven and easily noticed as the user flips between Web pages. Solve this by using the style manual previously discussed—allowing a common standard for images, audio, and video. If you are repurposing material from other media, it is often necessary to request the original material, even if you have digitized versions.

Slow-loading Pages

If the site generally feels "sluggish," the size of image files should be tested; occasionally, an image may not be properly processed. Long lags on all pages may indicate that the ISP/IPP doesn't have the capacity or speed to handle the site.

Broken Links

As the size of a site increases and individual pages are added or deleted, the probability of a "broken" hyperlink pointing to a nonexistent page increases exponentially. With small sites, the developer can re-test links manually, but large sites should use an automated link checker like those discussed in Chapter 5.

Navigation Problems

Frequently, what seems like a great design on paper has problems in execution. Beta-testers will often find unexpected dead-ends and illogical juxtapositions of content. The only solution in these cases is to go back and remodel the site.

Cross-platform Tests

Beta-testers working with different Web browsers frequently report contradictory results. The most common problems occur with nonstandard HTML tags like tables and frames, and external programming like Java or VRML. During debugging, changes should be made to the pages to allow support for the maximum number of users.

Social Considerations for Developing Sites

To conclude the discussion of development, we consider some of the social problems peculiar to developing Web sites. Since such sites are frequently developed and maintained by individuals in scattered locations, there is a new set of communication problems not found with other media.

Visibility During Development

More than any other "new media," Web sites are open during their creation. Not only can visitors with the right address log in to see the site taking shape, but the Web browser also allows them to examine their code. Depending on the situation, Web developers may find themselves under closer scrutiny from their clients than they are used to. While feedback between the developer and the individual who will control the site is important, the close environment may lead to *micro-management* which makes it difficult to work creatively. In this case, the developer may want to specify certain times others can access the development site so that concepts are fully executed before subjected to criticism.

Avoiding "Feature Frenzy"

As your site develops, you will have to deal with the tremendous speed of Internet change and development. It is a sure bet that during site construction you or someone associated with the site will see an ad touting the essential "next great thing that everyone needs" on their Web sites in order to "remain competitive." It is important to remember that basic Web pages written in HTML are the core of your Internet presence and the part that the user will spend the most time on. Concentrate on getting the site up with real entertainment, instead of making radical shifts to accommodate the newest gizmo. Remember: In the final analysis, it is *content*—not gadgetry—that brings visitors to your site.

Responding to Complaints

If you are developing a site for someone new to the Internet, you may find unwarranted criticism directed toward you. For example, the developer may be criticized for updating pages too slowly, when the problem is actually caused by *cached* older copies of the pages on the client's computer. If the client is using an outdated browser that doesn't display the site properly, the client may complain about a lack of features or formatting problems. Another client may complain that the site is "down," when the problem is actually mis-configuration of the local computer. In such cases, the developer should research the problem and explain the reasons for it clearly to the client. The developer should also encourage the client to explore other Web sites as well, since most people rapidly learn to distinguish general Internet problems from those specific to their site.

In one case which has undoubtedly been repeated many times, the developer of a medium Web site began the project before the client had an Internet connection. After developing the site for months in relative isolation, the developer suddenly received an angry call from the client who claimed their site "wasn't up." Upon questioning, the developer determined that the client had tried to connect to the site but kept getting "not found" errors from the connection software. Concerned about keeping the client happy, the developer continued to supply support instead of referring the client to the Internet Service Provider. After a half hour of careful questioning, the developer asked where the modem was plugged in. There was a long silence at the other end of the line and the client said, "You mean the antenna? There isn't any." It turned out the client was unaware that in order for the connection to be secured, the modem had to be plugged in.

Now that you've created the initial version of your site, you will want to effectively launch, maintain, and—in some cases—collect revenue. The subject of the next chapter is how to convert your site into an ongoing entertainment resource.

PART III

AFTER THE CURTAIN RISES:

Keeping Your Site in the Spotlight

http://kspace.com/intertainment

CHAPTER 7

SURF'S UP BUT WHERE'S THE BEACH?:

Netpublicity and Marketing for Intertainment Sites

A common misconception among Web site developers is that millions of surfers will immediately visit their site simply because it is on the Internet. While the Internet consists of millions of people who *might* visit any one site, there is no guarantee that even a modest fraction of this audience will just happen to "stumble" upon it. The Web transcends space and time; surfers are in control of what entertainment they choose and when. This is dramatically different from traditional mass media, where a time slot ensures a significant fraction of the audience. Although a Web site is "on the air" 24 hours per day, it is just one of hundreds of thousands competing for the prospective audience's attention. The need for promotion is old news to the entertainment industry. On the Internet, publicity takes a new form—here referred to as *netpublicity* to distinguish it from efforts in other media. This chapter shows how to let the Internet audience know where to find your newly launched entertainment on the Web and how to direct marketing efforts toward attracting your specific (or *niche*) audience.

What Is Netpublicity?

The purpose of netpublicity is to attract as many site visitors as possible who will be interested in experiencing the content you have to offer. In Web terms, you want to increase audience traffic (or *hits*) to your site and also ensure that the types of people you attract are likely to become loyal visitors. (See Chapter 8 for more information on encouraging repeat visits and the formation of a loyal community.) Since methods for attracting a niche Internet audience are still relatively untested, a mixture of random netpublicity and targeted marketing is necessary, at least during the initial round of promotion.

> ***My assistant spends one entire day each week just contacting other music sites and telling them about our company and our services. Just when we think we've contacted everybody, every week, there are thousands of new sites. In the Hollywood or Nashville music business, you meet the twenty major players, and they just play musical chairs. A generation later, their children replace them. But the Net provides an endlessly expanding marketplace.***
>
> —MOLLY-ANN LEIKIN, SONGWRITING CONSULTANT AND HIT SONGWRITER
> http://websites.earthlink.net/~songmd/

How Netpublicity Works

Before discussing the details of a netpublicity campaign, it is necessary to consider the special nature of Web-based promotion in greater detail. The netpublicity model is formed out of an environment where the audience has the unique characteristics associated with being *prosumers* and *hunter-gatherers* (see Chapter 2). In such an environment, netpublicity encourages the audience to make a virtual trip to a Web site. Beaming messages to the audience members' virtual homes (e.g., sending unsolicited email or advertising on television) is possible on the Internet, but it is treated as a breach of personal privacy and is far less efficient than might be expected.

The basic netpublicity method consists of *posting* information about your Web site to various areas on the Internet. Unlike other media, the promotions placed by the netpublicist do not have to function as full-fledged ads or press releases. Since a single sentence or word anywhere on the Web can provide a *hyperlink* directly to your Web site, simply post the site name, logo, or short comment. One goal of netpublicity is to leave as many of these links as possible scattered through the Internet environment, where they will be discovered by the portion of the audience likely to be interested in them.

Depending on the location, postings may have several sizes. The most common posting is a simple hyperlink, with the name of the site and a short (under 50 words) description of the site. Some sites allow longer, more detailed postings resembling classified ads. Small *distribution* graphics provide a step up in eye appeal; these small images, usually only an inch across, are frequently used to indicate sponsorships or use of a particular vendor's hardware and software. The most eye-catching posts are graphic *banners*, which are typically narrow graphics spanning the window of the Web browser. Larger promotions, comparable to a full-page spread in a magazine, are almost unknown; since the post provides a direct link to the content, there is little reason to duplicate it at the posting site. The Internet supports three major types of postings, each of which is discussed in the following sections.

Free Postings

These sites do not charge for postings, and do not require a reciprocal link back to your site. A brief posting is all that's needed, so a large number of postings can be made to these sites during a netpublicity project. Examples of free postings sites are "what's new" lists, search engines, yellow pages, "cool site" awards and reviews sites, and high and low traffic lists.

Reciprocal Links

The first and still very common method of posting hyperlinks involves a mutual exchange between two Web sites. Due to the effort required to establish them, these postings are generally highly targeted toward the specific audience for the entertainment site. These links are usually acquired through communication between site administrators hosting similar types of content.

Paid Advertising

Postings of this type require payment to a high-traffic Web site that offers ad space. Paid placements offer the highest potential for increased traffic; however, the cost is prohibitive for many independent entertainment professionals and companies.

Advantages of Netpublicity

Hyperlink postings have several advantages over real-world publicity. Unlike their physical counterparts (e.g., posters, billboards, and bus stop seats—and even traditional advertising), Internet promotion allows immediate access to the site being promoted merely by clicking on a text or graphic representation of the site. The Internet removes time and distance barriers while retaining a sense of place. Conventional advertising deluges consumers repeatedly, primarily to make them remember the entertainment, find its location, and raise general consumer awareness of the brand name. On the Internet, this entire process is compressed into a single decision to see what lies beyond the posting or ad. In effect, each posting consists of a virtual hyperlink "trap door" capable of teleporting the visitor directly to your content.

Since text-based hyperlinks cost virtually nothing to maintain—especially if the posting site accepts automatic submissions—postings are normally free. In fact, many sites actively encourage postings, since any site with interesting link collections is itself a valued type of content. Postings for a fee only occur on a few of the most highly-visited pages on the Internet (e.g., search engines). Since most postings are free, individuals and small development sites are not necessarily at a disadvantage relative to large sites. As long as a smaller entertainment site targets a niche audience, the number of postings necessary to effectively reach its audience may be relatively small. The trick of netpublicity is to leave the right trails: A successful campaign will put your site at the hub of a wheel with hundreds of virtual spokes guiding the audience to your site.

Do-it-yourself versus Outsourcing

One of the first decisions the Internet entertainment providers should make is whether to do the postings directly or hire an Internet-based publicity service. Netpublicity is not difficult or highly technical; effective netpublicity for entertainment sites can be performed with the same basic equipment used to create the individual *virtual production studio* described in Chapter 5. Almost all postings may be made through email or directly on the Web using fill-out forms. In-house netpublicity will allow a company's traditional publicity department to get a feel for the promotional opportunities on the Internet and learn to tailor its announcements to the Internet audience.

On the other hand, postings are *extremely* time-consuming; larger companies may find it more convenient to use an independent service for part of the work. To form a rough estimate of the time required, assume that each individual posting will take about five minutes to complete. With these assumptions, it will take almost eight hours for the netpublicist (working nonstop) to complete 100 postings. This may not be an efficient use of personnel, particularly on sites maintained by a small number of individuals. Commercial posting services typically charge between $1 to $5 per posting, which translates into roughly the pay for an entry-level member of the site team. A good combined strategy might be to use a netpublicity company for part of the work and have the in-house publicist or marketer take care of niche postings requiring special attention.

> ***My publicist, John Kruck, has been the single most important asset to our Internet strategy's success. John has taken the idea of use of the "Net" to completely unique and often unconventional levels.***
>
> —GARY TANIN OF SUBLIME NATION, ALTERNATIVE POP MUSICIAN
> http://kspace.com/sublime

If you decide to outsource, do some careful research before choosing a netpublicity service. As discussed in Chapter 3, traditional publicity firms and individual publicists have been slow to get on the Internet. Only a few traditional PR firms have a track record for major Web site promotion. An example of such a firm is Niehaus Ryan Haller Public Relations, Inc. (http://www.nrh.com) which has managed the promotion of well-known Internet companies including Spry (http://www.spry.com), Yahoo! (http://yahoo.com), and GNN (http://www.gnn.com). If your needs are more modest, your best bet is one of the hundreds of new startups which make netpublicity their primary interest. In addition to postings, their services may include additional features, such as help in creating press releases. For example, our Multispace Internet Services (http://multispace.com) netpublicity department handles press release authoring, promotional kit assembly, promotional software, as well as netpublicity postings and reciprocal links. Other well-known netpublicity services include the Global Internet News Agency or GINA (Figure 7.1), WebPromote (http://www.webpromote.com), and AAA Internet Promotions (http://websitepromote.com).

To find these companies, begin posting yourself; most of them offer some form of *freelinks* page as a way to promote their own service to tired netpublicists who may be wishing they were doing something else at that very moment! During your search for a netpublicity company, try asking the following questions.

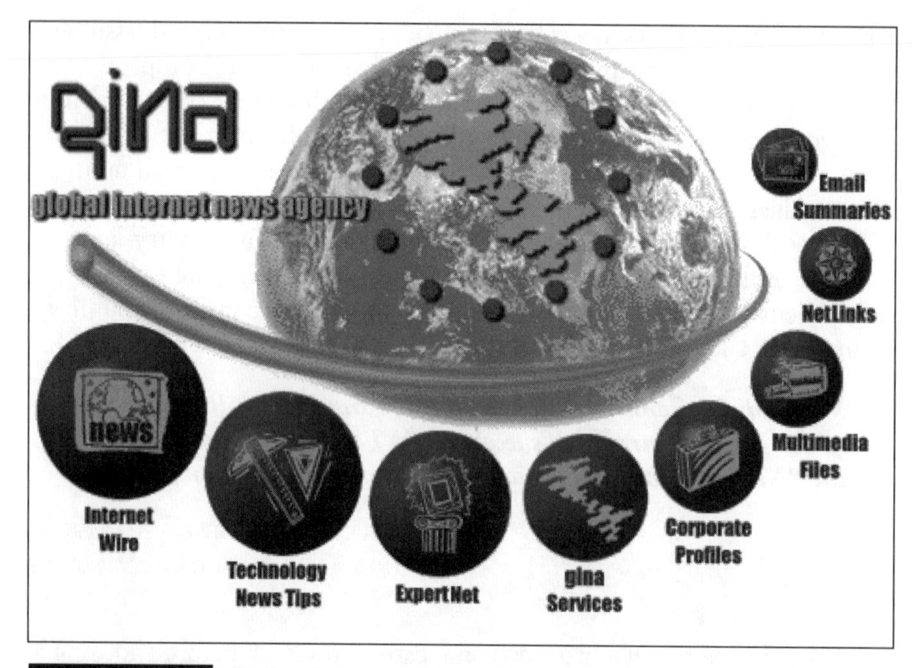

FIGURE 7.1 Global Internet News Agency (http://gina.com).

Does the Service Help Write Net-friendly Releases?

An experienced netpublicity service should be able to take your existing promotional material and develop net-friendly postings from them. Doing this indicates that the posting service sufficiently understands your site to post effectively. If this is not the case, the posting service may place listings in inappropriate areas far removed from where your target audience hangs out (e.g., listing a storytelling site as a business resource) .

Does the Service Provide a Record of Postings?

Incredibly, many small services do not provide reports of their work. Insist on receiving a full report of posting, classified by type and displaying the posting URL. If the posting service prepared your promotional blurbs, ask for these to review before the service begins posting.

Does the Service Provide for Commercial Postings?

Smaller companies may not have the administrative resources to keep track of ads or paying links. If you plan to spend significant amounts on ad postings, it is better to go with a service which specifically brokers ad space on high-traffic sites.

Can the Service Provide a *Checkback* Service?

Even after a post is made, various reasons may prevent it from actually appearing. Some of the more expensive services such as 1,2,3, GO! (http://www.mgroup.com/123go) specifically guarantee that each posting is actually recorded by continually checking back with the posting location and re-submitting, if necessary. Be aware that some popular postings sites take several weeks to review the postings before listing them.

Preparation for Netpublicity

Whether the actual postings are done in-house, the site's local netpublicist needs to carry out several steps before work can begin: prepare publicity material, identify the market, determine traffic goals, prepare a keyword list, and create a netpublicity database. Each of these is discussed in the following sections.

Prepare Publicity Material

Working from press releases and other material, compile a series of promotional *blurbs* ranging in size from a complete paragraph to a single sentence. In each case, create succinct, easy-to-read copy that will motivate the audience to visit the site. Once the copy is created, save it into a text-only (ascii) file for use during posting. In many cases, it is also a good idea to prepare small *distribution* graphics which can be used to link back to your site.

Identifying Your Market

Based on the overall concept for the site, determine what portion of the Internet audience will be interested in accessing your Web site. In doing this, analysis of the general demographics and profiles of the audience (see Chapter 2) are very helpful. Once the subgroup within the total Internet audience is identified, determine which Web sites the group is likely to visit.

Determine Your Traffic Goals

By examining the original site concept (see Chapter 4), estimate how many daily visitors you would like to support. Visitor numbers should be realistic and take into account the capabilities of the Web server's ability to process requests for content (see Chapters 5 and 6). For personal pages hosted on an ISP, a goal of a few hundred visits a day is reasonable. Sites hosting alternative or independently produced entertainment (e.g., a small record label) should try to reach several thousand hits daily; large media sites may command daily access anywhere between ten thousand to a few million hits. Sites with streaming audio and video need to translate visits per day into another parameter: How many visitors will be logged on at any one time? If the desired number exceeds the number of audio and video streams the Web server supports, some visitors will be "locked out" of service.

Prepare a Keyword List

Many individuals using search engines type single words to locate interesting sites. In developing the publicity program, the netpublicist should determine what words this audience is likely to use when looking for entertainment provided by the Web site. For example, an entertainment site featuring regular visits by celebrities might want to include the celebrity names in the keyword list. Also, include more common terms in the list that apply to your site (e.g., chat, art, music). Some posting services will request a list of keywords. Others, such as some search engines, will look at individual pages on your Web site for keywords. To ensure that the Web site pages contain appropriate keywords, coordinate with the site developers. Keywords may be part of text on the site or invisibly incorporated by using the *META* tag in HTML as follows:

```
<META name="description" content="the world's loudest rock band">
<META name="keywords" content="rock, noise thunder, mosh, music" >
```

This method conceals the keyword list from visitors actually on the Web site, while providing them to Web spider programs such as Infoseek (http://www.infoseek.com). Although words contained within site graphics can't be used as keywords, text within the *ALT* command can be read by search engines.

One special keyword will be useful in tracking the success of your netpublicity. Select a word or short phrase that is *unique* to your Web site (e.g., trademarked company name) and appears on many of its pages. Use the word in as many of your postings as possible. Later, by doing a search for this word through a search engine, you will get an estimate of how many times your Web site is mentioned elsewhere on the Internet.

Create a Netpublicity Database

Due to the relative newness of the field, there are no software tools available specifically designed to help the netpublicist. Since detailed records will be necessary for later evaluation of the netpublicity effort, you should configure a standard database (such as dBase or FileMaker) or spreadsheet (such as Lotus or Excel) to keep track of your progress. A netpublicity database should contain information on sites selected for posting—including name, date, and purpose. If possible, routines or macros should be created to search the database by date and URL.

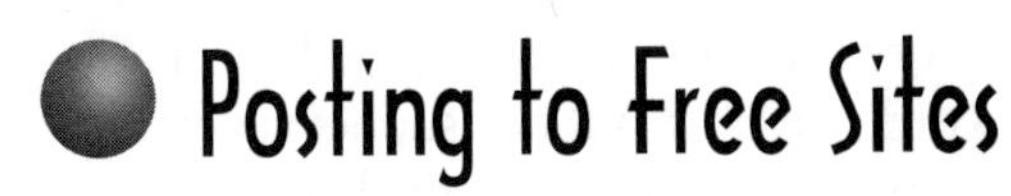

Posting to Free Sites

Once the preliminary work is complete, the next phase involves finding sites for posting and sending information to them. The majority of sites accept one-way posts at no cost. In most cases, postings are highly automated and proceed without intervention of the site operators. A few sites may require that the netpublicist send email to the administrator to state the reason for posting. The following sections cover the various types of free posting sites that are of particular interest to Internet entertainment providers.

"What's New" Lists

These lists are maintained specifically for posting Web sites that have just been launched. Since so many Internet users routinely check *what's new* lists for fresh content, these lists can generate a very large initial burst of traffic for your site. The original NCSA What's New list (http://www.ncsa.uiuc.edu/SDG/Software/Mosaic/Docs/whats-new.html) created for Mosaic in 1993 is still popular and it complements the NCSA/GNN counterpart at (http://gnn.com/gnn/wn/whats-new-form.html). Other major what's new pages include the Netscape What's New Page (http://home.netscape.com/home/whats-new.html), What's New Too! (http://newtoo.manifest.com), What's New in Europe (http://www.ukshops.co.uk:8000/whatsnew/announceit.html), and Starting Point (http://www.stpt.com).

Search Engines

Next to the Netscape home page, search engines have the highest traffic of any Web site on the Internet. Search engines are nothing more than enormous, searchable databases of hyperlinks. These databases are kept current through direct postings by netpublicists and/or automated searches of the entire Internet by *spider* programs. It is extremely easy to post to most of these engines; nothing more than your URL and a brief description of your site is required. After posting, the local spider visits the URL and indexes every page on the site. Since the search engine's spider will *eventually* find your site's page, the main purpose of posting is to move your site further up in its schedule and to ensure that the correct category and keywords are posted. Some major search engines include Alta Vista (http://www.altavista.com), Yahoo! (http://www.yahoo.com), Lycos (http://www.lycos.com), WebCrawler (http://www.webcrawler.

com), excite (http://www.excite.com), Infoseek (http://www.infoseek.com), and OpenText (http://www.opentext.com).

Among the popular search engines, Yahoo! is unique in that it relies solely on postings and displays a short description to be added to the post. In addition to allowing keyword searches, Yahoo! supports a very large number of lists arranged by topic. The usefulness of this organization has made Yahoo! the most popular search engine on the Net and a must for postings. Due to Yahoo!'s topic-based organization, it is important to find the best place to post the mere two links it allows per site. Before posting, search Yahoo! using keywords your audience is also likely to use and note what topic areas appear. After posting, confirm that the posts are actually visible in Yahoo!; a significant fraction of posts are rejected or assigned to different topics.

Yellow Pages

Following a directory model borrowed from the physical world, numerous sites have been created which refer to themselves as *yellow page* or *white page* lists. Some of these sites assume that visitors are posting business listings rather than entertainment sites; however, it makes sense to list entertainment here as well. Yellow pages typically allow postings containing more information than other lists, including extensive contact information. Examples of yellow page sites include the Big Book Directory (http://www.bigbook.com), the New Riders' Yellow Pages (http://www.mcp.com/newriders/wwwyp), and the GTE Super Pages (http://wp.gte.net).

Cool Site Awards and Reviews

If you consider your site outstanding (who doesn't!), it is extremely important to submit it for review to as many awards sites as possible. On the Internet, there is no simple "top ten"; instead, there are hundreds of sites whose primary business is to review and rate other Web sites. Posting to these sites is essential for recognition by the Internet audience. If your site is picked as a *cool site* by one of the major award or review sites, you can reliably expect your traffic to increase by thousands of visitors per day. Most award sites also provide a graphic logo that you can display on your own pages. Netpublicists should always include requests to The Original Cool Site of the Day (Figure 7.2), the Point Top 5% (http://www.pointcom.com), America Online's What's Hot (http://www.blue.aol.com/hot), Magellan (http://www.mckinley.com), and the Yahoo! Cool Site of the Day (http://www.yahoo.com/picks/daily).

Will the Internet ever have a single awards program comparable to those found in traditional entertainment? At present, momentum seems to be shifting in the opposite direction, as hundreds of new *cool sites* lists appear daily. Creating a cool site list on your own site is *itself* a good way to attract traffic. Since many smaller cool sites lists cater to specific niche audiences, postings to these lists may bring in more of your target audience. An example of a niche cool site list is Top 5% of Music Sites on the Net (http://www.hofstra.edu/~vmaffea1/top5music.html).

A rapidly growing category of cool sites allows users to vote on submitted sites, in effect providing an audience ratings system. One example of these sites is MCA's Zapper's Lounge (http://www.mca.com/tv/zap), which treats site ratings as a virtual game show. Sites are ranked by the number of voting rounds they last through. Other audience-generated ratings can be found at TV Net (http://tvnet.com) and Hollywood Online (http://www.hollywood.com).

Unlike posting to search engines and directories, Net custom requires that you post the award icon from a cool site on your home page. If you receive a large number of awards, the profusion of icons will begin to slow down page loading *and* could detract from your site's artistic design; in that case, consider making a special "awards page" for the icons. For example, Kaleidospace links to its awards page from a star icon on its home page. The advantage of a separate page is that you can also provide information about each award and links to reviews if present.

High-traffic Lists

This huge group of lists with relatively high traffic should form a major part of a netpublicity program. Many of these sites have well-organized directo-

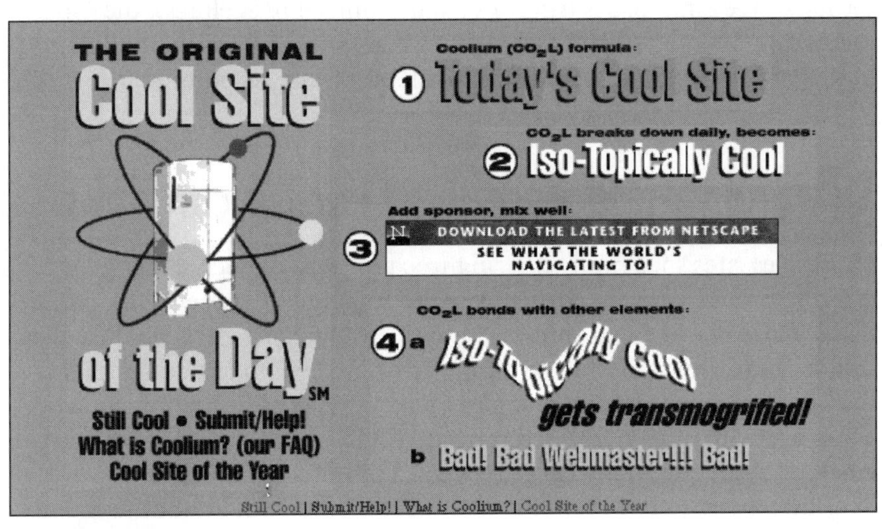

FIGURE 7.2 The Original Cool Site of the Day (http://cool.infi.net).

ries (similar to Yahoo!) like Webula (http://www.eg.bucknell.edu/cgibin/webula) and LinkMaster (http://linkmaster.com/addlink.html). Some sites, such as Submit It! (http://www.submit-it.com) and AAA Internet Promotions (http://www.websitepromote.com/home.htm), partially automate the process of submitting to multiple sites by sending data from a single form to dozens of locations.

Besides general lists, there are a large number of entertainment and media-specific lists available for posting. A representative example is Casbah (http://casbah.dmn.com), a comprehensive searchable directory of music releases and Internet sites. Postings aimed at entertainment professionals, including producers and screenwriters, find a home at The Hollywood Network (http://www.hollywoodnetwork.com).

Low-traffic Lists

Nearly all of the hundreds of thousands of personal home pages on the Internet have at least a few *cool links* compiled by the page owners. The value of posting to these locations—often referred to as *free-for-alls*—is relatively limited. Many of the current low-traffic automatic posting sites have been overrun with ads from get-rich-quick schemes and 900-number services. Personal pages are usually moderated, but the effort required to get a link may outweigh the benefit it will bring to the site. Probably the best strategy for handling low-traffic links is to make a small, steady number of postings over a period of months. Despite their other problems, small lists may retain a link for over a year before it is removed. Good places to search for low-traffic links include the M Group's FreeLinks pages (http://www.mgroup.com/freelinks), the Go Net-Wide directory (http://www.shout.net/~whitney/html/gopublic.html), and Expose (http://www.dev-com.com/~cmg/exppromo.htm).

Giving and Receiving Reciprocal Links

Besides sites specifically offering free postings, a much larger group exchanges links on a less formal basis. Mutual links between sites, particularly those that contain similar content, are the most effective links that can be made. Since they are typically associated with content—rather than posting-only sites—they tightly match the post to a target audience. Links are normally established by mutual agreement, mediated through email or other communication between Web site operators.

Newcomers to the Web may wonder why they would want to link to other sites, especially since sites with similar content are frequently their competitors. In reality, the benefits of traffic from other sites well outweighs any loss of visitors through the reciprocal links. Traffic may even increase globally for a set of sites sharing reciprocal links (resulting in a *neighborhood effect*, as shown in Figure 7.3). This is an example of *coopetition* frequently seen in the computer industry, where rival companies have joined for a common purpose. In the absence of coopetition, visitors coming from the general Web are likely to leave the same way—and disappear into the enormous maze of Web space. By contrast, reciprocal links between sites create a virtual neighborhood holding visitors for a longer period of time.

Due to the large amount of effort needed to establish reciprocal links, commercial *link brokers* are becoming a part of netpublicity. Examples include The Internet Link Exchange (http://www.linkexchange.com) and The Reciprocal Link Exchange (http://www.iaex.com/rlex/rlex.html). Both of these services register Web sites, which in turn promise to post each other's links or graphic *banners*. Another service potentially useful for finding sites with reciprocal links was recently announced by Rover (http://www.roverbot.com), a specialized search engine that returns the email addresses of Web site managers. Netpublicists searching for reciprocal links might use such a tool to compile a list of site administrators with content sufficiently similar to warrant reciprocal links and send email

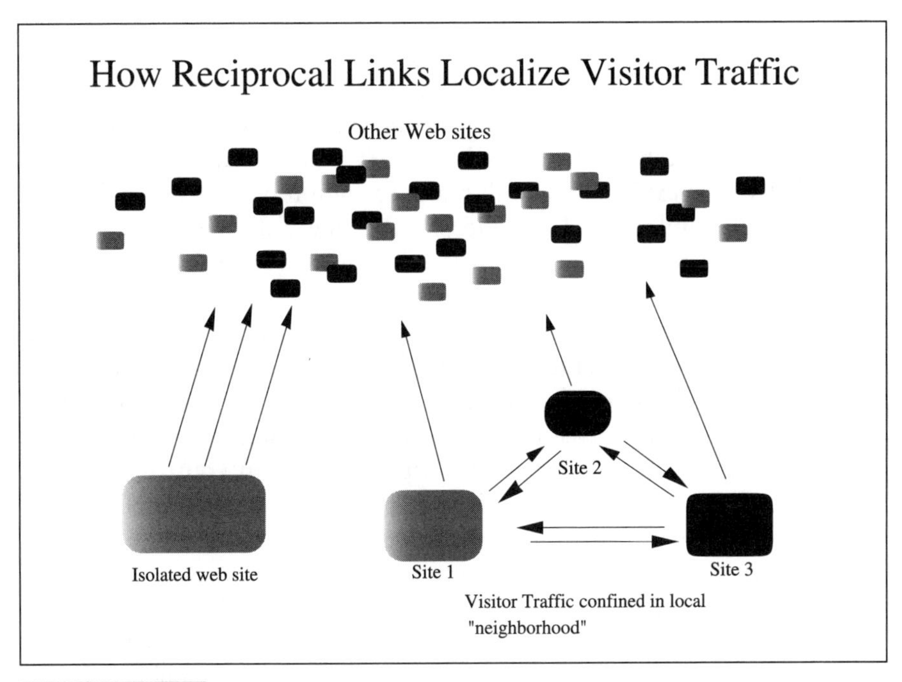

FIGURE 7.3 Neighborhood effect of reciprocal links.

queries to them. As with all unsolicited mailings, take extreme care not to indiscriminately *spam* uninterested audience members with your message.

Once your site is online, you will begin to receive numerous requests through your email boxes for reciprocal links. The netpublicist should check out candidates by logging onto the respective Web sites. If a link seems appropriate, the netpublicist should create a link to the site and send email requesting a reciprocal link. The other site should be monitored carefully to ensure that your link is actually posted; some site administrators are either backlogged or uninterested in actually posting your link. This is not evidence of criminal intent; it is easy to get backlogged with requests from sites who are interested in setting up reciprocal link arrangements. If you find yourself in a backlog situation, make sure to keep track of requests from other sites—and send the contact person a confirmation email once you have posted the site to your links area. At least once per quarter, do a link check on your own site (discussed in Chapter 8) to ensure that outlinks are all current and verify that the respective site managers are still maintaining links to your site. If you find that your site does not appear on some of these sites, send a message to those managers asking them to supply the posting and reminding them that they had originally requested a link from you. Following these rules can greatly increase the longevity of your postings.

Web Advertising

Web-based advertising is one of the hottest trends on the Internet. Jupiter Communication's WebTrack (http://www.webtrack.com) site estimates that yearly expenditures will reach $5 billion by the year 2000—up from about $40 million in 1995. Despite this, few entertainment sites have used a significant amount of paid advertising online. Larger sites with promotional budgets in the tens of thousands of dollars may consider placing paid advertisements on the highest-traffic Web sites. While a few sites have negotiated directly for ad placement on high-traffic sites, ad agencies are rapidly professionalizing the process. Some ad agencies active in Internet publicity for entertainment sites include Avalanche (http://www.avsi.com), DimensionX (http://dimensionx.com) and Razorfish (http://www.razorfish.com), who have worked with the XXIII Olympiad, Sega, and Time-Warner, respectively.

A good resource for online ad information is the WebTrack Adspace Locator (http://www.webtrack.com/sponsors/sponsors.html), which lists Web sites accepting advertising. WebTrack's descriptions include rate cards, site traffic, demographics, and other relevant information. Netpublicists should also check out the Interactive Publishing Alert (http://www.netcreations.com/ipa), an online newsletter that features a searchable database of sites accepting advertising along with rates and audience demographics. Both of these sites are listing an increasing number of ad-supported entertainment sites, including industry magazines such as Billboard (http://www.billboard-online.com) and Premiere (http://www.premieremag.com). A few Web-only entertainment sites such as Pathfinder (http://www.pathfinder.com) and Mr. Showbiz (http://www.mrshowbiz.com) accept advertising. Ads on these sites cost several thousand dollars per month and vary depending on *click-through* (the percentage of the audience that actually clicks on the ad itself). Companies who are interested in buying ad space on multiple Web sites should check out Focalink's SmartBanner (Figure 7.4) or DoubleClick (http://www.doubleclick.net). When an audience member loads an ad page, it is dynamically transferred from the company's own *ad server* database. This highly centralized arrangement allows the advertiser to control how individual ad banners are delivered to and rotated on remote sites.

The value of paid advertising spots promoting Internet entertainment is currently limited. It is difficult to estimate the value of a promotional banner on any site except on high-traffic search engines, which run $10 to $40,000 a month for placement. While ad agencies experiement with flashy audio-video presentations to replace the current graphic banners,

FIGURE 7.4 Focalink (http://www.focalink.com).

the slow connection speeds of most Internet users render multimedia ads little more than a nuisance. Due to advertising's high costs, independent entertainers and small companies can use their publicity budgets much more effectively by making free postings and sending out press releases to the appropriate media outlets. In most cases, low-cost ads (e.g., $1,000 per year) on small, niche service directories provide very little extra value compared to free postings. If advertising is used, netpublicists will also need to worry about their audience's response to paid ads. While most of the Internet audience accepts ad banners as useful information, resistance is sure to grow as advertisers attempt to use more "in your face" methods (such as obligatory audio spots) and the audience adopts various *ad blocking* software technologies (see Chapter 9).

Non-Web Netpublicity

Netpublicity is one of the areas where entertainment sites will come into contact with the older, non-Web portions of the Internet. Despite having been around for a while, these areas excel at providing interactivity and direct contact with the audience. Use of these services will be especially effective for netpublicists who are used to working on a one-to-one basis. Unlike postings, which can be placed and left alone, non-Web netpublicity requires maintaining an ongoing discussion with interested audience members. The most common areas used by netpublicists follow.

Mailing Lists

Email-based discussion groups typically consist of list members willing to receive messages from the list owner and each other. Lists are distinguished by restricted postings; normally, only members can post messages and each member receives messages from *everyone else* on the list. Mailing lists also have an administrator who keeps track of membership and moderates postings to the list. Membership to these lists is always voluntary and most lists allow members to subscribe or "unsubscribe" at will. Currently, at least 50,000 mailing lists were available on the Internet covering almost every subject imaginable. Most new Web sites post to the Net-Happenings mailing list at http://www.mid.net/NET/input.html.

If you are running a small site, joining mailing lists may be a great help in introducing your specific audience to your entertainment. Research the topic of any list carefully before becoming a member and make sure the list accepts publicity-style postings. Inappropriate postings will anger your audience; as a list member you will receive hostile email from every member on the list. Check out the various lists of mailing lists at sites like Liszt

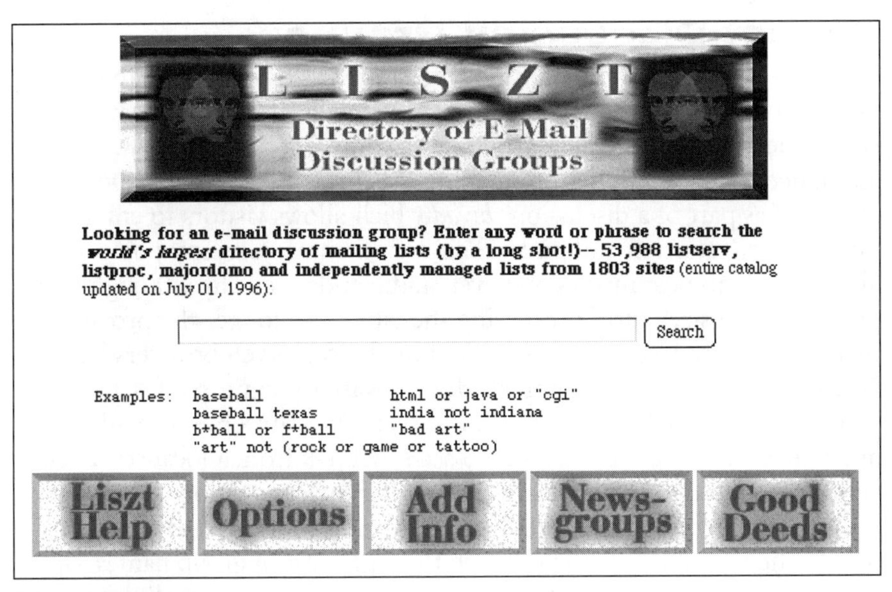

FIGURE 7.5 Liszt (http://www.liszt.com).

in Figure 7.5 and tile.net/listserv (http://www.tile.net/tile/lists/index.html), which provide searchable databases. Detailed summaries of many popular lists are available at the List of Lists (http://www.catalog.com/vivian/interest-group-search.html).

Sites operating their own Web servers should consider running their own mailing lists. Since lists allow communication between all members as well as the content providers, they are extremely effective at creating and supporting fans. Further discussion of how mailing lists can be used to build brand loyalty and fan bases can be found in Chapter 8.

Media Lists

These sites provide the email addresses of publications which accept electronic press releases. Once again, it is important to target your submission to the correct media source. Media lists are less common than mailing lists; Adam M. Gaffin's original Media List is no longer updated, but versions have been archived at many sites including http://www.webcom.com/~leavitt/medialist.html. This site contains email addresses for several hundred newspapers, broadcast stations, and weekly magazines which accept publicity releases. A large set of television-related email addresses is available at TV Net (http://tvnet.com). Currently, no email lists of radio stations exist, though this is partly offset by extensive archives such as BRS Radio Directory (http://www.brsradio.com), which includes an unsearchable but thorough list of email addresses for radio stations.

Usenet Discussion Groups

Usenet is the oldest and by far the largest discussion center on the Internet, with over 70,000 individual groups. Virtually all new Web sites should be posted to the newsgroup news:comp.infosystems.www.announce. Usenet differs from mailing lists in that posts and responses are listed as part of a discussion *thread* which allows visitors to enter an ongoing conversation and insert their own comments at any point. It is also possible to post images and even audio and video clips, though many groups have a size cutoff preventing the latter. No longer the province of text-only access, Usenet can be used directly from Web browsers like Netscape, but you must configure the software to point to a Usenet server (also referred to as an NNTP server). Most Internet providers allow their customers to connect to a Usenet *feed* from a local server and should be able to provide details for making the connection.

Like mailing lists, Usenet frowns on postings unrelated to the local topic. The netpublicist should search through a list of group names (search engine Deja News at http://www.dejanews.com specializes in Usenet) and read postings in those that look promising. Postings should avoid being overly "commercial"; they should be presented as friendly, knowledgeable discussions rather than sales pitches. Despite the noncommercial orientation of much of Usenet, posting can be very effective—especially for niche artists and musicians. On the authors' Kaleidospace site, some of the most effective publicity for individual artists has come from Usenet postings. An example is Kspace artist David Thomas Roberts (http://kspace.com/pinelands) who writes original ragtime music. When his area on Kspace went online, several postings were made to a Usenet group specifically devoted to New Ragtime. The result was immediate sales of DTR's CD and continued interest in his Web site.

 Inappropriate Netpublicity

Netpublicists—particularly those working for high-visibility entertainment sites that depend on audience goodwill—need to understand the distinction between appropriate and inappropriate postings on the Internet. The vast majority of the Internet audience detests unsolicited mass mailings or *spams*. While an audience member is frequently pleased to discover a cool link to your site in the exploration of the Web, the same link sent as *unsolicited* email to the member's private mailbox will receive a very different reception. While this may surprise new content providers, the prohibition against unsolicited advertising and promotion on the Internet is quite real and arises from the prosumer nature of the Internet audience. This audience wants control over finding its entertainment and does not appreciate being force-fed. Furthermore, site visitors have the same tools that content providers have to send messages. To put it another way, the Internet audience can do more than throw away junk mail: *They can throw it back*. This is a point which should not be taken lightly. Consider the outcomes of two types of unsolicited email messages sent to promote a Web site.

Short Announcement

In the first case, the content provider sends an email message a few sentences long describing the site. In most cases, audience members will simply delete the message.

Long Sales Pitch

If the content provider sends a long, *pitch-oriented* message, its main result will be to anger the recipients. The audience will retaliate, firing the message back—often hundreds of times—and post negative comments in discussion groups and Usenet. Since email is so easy to send, some of the recipients are likely to direct negative comments about the site to their friends or mailing lists of which they are members. If the site repeatedly offends audience members, it may end up on one of the various *black lists* for Internet advertising, of which The Black List of Internet Advertisers (http://math-www.uni-paderborn.de/~axel/BL/blacklist.html) is a well-known example. Entertainment sites, with their high visibility and dependence on public support, cannot have the bad press resulting from unsolicited email messages. *The message is clear: Don't do it!*

Other Marketing and Publicity Techniques

Besides the basic tools of netpublicity, many other methods can be used to effectively promote your Web site. Some of these rely on creating online events and resources to attract the audience; others are adapted from traditional publicity. The following provides just a few suggestions; a good netpublicist should be able to advise you on additional methods that are customized to your specific needs.

Creating Posting Resources

In the topsy-turvy world of the Internet, one of the best ways to promote your Web site is to create a list promoting other sites! Creating a What's New/What's Cool/free-for-all list is virtually guaranteed to draw traffic to your site. Lists can be made by directly coding in HTML or through automated programs like those available from Matt's Script Archive (http://www.worldwidemart.com/scripts). Posting resources are most valuable for small sites which might otherwise have trouble attracting visitors. By adding the resource, the site has changing content and increased interactivity—the hallmarks of entertaining Web sites. If your site provides niche entertainment content, you could easily attract traffic and prestige by creating your own posting area or awards site for that niche content.

Live Events

Cyberspace may be virtual, but a "live" event involving the site is often extremely effective at attracting the attention of local media. Live events provide a familiar context for press, particularly outside the Web, to report on your Intertainment. Many sites have received significant publicity in print simply by having a launch party for the project. Kaleidospace was launched offline at the Electronic Cafe International (http://ecafe.com) in Santa Monica, whose long-standing reputation in interactive media drew an audience able to appreciate the potential of the then (early 1994) obscure Web. Appropriate venues for launch parties include cybercafes, clubs, theaters, or large "wired" houses where guests can use local computers to visit the site. If Internet broadcast equipment is available (see Part IV), the online audience can also participate in the launch and even converse with guests by email or through chat programs.

> ***I've put my Website on all promotional materials and tell people who I meet at my shows, inform the DJ's who play my music, write it on my business cards. . . . Fans and customers who are Net-savvy like the fact that I have a Web site.***
>
> —LAURIE Z., CONTEMPORARY INSTRUMENTAL KEYBOARDIST
> http://kspace.com/lauriez

Cross-promotion in Print Media

Despite the rapid growth of the Internet, the majority of the public continues to get much of their information about new Web sites through newspaper and magazine articles. Cyberspace has spawned literally hundreds of new magazines reporting on every aspect of the medium. As one might expect, most of these publications have an online component through which the netpublicist can contact them. Out of the many Internet-related publications, CMP's *NetGuide* (http://www.netguide.com) reaches the largest nontechnical audience and contains a large section with reviews of Web sites. Ziff-Davis' *Computer Life* (http://www.zdnet.com/complife) also reaches a large nontechnical audience. Mecklermedia's Internet World (http://www.internetworld.com) is slightly older and runs more technical articles in addition to popular discussions of the Web. Even the Yahoo!

search engine has launched a real-world feature magazine, *Yahoo! Internet Life* (Figure 7.6). These magazines have circulation in the hundreds of thousands; getting exposure in them may have a major effect on the popularity of your site. If your site has an innovative concept or feature that might be worth a review or story, contact an editor and suggest an idea.

Though they were initially slow to catch on, traditional computer magazines with a large general audience such as Byte (http://www.byte.com) and Macworld (http://www.macworld.com) now have extensive Internet sections and may be worth checking out as well. Netpublicists should also consider industry trades such as The Hollywood Reporter (http://hollywoodreporter.com), Variety, and Billboard (http://www.billboard-online.com). Popular celebrity-driven magazines such as *Entertainment Weekly* and *People* (http://pathfinder.com) have begun to report

FIGURE 7.6 Yahoo! Internet Life (http://www.zdnet.com/yil).

on Intertainment; if your site contains content from high-profile artists, you may find interest here.

Cross-promotion through Products

Another extremely effective method for promoting Web sites is to list URLs on entertainment products or offline ads. Anyone checking the small print in movie ads has noticed the increasing number of Web address listings. Providing the URL in a print ad allows the Internet audience to access further information about the film. While larger sites may benefit from cross-promotion outside the Web, its value is even greater for independents. For example, musicians should make sure that their Web address is clearly stated on their CDs and cassettes. This way, anyone purchasing the product can immediately find out the latest news about the artist, join fan clubs, and even purchase new albums offered on the Web. Filmmakers may print their URLs on videos and mention the site at theatrical screenings. Visual artists may include their URLs on business cards or portfolios and display them at exhibits. For independents looking for professional representation and support, adding a Web address to a portfolio allows immediate contact from online industry reps. In the future, Web addresses may be added

FIGURE 7.7 The Dove Foundation (http://www.dove.org).

to virtually all consumer products. In a recent announcement, Hasbro Europe indicated that it was going to print the URL for Action Man (http://www.actionman.com) directly on the Action Man doll. In this way, the G.I. Joe-like character will receive the necessary Web traffic to help his fight against evil!

Endorsements

In order to bring in a specific audience appropriate to the site's entertainment, the netpublicist can solicit direct testimonials from appropriate individuals and groups. If, for example, the site is aimed at children, it may be possible to get an award from family groups both on and off the Web. An example of an organization that awards a seal of approval for family-oriented entertainment sites is The Dove Foundation (Figure 7.7). Art and music sites may look for similar endorsements from reviewers or well-known artists. However, celebrity testimonials are an untested area for Web promotion. Considering the sophistication of the Web audience (Chapter 2), endorsements are only likely to work if they are believable (e.g., the personality involved seems likely to have Internet access and have an interest in the site's content).

 Assessing Your Publicity Effort

As previously mentioned, the netpublicist should keep track of the location and date of individual postings as the project progresses. Thus, postings are correlated with changes in traffic on the Web site. If paid ads are being run on remote sites, it will be necessary to have access tracked independently by an auditing agency such as I/PRO (http://www.ipro.com) or Netcount (http://www.netcount.com). The report should also indicate whether a particular site was unusually slow or showed signs of poor maintenance. After the first wave of publicity is completed, evaluate the results. Following are some simple methods the netpublicist may use to evaluate the effects of postings.

> ***I've included my site address in my bio, spoken to friends and other artists about it. Reactions have ranged from 'What's the Internet? I've been wanting someone to explain it to me' to 'Give me your address and I'll take a look at your site.'***
>
> —EBAN LEHRER, REALISTIC AND SURREALISTIC PORTRAIT ARTIST
> http://kspace.com/lehrer

Overall Traffic

Rough estimates of the number of visitors can be determined by examining access statistics to the Web site, which can be provided by the administrator for the Web site software. (Creating these statistics from raw data is discussed further in Chapter 8.) For netpublicity, the relative (rather than absolute) number of visits is the significant figure. Starting before netpublicity begins, access statistics should be noted on a daily or weekly basis. Effective netpublicity programs should raise site traffic several-fold for a few weeks, after which access slowly drops to somewhat lower levels (Figure 7.8). Since the actual posting of submissions by the netpublicist may be delayed for weeks, traffic should be monitored for several weeks after the first wave of postings are complete. Once traffic begins to drop, a new round of postings may be initiated.

If traffic rates do not rise significantly, examine the nature of the postings closely. The lack of interest could be caused by the tone of the postings (e.g., sales pitches), their location on the Internet, or their rapid removal by the administrators of the posting site. Postings are sometimes removed if they do not conform to local policy (e.g., no posts from sites containing adult content) or because the posting list is simply too large. If the postings are in place, the most likely problem is that your intended audience never saw them. If your entertainment has niche appeal, it may take several rounds of netpublicity to identify your audience's online haunts. If it seems likely that the intended audience really sees the postings, try re-writing the post content to reflect different aspects of the entertainment on your site. For example, a celebrity site might choose to emphasize

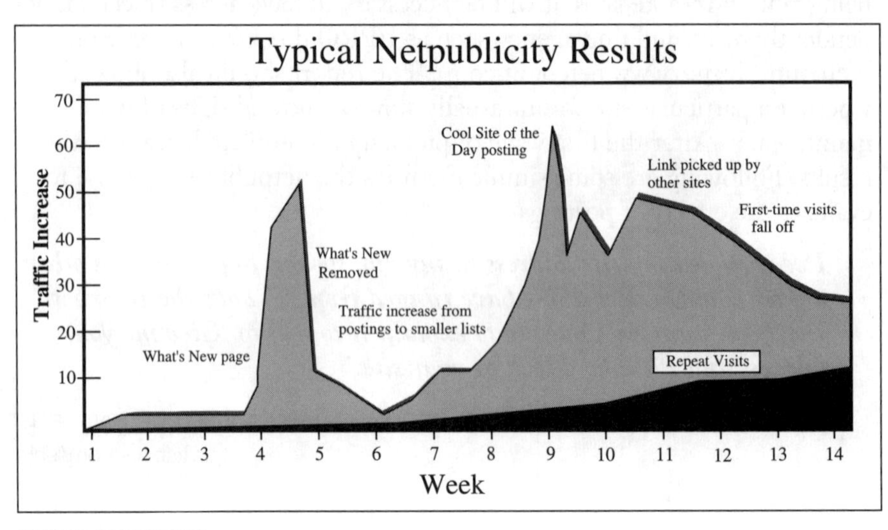

FIGURE 7.8 Effect of netpublicity on a Web site's traffic.

its chat rooms rather than the celebrity pages. With continued adjustment, a site may gradually be brought into tune with its intended audience.

Queries and Comments

A rise in queries from your audience may indicate that netpublicity is being targeted correctly. Email is the most direct measure, particularly if the site encourages response from visitors. If the site provides fill-out registration forms, the netpublicist should ensure that the forms ask the visitors where they heard of the site. The same question should be directed for queries by phone or other non-Internet means, especially if the site promotes products or services outside the Web.

> ***Most of our peers are, at the least, interested in what the Internet scene is all about in regards to independent product distribution. But I would say that most of the "buzz" about any particular site is communicated by personal contact between friends and colleagues—unless you've got no life, or are independently wealthy.***
>
> —MICHAEL GRODSKY OF THE POST AVANT-GARDE PUNK BAND DYNAMO HUM
> http://kspace.com/dynamo

Search Engine Tests

At the end of the initial period (approximately two months), the netpublicist should use several of the major search engines to look for unique keywords associated with the site. To do this quickly, use tools that search all the major engines at once, such as Metacrawler (http://www.metacrawler.com). By counting the number of hits returned by the search engine, estimates of the number of links pointing back to the site can be made. By comparing search results over time, it is also possible to see if the links are being removed or whether audience members who appreciate your site are making additional postings. Recently, WebCrawler (http://www.webcrawler.com) added a feature that allows site operators to determine which other sites in the WebCrawler database contain backlinks to them.

Sales

Good netpublicity—by increasing audience awareness of products sold by a Web site—can easily raise sales. This is particularly true if the product's name was included in the postings. Make sure that product postings use keywords the audience is likely to use searching for them. If well-known names are associated with the products, these should be included as well. Netpublicity effects on sales are particularly pronounced for products that are no longer available in retail outlets (e.g., out-of-print books) or appeal to a small but highly motivated niche audience.

Now that an audience has discovered your site, the next step is to ensure that your entertainment continues to be fresh and exciting each time people visit. The next chapter shows how providing maintenance, content updates, and site-audience interactions can turn the casual visitor into a member of a motivated and growing fan base.

CHAPTER 8

FROM BILLBOARD TO HANGOUT:

Developing a Fan Base and Maintaining Your Site

Now that you have raised your traffic and awareness of your site through netpublicity and marketing, you will want to ensure that your audience keeps coming back for more. Site visitors have little reason to come back unless they believe that there will be new, stimulating content. Due to its fundamentally interactive character, the Web is ideally suited to providing content updates and site modifications that will bring the audience back on a regular basis to "hang out" and ultimately become members of a community that you have created.

> ***Give me a REAL REASON to come back, or I won't.***
>
> —PAT ORTMAN, CREATIVE DIRECTOR, EMPTY STREET PRODUCTIONS, INC.
> http://www.generationx.com and http://www.emptystreet.com

From its beginnings as a physics laboratory experiment, the Web was designed to be a dynamic medium. Unlike read-only media such as CD-ROMs, a Web site may be modified at any time—and any changes are immediately available for online distribution. Despite this potential, a surprising number of Web sites (once one moves past the oversized animation sequence on the home page), do not change after their initial construction. While this may not pose a problem for an archive or online tutorial, it is unacceptable for Internet-based entertainment. What counts on your site is not the visitors' initial impression, but the one they have when they *leave* the site. Is there a reason to come back? If the visitors have exhausted the content and believe that nothing new will be added, they are unlikely to return. For temporary sites designed to promote a short-lived event, this may not pose a serious problem. However, for sites presenting long-term entertainment, maintenance and updates are essential. More than any other group, entertainment sites face the greatest challenge on the Web today—converting casual visitors into regularly returning fans.

The following discussion considers the various ways in which content providers and developers can create a dynamic Internet presence that directly involves their audience. More than any other medium, the Internet demands such treatment. The removal of barriers to distance, time, and distribution results in a demand for continual updates of content, as well as interaction between content providers and audience members. Pictured in this way, the Internet is less a technical *tour de force* and more a resurgence of the human dimension in entertainment. "Content is king" is a frequent comment within the entertainment industry. On the Internet, however, content takes a close second to community.

The first section of this chapter illustrates methods that will help the entertainment providers determine who is interested in their entertainment. This knowledge is put to use in the second section, which describes various ways in which entertainment providers can modify and add services to their site to give the audience what it wants. The final section explores methods which may help meld the audience into a community.

Knowing Your Audience

During concept development (Chapter 4)—and again during the initial netpublicity associated with the site launch (Chapter 7)—it was necessary to make assumptions about the audience based on general demographics. Once the site is open and receiving visitors, it is possible to determine more about the audience by analyzing the record of their visit. To serve their audience, content developers need to answer the following questions.

Who Are They?

Audience identification includes national origin, age, income, and other personal demographic information. Some of this is available in published Internet demographics (see Chapter 2), but collecting custom demographics for your site requires cooperation between the content provider and the audience.

Where Do They Come From?

Location affects the type of entertainment you provide. For example, if you find that most visitors are surfing in from large corporate networks during their lunch hour, you may tailor your interface differently than if late-night home users predominate. Sites with significant amounts of international traffic need to support their audience by creating cross-cultural interfaces, so that everyone can find their way around. A site with long sound and video downloads will be more easily accessed and enjoyed by students (who have free, high-speed Internet access) than by professionals using ISDN connections during peak business hours.

How Did They Get to Your Site?

Most Web servers record information which gives the last URL that your visitors accessed prior to entering your site. This information allows the site maintainers to find out which Web sites are contributing most to their content. Access analysis can also reveal whether most of your visitors come through your home page or jump to arbitrary locations within your site.

When Do They Visit Your Site?

Some sites are popular as a mid-day distraction, while others encourage lengthy late-night visits. Since the speed of the Internet—like other networks—decreases during peak hours of use, sites that have "prime time" access will want to design differently than those who receive their visits mostly during off-hours.

What Do They Like about Your Site?

Knowing the details of audience movements within your site can tell you if certain content has particular appeal. Are visitors following a few paths within the virtual landscape or are they being encouraged to explore all the site has to offer? It can also reveal whether the design of the Web site channels visitors away from material they would otherwise enjoy or frustrates them by trapping them in virtual *cul de sacs*.

Do They Come Back?

The ultimate goal of entertainment in an interactive media is to create an audience that feels it is part of the entertainment experience, even after it leaves the site. Success in creating such an environment will be reflected in frequent returns; knowing when and why your audience returns lets you update content appropriately. Proof of a stable, committed audience is also appealing to advertisers, financiers, and general business relationships that could make your Web-based entertainment an economic success.

Web Access Logs

By default, a Web site records information every time a visitor accesses its content. Each request, or *hit* is automatically written to an *access log* file. Due to the modular nature of the Web, hits do not correspond to individual visitors or even Web pages, but indicate downloads of individual text, graphic, or multimedia files. Since the same information is available to the Web server *prior* to responding to the visitor's request, advanced sites can use access information to deliver customized Web pages on-the-fly.

Properly analyzed, access statistics can show how to customize the Web site to the audience and provide tracking information to customers. Here's an example of a raw access log entry:

```
252-121.deetya.gov.au - - [04/Jul/1996:19:41:29 -0700]
kspace.com "GET /music.sys/Didrichsen/sounds/manowar.ram/ HTTP/
1.0" 200 15402
```

This cryptic information may be broken down in a fairly straightforward description of the access event.

Internet Address (252-121.deetya.gov.au)

This is simply the Internet domain name of the *computer* used to access the Internet. Web software does not record the email address, much less the actual name of the person accessing a site.

> ***One night I was talking to someone from Brazil and someone from Finland. In my next status report from Kspace I had downloads from both countries!***
>
> —Wade Laszlo of the hard rock band The Unholy
> http://kspace.com/unholy

Files, Directories, and Programs (/music.sys/Didrichsen/sounds/manowar.ram)

This information lets you know what areas of the Web site are being visited most frequently, as well as external programs running interactive features like order forms. In the previous example, the file being accessed is the Man-O-War RealAudio sample for Susan Didrichsen (http://kspace.com/didrichsen)—an artist in the Kaleidospace Music Kiosk.

Geographic and Organizational Distribution of the Audience (deetya.gov.au)

Since the Internet address of the audience member lists the kind of organization the computer is connected to, you can determine if your audience comes from a corporation or educational institution. The same information can identify the country of origin. In the previous example, the visitor who accessed the sound file came from the Department of Employment, Education, Training and Youth Affairs (deetya), a government organization (.gov) in Australia (.au).

Time and Date of Access ([04/Jul/1996:19:41:29 -0700])

Access logs automatically record when visits occur, down to the second. In addition to the standard information previously mentioned, most Web servers record additional parameters in separate log files, as follows:

- Movement Through the Site: Each time visitors select a page on the site, their Internet addresses are recorded. Correlation of each access makes it possible to trace the visitors' movements.
- Previous Location: Additional information, sometimes written to a separate referer log indicates the last Web site the audience member visited before coming to yours.
- Software: Web servers can record the type of Web browser the visitor uses to access the site (sometimes in a separate *agent log*). This provides information about the visitor's hardware and software capabilities and limitations.
- Error Messages: Error logs allow the administrator to pinpoint a variety of potential problems. Server errors reveal problems such as incomplete downloads, "broken" hyperlinks, and software malfunctions. Client errors indicate problems in the visitor's browser software or attempts to access restricted information.

Methods of Log Analysis

If you are running a Web server in-house, access log information resides in a file situated on the Web server's hard disk. These files are often huge; large media sites can generate files containing hundreds of millions of entries in only a few days. If your site is being hosted by an Internet Service Provider or Internet Presence Provider, you may not have direct access to the file, but you wouldn't want to! In order to be useful, the cryptic entries made in the often enormous access log need to be converted into a more easily understandable format.

ISP, IPP, or Meta-site Administrator

Most ISPs and IPPs will provide basic access reports to their audience (as will administrators of large meta-sites containing individual artists and companies). Anyone running a Web site using one of these services should ask for basic access logs, if they're not automatically generated. Information in these logs tends to be generic and relatively limited. While the report itself may be limited, numerical information may be imported into spreadsheets or database programs for further analysis.

In-house

A wide variety of programs that can produce custom reports specifically for Web access exist. These programs have several advantages over basic analyses. Most allow more sophisticated reports to be generated from the data and often produce easily understood graphic displays. In order to function, these programs must be installed on the Web server or a computer connected to it via a high-speed line. Sites on a limited budget

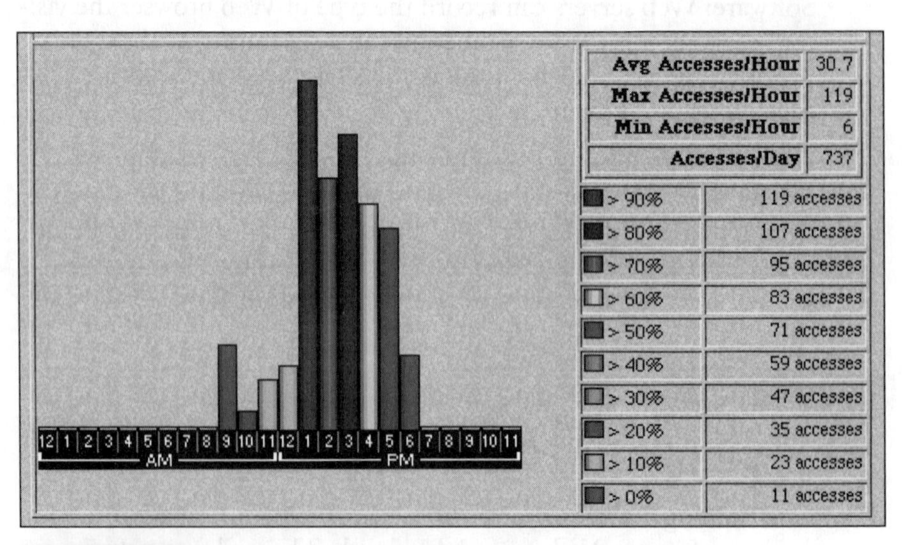

FIGURE 8.1 Sample output from AccessWatch (http://www.accesswatch.com).

should investigate the many free and shareware programs available on the Internet, examples of which include AccessWatch (Figure 8.1) and MK Stats (http://Web.sau.edu/~mkruse/mkstats). These programs create statistics for each of the information types available in the log data and transform them into graphical reports suitable for viewing through a Web browser. For operation, these programs require UNIX or Windows NT systems. Macintosh-based Web sites should check the Info-Mac Internet archive at ftp://sumex-aim.stanford.edu/info-mac/help/ for freeware and shareware analysis programs.

Fully commercial programs (usually around $600) provide even greater functionality. Unlike the programs previously mentioned, the commercial software stores access statistics in a custom database. This allows different data types in the access log to be compared to each other and to information in other databases. For example, some access programs correlate Internet domain names with names of actual companies, universities, and Internet service providers. This information could be used to create a report of access to your site by city. Examples of commercial analysis programs for Windows and UNIX servers include net.Genesis' net.Analysis (http://www.netgen.com), OpenMarket's WebReporter (http://www.openmarket.com), and e.g. Software's WebTrends (http://www.webtrends.com).

Log Analysis Services

Companies that do not have the time or resources to analyze their own Web traffic may outsource the work to log analysis services. These companies remotely monitor your Web site and store access data into large relational databases. Charges are rate-dependent, typically about $200 per month for medium-traffic sites and up to $2,000 per month for sites with over 1 million hits per day. The chief advantage of these services is the advanced, highly customized reports they can provide for the client. Industry leaders include I/PRO (http://www.ipro.com), NetCount (http://www.netcount.com), and IntersÈ (http://www.interse.com). I/PRO maintains a database which can correlate commercial Internet domain names with detailed company information such as location, number of employees, and type of business. Since data from a series of reports may be consolidated, it is possible to spot long-term trends in access to particular types of content. Since commercial services pool data from individual clients into a large demographic database, information from your site may be compared against the aggregate database of other sites. This comparison allows your site administrators to rank their performance relative to others in their industry.

Auditing Services

If you plan to use your access statistics for the purposes of selling ad space and justifying budget requests, it is important to have third-party verification of the statistics. Many ad agencies will not accept statistics generated by site administrators; they require outside verification. Commercial analysis services may also provide auditing services and have teamed up with well-respected organizations to enhance their credibility. Currently, I/PRO offers its I/AUDIT service in conjunction with Nielsen Media Services (http://www.nielsenmedia.com) and Netcount has partnered with Price-Waterhouse (http://www.pw.com) to offer similar features.

Smaller sites might be interested in using the services of the Internet Audit Bureau (http://www.internet-audit.com/intro.html). This free service installs a counter on your home page which registers each time the page is accessed and forwards it to the IAB database. Users log onto the IAB Web site to see their statistics. This is an excellent solution for personal sites on ISPs and other providers that do not allow installation of custom analysis software. Unlike other services, IAB only counts access to a single page on your site. A similar service is provided by Webcounter (http://www.digits.com).

 Analyzing Repeat Visits

The methods of site analysis previously described are entirely anonymous. All that is known about the visitors are their computers' addresses and, in some cases, where they work or go to school. In addition, access statistics reflect averaged values, rather than the preference of individual visitors. To further understand the Web site audience, several methods were created to uniquely identify and track individual visitors. One method uses software to anonymously register visitors. The second method parallels measurement systems in other media such as television and uses voluntarily provided personal information from a subset of the overall audience.

Address Correlation

The simplest method for identifying unique visitors is to collect all entries of a particular Internet address in the access log, and produce sub-logs for each occurrence. Certain products, such as Open Market's (http://www.openmarket.com) Web server, offer this feature. While this method works well for many visitors, it fails for some online services such as America Online and certain ISPs that use a secondary computer (known as a *proxy server*), which assigns a single Internet address to their members. Since

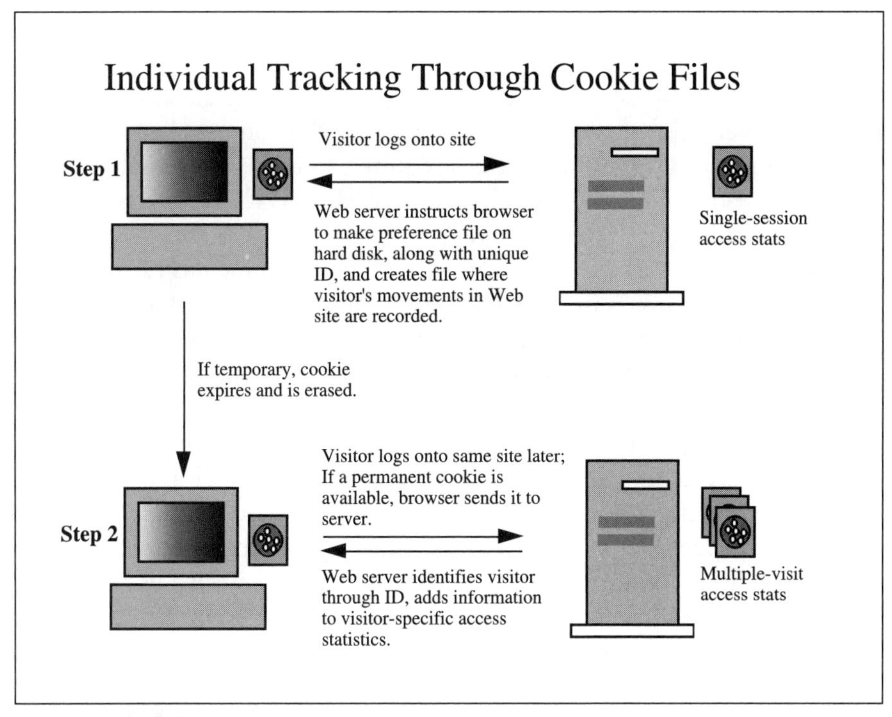
Individual Tracking Through Cookie Files
Step 1
Visitor logs onto site
Web server instructs browser to make preference file on hard disk, along with unique ID, and creates file where visitor's movements in Web site are recorded.
Single-session access stats
If temporary, cookie expires and is erased.
Step 2
Visitor logs onto same site later; If a permanent cookie is available, browser sends it to server.
Web server identifies visitor through ID, adds information to visitor-specific access statistics.
Multiple-visit access stats

FIGURE 8.2 Diagram of temporary and permanent cookies.

these visitors form a substantial fraction of the total Internet audience, address correlation cannot provide comprehensive statistics.

Cookies

To provide a greater capability for Web sites to track their visitors, Netscape (http://www.netscape.com) developed the *cookie* system during 1995. Cookies essentially provide anonymous, automatic registration of each visitor to your site. As shown in Figure 8.2, when visitors access a Web site that uses cookies, their browser software is given a unique identifier which is stored on their local hard disk. The next time they access the site, the browser presents the stored cookie file to the server. While cookies do not provide specific information about the visitor, they do allow access statistics to be correlated across multiple visits to the site.

Using this information, analysis software may show differences between casual and frequent visitors of content on the Web site. In fact, since each individual can be identified, the Web server can deliver customized pages made specifically for the individual. For example, a fan of an entertainment site who frequently accesses the video department might be presented with video-specific information upon entry into the site. By showing only the links that interest the visitor, large Web sites with many departments may reduce the clutter of their home pages. Another use for cookies is in online contests: By storing a cookie, visitors may be prevented from repeatedly re-entering the contest. A good resource for the programming tricks required to make customized systems work can be found at Andy's Netscape HTTP Cookie Notes (http://www.illuminatus.com/cookie).

Ever since cookies were first introduced, controversy has existed over their use. Since cookies provide the cyberspace equivalent of wildlife tracking collars, many feel that they violate the privacy of the Internet audience. To cope with these issues, most sites containing cookies now publicly announce that they use the cookie system and promise to keep the information private. Netscape has also introduced a *temporary cookie* which expires after a given period of time. A good discussion of some of the ethics of cookie use is available at Malcolm's Guide to Persistent Cookie Resources (http://www.emf.net/~mal/cookiesinfo). Audience members who don't want their movements tracked may also use cookie-blocking software developed by PrivNet (http://www.privnet.com) and others to keep their movements confidential.

Registration, Surveys, and Guestbooks

Cookies can only identify a Web browser, not the person behind it. The difficulties of analyzing anonymous tracking will increase as the Internet audience accesses the Web through information kiosks and laptop computers. As in other areas, the best information about the entertainment audience comes from freely given information from individuals. Increasing numbers of Web sites have turned to user registration to collect their demographics. In this case, individuals may provide information impossible to find through other methods. I/PRO offers a commercial service called I/CODE for this purpose. Audience members visiting Web sites voluntarily sign up for I/CODE—providing confidential, but extensive, personal information. Thereafter, their visits to I/CODE-enabled Web sites may be easily tracked, accumulated in a single large database, and compared to general access statistics. As a result, extremely accurate reports are prepared on Web site usage versus product preferences, income, age, and gender. This information may be used to tightly conform your entertainment to your audience. It may also aid in changing the content and/or appearance of your site to broaden its appeal.

To make a registration system work, you may have to provide an incentive for audience members to supply their information. A common way of doing this on Web sites is to host a contest and use registration as an option for joining. For example, on the Discovery Online Web site (http://www.discovery.com), special services including bulletin boards require the visitor to sign in and provide demographic information.

 Adjusting Your Site to Your Audience

Once you have identified the features of your audience in detail, analyze the site's content—with the goal of making additions and updates. Using this information, you can improve your site through *structure* (making it easier and more intuitive for the audience to navigate through the Web pages), *dynamism* (providing a continual flow of new content to enhance the audience's experience), and *community building* (promoting interactivity between the audience and the content, entertainment providers, and other site visitors).

Structure

Since the majority of your audience pays the provider for time spent exploring your content, make their page-by-page movement as efficient and painless as possible. A major component of your access statistics indicates the relative frequency that each portion of your site is viewed. In some cases, you will have information showing the actual path visitors took through your site. Chances are that your site's traffic flow will be at odds with your original road map. To correct this, modify your internal page formatting and/or the navigational structure linking separate pages. These structural enhancements convert your initial organization into one that more accurately matches the audience's needs and preferences. As VRML continues to extend Web sites into the third dimension, structural design will reach a new level of complexity, so it pays to create a good foundation in your current pages.

> ***I do* not *have to educate the masses anymore. Most people (thanks to the mainstream media) know how the Internet can save you time, money and energy! Example: If you cannot travel to XYZ Company or travel to a foreign land. . . one can view it on the Internet. Companies can instead give out their Web site address and save money by* not *having to mail out a company brochure.***
>
> —Marie Nelson, Internet Web listings and information technology provider, Electrosonic Systems, Inc.
> http://usa.electrosonic.com

Getting Visitors Past the Home Page

One of the most important things to check in your analysis is the number of visitors who get beyond the "front door" of the site. Many site operators, to their surprise, have found that the vast majority of their potential audience loads their home page and promptly leave. If such a trend appears in your statistics, there are several possible remedies. Examine the appearance of your home page. If it doesn't seem like a "front door," you may want to redesign its appearance so that it forms a single *frontispiece* to a secondary home page leading to the main site. This arrangement creates the psychological feeling of having stepped through and closed a virtual door; it often encourages a visitor to explore further before leaving. A simple frontispiece design with limited colors also reduces downloading time, keeping visitors on slow connections from leaving in frustration before they get in the door. Many sites have adopted the *frontispiece* model, including american recordings (http://american.recordings.com), Ecospace (http://ecospace.com), and HotWired (Figure 8.3). The latter's frontispiece changes daily and its clever design encourages visitors to return each day. An extreme example of the frontispiece approach is found at the Joe Boxer site (Figure 8.4), where the visitor must page through several frontispiece screens before reaching the main menu. By the time you get to the juggler at the carnival, you don't want to leave!

If possible, reduce the number of choices on the home page (or secondary home page) so that the site's purpose is clear to the visitor. By doing this, you will have more space to explain what each department of your site provides. If your site contains large numbers of distinct entertainment providers, design the departmental pages so that they can function as home pages in their own right. Including an exhaustive site index on your main home page may result in no selections being made at all—especially if your site has not had a chance to develop branding on the

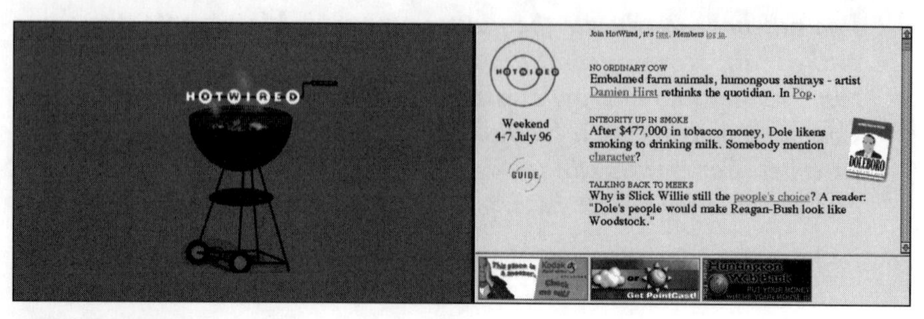

FIGURE 8.3 HotWired — Frontispiece and main menu (http://www.hotwired.com).

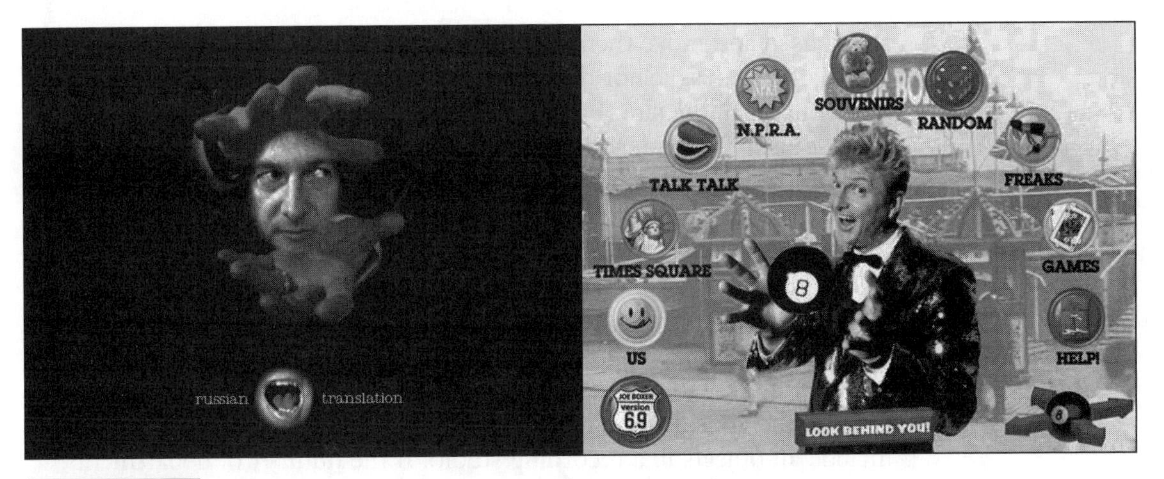

FIGURE 8.4 Joe Boxer — First frontispiece and main menu (http://www.joeboxer.com).

Internet. Finally, you might include a teaser in the form of a question or announcement pointing to a contest or linking to a series of screens (as in the Joe Boxer site, previously mentioned) that takes the site visitor on a mini-journey to your main menu. Another teaser is provided by the popular Java *tickertape* applet—which is often used on home pages to convey a philosophical statement, joke, or greeting that sets the tone for the visitor's experience.

Eliminating Dead Ends

If you notice that most visitors exit your site from a particular page, check your coding to see whether the visitors have become *trapped.* Although visitors can always retrace their steps by using the "Back" button on their browsers, improperly designed pages can prevent them from moving forward to deeper areas of the site. Many visitors will become frustrated at this point and leave the site rather than attempt to figure out a way around the virtual wall that blocks their path. Some of the most common causes of this problem are missing or bad links and navigational toolbars (see Chapter 6). In some cases, the correct links and toolbars may be present but are hard to find because of their size or positioning on the page.

Reducing Interface Complexity

Just as an overly complex home page may prevent the audience from entering your site, an elaborate site interface may discourage further exploration. If your visitors seem to make a few random jumps within the site before abruptly leaving, this may be the reason. If this problem appears in your access statistics, you should determine which links are rarely used and move them to secondary locations. Frequently, many areas conceived as major departments during the concept and development phases of the site (Part II) get little traffic. If your pages are still too confusing, consider rotating page contents every few minutes. For example, a site containing a large number of original works of art could rotate each work on the home page—converting spatial complexity to temporal complexity.

As another option, increase the strength or expand upon the graphical metaphor used to navigate your site. For example, consider a music site that uses the graphical image of a mixing console on its home page. If the number of areas in the site exceeds the number of faders and other controls on the console, you might consider enlarging the metaphor to include all objects in a recording studio. If the number of departments isn't necessarily increasing, but the amount of material per department continues to rise, make sure that your metaphor still adequately describes the material. Navigation may be streamlined by providing a button on every page linking to a site-specific search engine (see Chapter 5). If your site has a limited budget, consider installing Excite's free software (http://www.architext.com) to provide searching ability.

Support for the Global Audience

If your access statistics indicate that a significant portion of your visitors come from outside the United States, consider ways to support them. One such solution is multilingual pages, though the expense of some translation services can easily become cost-prohibitive. If your visitors use a different alphabet, consider providing links to international character sets for the Web browser. For Web page translation, check out services such as International Translators and Interpreters (http://www.awinc.com/np/translate).

Design graphics ensure that they are correctly interpreted by an international audience. Look for signs of ethnocentrism in your images; you may be reflecting hidden assumptions which could be nonsensical or even offensive to some cultures. For a good resource on the meanings of symbols and signs, check Martin Ryder's Semiotics research page at the University of Colorado at Denver (http://www.cudenver.edu/~mryder/itc_data/semiotics.html).

Embed Entertainment within Informational Links

While your goal as a content provider is to deliver entertainment, recognize that embedding your content within informational resources helps to attract and keep an online fan base. One of the great appeals of Intertainment is that it may be connected with informational resources which expand the audience's knowledge. If your audience is coming primarily from educational or archive sites, or appears to be exploring your site with great thoroughness, linking to Web sites related to yours may satisfy audience curiosity. For concerns about losing your audience by providing too many outlinks, request *reciprocal links* (Chapter 7) from each of the other sites. If you don't mind forcing new browser windows to pop up each time someone accesses another site (leaving your original site window intact underneath them), you might want to reference outlinks using the TARGET= "new" tag.

Dynamism

Part II discusses various ways to enhance the Web site interface (e.g., audio, video, and multimedia). While these techniques help convert static Web pages into active documents, they are empty motions unless the site's actual *content changes* frequently. *Dynamism*, defined here as frequent content updates, is essential if you want return visits to the site. The following are a few common methods for updating content.

Graphic Design and Format Updates

With the rapid increase in the graphical capabilities of the Web, entertainment sites must periodically rework their graphical content to maintain a cutting-edge look and feel. Figure 8.5 shows an example for an artist on Kaleidospace. Over a period of time, backgrounds were added,

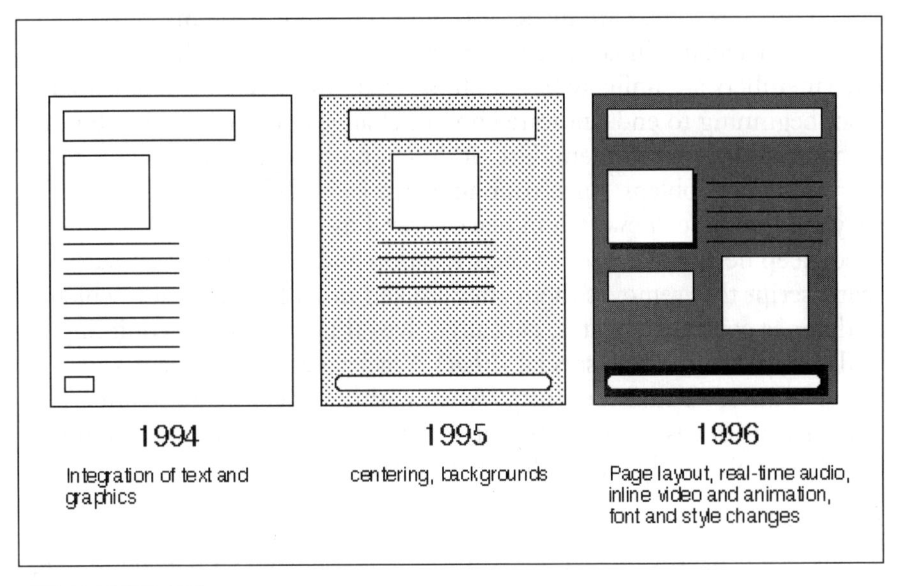

FIGURE 8.5 Kspace artist page development—1994, 1995, 1996.

text headlines were converted to drop-shadowed graphics, objects on the page were rearranged, and simple icons were replaced with more three dimensional navigation tools.

Changing graphics and formatting may be especially helpful in retaining an audience on smaller Web sites. Many smaller sites created by independents are abandoned without warning, but remain online as virtual "ghost towns." Due to this, the Internet audience interprets periodic design changes on independent sites as evidence of continued activity and professionalism on the part of the content providers.

Date and Time Counters

To make your site change from day to day, simply include an automated program on your home page. A straightforward example of this is the popular *counter* program which records access to the page along with current date and time information. An enormous number of counter programs have been written and are available for free on the Internet. Sample CGI-based counter and date programs may be found at The Web Engineers Toolbox (http://www59.metronet.com/cgi), and Java-based counters and date-time lists are available at the Gamelan site (http://www.gamelan.com). The counter concept may be extended by providing more information about the date and time, such as a quote of the day or description of the day's significance (such as a holiday).

Graphical Tags on Updates

When updates to text are made, it is important to call attention to them—particularly in large sites with complex interfaces—because audience members are unlikely to search for changes by reading a document from beginning to end. Indicate content changes by placing a small new or hot graphic next to them. Use of these graphics presents a significant management problem, since your audience is unlikely to be impressed if they see the same "new" tag in place several months later! If tags are used, keep detailed records of their location and/or construct an automatic script that removes them after a given time. Kaleidospace, which undergoes constant updates, partially solves this problem by confining update information to a special *What's New?* page. Kaleidospace and Time-Warner's Pathfinder (http://www.pathfinder.com) also maintain audience awareness by sending out update newsletters by email to those who have voluntarily joined their mailing lists.

Internal Ad Rotation

While Web advertising is often assumed to come from an outside source, nothing prevents a large site from setting up banner-style promotions for departments, products, or individuals represented on the site. For example, a large media site might rotate banners advertising new articles from different departments and a meta-site representing independent artists and musicians might run ads for individual home pages. Automated rotation systems can be developed with sophisticated, high-end applications like Netscape's Livewire Pro (http://www.netscape.com/comprod/server_central/product/livewire), but this approach is more complex and expensive than necessary for smaller sites. One possible system for supporting internal ads for smaller sites is supplied by Clickables (http://www.clickables.com) for under $50. (For information on high-end commercial ad rotation software, see Chapter 9.)

Columns and Reviews

If the entertainment featured on your site is unique, niche, or relatively unknown, consider taking an authoritative position and become a columnist or reviewer. This establishes the site as the reference and source for the entertainment you provide and audiences will return to read the latest commentary. An alternative method of supplying reviews is to allow visitors to submit reviews to the site, which encourages contact from the fan community. Providing reviews or commentary on your site doesn't demand fancy programming, but does require good writing and editing skills. Since the audience will expect new information on the site, the editor must have the time and resources to write for this ongoing *cybercolumn.*

Live Audio and Video Feeds

One of the most interesting features of the Web is its potential to provide "live" audio and video feeds from any location in the world. Web-based cameras have become extremely popular and are found on hundreds of Web sites (see the "spy cameras" section in Yahoo! for examples). This Internet version of a closed-circuit television can be surprisingly simple to set up. Inexpensive color cameras like the Connectix QuickCam (http://www.connectix.com) can provide still images or live video for under $300. With appropriate software extensions such as WebCamToo (http://www.mmcorp.com/~binky/index.html) or Cannibal Island Software's ShutterBug (http://goldfish.physics.utoronto.ca/Cannibal.html), a series of images can be relayed from the camera to the Web server and displayed on Web pages. Due to the bandwidth limitations of much of the audience, most *webcams* update their images every few minutes and are mounted in areas displaying slow but interesting changes. A good example of effective use can be found at Global Interactive's (http://www.gointeract.com) live event site. Its Tahoe Live (http://www.gointeract.com/tahoelive) shows skiing conditions on mountains in the area (Figure 8.6) and supports the travel and leisure orientation of the site. For larger sites

FIGURE 8.6 Tahoe Live (http://www.gointeract.com/tahoelive).

promoting traditional entertainment, a tremendous opportunity exists for providing dynamic content by taking Web-based cameras "behind the scenes" of film, television, and music production—though certain legal issues will need to be resolved (see Chapter 13).

Unlike video, live audio feeds are almost unknown—despite the widespread availability of the required software and the number of virtual radio stations. Possibilities for live audio would include a microphone mounted in a music club, ambient sound from exhibitions and conventions, or speeches and interviews. (For more information on video and audio streaming, see Chapter 10).

Community Building

Since its inception, the Internet has excelled in creating virtual communities that share common interests. As the audience for your site grows, you should begin adding services which allow your visitors to go beyond simply experiencing your content to engaging in direct, two-way participation. In addition to interacting with the content itself, your site can also encourage feedback between the audience and the entertainment providers, and communication among the audience members. In the most engaging Web sites, content forms a nucleus for strong connections between site, content provider, and audience—and the resulting community forms the basis for moving entertainment into new forms (see Chapter 12).

User-driven Content

One of the most effective ways to encourage feedback from your audience is by soliciting content provided by visitors. Typically, CGI-type programs (see Chapter 5) allow the audience to submit information which appears directly on the Web site. Examples of effective content include discussion groups for online fans and audience polls. Dujour (http://www.dujour.com) is an excellent example of a site which relies heavily on visitor input. It uses an extensive set of custom scripts to collect and process a large number of user-submitted riddles, jokes, and puzzles. Periodically, the scripts correlate riddles with correct answers and post the winners on the site. The extensive use of automation coupled with user input allows a small number of people to maintain a Web site with complex and rapidly changing information. Other user-driven sites include the Internet University's Pop Culture Quiz (http://www.internetuniv.com/contests/npopquiz.htm), TV Net (http://tvnet.com), and HitsWorld (Figure 8.7). The latter site is particular interesting because it creates its "Top 20" music list by compiling favorites from a large number of personal home pages. HitsWorld also runs other interactive features, including a poll where the audience can pick future music hits.

Get quick access to charts
with Hits World Bookmarks
May Album Reviews are here
firefly
HitsWorld
the #1 music source
We track about 500 songs every week on radio and your personal hitlists. Link to lyrics, sound and more!
Internet Top 50
International Charts
From the Netherlands to New Zealand, discover who's ruling the albums and singles charts around the world!
Join hundreds of players Predict future hits today!
HitPicks Charts Game
Personal Charts
Let your voice be heard! You rule these charts!
Check out what is on top of over 100 different radio charts around the U.S. & Canada, all categorized geographically and by format
Radio Charts and Playlists
HitsWorld Spotlight
Looking for what's happening on the national music scene? Check out national charts including Casey's Top 40 and Billboard's charts here.

FIGURE 8.7 HitsWorld (http://www.hitsworld.com).

Contests and Events

Time-limited events such as contests can help to solidify site visitors' interest in your content. The authors' Kaleidospace site was able to bring new awareness to its Screening Room area by running a contest for independently produced films. Both filmmakers and the general audience visited the Screening Room to learn the results of the contest and view video clips created by the winners. Contests on other Web sites have asked their audience to name the site mascot or answer trivia questions. France Online (http://www.france.com), an independent site specializing in travel and leisure information, ran a contest called Web D' Or that allowed audience members to rank French Web sites. Operating for several weeks, it rapidly made France Online the most popular French site on the Internet. The event-oriented nature of the promotion, combined with a voting deadline, encouraged large numbers of audience members to visit the site as soon as they heard about it. If Web D' Or had been run as an ongoing feature of the Web site rather than a one-time event, its impact would likely have been much lower.

Scavenger hunts form an increasingly popular class of audience-interaction games on the Web. At the start of a hunt, the content provider hides tokens on a variety of Web pages on participating sites. The game's players then cruise the Web, accumulating tokens which allow them to win prizes when they return to the original site. Scavenger hunts have been emphasized by game sites such as Riddler (http://www.riddler.com), which sends out frequent invitations for sites to participate in its scavenger hunts. For smaller sites, the increase in the number of visitors received could be quite significant.

Online Chat

Chat is one of the most powerful methods of increasing the interactivity of your site. It is relatively easy to implement programs such as WebChat (http://www.IRsociety.com/wbs.html); it requires no additional helper or plug-in applications to function. More sophisticated systems include the Java-based Earthweb (http://chat.earthweb.com) and the three-dimensional environments of The Palace (http://www.thepalace.com). While many sites run an unmoderated "open" chat, moderated chats are more effective in developing audience interest in the content of your site and developing a relationship between the audience and the content providers. As an example, the authors' Kaleidospeak (http://kspace.com/chat) chat room features weekly interviews with independent artists and site visitors. Due to this program, site visitors develop a personal rapport with the site administrators as well as the artists and musicians showcasing content. Kspace artists have also begun to use the chat room as a way to communicate with each other (as shown in Figure 8.8). While chat software is relatively easy to install and use, it is important to provide personnel who can monitor the room during use. On popular *open chat* sites such as TV Net (http://tvnet.com) and ESPNet Sportszone (http://www.sportszone.com), it becomes necessary to recruit chat "cops" to make sure the rooms are being used appropriately.

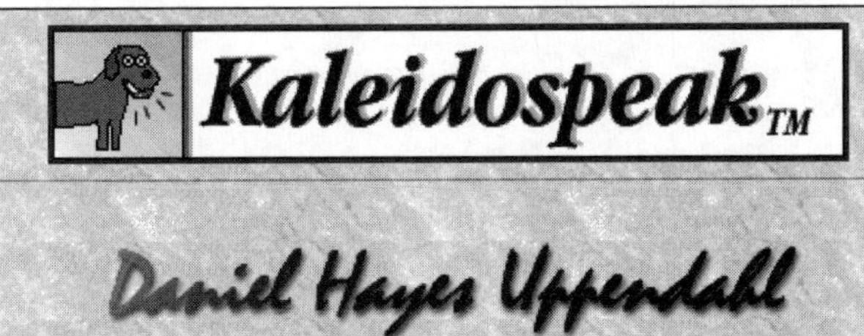

Kaleidospeak chat May 16, 1996

Jeannie Novak
Hi RonB: We're chatting with Daniel Hayes Uppendahl, photographer, who is showcasing his body piercing projects - CORPUS TRANSFIXUM (CD-ROM) and photographic prints - on Kspace at this **button** Daniel is also displaying part of his commercial photography portfolio.

Unpierced
Daniel, I agree with what you are saying about not judging people for any reason, but don't you think that the eyebrow ring has become the Nirvana t-shirt of 1996?

Phil
Daniel, Jeannie told me about the film you showed. Could you tell us a bit about the clip, since it will soon be on Kspace also? It sounded very ethereal.

Eban
What does "CORPUS TRANSFIXUM" literally translate to?

Daniel Hayes Uppendahl
Jeannie: People on the internet give me a great deal of positive feedback. Outside the internet, I have mixed reactions. I've been told by some, the project is sick and some have found it unnerving, but of course, most people have had positive reactions.

Ibsinn
I don't understand the eyebrow ring much, since it's hardly noticeable.

Daniel Hayes Uppendahl
Eban: Latin for "pierced (Transfixum) and body (Corpus)"

FIGURE 8.8 Kaleidospeak chat transcript fragment.

Pete
All: What do you think make people react negatively to piercing? Is is an association with S & M, a feeling that it is "primitive" or something else?

Pat
"Body transformation" right? Did someone earlier mention something about the similarities between S&M and piercing?

Eban
How do react when people say your work or you are sick?

Anonymous
Enters the room ...

Unpierced
Ibsinn, earlier you said that you were thinking of getting pierced, where were you thinking of?

Daniel Hayes Uppendahl
Phil: I'd love to say more about the film. Jeannie & Pete saw a five minute clip of a larger project. Some of the influences of the work would be Butoh (surrealistic dance from Japan), with a little bit of Samuel Beckett thrown in. It's a black & white film exploring the underworld of the psyche.

Eban
I would think that some are just reacting to the fact that is out of the norm (kinda like when long hair for men was first being seen)...?

Ibsinn
I was actually thinking of the nose because I like how it looks. As I said before, I don't really understand the philosophy. I'm not doing it to copy anyone. It just feels right for me.

Amanita
Dan: Beckett & Butoh....that is a winning combination!

Eban
Daniel: What forbidden images are you using in your film?

FIGURE 8.8 *Continued.*

Email-based Discussion Groups

In the previous chapter, email-based mailing lists were presented as an effective means for attracting an audience to your site. If your entertainment has a dedicated or cult following, use a site-specific mailing list to support ongoing community building content for your site. Since these lists are email-based, they may support thousands of members without major hardware allocations. Software for mailing list management is relatively inexpensive, but most must be installed on a UNIX-style workstation (see Chapter 5) for their operation. Popular packages for maintaining lists include Majordomo (http://www.greatcircle.com/majordomo) and Lyris (http://www.lyris.com). A Macintosh version of Majordomo has been developed by Leuca Software (http://leuca.med.cornell.edu/Macjordomo), and a commercial Macintosh product called Liststar is offered by Quarterdeck Software (http://www.starnine.com/liststar/liststar.html).

Personal Home Pages

A few sites allow visitors to actually create their own local home pages, usually through CGI-style scripts accessed by fill-out forms. Home pages can help a visitor to your site establish a strong personal identity, both for the content provider and the other members of the audience. Like chat, having home pages virtually guarantees that your audience will treat your site as a "hangout," particularly if other visitors can leave messages there. An outstanding example of a site providing home pages to its audience can be found at Firefly (see Figure 8.9).

FIGURE 8.9 Firefly (http://www.firefly.com).

Visitor Demographics

A seldom explored concept for community building sites is to provide on-the-fly statistics of user activity on the Web site. In order to implement the system, the site programmer will need to create a custom program which continually runs demographic analysis each time a visitor selects site content. Seeing this information, the visitor will instantly feel that the site is a community and be encouraged to join it. Live demographics work best with high traffic and search engines like Magellan (http://www.mckinley.com) have or are considering implementing real-time demographic pages.

Using Intelligent Agents

Agents apply information given to the Web site by an audience member to construct a virtual copy of their likes and dislikes. One of the best examples of such sites in the entertainment area can be found at Firefly (http://www.firefly.com) and RARE personal entertainment recommendations (http://www.surf.com/rare/home.html). These sites work by constructing a model of entertainment and lifestyle preferences of visitors through a questionnaire. This information is used to construct an agent that reflects the visitor's interests with regard to art, music, film, travel, and even business. As an example, your musical tastes can be used by an agent to recommend artists and recordings available for purchase. Agent sites promote an online community by recommending other audience members who have similar tastes. The intelligent agent approach goes a long way toward adding more person-to-person interactivity which is a unique strength of the Internet.

Collaborative Art

Continued developments in Web software are leading to the creation of environments in which multiple visitors can participate to create a larger artistic whole. Current examples include *graffiti* art panes on which visitors to Web sites such as the Virtual Graffiti Wall (Figure 8.10) and Real Grafitti (http://militzer.me.tuns.ca/graffiti) can "spray paint" their own work and modify the work of others. As Web-based virtual worlds become more common (Chapter 12), it will be possible to allow the site's emerging community to create its own environment within the site.

Meta-sites like the authors' Kaleidospace site have a dual responsibility to the general audience, and the hundreds of artists and musicians using the site for promotion, distribution, and placement. As one of the first Web sites to host significant numbers of artists, Kaleidospace has had much experience managing the several hundred independent artists and musicians on the site. Since the goal of Kspace

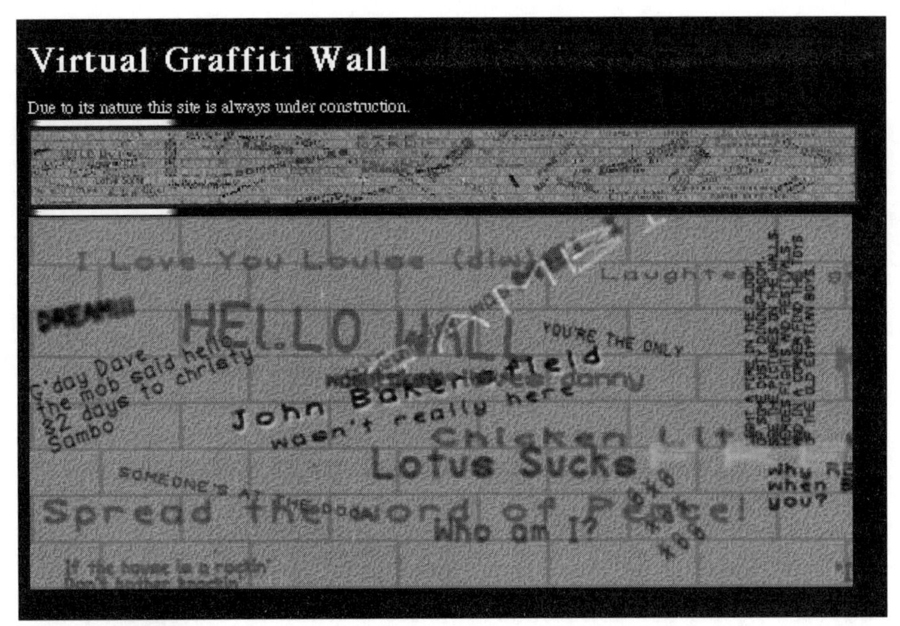

FIGURE 8.10 Virtual Graffiti Wall (http://www.sorceror.com/thewall.html).

extended beyond creating Web pages, an artist support policy was implemented early at several levels. The first level ensured that the artist received a constant stream of information about what was happening with the Web presence, even if the artist did not have an Internet connection. To this end, an automated script broke down the site's access logs into files for individual artists, which were emailed or faxed to the artists. Frequently, statistics indicated strengths of a particular artist which could be used to increase promotion and sales. The second level of support gave the artist access to services on the Web site itself. These included support for secure online ordering of products and access to the Kspace chat room for moderated discussions between artists and their audience. The final area provided support for community. Though far from complete in mid-1996, the goal was to facilitate contact among Kspace artists and interaction between the artists and site visitors (including prospective customers and industry contacts) with the goal of building an online community. These efforts included the creation of additional niche-oriented sites, customized searches, co-op advertising, and live events and collaborative projects featuring Kspace artists.

 Behind-the-Scenes Maintenance

In addition to the publicly available content maintenance and updates, keeping the site running smoothly requires daily work at the behind-the-scenes level. These tasks normally include the site's content developers as well as hardware and software adminstrators. While a complete discussion of many of these issues is beyond the scope of this book, the following presents some common problems and possible solutions with regard to Web site operation.

Monitoring Site Availability

Almost everyone has experienced messages such as "server not responding to requests" when trying to visit a site. In some cases, the problem occurs outside of the site administrator's network. For example, the audience member's local Internet connection malfunctions or an overload occurs at one of the Network Access Points (NAPs) that interconnect long-distance lines. However, in other cases the problem may originate within the site administrator's network—such as an overloaded or "crashed" Web server. This problem most frequently occurs when more people attempt to access the Web site than the equipment can handle (typically about 100-200 visitors at once for most commercial servers). It manifests itself by long waits to connect and extremely slow downloads of Web pages. If you receive consistent complaints or notice slowdowns yourself, the only recourse is to inform the person administering the Web server hardware. Ideally, you should have at least one person available 24 hours a day to keep an eye on the network, but in some cases this is not possible. If you do not have 24-hour network administration available to you, use special-

FIGURE 8.11 Caravelle (http://www.caravelle.com).

ized automated software such as WebWatcher from Caravelle (Figure 8.11) to monitor the network for you. WebWatcher and similar products may be operated from desktop computer systems and set to monitor a local or remote Web server, allowing content developers or project executives to monitor the site directly.

Fixing Broken Links

Even though the use of HTML editors and other site management tools (Chapter 5) to create Web pages has reduced the frequency of broken links, it usually only takes a few minutes of searching through most sites to discover missing graphics or media files. Site maintainers should periodically check the site as a whole, either by using their management software or by direct patrols with their Web browsers. Keep in mind that while management tools may detect missing files, they cannot distinguish files saved incorrectly to the server (e.g., movies saved as text).

Configuration Pages

If your site uses any features beyond basic text and graphics, some of the audience members may have trouble using them. One common problem comes from site visitors using Windows software who may be confused by QuickTime videos common on most Web sites. To solve this problem, the site administrators need to include information on the use of QuickTime for Windows. Similar problems will occur whenever a site uses specialized plug-ins, Java, or VRML. As each new feature is added to your Web site, make sure that online help is available to cut down on the number of confused email messages.

Maintaining Browser Compatibility

Keeping up with the frantic pace of innovation in Web-related software presents a major challenge to site administrators and designers. During 1996, the product cycles for Web browsers (driven by rivalry between Netscape and Microsoft) dropped from a year to a few months. This rate of change, unprecedented in the industry, can make it hard for Web site administrators to keep their sites compatible with the latest advances in browser technology. The site maintainers should periodically download the newest browsers and test their site for problems.

Backups and Historical Site Archives

While backups of the individual files of your Web site are the responsibility of the ISP/IPP or local hardware administrator, it is important to confirm that your data is actually saved. With smaller Web sites, the site developer is essentially at the mercy of the ISP or IPP providing the backup service. Due to this, independent developers should maintain a local copy of the site on their development system. It is usually impractical to do this for larger sites, which may have tens of thousands of entries. In this case, the local hardware administrator or remote ISP/IPP hosting service should make site backups to tapes—typically a data version of 4mm DAT cartridges. Ask the adminstrator periodically to provide additional backups for storage of up to a year. Not only does this ensure that no data is lost, but also it provides an historical archive of the site's development—which may someday be important in deciding copyright and other legal questions (see Chapter 13).

 Social Maintenance

As in any other business relationship, the site administrators will receive a steady stream of queries from other Web sites, clients, customers, and vendors—both by email and traditional means such as phone or fax. While planning a maintenance schedule, make allowances for these social tasks. The following lists some of the major areas likely to require social maintenance on entertainment sites; as you run your site, you will likely want to create a similar list. Typically, one or more persons must be responsible for social maintenance, and communicate comments and recommendations to the rest of the development team.

> ***As in any business, the personal touch is still the most effective sales tool. In the music business, we're artists. We're not anonymous bits of RAM—we have hearts and feelings and need personal attention. That's what I give my new clients on the Net that they can't get anywhere else. I find I can carry on an email relationship with a potential client for weeks, and they're still unsure about working with me. But if I ask that client to call me so we can chat and see if we're right for each other, I can clinch that relationship in a three-minute phone call. So the Net is a good way to find potential clients, but the personal touch still closes the deal.***
>
> —MOLLY-ANN LEIKIN, SONGWRITING CONSULTANT AND HIT SONGWRITER
> http://websites.earthlink.net/~songmd/

Client Support Programs

If you run a meta-site which showcases multiple entertainment clients, you should develop methods of staying in contact with them. Clients should receive regular email from you that keeps them informed of site-specific news, access statistics, and sales reports. If you charge artists and entertainers to put their material on your site, consider setting up a referral program to support your existing clients. "Live" support is also extremely valuable to most independent entertainers who appreciate personal contact and support, such as your attendance at their exhibitions, performances, and screenings. Your staff should be familiar with your clients' work and be able to discuss it with them as well as with customers interested in purchasing it. As Intertainment advances, meta-sites may begin to resemble artist management companies (see Part V), so a site which cultivates good personal relationships with its clients is most likely to succeed in the long run.

Customer Support Programs

A general problem for the entire Internet industry is customer support, which must improve before such dreams as online commerce can be fully realized. Successful sites will get many repeat customers; the maintainers of these sites need to keep detailed records to support them. For example, a previous visitor to a site should be able to fill in a password or ID code to order more products. As with clients, customer support should also extend off the Web. Since many people feel a need to talk directly with someone while ordering goods or services (especially high-ticket items such as original works of art), merchandising Web sites should provide a toll-free number to complement secure online ordering. Furthermore, even if a secure online ordering system is available, it does not ensure that everyone will use it. For example, despite the existence of a secure Web server, fully half the orders on Kaleidospace are received by phone, fax, snail mail, or email.

Responding to Visitor Queries

As a site becomes larger and more complex, many site managers find that they must assign an individual simply to pick through email responses and forward them to the appropriate groups. You will probably want to create a set of mailboxes that act as online filing systems or departments (such as "updates," database," and "jobs") to easily implement an internal forwarding system. If your site consistently gets a lots of messages with essentially the same questions, consider setting up automated scripts to supply automated email responses. While less personal than a "live" answer, it is much better than simply ignoring the messages altogether or delaying responses. Automated responses work well in the "info," "links," or "orders" mailbox of the site, since most visitors will assume that responses from these boxes will be automated. Even if you don't use automation, your administrators should have a series of templates which they may use as a framework for constructing replies.

Privacy Issues

If your site is processing orders, collecting customer demographics, or simply responding to email, you will frequently find yourself in possession of sensitive information. It is essential that you respect your clients' and audience's right to privacy. Make sure that demographic information is completely anonymous or that access to it is strictly controlled. If you are storing demographic information in a database, it should either be encrypted, stored on a machine disconnected from the Internet, or contain names and addresses replaced with arbitrary codes. Similar considerations apply to credit card information.

As your audience, clients, and customers increase in number, you are likely to be contacted by individuals both on and off the Internet who want to buy your demographic information or email addresses. While mailing lists are commonly sold to direct marketers in other media, this is a very bad idea on the Internet—since the audience can convey their anger by striking back (see Chapter 7). If you don't release mailing lists, make sure you inform your customers of this so they don't blame you for unsolicited advertising sent their way.

As we will see in Chapter 9, it is possible to collect a considerable amount of information about your site visitors. With the introduction of privacy software from companies like PrivNet (http://www.privnet.com), some of your visitors may actively prevent you from collecting information about them. Some individuals have suggested that site adminstrators respond to this by preventing anyone using privacy software from accessing their site. In the authors' opinion, this would be a serious mistake for sites providing entertainment content. Rather than shutting out audience members, consider implementing fill-out forms for collecting voluntarily supplied audience information. In this way, you will be developing a closer relationship with your audience, rather than shutting them out!

Unauthorized Use of Your Site's Programming

Due to the nature of the Web, other sites can process their own information by calling a program on your computer. Sometimes this is intended—as when search engines encourage other sites to create a local page on their server with code linking directly to the search engine. In other cases, site developers who can't create their own software will try to borrow yours. Careful analysis of the access log will allow administrators to detect unauthorized use of your programs. Usually, an email message to the administrator of the offending site is enough to stop the problem.

Unauthorized Use of Site Interface and Content

A surprising number of people on the Web assume that because something is posted on a Web page it is free for unlimited use. Unauthorized copying of graphics from Web sites is a common event; most offenders are non-artists who treat other sites as a source of clip art. Since the intent of the copier is usually harmless (e.g., creating a fan site), a message from your Web administrator is usually sufficient to solve the problem. The administrator should explain that the copied material is not free and possibly provide alternate distribution graphics which can be used in its place. Further discussion of the legal implications of distributing content through the Internet can be found in Chapter 13.

Dealing with Hackers, Spammers, and Potty-Mouths

These irritating members of the Internet community will confront every Web site sooner or later. Of the three, *hackers* are best known due to widespread sensationalization by the popular media. The launch of a new Web site, particularly if a high-profile media company is involved, is a natural invitation to people who want to break into the site. The vast majority of these efforts are clumsy and can be fended off with a minimum of security. Make sure that the system administrator has installed basic security screens or firewalls. The administrators should conduct periodic reviews of the programs running on the Web server. Security should extend to the physical world as well. Since computers are valuable property, sites run in-house need to ensure that equipment doesn't "walk away." Smaller site operators should request information on the security their ISP or IPP provides.

Spammers (individuals who flood the Internet with unsolicited email) were mentioned in Chapter 7 as the chief practitioners of a bad type of netpublicity. With respect to Web site maintenance, spammers pose the greatest problems to meta-sites that host the home pages of multiple entertainers. A typical spammer might send email promoting an unlikely business opportunity to everyone on the site. Since spammers rarely listen to reason, the best solution is to install "anti-spam" software developed by PrivNet and others. On Kaleidospace, a custom-automated script detects and eliminates spams from each artist's public email box and forwards the remaining information to the artist's private mailbox. While automation can detect blanket email attacks, it cannot stop spammers who target a subgroup of your Web site clients. Rather than find their own content, some independent site operators will attempt to solicit artists and musicians away from other meta-sites. The best defense against such actions is to make your clients feel as if they are part of a community, so they won't be tempted to go elsewhere.

Potty-mouths (their behavior does not dignify a more sophisticated name) are the easiest of the three groups to deal with. This group includes individuals who use offensive language, as well as those who repeatedly complain or post long *flames* (long-winded diatribes against your site). Common offenders include nit-pickers, know-it-alls, undersocialized netheads, and sometimes a person who is having a *very* bad day. Occasionally, a potty-mouth is a disgruntled or jealous Web designer who decides to attack your Web site verbally for imagined gain on their part. Whatever their origin, they can cause problems—especially if you run interactive services like posting boards or chat rooms. While software may allow potty-mouths to be "turned off," a better course is to simply ignore them. Since the goal of their behavior is attention, lack of it will induce them to go elsewhere.

In the next chapter, the discussion of the operation of an entertainment-based Web site continues—moving to the bottom line of generating revenue for your site!

CHAPTER 9

WHERE'S THE CASH COW?

Making Your Site Pay

I view the Internet as an entertainment medium as well as a marketplace—much like the early village markets which provided a meeting place to exchange ideas and to trade and barter goods.

—BOBBY LEE CUDE OF HARD HAT RECORDS—NEW BROADWAY MUSIC
http://kspace.com/hardhat

As late as the end of 1994, the authors and other content providers on the Web were frequently told that they *weren't allowed* to run commercial services on the Web. How this situation has changed! By mid-1996, commercial services were the *only* Web sites many people had ever seen, and large and small Web sites were furiously searching for a revenue model that could make their content pay for itself. While Intertainment is booming, revenue sources have been slow to appear—and many feel that most Web sites will have difficulty making ends meet for some time to come. In a recent study by Forrester Research, Inc. (http://www.forrester.com), it was predicted that the typical large media site (with about $150,000 in development costs) will not generate a profit until the year 2000. Forrester bases this claim on the fact that expenses for developing Web-based content are increasing more rapidly than available revenue. Most of the cost increases derive from site marketing and promotion, since technology costs have remained constant.

Despite these grim pronouncements, a large number of entertainment sites are running as real businesses and making a profit off the Web. Many of the most profitable sites are quite small, which demonstrates that size is not a predictor of economic success. This chapter is devoted to showing how Intertainment can make money. It describes the various resources available for revenue generation by the four major commercial methods: sponsorships, sales, subscriptions, and advertising. Discussion of the general issues involved in running a business is beyond the scope of this book; see the outstanding summary at Wilson Internet Services (http://www.wilsonweb.com) or one of the many books available in stores. As with the real world, you should check out any business you contact for goods and services online through resources like the Better Business Bureau (http://www.bbb.org/bbb).

Choosing a Revenue Model for Your Site

The revenue model you develop for your Web site can have a major impact on how you create your content. For example, if your site is supported primarily by advertising or sponsorships, you may find it difficult to post controversial content which might result in losing your sources of revenue. Sales-based sites will have to set up for high volume in order to make significant amounts of money. Subscription-based sites must have content sufficiently compelling to overcome the audience's resistance to paying for Web content. Most Web sites will need to mix the various methods in order to break even. As the Web matures, a site's revenue model of choice will most likely be based on the type of content that site provides. A site containing repurposed content from other media will normally receive sponsorship, but may be able to raise additional revenue through ads. Integrating specialized information into a site's entertainment value may help to build subscriber bases. If the site offers entertainment that may be joined outside of the Web (e.g., music, visual art, film, passes to real world events), a direct sales and payment-per-product model may be maintained.

> ***Large companies spend millions on their Internet strategies, but they usually still don't "get it"—do you really want to click on silly Web-ized ads for toothpaste? No way!***
>
> —Pat Ortman, Creative Director, Empty Street Productions, Inc.
> http://www.generationx.com and http://www.emptystreet.com

Sponsored Sites

These sites currently make up the largest group of entertainment sites on the Internet. While the adage that "nobody makes money on the Internet" is not true, most sites require outside support in order to maintain operations. Fortunately, the relatively low startup and maintenance costs for Web sites allow a variety of solutions which large and small sites alike may implement.

Out-of-pocket

Since basic site maintenance on a remote ISP/IPP costs $10 to $200 per month, it is practical to develop and maintain smaller entertainment sites directly out of individual or group pockets. For independent musicians, artists, and filmmakers, the promotional value of the site can easily outweigh these relatively low costs.

Underwriting

Nonprofit organizations or sites pushing technological or social boundaries with their content may be able to develop sponsorships similar to those used to subsidize programming on public broadcasting. In some cases, they may secure sponsorship for a Web site from the same organizations that underwrite them in other media. As the Web becomes more widely recognized, a proposal for a site may actually be an asset for larger projects. For example, independent filmmakers might investigate the services provided by The Bay Area Video Coalition (http://www.sirius.com/~sstark/org/bavc/bavc.html) or Visual Communications (http://vc.apnet.org/~viscom). If you are new to sponsorship, see a training course or book detailing sponsorship. Sponsor consultants have recently come online; SponsorVision (http://members.aol.com/sponsorvis/index.html) is a good example of an organization providing this service.

Commercial Sponsorship

A significant number of companies, particularly those in the computer industry, help to sponsor high-profile Web sites providing entertainment content. An early example of commercial sponsorship was the Internet Underground Music Archive (http://www.iuma.com), which received sponsorship from Silicon Graphics (http://www.sgi.com). More recently, both Sun Microsystems (http://www.sun.com) and Apple Computer (http://www.apple.com) have sponsored Web sites "powered" by their respective hardware. Sites seeking commercial sponsorship will normally need to demonstrate either high access by the Internet audience or innovative programming and content which shows off the capabilities of the sponsor's systems.

Financing

In some cases, your entertainment concept may require a large amount of money to implement and/or uses patentable technology. If this is the case, you may want to secure financing. Currently, the financial community is moving from support for Internet software and hardware companies toward content providers. An example of this change is seen with the recent public offering for C|Net (http://www.cnet.com), a popular combined Web site and cable channel. While a detailed discussion of the process of acquiring financing is beyond the scope of this book, there are many offline and online resources for new Web businesses. An example of a service showcasing companies for financing can be found at Moneyhunter (http://www.moneyhunter.com). The site offers resources, including a business plan template, a "golden rolodex" of investors, and the chance for entrepreneurs to participate in its cable TV show. The publishers of *Red Herring Magazine*'s herring.com (Figure 9.1) offer the Entrepreneur's Resource Center, which provides a guide to funding through venture capital, and investment and commercial banks—along with legal and accounting resources. In order to pursue financing at this level, you will need to prepare detailed business and marketing plans. If you are interested in hiring a service to prepare your plan, do some research to ensure that the service understands the Internet well enough to address the particular needs of business conducted online. Watch for a new industry specializing in Internet business plan development in the near future.

Subscription-based Sites

In 1995, many companies tried converting their Web sites to services charging membership fees, only to cancel their plans when they experienced major drops in traffic. Currently, the subscription model is enjoying a revival as content on some sites becomes compelling enough for the Internet audience to pay for the service, and database registration and tracking programs (Chapter 5) become easier to implement. Subscription models are likely to become more popular as methods are developed to allow *micropayments* for access to content (see discussion later in this chapter).

Major entertainment-related sites including Time-Warner's Pathfinder (http://www.pathfinder) and Playboy Enterprises (http://www.playboy.com) are developing new subscription models with rates comparable to consumer expenditures on magazines. Many game sites are developing subscription models, most notably the ImagiNation Network's CyberPark (Figure 9.2)—which is moving its gaming community to the Internet after several years of operation as an independent online service. ESPNet SportsZone (http://www.sportszone.com) continues to support high subscription levels for its premium content (currently $4.95 per

FIGURE 9.1 *Red Herring Magazine*'s herring.com (http://herring.com).

month or $39.95 per year); subscriber-only areas are marked with a ticket icon. Mixing free and pay areas of the site's content on the same page keeps overall traffic high and helps to encourage uncommitted visitors to

FIGURE 9.2 ImagiNation Network's CyberPark (http://inngames.com).

subscribe. Smaller sites may benefit from subscriptions as well; niche sites and newsletters with tightly focused content are likely to be successful at charging subscriptions for their content.

Chat presents a significant and relatively unexplored area for subscription models. Since content in chat rooms is created largely by visitors, chat does not require expensive content development and may, therefore, offer revenue potential to small sites with limited development budgets. Anticipating a rise in subscription-based chat rooms, The Palace (http://www.thepalace.com) has instituted licensing fees for commercial use of its chat software. Subscription models will apply equally to virtual-reality based Web sites, which provide exploratory environments featuring both objects and individuals.

With the rise of streaming audio and video, the pay-per-view system is being investigated by companies such as MediaCast (http://www.mediacast.com). In principle, online events involving high-profile celebrities could sell virtual tickets to the Internet audience. Most of the methods being used to enable electronic currency (see later discussion) may be readily adapted for virtual ticketing. Creating the immediacy characteristic of live events is problematic for pay-per-view schemes, since the Internet will not support full-motion and full-screen video for several years. In the interim, cybertickets could be sold to online chats hosting a celebrity. Another possibility for pay-per view is to create contests that can be represented without video, such as tokens on a boardgame.

Advertising-supported Sites

If your content is interesting to your audience but does not lend itself to the subscription model, advertising may provide an alternate source of revenue. Most industry experts agree that advertising will become a major source of revenue for the Web. According to predictions made by Jupiter Communications (http://www.jupiter.com), Web advertising will rise from its 1995 levels of about $50 million to $2 to 5 billion by the year 2000. Interestingly, the same report predicts that Web ad revenues will rise higher than radio, but will still be a fraction of print and television advertising. Interest in online advertising continues to grow and Advertising Age (Figure 9.3) helped to legitimize the industry by launching its own major Web site.

FIGURE 9.3 Advertising Age (http://www.adage.com).

WebTrack's Advertiser Rankings for 1995

WebTrack's Top 10 Web Advertisers

1995 Q4 Top Web Advertisers (based on placement spending)

Rank	Advertiser	1995 Q4$
1.	AT&T	567,000
2.	Netscape	556,000
3.	Internet Shopping Network	329,000
4.	NECX Direct	322,000
5.	Mastercard	278,000
6.	American Airlines	254,000
7.	Microsoft	240,000
8.	c|net	237,000
9.	MCI	231,000
10	SportsLine	218,000

WebTrack's Top 10 Web Publishers

Q4 Top Web Publishers (based on placement revenue)

Rank	Publisher	1995 Q4$
1.	Netscape	1,766,000
2.	Lycos	1,296,000
3.	InfoSeek	1,215,000
4.	Yahoo	1,086,000
5.	Pathfinder	810,000
6.	HotWired	720,000
7.	WebCrawler	660,000
8.	ESPNET SportsZone	600,000
9.	GNN	594,000
10.	c|net	540,000

http://www.webtrack.com/research.html

FIGURE 9.4 Llist of Web Track sites with most ad revenue.

Measuring the Value of Your Site

For advertisers, the value of your site lies ultimately in the absolute number of people that visit it and look at their ad. Two methods of measurement are currently in use on Web sites. *Impressions* simply count the number of times a Web page bearing an ad has been downloaded (and presumably viewed). An increasing number of advertisers also count *click-throughs*, which measure the number of times an audience member actually selects an ad banner and visits the advertiser's site. Once you have reliable statistics on your site's traffic flow (see Chapter 8), you can

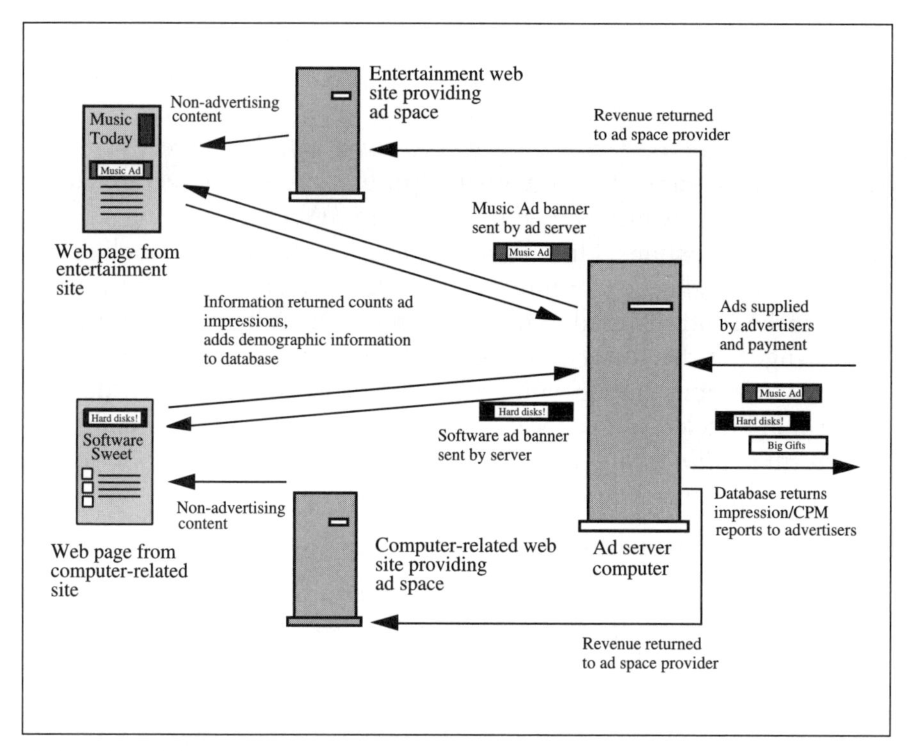

FIGURE 9.5 Diagram of how ad servers work.

compute an ad cost based on CPM, which is the cost per thousand impressions. Currently, Web sites charge anywhere between $3 and $300 per CPM, with $20 to 30 per CPM as the average. In the near future, Web-based ad pricing will likely move beyond static rate cards and be priced individually based on the product being sold, the content on the Web site taking the ad, and the response from the audience desired by the advertiser. Figure 9.4 shows Web Track's advertiser rankings for 1995.

What Advertisers Expect

In order to make your site an attractive place to put ads, you will have to meet standards which assure your advertisers are getting what they pay for. Most advertisers contract for a specific number of impressions. Examine your access (Chapter 8) and make sure you can really deliver the number of clicks the advertiser wants. Since Internet advertisers are usually sensitive to the audience's resistance to unsolicited advertising, categorize ad space on your site according to popularity, subject matter, or site-specific visitor demographics. After the ad runs, advertisers will request detailed audience breakdowns of the type of click-throughs they received on their pages.

Running and Maintaining Ads In-house

If you have invested in a large in-house network and have experience dealing directly with advertisers, you may elect to install ad rotation and tracking software (otherwise known as *ad server* software) directly on your site (see Figure 9.5). NetGravity (http://www.netgravity.com) has created AdServer, which is used by many large Web sites placing ads from multiple vendors. The software provides a graphical scheduling calendar for managing ad placement and rotation, and allows click-throughs to be tracked and reported to the advertisers. The AdServer software can also change ads the visitor sees based on page context. For example, if the visitor is searching the site with "video" as a keyword, an ad for video sales could be selected to appear along with the results of the search. This form of *affinity* targeting is in the spirit of the Internet—offering relevant information instead of unsolicited sales pitches.

Centralized Web Advertising Services

Web ad agencies offer the possibility for entertainment sites to earn money from advertising without the hassles associated with rotation programs and auditing. DoubleClick (http://www.doubleclick.net) provides a good example of these services. Web sites that join DoubleClick (membership is about $1,000) tap into its centralized ad server software rather than installing their own programs. In order to use the ad server, the site developers work with the ad agency to develop a categorization of the overall Web site carrying ads and the individual pages ads will be placed on. The Web site accomplishes this by placing a link to the ad, which is actually located on DoubleClick's Web site. Like NetGravity's software, DoubleClick allows affinity targeting of ads. When the page bearing the ad is loaded by an audience member, the ad server consults its database and delivers an ad that matches the page category.

For sites without sufficient traffic to attract large revenues, it may not make sense to pay the relatively high membership fees charged by high-profile ad agencies. Recently, various organizations have appeared that broker combined ad space from a large number of independent Web sites. One example of such a service is provided by the online game site Riddler through its Commonwealth Network (http://www.commonwealth.riddler.com). To sign up, content providers register with Riddler and install links to banner ads delivered from its ad server. Membership in the network is free. Currently, Riddler pays Web sites that join its network $7.50 per CPM and has already signed up nearly 1,000 smaller Web sites. A similar service was recently announced by DMN Media (http://www.dmn.com/media), which is specifically pooling ad space for music-related Web sites. DMN (which also hosts the Cabash music-specific search engine) also has free signup for its network and allows its members to keep approximately $14 per CPM. Since virtually any Web site can set up a similar network by purchasing ad server software, independent ad networks are likely to become common on the Web.

Content providers who are considering using online ads as a major revenue source should be aware that the future of Web-based advertising is far from certain. With the introduction of PrivNet's ad filtering software (http://www.privnet.com), it has become possible for site visitors to selectively block ads from appearing onscreen. While some online advertising services have dismissed this effort as a "prank" or temporary irritation, the fact remains that any of the dozens of services designed to filter adult content (such as SurfWatch at http://www.surfwatch.com) could easily be adapted to block advertising. All that is necessary is for surfers to decide that ads are "indecent" or "obscene!"

> ***[Ad-blocking software] will force Internet advertising to be less intrusive and in-your-face. The current model seems to be evolving towards "Let's make it bright and flashy and moving so they'll click on it." Cookie blocking is much easier than banner blocking.***
>
> —James Howard, President, PrivNet
> http://www.privnet.com

Direct Sales Sites

While much current attention in the entertainment industry has been focused on ad-sponsored Web sites, the expected growth of sales revenue is even more astounding. According to the *Trends in the WWW Marketplace* by ActivMedia (http://www.activmedia.com), Web-based sales are expected to rise from $436 million in 1995 to nearly $46 billion by 1998. A significant proportion of total sales are predicted to be from entertainment-related consumer product categories. An older but still valuable resource for the status of electronic transactions can be found at Sun Microsystem's SunWorld Online (http://www.sun.com/sunworldonline/swol-09-1995/swol-09-webbiz.html). The following are some of the methods and resources needed to sell online.

Product Sales and Commissions

If your site provides a service, such as enabling an online auction or selling third-party products, it can collect a commission or flat rate for having the product online. Kaleidospace began the era of independent arts and entertainer product sales in early 1994, and has since been

FIGURE 9.6 Music Boulevard (http://www.musicblvd.com).

followed by many other independent sites. Other independent sites have specialized in retail to the extent of becoming online stores. Music is a particularly common specialization of online entertainment stores, including CD Now (http://www.cdnow.com), CD Universe (http://www.cduniverse.com), and Music Boulevard (Figure 9.6). Online music stores have a significant advantage over their physical counterparts, since visitors may easily search through comprehensive catalogues with hundreds of thousands of selections. Following the lead of the independent retail outlets, established chains such as Tower Records (http://www.towerrecords.com) have recently come online and large media groups such as MGM/UA (http://www.mgmua.com) and Pathfinder (http://www.pathfinder.com) have begun selling magazine subscriptions and promotional products through the Web.

Selling Space on Your Site

Popular independent entertainment sites may also incur revenue by selling space, design and programming services to other entertainment content providers who sell products and services on the site. Examples of this arrangement may also be found in Kaleidospace, as well as many other virtual art galleries and music sites on the Web. On Kaleidospace, artists pay flat setup fees to have their areas created. After their material is online, artists can choose from one of two options. In the first case there are no monthly fees, but the site receives a commission on sales the artist makes through the Web. The second plan does not include a commission, but requires a flat monthly rental.

 Financial Transactions on the Web

All of the previous sales models are vastly enhanced if the Web administrators can take payment for entertainment products and content online. Surprisingly, an informal study conducted by WebWeek (http://www.webweek.com) in June 1996 indicated that only a minority of commercial sites are accepting transactions using advanced, secure Internet technologies. Only one-third of merchants are accepting orders securely, with the rest relying on credit card numbers sent through insecure email, phone, fax, or *snail mail*. The following sections describe programs used to collect payment information and various electronic cash systems which allow fulfillment.

Order Forms and Virtual Shopping Carts

If you plan to sell a small number of products or services through your site, orders can be handled through a simple fill-out form. When ordering, the audience member fills out contact and credit card information (if the site allows secure transactions) and the items desired. Sites with multiple products are increasingly enhancing basic order forms with a virtual *shopping cart*. On these sites, the visitor's selections are tracked behind the scenes and entered into a file. The visitor has the option of examining the contents of the shopping cart, adding or deleting items, and ordering them at any time. Many ISP/IPPs now offer shopping cart programs as an enhancement to their basic services, and commercial programs have been provided by companies like Netlink (http://www.netlink.net/cybernet/cybernet.htm) and Webpage Wizard (http://www.wpwizard.com).

Secure Credit Card Transactions

Despite media sensationalism, the Internet is a relatively safe place to conduct transactions—certainly safer than giving credit cards to strangers over the phone or at restaurants! Several vendors provide Web servers supporting secure transactions delivered from order forms or shopping carts. Operating systems supported included Windows NT and UNIX systems by Netscape (http://www.netscape.com) and O'Reilly (http://software.ora.com), Windows NT by Microsoft (http://www.microsoft.com), and Macintosh by Quarterdeck's Webstar (http://www.starnine.com).

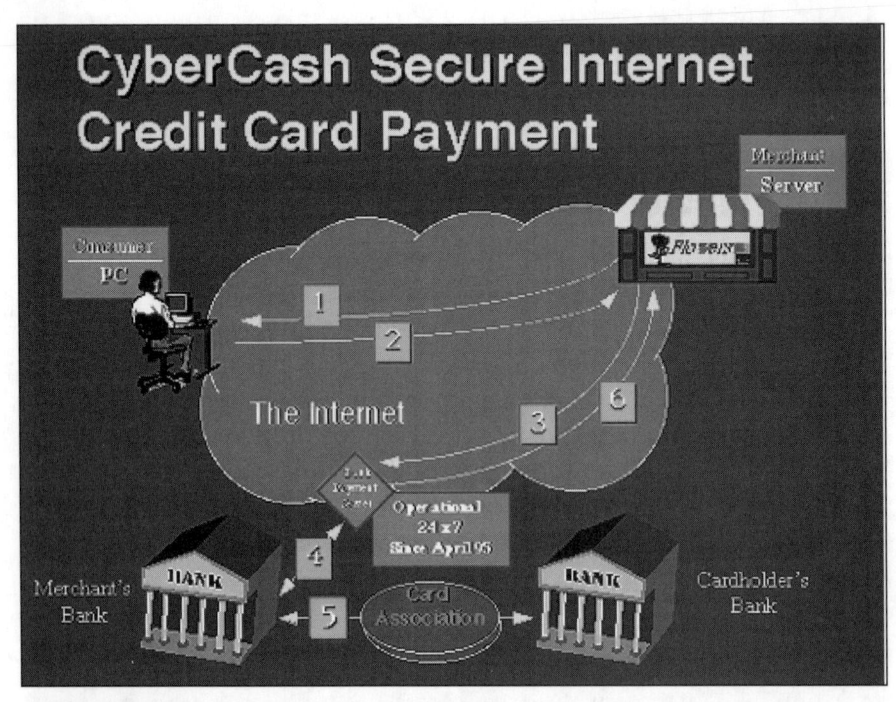

FIGURE 9.7 Diagram of micropayment system (provided by CyberCash at http://www.cybercash.com).

All these servers use a variation of *key escrow* encryption systems developed by RSA Data Security, Inc. (http://www.rsa.com). In order for the key system to work for secure transactions, two files are created: *public key* (widely available and installed in products such as Web browsers) and *private key* (held by the Web server and never distributed). To initiate a secure transaction, the Web browser sends a public key to the Web server, which then uses its private key to decode the message. As long as the private key is truly private, key encryption schemes can lead to virtually unbreakable security (see the discussion at http://www.netscape.com/newsref/ref/rsa.html).

Once installed, secure servers run without attendance, but the site administrator must periodically collect credit card numbers and clear old ones. To use these secure systems, you must also establish a merchant account—which is frequently difficult for new startups to obtain. To meet the needs of Web-based businesses, many companies including www.charge.com (http://www.charge.com) provide brokering services for small businesses trying to get merchant accounts. Check the Yahoo! Financial Services area for more information.

While secure browsers and servers provide an effective means of delivering payment between a customer and a Web site, they lack many

FIGURE 9.8 CyberCash (http://www.cybercash.com).

other features supporting micropayments, vouchers, smart cards, and virtual coupons—as well as business transactions including credit card authentication and banking services. Due to this, merchants are put in the unpleasant position of having to store sensitive credit card information for later forwarding. Ideally, this information could be transmitted directly to the bank or credit card company, without the merchant having to read the customer's credit information, as shown in Figure 9.7.

To support these services, a new protocol called Secure Electronic Transactions (SET) has been established jointly by Visa (http://www.visa.com) and MasterCard (http://www.mastercard.com). This agreement resolves an earlier conflict between competing protocols (Microsoft/Visa's STT and Netscape/MasterCard's SSL) for secure transactions. Companies including Netscape (http://www.netscape.com), Checkfree Corp. (http://www.checkfree.com), First Virtual Holdings, Inc. (http://www.fv.com), CyberCash (Figure 9.8), and VeriFone (Figure 9.9)—which creates in-store systems linking retailers with banks and credit card companies—will be using the new procedures to support virtual "wallets" which can store cybercash "cards" from different companies.

One of the advantages of "real" money is that it is anonymous; anyone can use the same dollar bill to make a purchase. By contrast, most of the secure protocols allow precise tracking of the customer making the transaction. Many privacy advocates, are concerned that banks and credit

FIGURE 9.9 VeriFone (http://www.verifone.com).

card companies will use electronic transactions to gather confidential information about individuals. To address this problem, several proposals have been made to create an anonymous form of electronic cash. This type of system, such as that offered by the Netherlands' DigiCash NV (http://www.digicash.com), leaves no audit trail and ensures anonymous, untraceable transactions. The Mark Twain Bank of St. Louis (http://www.marktwain.com) is using the DigiCash e-cash system to let individuals and merchants exchange U.S. dollars electronically.

Micropayments

The ideal pay-per-view system on the Internet would be able to charge very small amounts of money for transactions. This *micropayment* model, a variation of the subscription, distinguishes itself by the extremely small (fractions of a cent) charges necessary to support charging for digital information. Micropayments (sometimes also referred to as pay-per-piece) have the potential to be quite popular with consumers because of the low charges (a few cents per transaction). Most electronic money systems have micropayment schemes, such as Carnegie-Mellon's NetBill (http://www.ini.cmu.edu) and CyberCash's CyberCoin (http://www.cybercash.com). A wide variety of Web sites are considering microspayments, including Discovery Online (http://www.discovery.com), and Playboy (http://www.playboy.com). Rocket Science Games (http://www.rocketsci.com) will be creating virtual arcades using CyberCoin microspayments, which allow quarter-sized charges to be collected.

With their similarity to royalties, micropayments may be the future of Web-based entertainment, if schemes capable of securely processing large numbers of tiny transactions can be implemented. For example, a major media site receiving several million hits a day would have to process a comparable number of micropayments—probably using protocols from several vendors. To centralize micropayments, companies like Clickshare Corp. (http://www.clickshare.com) have developed a centralized system to handle micropayments across large numbers of Web sites. The advantage of the system is that the consumer receives a single bill for what might be thousands of individual tiny transactions with dozens of merchants. In order to work, Clickshare will have to get the cooperation of Internet access providers, since they do the actual collection of funds.

Phone-based Transactions

An alternative approach used in conjunction with a secure ordering system provides a toll-free number that customers can call to leave their credit card number. This method is particularly suited for companies selling physical products like CDs and videos. Even when a secure system is installed, many customers will prefer to use the phone. Due to the expense of the calls—especially if the site receives a significant number of international sales—sites will need to charge a processing fee that covers the calls. If your site does not have a physical product, you may still charge for access to content through systems like 900 Numbers Unlimited (http://www.best.com/~surfinet), which provides a set of 800 and 900 numbers that customers may call to receive access to restricted areas of a Web site. Each time a customer calls, the phone company bills the customer and passes a portion of the payment back to the Web operator.

Now that we've discussed the revenue models available on the Web, you should be able to maintain and expand your Intertainment business. By doing so, you have joined a rapidly growing group of entertainment Web sites. The next chapter examines the state of entertainment on the Web, including traditional entertainment, new forms of entertainment, and entertainment augmenting a site's products or services.

PART IV

THE MANY FORMS OF INTERTAINMENT

http://kspace.com/intertainment

CHAPTER 10

TRADITIONAL ENTERTAINMENT: Music, Broadcasting, Film, Publishing, Visual Art and Performance

An anonymous party guest exclaimed, "Why would anyone need the Internet? We have public television."

Despite the exotic nature of the medium, the Internet is proving to be a natural extension of traditional entertainment. With a potential audience growing at a rate of several thousand people every day, it seems that everyone in the traditional arts and entertainment industry is converting their content for cyberspace. Radio stations list their Web sites as often as their call letters, artists schedule major exhibitions for a worldwide cyberspace audience, and no newspaper movie ad is complete without a Web address. Throughout the traditional industry, content created for other media is being repurposed for the Web—from simple promotions to true extensions of the existing entertainment product. This phenomenon affects all levels: Large companies are rediscovering their audience, while smaller independents and individual entertainers find that they can truly compete in the promotion and distribution arenas. Company-specific Web sites allow consumers to gain more awareness of the company's relationship to its product, enabling traditional entertainment corporations to enhance their image and establish distinctive branding. The movement of traditional entertainment to the Web is no longer seen as a fad or marketing trick, but as an essential strategy of the new interactive age.

This chapter covers several areas of the traditional arts and entertainment industry that are being represented on the Web, including music, broadcasting, film, publishing, performance, and visual art. Each of these industries is discussed with regard to its current state, potential challenges, and future direction with regard to Intertainment.

Music

It's no secret that music is one of the driving forces behind Intertainment. Music has defined the cutting-edge of the Web ever since the first music sites went online in early 1994—only months after the release of the Mosaic Web browser brought multimedia to the Internet. It is possible that the abstract nature of music itself—as well as the professional music community's familiarity with synthesizers, MIDI, and other digital systems—has made it easier for the music industry to embrace the Web. After a year of incredible growth, mid-1995 found virtually every major record label represented on the Web—alongside the tens of thousands of independents who had already established their own sites.

Technology

With the introduction of real-time sound delivery by Progressive Networks' RealAudio (http://www.realaudio.com), the Web is rapidly taking on the characteristics of a play-on-demand jukebox operating without the *playlist* constraints of broadcast media. Real-time audio requires an expansion of the current Web server model (see Chapter 5) to include a second audio server. MIDI support from software such as LiveUpdate's Crescendo (http://www.liveupdate.com/midi.html) is becoming a hot trend, particularly when used to provide quickly downloaded music as ambient background on Web sites. Until the video equivalent of RealAudio software is available, music videos will still be limited to relatively short (10-30 second) QuickTime clips.

Major Labels

Since mid-1994, major and mid-sized labels have used the Web to provide extensive promotional material for their artists, including audio and video clips, interviews, reviews, concert and tour scheduling, fan-based

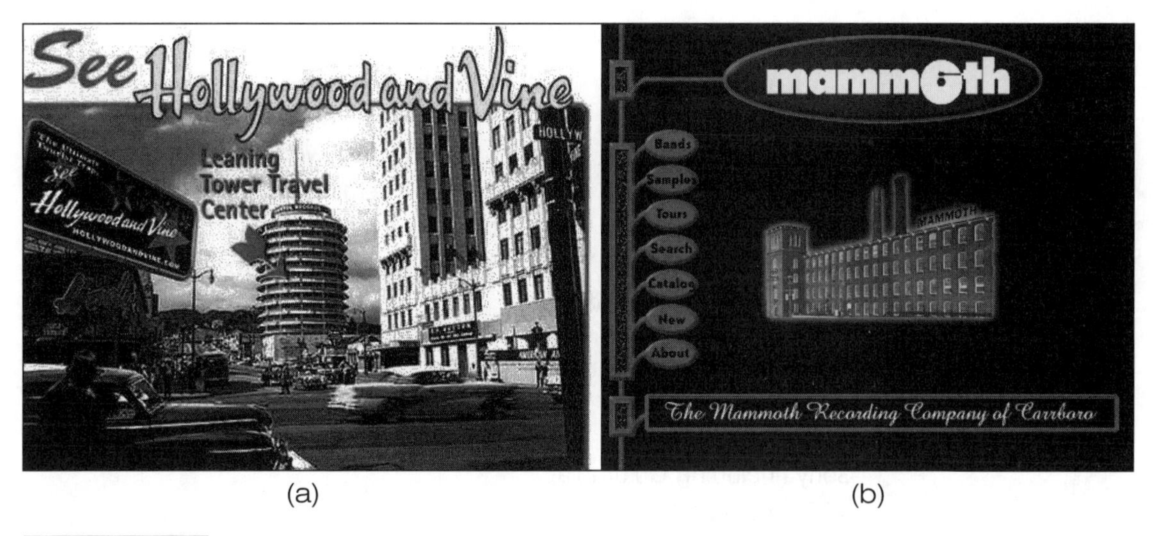

(a) (b)

FIGURE 10.1 (a) Capitol Records (http://www.hollywoodandvine.com); (b) Mammoth Records (http://www.mammoth.com).

mailing lists, and even live online chat. Some major labels, such as Polygram (http://www.polygram.com), have also launched online music magazines. Music sites are extremely popular with the Internet audience and most majors provide cutting-edge interfaces with advanced multimedia, as shown in Figure 10.1a. Since major labels already have extensive distribution, their Web sites are geared more toward promotion than online sales. Table 10.1 presents selected major labels on the Web.

Independent Labels

Independent labels follow the pattern of providing extensive promotional material for each artist. Since independents frequently have less extensive distribution, they have been more active in selling their products online. Figure 10.1b shows an independent record label. By combining their Web sites with effective netpublicity (see Chapter 7), many have been able to increase audience awareness—particularly for artists who seldom get radio play. Directories of independent labels can be found at Yahoo!, Kathode Ray Music (http://kathoderay.org/music) and The Partial List of Independent Music Labels (http://www.freenet.hamilton.on.ca/~ac991/indie.html). While larger independents such as american recordings (http://american.recordings.com) may run their own in-house networks, smaller labels typically create sites using basic ISP/IPP accounts (see Chapter 5). Since most labels are creating *label-oriented* sites, Internet promotion in particular has increased label identity for

TABLE 10.1 Selected Major Labels on the Web

Label	Web Address
Arista Records	http;//www.aristarec.com
Capitol Records	http://www.hollywoodandvine.com
EMI	http://www.emirec.com
Geffen Records	http://www.geffen.com
MCA International	http://www.mcamei.com
PolyGram (including A&M, Axiom, Hollywood, London, Mercury, Motown, Island, and Polydor)	http://www.polygram.com
RCA Victor	http://www.rcavictor.com
Sony (including Columbia, Epic, Legacy, and Sony Classical)	http://www.sony.com
Virgin Records	http://www.vmg.co.uk
Warner Bros. (including Warner Bros. Records, Elektra, Atlantic, and Reprise)	http://www.music.warnerbros.com

even the largest labels. Interestingly, the labels have concentrated on this as opposed to creating sites for specific album releases—in contrast to film studios, who have made it a practice to create sites devoted to film releases. Table 10.2 shows some selected independent labels on the Web.

Independent Musicians and Directories

Probably the greatest beneficiaries of the Web are the huge numbers of unsigned musicians and bands who have the ability to create an album but have limited distribution channels. The low entry costs for basic sites (see Chapter 5) have allowed tens of thousands of independents to promote, distribute, and showcase their work to consumers and industry professionals. Musicians on independent labels frequently create their own independent sites, augmenting the promotion provided by their label's Web site. In many cases, fan sites created for the musicians also contribute to their Web presence. However, the success of music on the Web has created its own problem: Individual artists and albums may be difficult to find among the thousands of sites listed in major directories. Fortunately, searchable music databases can be used to locate independents. Some, like the the Web Wide World of Music (http://american.

TABLE 10.2 Selected Independent Labels on the Web

Label	Web Address
american recordings	http://american.recordings.com
Chartmaker Records	http://kspace.com/chartmaker
DBK Records	http://kspace.com/dbk
Dominion Records	http://www.dominionrecords.com
4AD	http://www.4ad.com
Griffin Music	http://www.GriffinMusic.com
Hearts of Space	http://www.hos.com
Higher Octave	http://www.higheroctave.com
Mammoth Records	http://www.mammoth.com
Moonridge Records	http://kspace.com/moonridge
Nettwerk	http://www.nettwerk.com
Radioactive Records	http://www.radioactive.net
Rhino Records	http://pathfinder.com/rhino
Sin-Drome Records	http://kspace.com/sindrome
TVT	http://tvtrecords.com
Windham Hill	http://www.windham.com

recordings.com/wwwofmusic/index.html), are designed for the general audience, while others, such as Dr. Sounds Audio Prescriptions (http://www.drsounds.com), are designed specifically for use by industry professionals. Selected music directories are listed in Table 10.3.

> ***I think the Internet is challenging the "good old boy" networks of this industry. Independents can carry more weight now and we are more accessible than ever.***
>
> —PAT SHELBY, CONTEMPORARY CHRISTIAN MUSICIAN
> http://kspace.com/shelby

Meta-sites

Due to the difficulty of attracting sufficient traffic to individual music sites, many musicians establish their Internet presence on meta-sites that host moderate numbers of independent musicians and sometimes small labels. These sites are numerous and well-established; pioneering sites such as the Music Kiosk section of Kaleidospace (http://kspace.com) and the Internet Underground Music Archive or IUMA (http://www.iuma.com) formed the first wave of Web music during 1994. Besides increased traffic, meta-sites offer lower page development costs, access to shared

TABLE 10.3 Selected Music Directories on the Web

Directory	Web Address
The Casbah	http://casbah.dmn.com
Dr. Sounds Audio Prescriptions	http://www.drsounds.com
GEMM Music Search Machine	http://gemm.com
Harmony Music List	http://orpheus.ucsd.edu/harmony
Mammoth Music Meta-List	http://www.pathfinder.com/vibe/mmm/music.html
Music Search	http://www.musicsearch.com
Web Wide World of Music	http://american.recordings.com/wwwofmusic/index.html

services like secure order forms (Chapter 9), chat rooms, and promotion with other artists. Table 10.4 lists some independent music meta-sites.

Music Stores

Online music retail outlets take advantage of the unlimited "shelf space" in cyberspace to provide low-overhead sales of CDs and other musical products. Unlike label sites and meta-sites, they are not designed for casual exploration of promotional material. Instead, most sites are characterized by enormous (>100,000) selections searchable by keywords. All of these sites provide for secure online ordering of products. Examples include CD Now! (http://www.cdnow.com), CD Universe (http://www.cduniverse.com), Music Boulevard (http://www.musicblvd.com), and

TABLE 10.4 Selected Independent Music Meta-sites on the Web

Meta-site	Web Address
Artist Access	http://www.artistaccess.com
Artist Underground	http://www.aumusic.com
Euphoria World-Wide Records	http://euphoria.org/home
Eyeneer Music Archives	http://www.eyeneer.com/index.html
Gignet	http://www.gignet.com
Internet Underground Music Archive [IUMA]	http://www.iuma.com
Kaleidospace Music Kiosk	http://kspace.com
Sonicnet	http://www.sonicnet.com

TABLE 10.5 Selected Music Venues on the Web

Venue	Web Address
Genghis Cohen Cantina (Los Angeles)	http://i-site.com/~cantina/genghis.html
House of Blues (Los Angeles)	http://www.hob.com
moe's (Seattle, WA)	http://www.imusic./com/live/index.htm
Paradox (Baltimore, MD)	http://ubmail.ubalt.edu/~rmills/pdox0.html
Squeeze Box (New York)	http://www.squeezeme.com
Troubadour (Los Angeles)	http://www.troubadour.com
Yoshi's Nitespot (Oakland, CA)	http://www.yoshis.com

Molly Malone's (http://www.cd4less.com). Sites listed by the Harmony Equipment List (http://orpheus.ucsd.edu/harmony/instr/index.html) sell musical instruments and other equipment. Real-world retail stores such as Tower Records (http://www.towerrecords.com) are just starting to sell online and may experience significant competition from the startups which are already online.

Venues

Just like the general industry, music venues have been quick to appreciate the value of the Internet, as shown in Figure 10.2. Hundreds of music clubs run Web sites announcing calendars of upcoming events; it is only a matter of time before they begin selling tickets online (or through Ticketmaster [http://www.ticketmaster.com], which is currently not using its site to sell tickets but may do so in the future). A searchable database of live music listings is maintained at the Worldwide Internet Live Music Archive (WILMA) (http://www.wilma.com) and the San Francisco Live Music List (http://www.netcom.com/~skipmc/sfclubs.html). Some music venues have installed high-speed links to the Internet directly from the club, enabling two-way communication with the Internet audience. Table 10.5 lists selected music venues on the Web.

Music Publications

Many large media sites such as Pathfinder (http://www.pathfinder.com) run music sections with contents resembling those in news rack entertainment magazines. With so many musicians online, an audience for general magazines like Vibe Magazine Online (http://www.timeinc.com/vibe/VibeOnline!.html) and independent music magazines like Jim

FIGURE 10.2 Squeeze Me (http://www.squeezeme.com).

Santo's Demo Universe (http://www.popes.com:80/demou) and Aiding and Abetting (http://ns.cent.com/abetting) is rapidly forming. BAM Media's Music Universe (http://www.musicuniverse.com) contains the online version of *BAM*, as well as *The Rocket* (a Northwest music publication) and an area where site visitors may review new music submitted by independents. Table 10.6 lists some music publications on the Web.

Concerts and Festivals

A good archive for music festivals may be found at appropriate subdirectories in Yahoo! and in the Harmony Music Event List (http://orpheus.ucsd.edu/harmony/events/index.html). A searchable event list is maintained at Musi-Cal (http://concerts.calendar.com), which also allows concert postings. Live performance organizations such as the New Music Scene (http://www.nms.org and http://kspace.com/nms) actively promote their ongoing shows through the Web. Major music festivals such as Lollapalooza (http://www.lollapalooza.com), H.O.R.D.E. (http://www.polygram.com/horde), Milwaukee's SummerFest (Figure 10.3), and the New Orleans Jazz Festival (http://nojazzfest.com) also have developed Web sites that provide performance schedules and sneak previews of the shows. General concert tour schedules for major artists are available online from Pollstar (http://www.pollstar.com), along with information for ordering their contact directories, tour histories, and CD-ROM-based information. Many "ghost town" Web sites promote events that actually occurred years ago; they now function as inadvertent archives!

> ***As a result of an Internet inquiry, our label (MultiMusica USA) consummated an international distribution agreement with a label in Japan for Gary Tanin's Sublime Nation CD. . . . As a result of some of our internet promotion our CD, Sublime Nation, received a 3-star review in a nationally syndicated newspaper. . . via the Internet.***
>
> —GARY TANIN, ALTERNATIVE POP MUSICIAN
> http://kspace.com/sublime

TABLE 10.6 Selected Music Publications on the Web

Publication	Web Address
Addicted to Noise	http://www.addict.com/ATN
Aiding and Abetting	http://ns.cent.com/abetting
BAM Music Universe	http://www.musicuniverse.com
Billboard	http://www.billboard-online.com
Cash Box	http://online.music-city.com/cashbox.html
Contemporary Christian Music	http://www.ccmcom.com
Dirty Linen (folk)	http://kiwi.futuris.net/linen
Guitar World	http://www.guitarworld.com
HardCORE (rap)	gopher://fir.cic.net/11/Zines/HardCORE
Keyboard	http://www.keyboardmag.com
Modern Drummer	http://www.moderndrummer.com
Jim Santo's Demo Universe	http://www.popes.com:80/demou
Streetsound Music Arcade	http://streetsound.com/zone
Vibe Magazine Online	http://www.timeinc.com/vibe/VibeOnline!.html
World Party Music	http://WPMusic.com

FIGURE 10.3 SummerFest (http://www.summerfest.com).

A&R and Placement

With the appearance of A&R and other industry reps, musicians are increasingly using their Web sites as globally accessible "demo tapes," saving the time and expense of mass mailings—and often going around the "no unsolicited material accepted" rule. Online placement services that review music and shop record deals include Taxi (Figure 10.4); and Main Street Management (http://www.multi-medias.ca/Mainst/index.html). *Crisp Magazine*'s Cyberstudio (http://www.crispzine.com) bills itself as a connecting point between the industry and independent musicians, artists, and designers, and features commentary by A&R executives as well as stories on how independents are promoting themselves in the industry. Other placement services include booking agents like Concerted Efforts (world music, zydeco, blues, folk, ethnic, jazz, soul, rock, gospel, comedy ; http://members.gnn.com/concerted/home.htm) and Mars Talent Agency (50s and 60s acts; http://users.aol.com/marstalent/private/mars.htm).

FIGURE 10.4 TAXI (http://www.taxi.com).

> ***I'm currently negotiating a prospective record deal as a result of a solicitation made on a newsgroup on the Net.***
>
> —Bernard Yin of the salt-water damaged alternative rock band Brazil 2001
> http://kspace.com/brazil

Professional Organizations and Services

As thousands of musicians jumped onto the Internet literally overnight, professional organizations were hard-pressed to follow. The National Academy of Recording Arts and Sciences or NARAS (http://grammy.com)

contains historical information and the official Grammy site, and the National Academy of Songwriters (http://kspace.com/nas and http://i-site.com/~nas/nashome.html) contains an online version of the *Songwriters Musepaper*, as well as the ability to join the organization and its online mailing list. Music publishers such as EMI Music Publishing (http://emimusicpub.com) have also created sites promoting their publishing and licensing services for soundtracks, commercials, plays, and multimedia. Major performance rights organizations such as BMI (http://www.bmi.com) and ASCAP (http://www.ascap.com) are also available. Finally, several music libraries are online—including Scoring Services (http://www.scoring.com) and Impact Music Library (http://www.studioland.com). In the future, these services may be able to distribute music via micropayment systems directly over the Web.

Future Trends

The music industry's use of the Internet is changing rapidly as new technologies appear and musicians become more aware of its potential. While not exhaustive, the following are some trends to watch for during the next year.

Music as Part of the Web Experience

During the short history of music Intertainment, audio has been provided as a direct promotion to sell a musical product. Since music is becoming more integrated into the overall Web experience, many sites now run background or ambient music for mood enhancement. As this practice becomes more common, it will lead to new forms of electronic licensing, royalty systems, and increased online revenue.

Complete Music and Performance Videos

Most Web video clips are limited to small (160 x 120 pixel) sizes and 20 to 30 seconds of playing time. Recently, NAMS 2000 (http://www.mw3.com/nams) released a custom player for full-length, highly compressed videos in their proprietary VAOD format. Playing back at 320 x 240 resolution, the videos average five megabytes for five minutes of playing time. As systems like this become widespread, providing full-length performance and music videos will become a reality. (The requirements for delivering video through the Internet are discussed more fully in the broadcast section that follows.)

Online Ticket Sales

The same distribution model used to sell music products online may be used to sell tickets to concerts and tours. Kaleidospace and other independent sites already provide this as a service to independent musicians—but as micropayments become common in 1997, it is likely to become more widespread.

Cyberconcerts and Musical Events

With the introduction of real-time audio and virtual reality (see Chapter 12) systems, the stage is literally set for running live concerts on the Internet. Concert development is already underway by groups such as Mediacast (http://www.mediacast.com). Cyberconcerts will include live audio and a visual counterpart—consisting of live video from the concert and/or a virtual reality environment in which the concert "mirrors" itself in cyberspace.

Online Auditions and Collaborative Music

As the music community increasingly uses the Internet as its preferred communication medium, expect musical collaborations where a series of artists build on basic musical tracks. Also, look for online jam sessions between remote musicians using MIDI systems, though these may suffer from "lag time" between the two locations. Finally, musicians will make use of search engines to scout out other musicians.

Direct Distribution of Musical Product

The virtual radio stations discussed in the broadcasting section that follows can only deliver sound at the fraction of the quality of audio CDs. Currently, complete high fidelity downloads of entire songs or albums take too long to be a practical distribution mechanism for music. As the speed of the Internet increases with new technology (see Chapter 15) and micropayment systems become more widespread, pay-per-download models will become possible. Retail outlets need to become Internet-aware so that they can compete in this arena.

Broadcast: Radio, Television, and Cable

The broadcast industry is based upon the delivery of a high-bandwidth, continuous, non-interactive linear narrative—and, as such, it is fundamentally dissimilar from the interactive, low-bandwidth world of the Web. Music has adapted well to the Internet because it is a non-linear, abstract medium, which is still effective if provided as a set of low-resolution clips. However, broadcasting is more conducive to a literal repurposing of content; this is currently practical on the Internet for radio (audio), but not television and cable (video). As real-time technologies have advanced and the public has begun to compare the Web to radio and television, the industry has become increasingly interested in using the Internet for distribution of its current entertainment.

Technology

RealAudio and similar systems have enabled the delivery of audio-only programming, which has encouraged radio stations to begin delivering their standard programming online. However, sending video to a significant number of the Internet audience has been very difficult. During 1994 to 1995, the difficulty of squeezing *any* moving images through a phone line seemed an insurmountable problem. Proprietary player software systems such as NetTOOB (http://www.nettoob.com) use variations of *MPEG (Motion Picture Expert Group)* for video compression; other technologies such as *wavelet compression* developed at the Houston Center for Advanced Technology (http://www.harc.edu) create data which *streams* out in real-time over low-speed Internet connections. With developments by VDONet Corp. (http://www.vdo.net) and Xing (http://www.xingtech.com), the best of these technologies can deliver a small color image running at a few frames per second through a 28.8 modem line (provided the visitor has high-end computer equipment in the Pentium/PowerPC class). Even with these improvements, Internet video delivery suffers from severe constraints on audience size. Computers that handle tens of thousands of daily visitors to their Web sites are overloaded by more than 100 broadcast users. The problem is so great that considerable research is going into *multicast* technologies which split the broadcast signal among a large number of *reflector* computers to increase the audience capacity. VDONet recently began working with NBC and PBS to develop a multicast system; the group is establishing technology centers in New York and Palo Alto. Whatever the outcome, Internet broadcasts will be limited to audiences of a few thousand for several years to come.

> ***Once you've got digital video telephone, and this could mean CU-See Me or whatever on the Internet, then video on demand and music on demand are there. . . . You could say, 'I want to hear Louie Louie on the radio all day long' and then check it out and find some radio station in Seattle that plays nothing but Louie Louie and dial them up. You could get whatever you want, and the whole circuit of stations and licenses and radio broadcasting is going to have to be completely rethought because its usefulness will be completely different.***
>
> —Jim Pickrell, Owner, Leonardo Internet
> http://www.leonardo.net

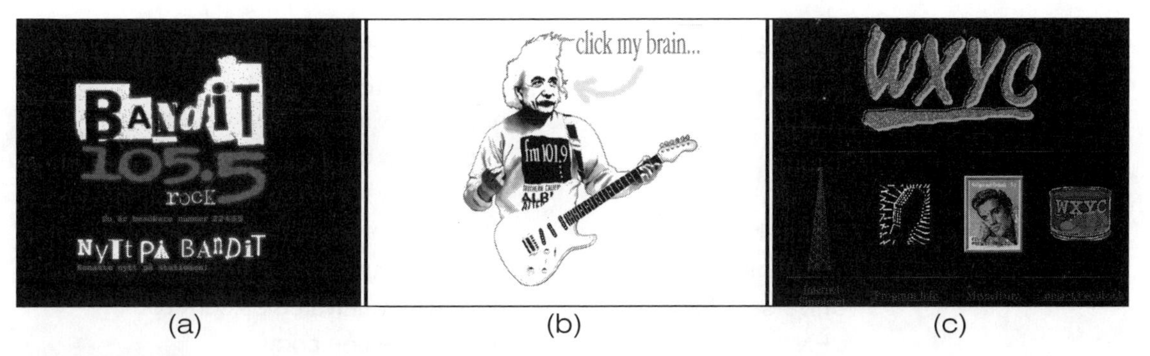

FIGURE 10.5 (a) Bandit 105.5 from Sweden (http://www.bandit.se); (b) KSCA from Los Angeles, CA (http://www.ksca.com); (c) WXYC from Chapel Hill, NC (http://sunsite.unc.edu/wxyc).

Virtual Radio Stations

Imitation is the sincerest form of flattery; nowhere is this more evident than in the meteoric rise of radio stations delivering their broadcasts over the Internet. To acquire a global audience, a radio station merely needs to convert its current feed to RealAudio format. Radio excerpts may be provided for play-on-demand or live feeds may be delivered virtually unchanged onto the Internet. While hardware requirements are fairly high (fast workstations with T1 access or greater as described in Chapter 5), free software such as Cyber 1 (http://www.cis.ufl.edu/~jselbie/cr1.html) and commercial products such as Terraflex (http://www.thedj.com) provide complete "virtual DJ" packages needed to get radio stations online. Public radio networks such as National Public Radio (http://www.npr.org) have Web sites; the latter created a site early in the Web's history that now provides extensive real-time audio online. A good list of commercial, college and independent radio stations on the Web is maintained by Stanford's KZSU (http://kzsu.stanford.edu/other-radio.html). One remarkable feature of virtual radio is that every station is international; for example, consider that the Swedish station Bandit 105.5 (http://www.bandit.se) may be heard anywhere in the world 24 hours a day. See Figure 10.5 for examples of virtual radio. The transmission of traditional broadcast radio signals through the Internet raises major questions of intellectual property and advertising that need to be addressed in the near future.

Existing radio stations are joined by a large number of Internet-specific audio broadcasters such as Virtual Radio (http://www.microserve.net/vradio) and Audionet (http://www.audionet.com). Visitors to the

TABLE 10.7 Selected Television Networks on the Web

Network	Web Address
ABC	http://www.abc.com
CBS	http://www.cbs.com
NBC	http://www.nbc.com
Fox Network	http://foxnetwork.com
PBS Online	http://www.pbs.org
Universal Channel	http://www.univstudios.com/tv
UPN	http://www.upn.com
WB	http://tv.warnerbros.com
WGN	http://www.wgntv.com

Internet Jukebox (http://interjuke.com) may hear transistor-radio quality downloads of entire albums using RealAudio software. Some additional sites of interest include the Airwaves Radio Journal (http://www.airwaves.com), Classical Music Stations on the Web (http://www.cybercom.net/~umar/classic.html), Religious Broadcasters Online (http://www.nrb.com/nrb), Pacifica (http://www.pacifica.org), and Talk America (http://www.talkamerica.com).

FIGURE 10.6 ABC television (http://www.abc.com).

FIGURE 10.7 *The Rosie O'Donnell Show* (http://rosieo.com).

Network and Independent Television

Both network and independent television channels have established Web sites that provide program listings, descriptions, and promotions, as exemplified in Figure 10.6. U.S. and international network directories are available at sites such as TV Net (http://www.tvnet.com), United Artists Programming (http://www.uaep.co.uk/pages/tvpages.html), and WebO-Vision (http://www.webovision.com). Individual broadcast show sites are listed in TV Net's Ultimate TV List (http://tvnet.com/UTVL) and the New York Times TV Host Online (http://nytimes.com/etv). In addition to established networks, Web-only broadcasting services such as InterneTV (http://www.internetv.com) and Netcast (http://www.ncc.net) are in various stages of development. Table 10.7 lists selected television networks on the Web.

Networks typically provide individual Web pages for their shows within the networks' larger Web sites. While some have created Web sites for individual shows, such as *The Rosie O'Donnell Show* (Figure 10.7), the broadcast industry—like the music industry—has generally not followed the film industry's lead in creating an online experience associated with a specific show. The most likely reason for this is that, although a film contains a storytelling element (as does the linear narrative of a

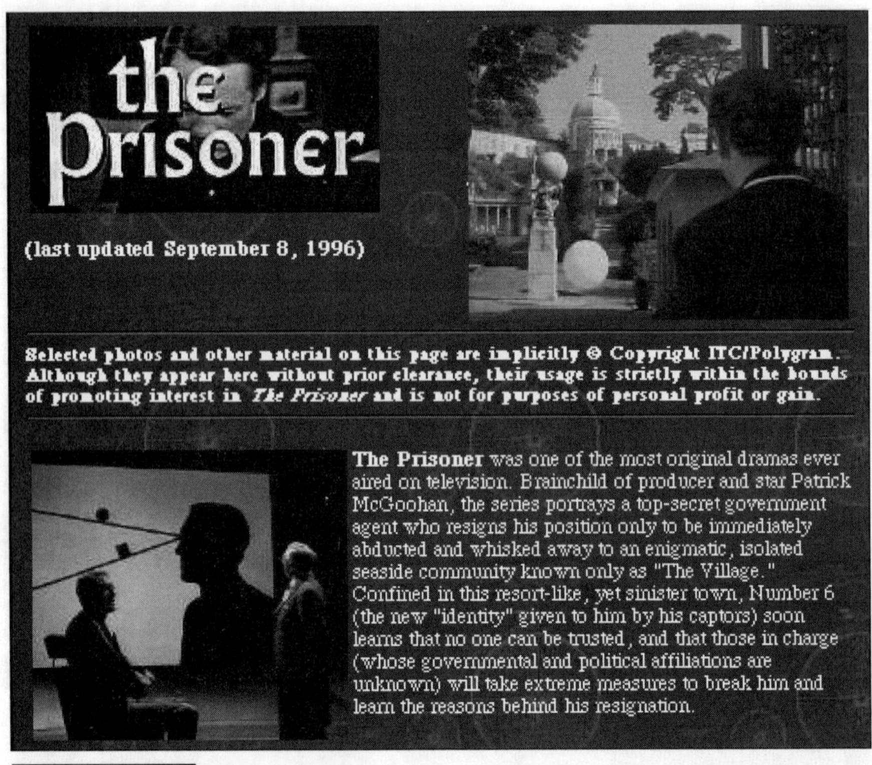

the prisoner
(last updated September 8, 1996)
Selected photos and other material on this page are implicitly © Copyright ITC/Polygram. Although they appear here without prior clearance, their usage is strictly within the bounds of promoting interest in The Prisoner and is not for purposes of personal profit or gain.
The Prisoner was one of the most original dramas ever aired on television. Brainchild of producer and star Patrick McGoohan, the series portrays a top-secret government agent who resigns his position only to be immediately abducted and whisked away to an enigmatic, isolated seaside community known only as "The Village." Confined in this resort-like, yet sinister town, Number 6 (the new "identity" given to him by his captors) soon learns that no one can be trusted, and that those in charge (whose governmental and political affiliations are unknown) will take extreme measures to break him and learn the reasons behind his resignation.

FIGURE 10.8 *The Prisoner* (http://www.inmind.com/people/teague/prisoner.html).

television show), television and radio have stronger channel and station identification. The television and radio audience usually memorizes the programming associated with the media companies involved. (As mentioned in the music section, the reaction of many labels to the Internet has been to increase their audience's label identification by concentrating on building sites associated with the label as opposed to the album or even the artist. This marks a change in the way the audience is reacting to labels, but channel and station identification in the broadcasting industry is nothing new.) A few extremely popular shows, such as Fox's *The X-Files* site (http://www.foxhome.com/trustno1), display features common on movie Web sites, including online games and video clip archives.

Fan Sites

While the networks usually do not create program-specific sites, they do exist—as a surrounding Web of fan-created sites which frequently number in the dozens per individual show. Fan sites broaden the TV universe by allowing many vintage shows which are no longer in syndication—ranging from *The Honeymooners* (http://www.intercall.com/~python/

honymoon/honymoon.htm) to *The Prisoner* (Figure 10.8, to *Twin Peaks* (http://www.city.ac.uk:8080/matthew/twin-peaks)—have an afterlife on the Web. Many fan sites such as the Babylon 5 Creative Mailing List (http://www.anxst.com/b5/story) feature fan-created fiction, which is becoming popular entertainment in its own right. The impact of these sites is unprecedented: For the first time in history, fan material is available in the same medium as the original programming. Other fan sites provide reviews, commentary, and advocacy groups supporting plot changes for popular shows. For example, a category of fan sites for *The X-Files*—called "Relationshippers"—consists of members who are "lobbying" for an on-air relationship to occur between the two main characters (agents Scully and Mulder).

Cable Television

Cable networks already experienced in creating content for specific audiences have taken well to the Web; many advertise their Web sites continuously during regular programming. Figure 10.9 is an example of a cable network Web site. Like network and movie sites, cable shows like HBO's *Tales from the Crypt* (Figure 10.10) may have their own Web sites;

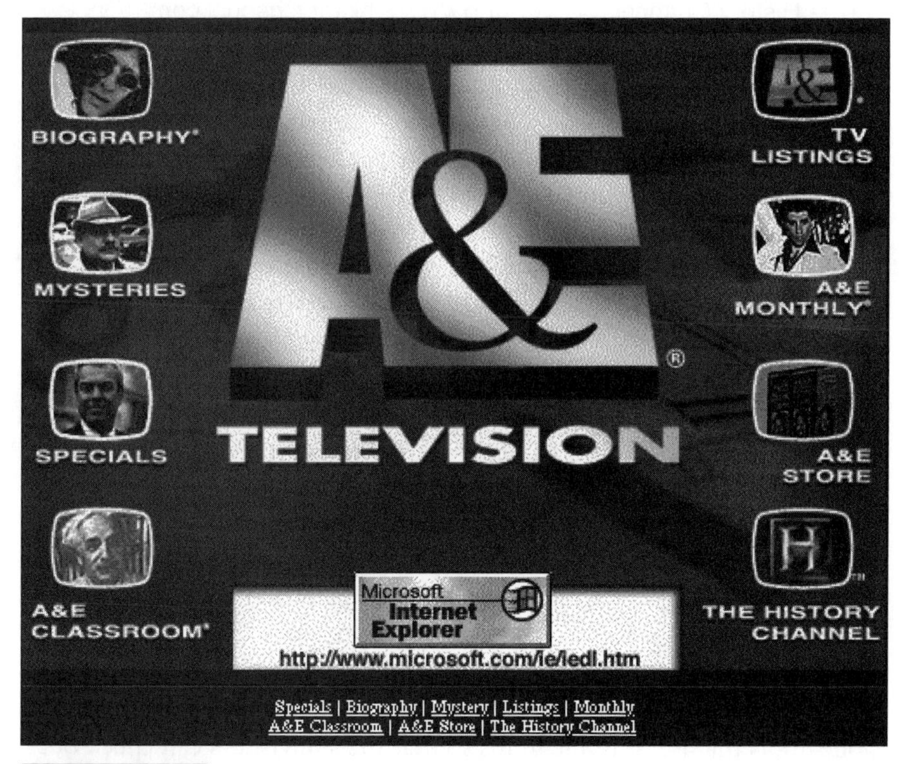

FIGURE 10.9 A&E (http://www.aetv.com).

TABLE 10.8 Select Cable Networks on the Web

Network	Web Address
A&E	http://www.aetv.com
American Movie Classics	http://www.amctv.com
BET NetWorks	http://www.betnetworks.com
Bravo	http://www.bravotv.com
Cartoon Network	http://www.filmzone.com/SpaceGhost/cartoonnet.html
Cinemax	http://www.cinemax.com
CNN	http://www.cnn.com
Comedy Central	http://www.comcentral.com
Discovery Channel	http://www.discovery.com
Disney Channel	http://www.disney.com/DisneyChannel
E!	http://www.eonline.com
Family Channel (FAMfun!)	http://www.famfun.com
fX	http://www.fxnetworks.com
HBO	http://www.hbo.com
The History Channel	http://www.historychannel.com
Independent Film Channel	http://www.ifctv.com
Lifetime	http://www.lifetimetv.com
The Movie Channel	http://www.viacom.com/tmc
Much Music	http://www.muchmusic.com/muchmusic and http://www.muchmusic-usa.com
MTV	http://www.mtv.com
Nick at Nite	http://nick-at-nite.com
Nickelodeon	http://www.viacom.com/nick
Nostalgia Television	http://www.nostalgia-tv.com/home
Playboy TV	http://www2.playboy.com/entertainment/playboy/pbtv/index.html
Sci Fi Channel	http://www.scifi.com
Showtime	http://www.showtimeonline.com
Sundance Channel	http://www.sundancechannel.com
Turner Classic Movies	http://www.turner.com/tcm
USA Network	http://www.usanetwork.com
VH-1	http://vh1.com

however, they are usually part of the cable network's larger site. A common form of interactivity on many of these and other traditional television sites is the use of frame grabs so that the site visitors can check out "what's on" at that very moment; these are available at several sites, including Comedy Central (http://www.comcentral.com) and Turner

FIGURE 10.10 *Tales from the Crypt* (http://www.cryptnet.com).

Classic Movies (http://www.turner.com/tcm). Table 10.8 lists selected cable networks on the Web.

Recognizing the news and entertainment potential of the Internet early, C|Net (http://cnet.com) created a specialized cable channel which reports on news that focuses on various aspects of communications and technology. The cable channel was paired with a large news-oriented Web site; the cable and Web "channel" frequently ran similar content. The resulting dual presence in cable and cyberspace has made C|Net one of the most popular Web destinations; this startup company demonstrated it by going public. More recently, NBC and Microsoft teamed up to develop their own parallel Web site and cable channel called MSNBC (http://www.msnbc.com). Both networks plan for increasing synchronization of cable and Web content, so that an audience member watching one can immediately switch to the other for more information.

> ***By being involved in local TV News I saw that people were very angry and frustrated with television. Unfortunately most people did not have a medium or forum to express their anger and thoughts. I felt that if I could create an online forum where people could exchange ideas and vent about television it would make them feel as though they had a little control of their one-way TV sets.***
>
> —David Cronshaw, Creator, TV Net
> http://tvnet.com

Program Guides

In addition to network sites, programming guides are quite popular. Despite the entry of traditional directories like TV Guide On.Line (http://www.iguide.com/tv/), most guides come from outside the traditional broadcast environment. Popular guides include independent sites like TV Net (http://www.tvnet.com) and developers such as Apple Computer's QuickTime Live! (http://live.apple.com) and Progressive Networks' Timecast (http://www.realaudio.com/timecast) provide information about audio and video broadcast events shows, including international listings.

Broadcast-model Web Sites

Abandoning the idea of running video over the Internet, companies such as Pointcast (http://www.pointcast.com) have adapted the broadcast model to a relatively slow delivery of information and images. The Pointcast system consists of a specialized Web browser that automatically connects to Pointcast's main site and continually downloads data without user intervention. The slide show format of the broadcast fits perfectly with a screen saver; most users configure Pointcast to run continually in the background on their computers. The tremendous popularity of Pointcast indicates that the Internet is useful for certain types of broadcast, even at its current speeds.

TV and Web Hybrids

Some groups have tried to integrate broadcast television with the Internet. Intel and NBC's ambitious Intercast (http://www.intercast.org) program integrates television shows with a Web site supplying up-to-the-minute information about the program. Intercast's first extended broadcast came from the Olympic games; several major networks intend to offer Intercast programming in 1996. Intercast embeds HTML code in the TV signal and allows it to be displayed on a computer simultaneously with the TV show. Since the signal is delivered through television, the Web pages are not interactive—though the computer can access Intercast and Web pages on the Internet at the same time. Intercast requires custom hardware and software in order to function properly; it is currently available for only a small portion of the total Internet. While the idea has obvious merit, Intercast is competing with a variety of Web sites offering similar but truly interactive news and informational services. It remains to be seen whether synchronization with a television signal will make it the service of choice for the Internet audience.

Professional Organizations and Resources

A few sites like TV Net (http://tvnet.com), TV Week (http://www.iguide.com/tv), Media Planet (http://www.faludi.com/mediaplanet), and Don Fitzpatrick Associates (http://www.tvspy.com) provide contact information for broadcast industry professionals, job listings, and industry-specific bulletin boards. Cable industry news is provided by Cable Online Industry News (http://www.cable-online.com) and The TV Rundown (http://www.tvrundown.com) provides a similar resource for the entire industry. Other broadcast resources include the American Federation of Television and Radio Artists or AFTRA (http://www.aftra.com), American Film and Marketing Association (http://www.afma.com), a trade association for independent television and film production companies, and Radiologon (http://www.radiologon.com), a site geared to radio professionals. Table 10.9 provides a selected list of professional organizations and resources on the Web.

TABLE 10.9 Selected Professional Broadcasting Organizations and Resources on the Web

Organization	Web Address
Academy of Television Arts & Sciences	http://emmys.org
American Federation of Radio and Television Artists [AFTRA]	http://www.aftra.com
Cable Online Industry News	http://www.cable-online.com
Don Fitzpatrick Associates	http://www.tvspy.com
Federal Communications Commission [FCC]	http://www.fcc.gov
Media Planet	http://www.faludi.com/mediaplanet
National Association of Broadcasters	http://www.nab.org
Radiologon	http://www.radiologon.com
Society of Broadcast Engineers	http://www.sbe.org
TV Net	http://tvnet.com
The TV Rundown	http://www.tvrundown.com
TV Week	http://www.iguide.com/tv

Future Trends

Despite progress in Internet broadcasting, the problems associated with adapting an essentially two-way media for one-to-many broadcasting present formidible challenges to the existing industry. The problems are acute for broadcast since—unlike movies which may be viewed at any time—the broadcasting industry often requires bandwidth at the moment the event is occurring.

Replacement of the MPEG Standard

While MPEG-2 currently forms the digital video standard favored by broadcasters, many problems stand in the way of using it on the Internet. Current MPEG schemes assume unrealistically high bandwidth (e.g., 15-20 times faster than the fastest consumer modems) and are less effective at the low data rates characteristic of the Web than other compression standards like wavelet technology. In order for broadcasters to be successful in the near term, they must be willing to consider alternate data compression technologies.

Non-broadcast Internet Use by Broadcasters

The explosion of fan sites and discussion groups on the Internet point to another way broadcasters can use the Internet. Whereas a network station might receive a few dozen letters monthly, the same network's Web site could easily accept thousands of email messages in the same time. Fan sites provide free promotion for broadcast shows and are pools for potential new writing talent and story concepts as well. It seems likely that broadcast radio and television will use their Web presence increasingly to create a back channel for consumer response.

Slow-broadcast Solutions

In the near term, various slow-broadcast solutions like Pointcast will be the dominant form of broadcast on the Internet. Already, signs of adaptation to slower broadcast models are visible as major network Web sites increasingly resemble online magazines in their format and content. Instead of broadcasting complete scenes, the sites will provide constantly updated text and simple graphics describing the scene. As speeds increase, live transmissions will become more common—particularly *microcasts* aimed at small audience groups.

Long-term Advantage

As discussed in Part III, a Web site is a process rather than a thing—and content providers used to constant change and updates will be able to use the medium more effectively. Compared to film and traditional multimedia, broadcasters are more experienced with being online all the time and will be able to apply this understanding to the Web in the long run.

Film and Video

Studios and independent filmmakers were initially cautious in repurposing their content for the Internet. While the Web was capable of displaying graphics during the first half of 1994, the tiny iconic images that appeared on the home pages of most sites seemed incapable of delivering the rich, visual impact of a feature film or even small-screen video. By mid-1995, the first film sites had appeared; most were created by major studios in order to promote feature releases. Despite the enormous potential for independent film promotion and distribution on the Internet, few resources currently exist. Film venues, publications, and representation and management are currently just beginning to go online, and—with the introduction of real-time video techniques and the formation of a critical mass of film professionals on the Internet—use of the Internet by the entire film industry is likely to rise.

Technology

Since films are finished works (unlike broadcast content), the technical problems with their delivery involve the ability to dramatically compress the content for fast downloads—or delivering it continuously in real-time or streaming modes. Internet movies frequently use Apple Computer's QuickTime format (http://www.quicktime.com), along with the proprietary compression systems previously discussed for broadcasting. One advantage of film technology is that movie content is usually not as time-sensitive radio and TV broadcasts—so long download delays are more acceptable.

Film Studios

Promotional film sites are the most obvious form of film industry representation on the Internet, as shown in Figure 10.11. The industry has embraced the Internet as a promotional medium, as seen in the real world by providing film URLs in television commercials, billboards,

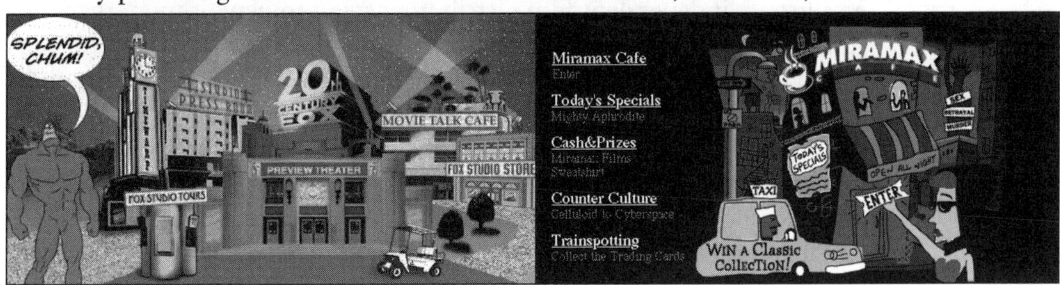

(a) (b)

FIGURE 10.11 (a) 20th Century Fox (http://www.fox.com); (b) Miramax (http://www.miramax.com).

TABLE 10.10 Selected Film Studios on the Web

Studio	Web Address
Disney	http://www.disney.com
Fine Line Features	http://www.flf.com
MCA/Universal	http://www.mca.com
MGM/UA	http://www.mgmua.com
Miramax	http://www.miramax.com
New Line Cinema	http://www.newline.com
October Films	http://www.octoberfilms.com
Paramount	http://www.paramount.com
PolyGram Filmed Entertainment	http://www.polygram.com
Sony Pictures	http://www.sony.com
Trimark	http://www.trimarkent.com
20th Century Fox	http://www.fox.com
United International Pictures	http://www.uip.com
Warner Bros.	http://www.movies.warnerbros.com

theater previews, and newspaper advertisements. Before a theatrical release, almost every feature film is previewed by Internet surfers through an autonomous promotional Web site. Since film is a visual medium, these sites push the existing multimedia capacity of the Internet to the limit, featuring advanced programming (Chapters 5 and 6) and interactive game elements. In addition, all major film studios have Web sites of their own and—just like the music and broadcasting sites—have succeeded in enhancing their image through their online counterparts. Table 10.10 lists some film studios on the Web.

Small Distributors and Retail Chains

As a group, independent film distributors stand to benefit more than almost any other group from the Internet—and a growing group of sites is providing effective contact between the industry and the Internet audience. Expanded Entertainment (http://kspace.com/expanded) provides video compilations of animation from around the world and Moving Images Distribution (http://www.movingimages.bc.ca) provides a complete catalog of over 400 independently produced Canadian films. Video rental and retail stores such as Blockbuster Video (http://www.pwr.com/blockbuster) are just beginning to get onto the Web and do not support online sales at present. Sales of film and other memorabilia are available at the Hollywood Movie Store (http://hollywoodnetwork.com/Moviestore).

FIGURE 10.12 Society of Keanu Consciousness (http;//www.empirenet.com/~jahvah/skc/skc.html).

> ***This is simply the start of another medium, much as radio made stars and humanized people like Burns and Allen. Internet will make its own 'stars.'***
>
> —CHAZ MCAULEY, FOLK ROCK NOVELTY MUSICIAN
> http://kspace.com/mcauley

Actor Fan Sites

Most of the major and independent studios have developed official sites for high-profile performers. While these sites frequently function separately from the studio sites, it is relatively uncommon for celebrities to be directly involved in the development of their site. The majority of film sites are created by fans, who often provide the only Web presence for vintage, cult, and classic films. Fan sites also exist for virtually any film personality; these are usually sponsored by their existing fan club. Sites featuring currently popular film celebrities include the well done Society of Keanu Consciousness (Figure 10.12) and sites for Sandra Bullock (http://www.kaiwan.com/~sirfitz/bullock.html), Jim Carrey (http://www.halcyon.com/browner), and Patrick Stewart (http://www.ourworld.compuserve.com/homepages/psas). A good directory for entertainment-related fan sites is available at The Network of Entertainment Fans (http://www.tnef.com). The popularity of fan sites has attracted the attention of developers of "official" celebrity sites; the more Internet-aware studios such as Fine Line have encouraged fan participation in helping them to develop appropriate Web sites for their personalities.

Independent Filmmakers

Currently, independents lag behind major studios in their use of the Web, but the gap is closing as they discover its potential for open, low-cost promotion and distribution. An example of an independent filmmaker site can be found at Matt Sesow's page, shown in Figure 10.13; he was also a winner of a recent filmmaker's contest hosted by the Kaleidospace Screening Room. Additional material is available at http://kspace.com/sesow. Interesting resources for independent film are maintained at Cinema Connection (http://www.webcom.com/~3e-media/TMC/tccframe.html), Indy Cine (http://www.digimark.net/st/), and IndieZine (http://telluridemm.com/indizine.html). Directories for individual films such as Chaos Entertainment's Drawing Down the Moon (Figure 10.14), can be found at Yahoo! in the Independent Titles subdirectory.

Another outstanding resource for budding filmmakers is Cyber Film School (http://www.cyberfilmschool.com), which provides a complete educational resource for screenwriting and filmmaking. Individual directors and actors are listed in searchable databases like Videopro (http://txdirect.net/videopro) and links to fan pages can be found at sites like Johnny G's Independent and Cult Film Page (http://www.netcom.com/~johnnyg2). Independent production studios have just begun to go online; a few like Hollywood's Los Angeles Film Factory (http://www.lafilmfactory.com) are providing listings of their services.

Resources and Reviews Sites

These sites provide critical commentary and interviews with individuals involved in filmmaking. Feature films and links to *official*

FIGURE 10.13 Matt Sesow (http://members.aol.com/msesow).

FIGURE 10.14 Drawing Down the Moon (http://www.netins.net/showcase/ddtm).

sites are provided at resources like Time-Warner's movie review database on Pathfinder (http://www.pathfinder.com/pathfinder/reviews/movies.html) for *Time* and *Entertainment Weekly*, MovieReviews' Circle of Critics (http://moviereviews.com), Mr. Showbiz (http://www.mrshowbiz.com), and MovieCritic (http://www.moviecritic.com)—which provides reviews for a large number of films, along with links to their *official* sites. Reviews are also available from the hundreds of independent online newspapers such as Zone Interactive's Mr. Cranky Rates the Movies (Figure 10.15) and many personal sites such as Mr. Brown's Movie Page (http://members.tripod.com/userland/M/MrBrown).

For comprehensive searches of virtually all movie material on the Internet, the best resource is the Internet Movie Database (http://www.imdb.com). This site provides well-organized searches based on names, plot, performers, and quotes. Listings of many independent studios are available through Movienet (http://www.movienet.com) and Movies.net (http://www.movies.net). FilmZone (http://www.filmzone.com) provides a database of links to film sites, as well as an extensive collection of reviews and interviews. Another important trend is at MovieLink (http://www.777film.com), the online counterpart to MoviePhone that provides basic promotions for some films while allowing online ticket ordering for many others.

FIGURE 10.15 Mr. Cranky (http://internet-plaza.net/zone/mrcranky).

Publications

Many film and television publications (Hollywood industry trades and *gossip* magazines) are available on the Web as *e-zines*, including Premiere (http://www.premieremag.com) and Entertainment Weekly (http://www.timeinc.com/ew). In addition to online newspapers and popular magazines, several specialty publications such as Flicker Alternative Cinema (http://www.sirius.com/~sstark) and Animation World Magazine (http://www.awn.com) focus on specific aspects of the industry. Professional publications include Box Office Magazine (http://www.boxoff.com), Filmmaker Magazine (http://www.filmmaker.e-domain.com/filmmaker.html) and The Hollywood Reporter (http://www.hollywoodreporter.com).

Professional Resources and Artist Representation

Sites that specialize in providing contacts within the movie industry are among the fastest-growing on the Web. Some of these sites, such as WebMovie (http://www.webmovie.com), Film.com (http://www.film.com/film), or The Film and Video Internet Gateway (http://www.idir.net/~mlande/film), are devoted to providing information for film professionals of all types. Others like eMoon (http://www.hollyvision.com/emoon) specialize in providing directories for film crew, equipment, and services.

Filmmakers looking for the perfect location may check out one of the numerous film board sites or the Association of Film Commissioners International (http://www.afciweb.org), a nonprofit organization serving the needs of on-location film, television, and commercial production. Lectures on Hollywood deal-making are provided in real-time audio by the Hollywood Broadcasting Network (http://hollywoodnetwork.com/Live). Some other resources include The Reel Directory (http://www.connectmedia.com/reeldir.html), a Bay area film production guide, and Native Resources (http://www.kusm.montana.edu/NativeVoices), a Public television workshop giving Native Americans access to media resources. Production studios and resources, another class of site, are rapidly growing on the Web. Stock footage is available from Footage.net (Figure 10.16), and film music resources are covered by www.filmmusic.com (http://www.filmmusic.com)—an independent site that also features reviews and interviews with film composers.

In addition to Kaleidospace (http://kspace.com), there are several meta-sites that focus more on placement services for performers and are designed to attract interest from production companies and other professional groups. Sites like The Talent Network (http://www.talentnet.com), Actors Online (http://www.actorsonline.com), Hot Shots Talent (http://www.modelslynk.com), and The Virtual Headbook (http://www.xmission.com/~wintrnx/virtual.html) have attempted to create directories and meta-sites similar to the *head shot* books common in the industry. In most cases, admission to sites is based on paid subscriptions.

Sites such as Studionet (http://studionet.com) provide information for production support including photographers, agents, and hair and makeup stylists. As image-oriented search engines become widely available (see Visual Art later in the chapter), it will be possible to progressively search a worldwide actor database for people exactly matching requirements for film and other visual entertainment. New sites like the Casting Guild's Casting Call (http://www.castingcall.com) and The Hol-

FIGURE 10.16 Footage.net (http://www.footage.net).

lywood Mall's casting call section (http://www.hollywoodmall.com) provide lists of casting calls for union, non-union and student film, commercials, stage and TV productions. Larger talent agencies such as the Creative Artist Agency (http://caa.com) are just beginning to come online.

Professional Organizations

Several film organizations such as the Director's Guild of America (DGA), Screen Actor's Guild (SAG), International Animated Film Society (ASIFA) (http://www.awn.com/asifa_hollywood/index.html), Motion Picture Association of America (MPAA), and Academy of Motion Picture Arts and Sciences (AMPAS) have established sites on the Internet for their members. These sites contain information on history, membership, and award ceremonies (e.g., AMPAS' Oscars) associated with each organization. Independent filmmakers will be interested in The Web Cinema Group (http://www.webcinema.org), a nonprofit group dedicated to helping

TABLE 10.11 Selected Film-related Industry Professional Organizations on the Web

Organization	Web Address
Academy of Motion Picture Arts and Sciences [AMPAS]	http://www.oscars.com
American Federation of Television and Radio Artists [AFTRA]	http://www.aftra.com
American Film Institute	http://www.afionline.org
American Film and Marketing Association	http://www.afma.com
Directors Guild of America [DGA]	http://www.dga.org
Independent Film and Video Alliance	http://www.ffa.ucalgary.ca/ifva/index.html
International Animation Association [ASIFA]	http://www.swcp.com/~asifa
Motion Picture Association of America [MPAA]	http://www.mpaa.org
National Film Board of Canada	http://www.nfb.ca
Screen Actors Guild [SAG]	http://www.sag.org
The Web Cinema Group	(http://www.webcinema.org)
Writers Guild of America [WGA]	http://wga.org

FIGURE 10.17 Cannes Film Festival (http://www.festival-cannes.fr).

independents to finance, create, producte, distribute, and market independent film. Startup Web sites like the Hollywood Network's Interactive Studio (http://hollywoodnetwork.com/Studio) also offer membership in their Web-specific producers, writers, and screenwriters network. Table 10.11 provides selected film-related organizations on the Web.

Film Festivals

Web sites devoted to film festivals and other film and video events can introduce the Internet audience to new material frequently unavailable at the corner theater. Major festivals online include The Cannes Film Festival (Figure 10.17), Sundance '96 (http://www.sundancefilm.com), as well as more specicalized gatherings like the New York Gay and Lesbian Film Festival (http://www.newfestival.com). Independents can check out The Los Angeles Independent Film Festival (http://www.laiff.com) and the Gen Art Film Festival (http://www.genart.org). One of the most interesting festival sites is the Virtual Film Festival (http://www.virtualfilm.com). Working with Apple Computer's QuickTime Live! (http://live.apple.com) in 1996, this group conducted a variety of live cybercasts from film festivals including Sundance and The Florida Film Festival (http://enzian.iserver.com/fff_96/live.html).

Future Trends

As the speed of the Internet increases and filmmakers move to digital, non-linear film processing, interest in the Internet is sure to rise. The chief challenges include providing a way to actually view films through the Internet and developing a distribution model that benefits from the direct-to-audience sales potential of Web sites. Following are some of the trends anticipated for the film industry on the Internet.

Hyperlinked Video

Both Apple Computer and other groups are developing digital formats that allow hyperlinks to be applied to people or objects in the movie itself—as well as fast, arbitrary jumps within the video (see Chapter 15 for more discussion). This means that movies will increasingly be able to expand their stories beyond a closed linear narrative and provide true interactivity. At that point, film will integrate with the Web much more closely than is currently possible.

DVDs

The Digital Versatile Disc (DVD)—check the specs at http://www.sel.sony.com/SEL/consumer/dvd/index.html)—format allows high-definition, feature-length video to be stored on discs the size of current audio CDs. Unlike audio CDs, DVDs use data format common to the computer, film, broadcast, and music industries. With the introduction of relatively inexpensive DVD/CD players (~$600) late in 1996, it is likely that consumers will have access to the technology sometime in 1997. One possible consequence of the DVD revolution is that independent filmmakers will be capable of reproducing copies of their work with the same ease and low cost enjoyed by independent musicians. When this occurs, many independent filmmakers will be interested in distributing their works directly to their audience; thus, the Internet will provide the same promotion and distribution potential to filmmakers it currently supplies to independent musicians. (See Chapter 15 for more discussion of DVD.)

Expanded Movies

Promotional sites for movies frequently provide enough entertainment in themselves to suggest a closer connection between them and the film itself than promotion. In the future, Web sites may hold contests which may only be solved by viewing the film, expanded interactive adventures involving film characters, and even a chance for the audience to participate in developing sequels. In the near future, films may be designed that depend on Web access for full enjoyment by the audience! As real-time video becomes more practical, it will be possible to embed the film itself in the larger interactive universe of the Web site—and some people many never experience the film outside of their computer screen.

Publishing and Writers

The Writer's Guild of America (http://wga.org) now recognizes Web site writers as eligible to join their organization, signaling the traditional industry's increasing acceptance of the Internet. Writers and publishing companies can benefit from the wide exposure the Internet provides, including the potential for tiny production costs associated with electronic book distribution. However, traditional writers and publishers are only beginning to tap the potential of the medium, despite the large amount of entertainment-related writing already appearing on the Internet (see Chapter 12).

Technology

Virtually any Internet connection can deliver text corresponding to full-length novels in a short amount of time. The main challenge to writers has been visualization. Computer screens have a fraction of the contrast of printed paper, and online text is therefore more difficult to read. While most audience members have printers, the cost of printing a major work is higher than a copy of the book itself. Since text retains its value when copied (unlike images, which are usually lower-resolution than the real thing), writers also require systems which protect the book against unauthorized copying. To this end, *digital signatures* (check Netsurfer's security focus at http://www.netsurf.com/nsf/v01/03/nsf.01.03.html)—which allow unique identification of electronic documents and prevent secondary copying—are undergoing active development.

Publishers

Most book publishers have created Web sites online (see Figure 10.18); comprehensive directories listing many traditional publishers can be found at Publisher's Place (http://www.books.com/scripts/place.exe), Bookwire (http://www.bookwire.com), and The Internet Book Fair

TABLE 10.12 Selected Large Fiction Publishers on the Web

Publisher	Web Address
Avon Books	http://www.avonbooks.com
Bantam Doubleday Dell	http://www.bdd.com
Harper Collins	http://www.harpercollins.com
Putnam/Berkley	http://www.mca.com/putnam
Penguin	http://www.penguin.com
Random House	http://www.randomhouse.com
Simon & Schuster	http://www.simonsays.com

FIGURE 10.18 Bantam Doubleday Dell (http://www.bdd.com).

(http://www.bookport.com). These sites offer book previews along with information about the authors, buying (and sometimes reselling)—and additional features like virtual coffeehouses. Specialty publishers, such as Lone Eagle Publishing (http://www.loneeagle.com) and NBM Publishing (http://kspace.com/nbm), allow secure online ordering. Table 10.12 lists selected large fiction publishers on the Web.

Authors and Fans

Search engines such as Yahoo! list thousands of fiction authors. Individual sites are maintained by an astonishing mix of publishers, universities, fans and, in some cases, the authors themselves. A good example of this is found in sites for horror writer Clive Barker. His original Web site (http://kspace.com/barker) promoting his writing and original art was put up as part of the Kaleidospace Artist-in-Residence Program. In short order, a series of fan sites were established, which have now been linked in the Lament Configuration (Figure 10.19). In addition to promotions for real-world books, some authors have taken the plunge and written novels to be consumed directly online. In a recent example, author Joe Queenan used a preset title and one-line senario to create *Serb Heat*, an online, full-length novel that ran in serial on the Mr. Showbiz (http://www.mrshowbiz.com) Web site from April 30 to May 2, 1996. The material posted was actually a first draft and the Internet audience was encouraged to provide comments and criticism.

Bookstores

During 1994, the idea of online bookstores appeared to be taking off, as early efforts to create a system to pay for downloaded books were put into place. However, the expected takeoff in *e-books* did not materialize and many electronic bookstores have since gone out of business. More recently, with electronic cash and micropayment systems appearing on the Web (see Chapter 9), a resurgence of interest has occurred—and many book distributors are again testing the waters. Conventional book retailers can be found using the directories at Bookweb (http://www.bookweb.org), which also contains organizations such as the American Booksellers Association. New distribution outlets such as Mind's Eye Fiction (http://www.ghgcorp.com/mindseye) are selling serialized portions of novels to their visitors via a pay-per-download model. Similar payment systems are currently being reviewed for implementation on other book distribution sites, including the Kaleidospace Reading Room.

Professional Resources and Organizations

In addition to the Writers Guild (http://www.wga.org), professional organizations such as the National Writers Union (http://www.nwu.org/nwu), Horror Writer's Association (http://www.greyware.com/hwa), and Romance Writers of America (http://www.rwanational.com) have online informational sites. A directory of writers' resources is being developed at Inkspot (http://www.inkspot.com/~ohi/inkspot/home.html). A few book agents have begun to put up sites promoting their services, Strictly Book Promotions (http://www.inter-mall.com/publicist/sbp) is an example of a group providing publicity for small press and individual book releases. An excellent directory for comic book conventions can be found at comicshow.com (Figure 10.20), and general book fair directories can be found at The Internet Book Fair (http://www.bookport.com/htbin/welcome/9505.html) and Oliver and Gannon Associates' ShowFairsFestivals.com (http://www.showfairsfestivals.com).

FIGURE 10.19 Lament Configuration (http://www.ccnet.com/~fburke/lament.html).

FIGURE 10.20 Comicshow.com (http://www.comicshow.com).

Future Trends

Professional writers will undoubtedly increase their numbers on the Internet, though it is unlikely that traditional entertainment forms such as novels and short stories will be transferred to the medium in their current form. The introduction of micropayments will also cause major changes in writing online. With a secure method in place to be compensated for their work, more writers will consider providing stories or ongoing serials to the Internet audience. Currently, the future of Internet writing appears to lie in increased interactivity with the audience at all levels—including collaboration with the audience in the writing phase as well as turning linear narratives into multidimensional hyperbooks. These new writing forms are dicussed more fully in Chapter 12.

Following music, art is one of the hottest categories of the entire Internet. With support from university departments, the first noncommercial galleries went online as early as October 1993. Virtual galleries have continued to be created by academic departments, nonprofit organizations, commercial galleries, and small businesses. Thousands of art galleries are available that showcase work by famous masters, and contemporary fine and commercial artists. While sales of original art are minimal, retail prints, greeting cards, posters, and other reproductions such as t-shirts are popular in online stores. This growth of visual art on the Internet has resulted in increased awareness of fine and commercial art to a new audience, many of whom may have never visited a real-world gallery.

Galleries and Museums

Since the Web is well-suited for transmitting visual art, the vast number of online galleries and museums is not surprising. Some of these galleries are virtual representations of physical viewing space, while others are all-virtual and represent a new model for promoting and distributing visual art. Due to the large number of individual sites, many directories have evolved—including the Internet for the Fine Arts (http://www.fine-art.com) searchable database and 1000 Points of Art (http://members.aol.com/noahnet/art). World Wide Arts Resources (http://wwar.world-arts-resources.com) has created a definitive list of nearly 10,000 links to all aspects of visual art.

Individual galleries include the authors' Kaleidospace Art Studio (http://kspace.com) and the original Art on the Net (http://www.art.net), both established at the beginning of 1994. Additional galleries include the 2,600-member Chicago Artists Coalition (http://www.caconline.org/home.html) and the Canadian Native Arts Gallery (Figure 10.21). Most of these sites are run on a subscription basis; artists pay a one-time charge, monthly fee, and/or commission to display their work. Examples of online museums include The Krannert Art Museum (http://www.art.uiuc.edu/kam), one of the first arts resources to go on the Web, the Smithsonian's National Museum of American Art (Figure 10.22), and Le Louvre (http://mistral.culture.fr/louvre). Newer online museums include The

TABLE 10.13 Selected Galleries and Museums on the Web

Museum	Web Address
Art on the Net	http://www.art.net
The CAGE Gallery (Dutch)	http://asterix.urc.tue.nl/~rcrolf/cage/cage.shtml
Canadian Native American Art Gallery	http://firstnations.com/nativeart/NATIVEART.htm
Chicago Artists Coalition	http://www.caconline.org/home.html
Official Salvador Dali Museum (St. Petersburg, Florida)	http://www.webcoast.com/Dali
Guggenheim Museum	http://math240.lehman.cuny.edu/gugg
Kaleidospace Art Studio	http://kspace.com
Krannert Art Museum	http://www.art.uiuc.edu/kam
Le Louvre	http://mistral.culture.fr/louvre
Museum of Jurassic Technology	http://www.mjt.org
Palazzo Grassi (Venice)	http://www.palazzograssi.it
Philadelphia Museum of Art	http://pma.libertynet.org
Smithsonian National Museum of American Art	http://www.nmaa.si.edu
Web Museum	http://sunsite.unc.edu/wm

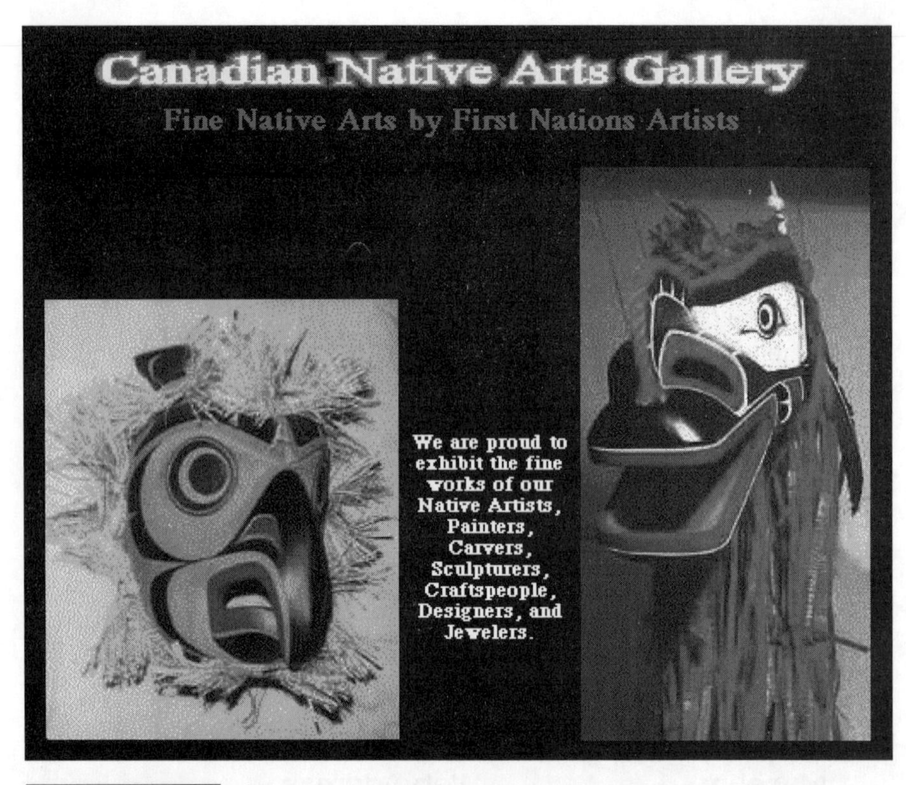

FIGURE 10.21 Canadian Native Arts Gallery (http://firstnations.com/nativeart/NATIVEART.htm).

Web Museum (http://sunsite.unc.edu/wm), which contains a complete online tour spanning several continents and Web sites, and the fascinatingly weird and humorous Museum of Jurassic Technology (http://www.mjt.org), which has existed in its physical form in Los Angeles for an uncertain duration. Table 10.13 shows selected galleries and museums on the Web.

Sites devoted to specific artists are available, including the Leonardo da Vinci Museum (http://www.leonardo.net/museum); this examplifies how Internet Service Providers (in this case, Leonardo Internet) use the arts and entertainment potential of the Internet to provide content value along with their access services (see Chapter 15). Like film stars, well-known artists do not often create personal exhibitions. One of the few examples is the personal site of Swiss artist H. R. Giger (Figure 10.23) which contains updates on his current work and an online chat room. The site also contains an email *hotline* where fans can report unauthorized use of the artist's work.

FIGURE 10.22 Smithsonian's National Museum of American Art (http://www.nmaa.si.edu).

Art Sales and Auctions

Fine art is being auctioned online by well-known organizations such as Christie's (http://www.christies.com), Sotheby's (http://www.sothebys.com), and Phillips (http://www.phillips-auctions.com). Animation collectors may want to check out Disney's Animation Art (http://www.artventures.com) for sales of rare animation cels. Other sites include Auctions On-line (http://auctions-on-line.com), which provides a comprehensive searchable database of auctions all over the world, and the European Art

FIGURE 10.23 H. R. Giger (http://www.hrgiger.com).

Forum (http://europeanonline.com/artforum), which includes photos in its indexed database.

Exhibitions and Festivals

Arts festival Web sites are almost as common as virtual galleries. Many large festivivals offer information and sample exhibits including the European Media Arts Festival (http://emaf.com), Art Chicago 1996 at Navy Pier (Figure 10.24), Burning Man Festival (http://www.istorm.com/burningmam), Festival of the Arts and the Pageant of the Masters (http://www.foapom.com), and Edinburgh Festival Fringe (http://www.presence.co.uk/fringe).

Professional Organizations and Foundations

Many regional, national, and international organizations are available through the Web, including the National Association of Fine Artists or NAFA (http://www.nafa.com), California Lawyers for the Arts (http://kspace.com/cla) and American Council for the Arts (http://www.artsusa.org). Art groups with a political or cultural agenda are particularly common. Many, such as Artists for Social Responsibility (http://www.visionsound.com/asr.html), take stances for human rights and against censorship, while others like Artists for a Better Image (ArtFBI) (gopher://gopher.tmn.com/11/Artswire/artfbi/) want to counter popular stereotypes of artists in society. Other new groups include the International Association of WebArtists (http://www.webartists.com), which is organizing visual artists working on the Web. Art foundations are also just beginning their march to the Web. A few organizations like the Global Arts Foundation (http://www.global-arts.org) and Art

FIGURE 10.24 Art Chicago 1996 at Navy Pier (http://www.scuba.com/~tha).

Matters, Inc. (http://www.artmatters.com), and National Endowment for the Arts (http://arts.endow.gov) represent this group.

Future Trends

Like other areas of traditional arts and entertainment, the visual arts community will continue to find new ways to display its work. While the current Web is capable of displaying many types of visual art, developments in hardware and software will help to fully integrate other aspects of the art community into the operation of the Web.

Online Auctions and Commissions

As the quantity and quality of online art increases, the Internet audience will feel increasingly more comfortable with online auctions. A possible outgrowth of this model is *virtual commissions*, where artists bid for the creation of commissioned works in an interactive online forum.

Three-Dimensional Displays

As various technologies for creating three-dimensional environments (Part II and Chapter 12) become common on the Web, it will be practical to display sculpture and other spatial art in a way which more accurately reflects its real appearance.

Visual Searching

Art on the Internet currently faces an overabundance of riches; there is so much art available that it is impossible for a prospective art buyer or collector to see more than a tiny fraction of the total art pieces available. While keyword-based search engines may recover the location of an artist's site—or even a particular art style or subject—until recently there was no way to search through the images themselves for characteristics of color, mood, and texture. Recently, however, graphical databases such as Virage's Visual Information Retrieval or VIR (http://www.virage.com) technology can classify pictures by color, size, and shape. Yahoo! has recently deployed its own Image Surfer (http://ipix.yahoo.com/isurf.html) in selected areas of its database with high image content. Deployment of this and similar technologies will allow audience members to progressively refine searches based on the appearance of the art.

Live Performance

Live performers and performance venues would not at first thought seem the likeliest candidates for Web counterparts. However, certain areas of the performance industry have been making use of the Web

FIGURE 10.25 Virtually Funny (http://virtuallyfunny.com/netcomic).

for show schedules, general global awareness, and sometimes even virtual performances.

> ***"[The Internet] has given us worldwide exposure. Our clients have been getting booked and called from all over and getting paid for their services."***
>
> —Susan Levin, Publisher and Owner, Speakers, Consultants, Entertainment Directory
> http://www.a2zpros.com

Comedy

Like independent musicians, unsigned performers have discovered the promotional value of personal home pages. Beginning with early efforts such as the Kaleidospace Center Stage, performers have provided resumes, excerpts, and even short video clips showcasing their perfor-

FIGURE 10.26 Merce Cunningham (http://www.merce.org).

mance abilities. One of the largest groups online consists of independent comedians, who often offer comedy in byte-sized clips. In addition to one of the only personal sites maintained by a celebrity—Rodney Dangerfield (http://www.rodney.com)—a great example of a comedian's site is independent performer Arthur Montmorency's Virtually Funny (Figure 10.25), where site visitors can participate in virtual heckling! Other comedy-oriented sites include Monty Python's PythOnline (http://www.PythOnline.com), which provides a focus to the 1,500 sites and discussion groups already on the Net. Outstanding sites have also been created by independent comedy groups such as the Australian-based The Men Who Knew Too Much (http://yoyo.cc.monash.edu.au/~lupulus/index.html). Video clips from a variety of independent comedians are available at Comedy on the Web or COW (http://www.comedybreak.com), and an extensive directory of other comedians and clubs is available at The Comedy Page (http://comedypage.com). Directories of performers of all types are becoming very common on the Web and they are similar in format to music meta-sites.

FIGURE 10.27 Survival Research Laboratories (http://www.srl.org).

Dance

While not well-suited for direct online delivery, dance nonetheless benefits greatly from the Internet's promotional and communication ability. Current sites feature home pages for companies, events calendars, and, in some cases, online ticket ordering. A general directory for dance of all types is maintained by Marv Vandehey at http://www.cyberspace.com/vandehey/dance.html. A large listing for modern dance is available at Amy Reusch and James S. White's Dance Links (http://users.aol.com/aablisting/modern.htm), and links for classical ballet as well as modern dance are available at CyberDance (http://www.thepoint.net/~raw/dance.htm). The DancePages Directory (http://emporium.turnpike.net/~dpd) is a worldwide geographic directory of information on choreographers and dance companies. Sites devoted to well-known dancers and choreographers are not common at this time; however, the Merce Cunningham site (Figure 10.26) is an excellent example.

Performance Art

Performance art groups are also becoming available through the Web. Well-known performance art online includes the site for Survival Research Laboratories (Figure 10.27), which offers performance schedules, a description of new outrageous machines constructed by the group, and videos of past performances for sale. Laurie Anderson's Green Room (http://www.voyagerco.com/LA/VgerLa.html) provides a series of Shockwave-based multimedia presentations sized for fast and slow Internet connections. The well-known STOMP (http://www.usinteractive.com/stomp) has a sophisticated site using Java, Shockwave, and RealAudio technologies.

Theater and Performance Spaces

Traditional theater seems far removed from the Internet, since many of the unique values of the medium are lost on a computer screen. Despite this, theaters have not been shy about jumping onto the Web—and directories in Yahoo! for regional theater list hundreds of shows and venues. Popular musicals such as *The Phantom of the Opera* (on Andrew Lloyd Webber's Really Useful Theater Company site at http://www.reallyuseful.com/Phantom) have dozens of fan sites that focus on every

FIGURE 10.28 Boston Rock Opera (http://www.wmedia.com/BROweb).

FIGURE 10.29 The Kitchen (http://www.panix.com/userdirs/kitchen).

aspect imaginable of the story and production. Other unusual and interesting theater sites include the Boston Rock Opera (Figure 10.28), the American Repertory Theatre (http://www.fas.harvard.edu/~art/), the more classical Fahrenheit Theatre Company (http://www.iac.net/~marjason/ftcindex.html) in Cincinatti, and the Indianapolis Civic Theatre (http://www.nchcpl.lib.in.us/ict/ict.html)—the oldest civic theater in the United States. The John F. Kennedy Center for the Performing Arts (http://www.kennedy-center.org) has an extensive site with historical, show, and educational information; the ability to order tickets online will be available in the near future.

Performance art venues such as Performance Space 122 (http://www.echonyc.com/~ps122) are also going online. PS122 is located in an abandoned school building in New York City's East Village; the site offers poetry, dance, performance art, and product sales for many of its artists. A resource for current performing arts may be found in New York at The Kitchen (Figure 10.29), which supports and promotes the cultural vanguard in music, dance, video, and performance. The Kitchen provides a performance space with an impressive history of outstanding performances by Laurie Anderson, Brian Eno, Robert Mapplethorpe, Philip Glass, David Byrne, and Peter Greenaway. Online, the Kitchen Web site lists internship opportunities, a place to purchase "Internet discount" season subscriptions, and even a form for submitting performance proposals. Despite the large number of independent comedians online, there are currently few sites devoted to comedy clubs. A few examples are The Comedy Store in London (http://www.londonmall.co.uk/comedy/) and The Punchline in Atlanta (http://www.punchline.com).

Professional Organizations and Resources

Some performance arts organizations online include the International Society for the Performing Arts or ISPA (http://ispa-online.org), American Association of Community Theater (http://www.aact.org), and National Association of Performing Arts Managers and Agents or NAPAMA (http://www.arts-online.com/napama.htm). The Tony Awards (http://tonys.org) is also well-represented with its high-impact site. The Web contains resources for costuming such as The Costume Source (http://www.ddi.digitial.net/~milieux/supplies/websupplies.html); set design such as SceneryWest (http://www.scenerywest.com); and stage lighting such as Electrics Land (http://www.clarkson.net/~hopke/stagecraft.html). Online ticket purchases are provided by Playbill Online (http://piano.symgrp.com/playbill) and The Theatre Network (http://www.interlog.com/~artbiz) provides an electronic magazine serving the needs of the international theater community.

Future Trends

Even with today's technology, performers can begin to provide their work in the enormous number of chat rooms on the Internet. To date, appearances by performers have been largely of the interview type, but the potential exists for virtual performance. In the near future, comedians are likely to set up virtual joke clubs where the performers can reach a much larger audience, while still holding the intimate appeal of a small club. With the advent of video streaming techniques, more live events will be seen over the Web—and more advanced techniques may allow performers to interact with their audience in real-time virtual, three-dimensional environments (see Chapter 12).

The previous exposition, while only scratching the surface, should convince anyone that traditional arts and entertainment have embraced the Web. In the next chapter, we move from the traditional arts and entertainment industry to recreational entertainment (including sports, travel, lifestyles, and leisure).

CHAPTER 11

RECREATIONAL ENTERTAINMENT: Cybercafes, Gaming, Sports, Travel, and Personals

One of the extraordinary features of Web-based entertainment—aside from its global reach and universal access—is the support it gives to recreational entertainment. In much of traditional entertainment (see Chapter 10), a large, relatively passive audience experiences the work of professional artists and performers. This stands in contrast to recreational entertainment (e.g., social dancing), where individuals or small groups create their own fun. On the Web, the distinction between the two types of entertainment is greatly reduced and recreational entertainment achieves a visibility only available in print media.

 Cybercafes

Cybercafes distinguish themselves from general venues with Web site counterparts by providing a two-way connection between the coffeehouse, pub, or other social space and the Internet. As such, they function as equalizers—allowing virtually anyone access to the Internet and its advanced technology without having to purchase and master the use of expensive hardware. The genesis of the current cybercafe movement actually occurred in 1984 when the pioneering Electronic Cafe International or ECI (Figure 11.1) opened its doors in Santa Monica, CA. Communication between ECI and other locations originally consisted of

FIGURE 11.1 Electronic Cafe International, Santa Monica, CA (http://www.ecafe.com).

videoconference-style connections. As the Web began to explode a decade later, other groups following ECI's lead developed a new form of cybercafe based on connections leading out onto the general Internet.

Technology

Off-the-shelf Internet hardware and software can be readily adapted for cybercafes. Usually, the systems are enclosed in protective cases (which also prevent theft) and additional software simplifies the process of going online. At present, most cybercafes follow a build-your-own plan for assembling their hardware, but resources like SF Net (http://www.sfnet.com) provide information for creating public-access terminals in cybercafes. Breakaway Presentation, Inc. (www.breakaway-presents.com) recently announced the availability of custom Internet *kiosks* and it is likely that cybercafe-specific hardware will be available in the near future. To help with cybercafe management, Cybertime (http://www.rockmall.com/cyber.htm) provides software for billing customers based on their time online. Their system includes a help system and a simplified login procedure for customers.

Cafes

Currently, the Yahoo! cybercafe list has several hundred cybercafes listed in countries throughout the world and other lists like Global Computing's (http://www.globalcomputing.com/cafes.html) cybercafe list and Mark Dziecielewski's Cybercafe Guide (http://www.cyberiacafe.net/cyberia/guide/ccafe.htm) provide even more examples. CyberJava (Figure 11.2) in Venice, CA provides a suite of services to its customers, including Web site hosting, training courses, numerous events (including a Friday night *X-Files* viewing party)—and, of course, good coffee. Its Web site follows other cybercafes in promoting its service to the world while providing instructions and interesting links to its customers. Other well-known and interesting cybercafes include the World Cafe (http://www.worldcafela.com) in Santa Monica, Tetris (http://www.dux.ru/guest/netcafe/Eng/CafeHome.html) in Russia, and Saga (http://www.saga.is) in Iceland. Some cybercafes like Geneva's Global Cafe (http://www.globalcafe.ch) also provide local travel guides, while others are even usurping the province of copy houses by offering color printing and reproduction services. Cybercafes with high-speed links to the Internet like the Netropolis Cybercafe (http://www.netropolis.co.uk) frequently broadcast concerts and other performances from their location.

Cyberpubs, distinguished by the presence of alcohol and the distinct atmosphere created, are also becoming common; some examples are Nutty's Pub (http://www.sd.cybernex.net/nuttys) in South Dakota and Six Bells (http://www.cityscape.co.uk/users/hd91/index.html) in Cambridge, England.

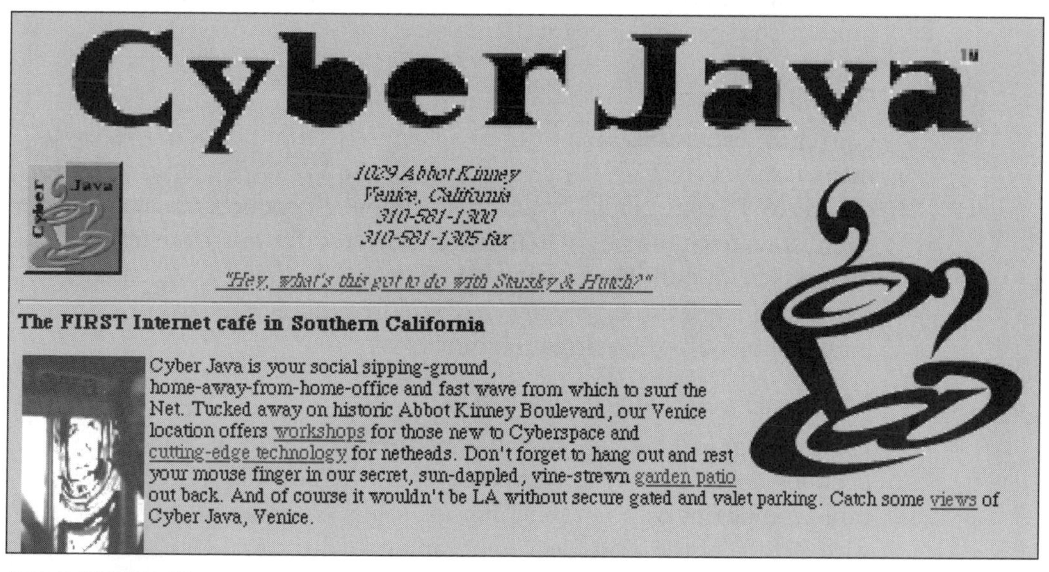

FIGURE 11.2 CyberJava (http://www.cyberjava.com).

I don't feel that cybercafes will be in direct competition with traditional cafes. Cybercafes should be thought about as a whole new business, where the concept of public computing and the Internet are centered around an atmosphere resembling those of traditional neighborhood cafes. I feel that if there is any business we are directly competing with, it would be businesses like Kinko's. It's the goal of the cybercafe entrepreneur to attract small businesses and work-at-home businesspeople to their establishment where business and Internet services are offered in a warm inviting atmosphere."

— Rom Agustin, Owner, CyberJava
http://www.cyberjava.com

Because of their close contact with those members of the public who haven't gotten online, cybercafes are ideal places to sell Internet services. In fact, several cybercafes like The Megabyte Coffeehouse (http://www.megabytecoffee.com) do provide ISP/IPP services, including email accounts and dialup connections. This significantly changes the characteristics of a cybercafe relative to conventional coffeehouses. Figure 11.3 shows The Hub Internet Cafe, a cybercafe in Australia.

Future Trends

Short of the government handing out free computers, cybercafes will provide Internet access to a significant fraction of the Internet audience. In such a position, it seems likely that they will be involved in several significant changes in the years ahead.

Retail Outlets

Currently, cybercafes are in the enviable position of providing access to many products that are only sold through the Web. It's a short jump for cybercafes to start taking inventory for popular products available on the Web. New technologies may even allow cybercafes to create custom products from multimedia downloaded from the Web (see Chapter 15). With such a system, cybercafes may rapidly become the best place to purchase niche and hard-to-find items.

Merging with Regional ISPs

Existing regional and "mom and pop" Internet service providers have been looking for a way to remain competitive, now that telephone and cable companies plan to offer Internet access. Integrating ISP services with a coffeehouse is an ideal solution for smaller providers; many will either start their own coffeehouse or merge with existing cybercafes.

FIGURE 11.3 The Hub Internet Cafe (http://www.thehub.com.au/hublife/hubcafe/).

Expansion of Other Venues

The cybercafe model is already spreading past coffeehouses to music clubs and other social gathering places. New York's The Cosmic Cavern (http://totalny.com/city/cosmic) and Belgium's Mirano Continental (http://netcity.be/mirano/index.htm) synchronize their virtual parties with real ones occurring in the club. Other possibilities include record stores and book stores, some of which already provide coffeehouse-style service.

Cyber Franchises and Chains

Though the time seems right for cybercafes to expand in a major way, existing franchise coffeehouses have been cautious about getting onto the Internet. In mid-1996 Starbucks Coffee (not currently online) announced its intent to study cybercafes for several months before making a decision about its own involvement. As most Internauts know, a few months' delay is equivalent to years of time in off-Net business. In contrast to the cautious approach of coffeehouse chains, many cybercafes actively seek to expand their business model. For example, CyberJava recently announced a partnership program with new cybercafes, while Cafe Internet (http://www.cafe-inet.com/realindex.html) is already building an international franchise and CafeNet (http://www.iep.com/net_cafe.html) seeks to build a chain of cybercafes throughout Latin America.

FIGURE 11.4 GameFORCE (http://www.amadeus.es/GameFORCE).

Gaming

The gaming industry is one of the oldest resources on the Internet; the rise of the commercial Web has generated an astonishing array of sites devoted to virtually every aspect of gaming. While some cutting-edge sites are pioneering online multiuser games (Chapter 12), the majority support traditional, board, role-playing, gambling, simulation, strategy, and computer gaming communities. The following sections provide a brief introduction to this fascinating area.

Game Directories and Resources

The popularity of games is so great on the Internet that sites which provide links to game resources are major entertainment attractions in themselves. The Games Domain (http://www.gamesdomain.com) provides a large, searchable database of fact sheets and virtual *walkthroughs* of traditional, computer, and online games. Games Domain and another popular site known as Happy Puppy (http://www.happypuppy.com) reserve portions of their sites for downloads of free and shareware games. Fan pages are listed in Games Domain and other sites such as GameFORCE (Figure 11.4). Specific game types include sites like the Simulation Gaming Home Page (http://world.std.com/~ctate/strategy.html), which specializes in links to historical strategy games. Bridge on the Web (http://www.cs.vu.nl/~sater/bridge/bridge-on-the-web.html), a niche site, concentrates on providing rules and strategy information for the classic card game.

Cartridge and Computer Games

Games of this type, with enormous yearly sales of hardware in the offline world, are well-represented on the Web. Major developers such as Sega (http://www.sega.com) and Nintendo (http://www.nintendo.com), new media divisions of companies like Virgin Interactive (http://www.vie.com), and independent software-only developers like Rocket Science (Figure 11.5) have all put major efforts into creating Web sites. Comprehensive directories include sites such as Video Games On-Line or VGOL (http://www.vgol.com), which features lists of electronic game companies as well as links to professional organizations, distributors, and magazines. Interestingly, while many of these sites provide reviews and online ordering, few have attempted to develop gaming services directly through the Web.

Role-playing

Traditional role-playing companies such as Steve Jackson Games (http://www.io.com/sjgames) are getting online. Typically, role-playing game (RPG) sites offer sales of new games, tournament listings, contact points with other gamers, and sometimes articles by staff. TSR, Inc. (creators of *Dungeons & Dragons*) is currently running an unofficial Web page at http://members.aol.com/tsrinc until the official site becomes available. Some developers are interested in extending the role-playing model to the graphical environment. The V. G. Engine (http://www.io.com/~

FIGURE 11.5 Rocket Science (http://www.rocketsci.com).

fenix/vgengine) is a worldwide group of game developers using the Internet to develop massive role-playing games. Other developers are rapidly advancing the high-speed role-playing of Internet MUD (Multi-user Domains); these are sufficiently different from traditional role-playing games and are discussed in Chapter 12.

Board Games

Hundreds of sites devoted to board games provide information, instructions, and tournament information. Some comprehensive archives include the WWW Backgammon Page (http://www.statslab.cam.ac.uk/~sret1/backgammon/main.html), Internet Chess (Figure 11.6 (a)), and Chinook Checkers (http://web.cs.ualberta.ca/~chinook/). As you might expect, there is a promotional site for Monopoly (http://www.monopoly.com), which contains historical information, instructions on how to play the CD-ROM version on the Internet, and a chat room for Monopoly fans. There is also an online version of Connect Four (Figure 11.6 (b)) developed by Virginia Tech student Joe Hines. Several fan sites for the popular games, Scrabble (e.g., Scrabble Club No. 21 in San Jose, CA) at http://www.yak.net/kablooey/scrabble.html and Risk (e.g., University of Rochester's http://www.cif.rochester.edu/users/tacoman/RISK/risk.html) exist also.

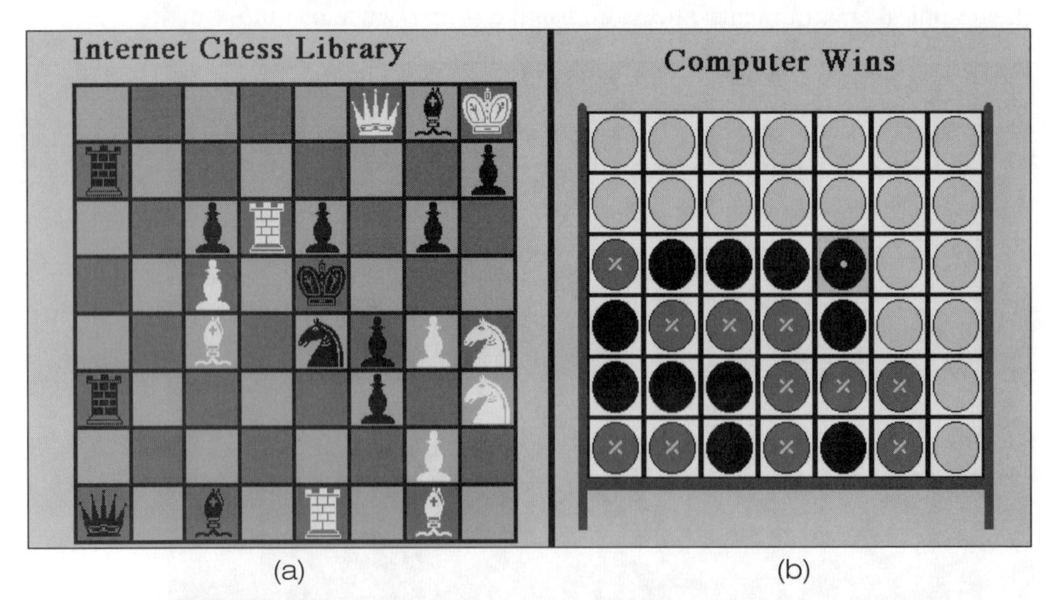

(a) (b)

FIGURE 11.6 (a) Internet Chess (http://caissa.onenet.net/chess/HTML/homepage.html); (b) Connect Four (http://csugrad.cs.vt.edu/~jhines/ConnectFour.html).

FIGURE 11.7 Reefer City (http://www.reefercity.com).

Like many other areas of entertainment, board games suffer a distribution problem; although thousands of new games are designed every year, only a fraction actually reach stores. In order to circumvent this bottleneck, many board games designers and small distributors are turning to the Web as a place to promote and distribute their games, particularly if their content is in some way controversial. An example of an independent game is found in Reefer City Productions' Reefer City (Figure 11.7), a board game whose object is the purchase and sale of marijuana. Other more conservative examples include Space Age Games' Space Race (http://www.thuntek.net/spacerace), a science fiction theme strategy game, and Curry Games, Inc.'s Initial Response (http://www.polarnet.com/users/curry), a celebrity naming game.

Puzzles

An archive of crossword and brain-teaser links is maintained at The Puzzle Depot (http://www.puzzledepot.com), which also runs online contests with prizes—but be wary of the Jumble & Crossword Solver (http://odin.chemistry.uakron.edu/cbower/jumble.html). There are online versions of classic puzzles such as Slider Puzzle (http://www2.smart.net/mcurtis-cgibin/slider.html); a version of the popular Rubik's Cube can be found at Gid's Cube (http://www.blueberry.co.uk/gid-bin/cube/).

Arcade

Through the use of Java and Shockwave programming (Chapters 5 and 6) the Web has revived classic arcade games, including Missile Commando (http://www.sdsu.edu/~boyns/java/mc) which is based on Missile Command, Gobbler (http://www.magnastar.com/games/gobbler) which is based on Pacman, and 3-D Pong (http://netleaders.com/Bounce.html) which is based on Pong. Real-world arcades are represented through game manufacturers such as National Tech Systems (http://www.mindspring.com/~nti1/Challenger.html), which produces the popular Challenger bar game, and distributors like Pocketchange (http://www.pocketchange.com), which retails both new and used arcade equipment, as well as other coin-operated games.

TV Game Shows

Reflecting the popularity of television, a variety of sites cater to widespread interest in game shows both past and present. Game-show-specific cable channels such as Sony's Game Show Network (http://www.spe.sony.com/Pictures/GSN/index.html) provide complete programming guides to popular game shows of the past, as well as interactive games with cash prizes. Many of the official Web sites such as JEOPARDY! (http://www.spe.sony.com/Pictures/tv/jeopardy/jeopardy.html) are surrounded by a swarm of fan sites. Directories for both types of sites are available at Game Show Central (http://studentweb.tulane.edu/~bfranci/gameshow.htm) and The Game $how Page (http://silver.ucs.indiana.edu/~wlambert/GameShows.html). Many of these sites are now running versions of the original shows online, including trivia polls and contact programs for former game show contestants.

Tournaments

Many large-scale competitions place sites on the Web to host the event. Tournament sites are available for bridge, chess, role-playing, computer, and historical strategy games; they have listings in Yahoo! and other specialized gaming directories. A typical site is available at the 1996 U.S. Masters Chess Tournament (http://www.redweb.com/usmasters), which provides a description of the contest with travel and other information. Due to their transient nature, individual pages are not listed here, though the Sugarbush, Vermont Tomato War (http://members.aol.com/TomatoWar/index.html) needs to be mentioned under any circumstance. This long-standing event held each Columbus Day, involves hundreds of participants hurling tomatoes with a variety of medieval devices.

FIGURE 11.8 *The Cable Guy* Sweepstakes (http://www.thecableguy.com/portal.html).

Sweepstakes and Contests

Sweepstakes are becoming common on the Web and many sites for feature films offer them as part of larger promotions. Many entertainment sites, particularly those for feature films, have created online games using characters and plot lines taken from the original work. Examples include MCA's Waterworld: Quest for the Mariner (http://www.mca.com/unicity/waterworld), based on *Waterworld*, and Sony's Entrapnet (http://www.spe.sony.com/Pictures/SonyMovies/Entrapnet/contest.html), based on *The Net*. Other examples include sweepstakes for The Hunchback of Notre Dame (http://www.disney.com/DisneyPictures) and The Cable Guy (Figure 11.8). Since many of these sites are available long after the film's theatrical run, they constitute an extension of the original story into a new arena.

While many companies are offering sweepstakes-style promotions as part of their Web advertising, The Prizes Domain (http://prizes.com) offers a variety of sweepstakes and accepts micropayments (see Chapter 9) for registration fees. The Riddler (Figure 11.9) maintains a large set of online games and gives out prizes to winners. State, national, and even international lotteries are also beginning to explore the Internet. A site for the New Jersey State Lottery (http://www.interlotto.com/pages/h3300.html) is complimented with lotto ticket buying clubs (http://members.aol.com/wwwlotto/private/index.html). Clearly, sweepstakes-style gaming will be a major part of Internet entertainment.

FIGURE 11.9 The Riddler (http://www.riddler.com).

Gambling

Internet games of chance hold the potential for profitable Web-based entertainment and raise major legal, social, and politicial issues (see Part V) inevitiably associated with a global gambling network. Like many other traditional entertainment industries, the sites representing well-known casinos are currently promotion-only. Casino Net (http://the-casino-net.com) provides the definitive resource for finding Web sites hosted by individual casinos such as the Tropicana Resort and Casino (Figure 11.10), as well as travel, shopping, entertainment, and tournament schedules. Other useful sites for casino information include Vegas.com (http://www.vegas.com) and The Vegas Daily (http://vegasonline.com).

There are several handicapping sites available on the Web. The William Hill site (http://www.williamhill.co.uk) provides daily odds for a variety of sports including football, golf, and horse racing. Currently, the company only accepts bets by phone, though an online betting version is in the works. Similar sites are provided by Lou Diamond Cybersports (http://www.cybersportslv.com). Competitive Edge (Figure 11.11) provides a variety of services on its site: Games and Tips Online is a resource linking to online games and a tip sheet for playing; Poker Player strives to be the definitive online magazine for poker, with tournament news, tips, and other information about the card game; Vegas Edge functions as a meta-site for many of the Las Vegas hotels and casinos; and Sports Edge is a sports and fantasy news periodical.

FIGURE 11.10 Tropicana Resort and Casino (http://tropicana.lv.com).

The ultimate goal of the gambling community is to extend its business into the online world. Due to strong legal concerns about a globally accessible gambling network, most of the activity has been outside the United States, with Web businesses operating from Monaco, St. Martin, St. Vincent, Barbados, Luxembourg, and Bermuda. An example of this

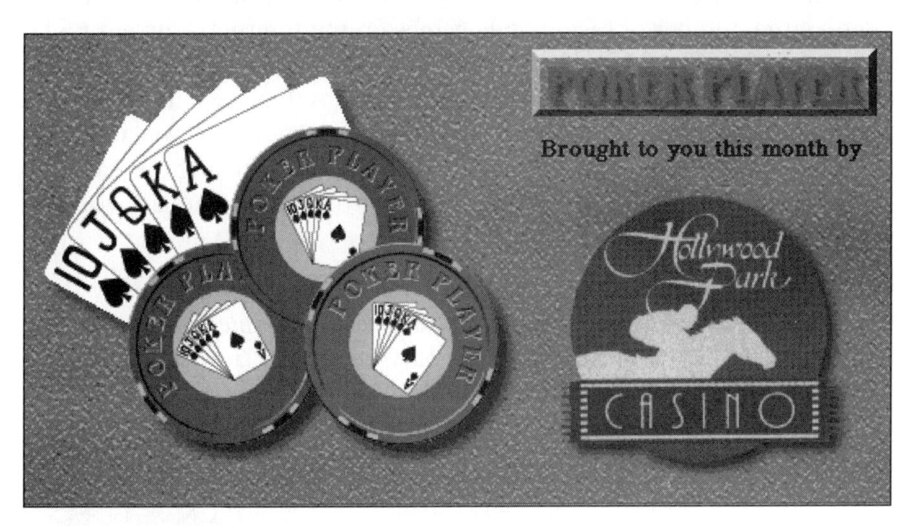

FIGURE 11.11 Competitive Edge poker player site (http://competitive-edge.com).

FIGURE 11.12 Virtual Vegas (http;//www.virtualvegas.com).

new business is Internet Casinos, Inc. (http://www.casino.org), which runs a large number of casino-style games on the Internet. Currently, games may be played for free, but prizes are awarded to winners. The online business plan of the organization indicates that they intend to charge for gaming once reliable electronic cash systems are available. The industry pioneer, Virtual Vegas (Figure 11.12), is taking the more ambitious approach and developing a total virtual entertainment world in which gaming is one of many activities.

> ***Virtual Vegas wants to be the place that people come when they want to play, relax, meet new and interesting people and be entertained. We are also working very hard to stay on the cutting edge of community and interactivity by enabling things like our Craps Game and Chat area using the Palace as well as our Onlive 3-D real-voice chat area.***

— John Bates, Director of Online Services,
Electromedia/Virtual Vegas
http://www.virtualvegas.com

Future Trends

As the sophistication of the the Web rises, games comparable in interface and response to cartridge and CD-ROM systems will become commonplace. These games are likely to become part of virtually every aspect of Internet entertainment. The introduction of electronic cash and micropayments will mark a watershed for the industry and demonstrate the true commercial potential of games on the Internet. Currently, many plans are underway to add Internet connectivity to computer games; it is not improbable that traditional board games will add similar connectivity in a relatively short time. This will hasten a general "blending" of traditional games, electronic games, and interactive entertainment into a single common form.

Sports

Like games, sports is an extremely popular topic on the Internet, with Yahoo! listing 10,000 individual sites. Huge numbers of sites report on professional sports; an equally large number provide information on recreational sports, organizations, and equipment vendors. A variety of sites offer everything from news, scores, and statistics to collectibles and memorabilia.

Directories

Start exploring sports on the Internet at America's Sports Headquarters (http://www.sport-hq.com). This site provides a searchable database of professional, spectator, and recreational sports and retail outlets, as well as a large number of sports-specific chat rooms. Specialty directories include the well-organized Brian's Sports Links (http://falcon.jmu.edu/~hamricba/slink.html). and the WWW Women's sports page (http://fiat.gslis.utexas.edu/~lewisa/womsprt.html). Other directories include encyclopedic information on a particular sport, such as Total Baseball (http://www.totalbaseball.com). Many directories also run opinion polls, chat rooms, and encourage visitors to rank their favorite teams and players.

Sports News

Several large sports media sites report up-to-the-minute information on regional, national, or international scores. Due to the popularity of the subject, the largest sites—including ESPNet SportsZone (Figure 11.13), CNN Interactive (http://www.cnn.com/SPORTS), Sportsline USA (http://www.sportsline.com), USA Today's Sports (http://www.usatoday.com/sports/sfront.htm), and Nando.net's sports section (http://www.nando.net/SportServer)—either charge for subscriptions or plan to do so

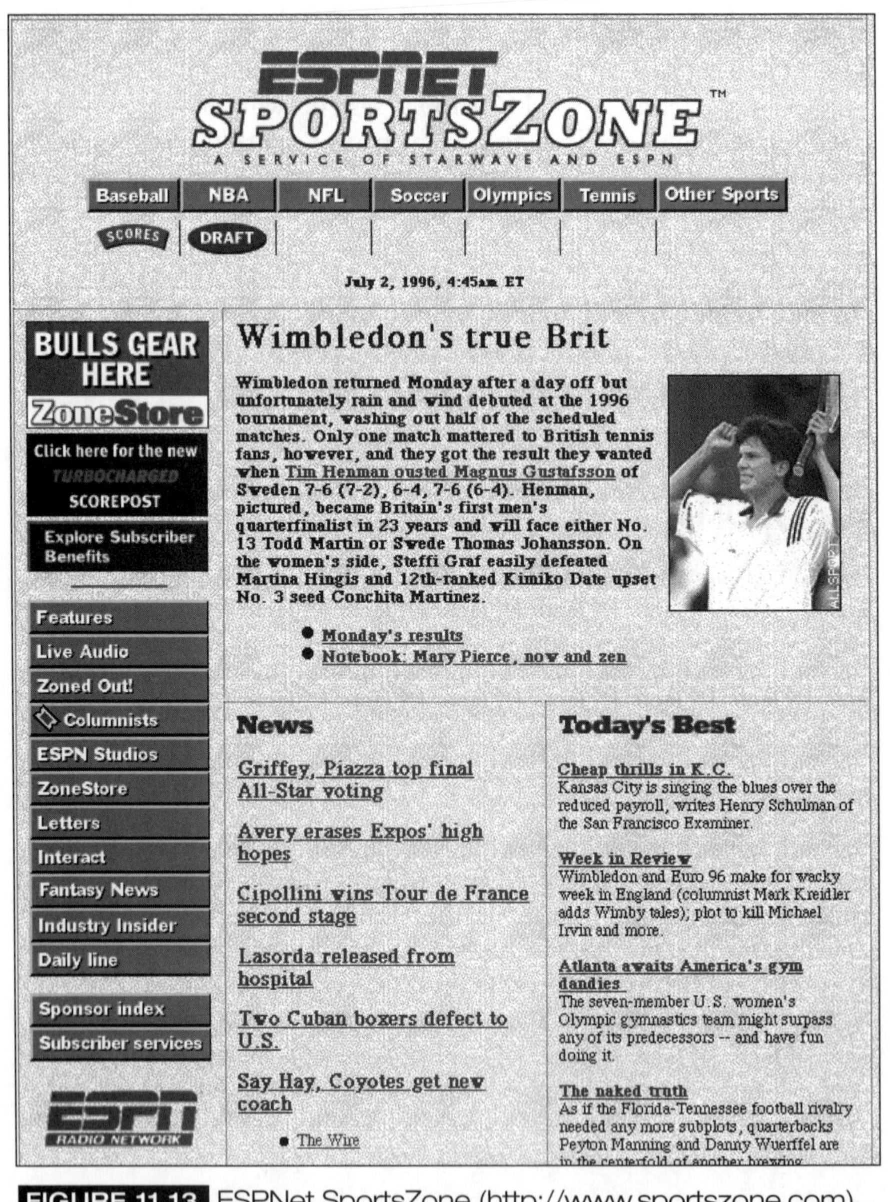

FIGURE 11.13 ESPNet SportsZone (http://www.sportszone.com).

in the future. ESPN's Web site, already one of the most popular destinations for surfers, had 450,000 users with 1.5 million hits during Superbowl weekend 1996. Competition between these sites is fierce; to date, the Internet audience has not selected a winner. Other, more personalized services such as The Mercury Mail (http://www.merc.com) provide customized sports news delivered by email for about $20 a year. Other useful sites include AllSports (http://www.allsports.com), which covers minor league baseball, and the Little League World Series (http://www.littleleague.org).

Typically, sports news sites report on as wide a variety of issues as possible. Since many audience members have very specific interests, the sites often allow paying members to customize their visits to the Web site so that the sports of interest are displayed prominently on the home page.

Major Leagues and Tournaments

Sports organizations, sometimes in conjunction with traditional broadcasters, are well-represented online. Official sites include the National Football League's Team NFL (Figure 11.14), Major League Baseball's @Bat (http://www.majorleaguebaseball.com), and the National Basketball Association's NBA.com (http://www.nba.com). In addition to their own pages, individual teams in each league typically have an official site surrounded by dozens of fan sites. All of these sites provide overlapping, but more specific coverage of the same information available at the sports news sites, as well as league and team-specific articles. Tournaments such as Wimbledon (http://www.wimbledon.org), Euro 96 (on Soccernet at http://soccernet.com/euro96), and Oh-Sumo Nagoya (on the Tokyo

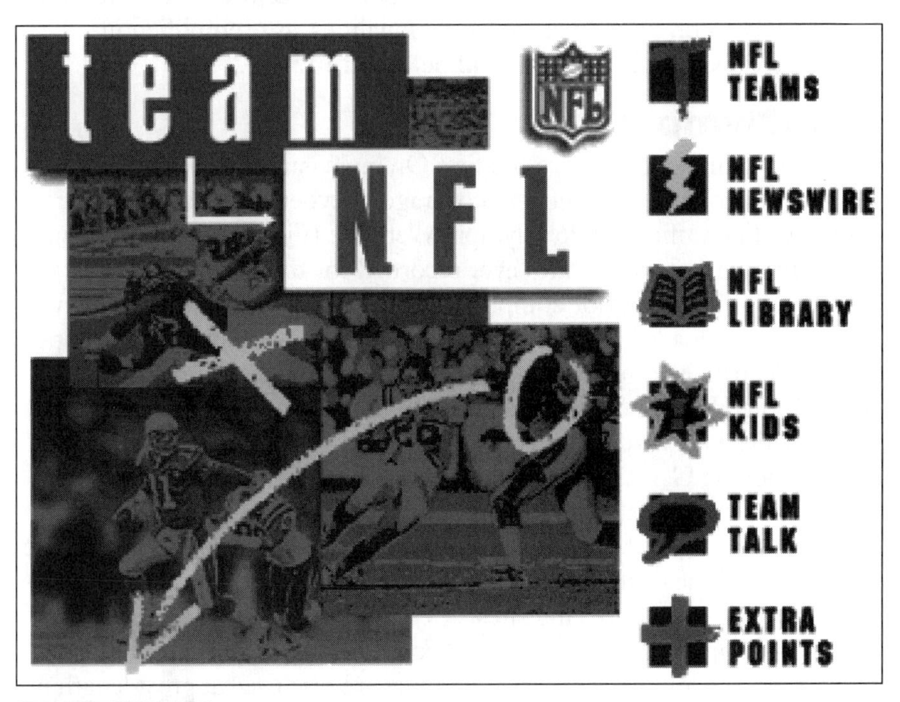

FIGURE 11.14 National Football League's Team NFL (http://www.nflhome.com).

FIGURE 11.15 Shaq World Online (http://www.shaq.com).

Broadcasting System's site—complete with RealAudio—at http://tbs.co.jp/radio/realaudio/sumo_nagoya/index.html) have official sites.

Chat rooms are extremely popular, and virtually all major sites run at least one for their audience. Unlike many other sites on the Net, people in sports chat rooms actually talk about sports! Recently, many sites have begun to focus on individual sports personalities, as exemplified in Shaquille O'Neal's Shaq World Online (Figure 11.15).

'96 Olympics

The 1996 summer games are the first Olympic games to occur during the short history of the Web and coverage in cyberspace has been extraordinary. The Official 1996 Olympic Web Site (Figure 11.16) received one of the highest traffic rates ever recorded for the Web—requiring specialized multiprocessor computers from IBM to handle the tremendous audience loads in excess of a million visitors per day. The site supported electronic commerce; nearly 40,000 tickets were purchased through the Web. In addition to direct reports on the games, the official site provides information on volunteer positions, travel, and coverage of the Paralympic Games for people with disabilities. The main site is surrounded by hundreds of official and non-official sites providing headlines, rankings, history, and commercial sponsor links. News from online broadcast and magazine sites forms an additional layer of coverage totaling thousands of interlocking sites.

The Olympics demonstrates how Web sites can create both a past and future presence for an event. Past Olympics are discussed at great length in several Web sites, of which NationsBank's 100 Years Looking Back (http://www.96games.com/history) provides especially detailed information

FIGURE 11.16 Official 1996 Olympic Web site (http://www.atlanta.olympic.org).

with a year-by-year calendar. While the next Olympic games are a few years in the future, it's not too soon to check out official sites for the Nagano Winter Games of 1998 (http://www.olympic.org/games/nagano), Sydney Summer Games of 2000 (http://www.sydney.olympic.org), and Salt Lake

City Winter Games of 2002 (http://www.olympic.org/games/saltlake) which are already available. Not content to wait, cities like Cape Town (http://www.ct2004.org.za) have already created host sites bidding to become the Olympic city of 2004—and other sites are bidding all the way to 2013.

Sports Handicapping

Sportswire (http://sportswire.com) provides an outstanding sports handicapping resource and is actively soliciting handicappers online. A branch of the Sports Network (http://www.sportsnetwork.com), it also provides a list of current "handicapping scams." Related informational sites include Real Sports (http://www.realsports.com) and The Sports Exchange (http://www.sportsexchange.com). With the success of these sites, it is a sure bet that their numbers will continue to increase. Numerous chatrooms at SportsChat (http://www.4-lane.com/sportchat) host informal handicapping and other casual sports conversation.

Recreational Sports

Thousands of sites, nearly all of them personal home pages, provide information, travelogues, links to agencies and sports vendors, and personal reviews of just about any sport imaginable. Unlike small sites in other areas of Intertainment, their pages frequently attract healthy lists of advertisers. The INFOHUB Recreation Page (http://www.infohub.com/TRAVEL/ADVENTURE/recreation.html) maintains a huge list of outlinks containing resources ranging from scuba diving to mountain climbing. Listings of sports and social clubs throughout the United States are available at the members-only The Social Cafe (http://www.social.com). Sites specifically devoted to "extreme" recreational sports

FIGURE 11.17 T@p Online's Extreme Sports Page (http://www.taponline.com/tap/sports/extreme/index.html).

FIGURE 11.18 Alternative Golf Workshop (http://altgolf.com).

like snowboarding and skydiving can be found at *Outside* magazine's online Extreme Magazine (http://outside.starwave.com) and T@p Online's Extreme Sports Page (Figure 11.17). A site that offers instructional services is The Alternative Golf Workshop (Figure 11.18).

Future Trends

With the widespread interest in sports information, as well as increasing advertising by manufacturers of sports equipment, sports sites appear to have one of the brightest—and most lucrative—futures on the Web. Since people who watch sports frequently play them as well, the audience is a natural for the prosumer world of the Internet.

Competition for Sports News Services

The largest sports services will feel increasing competition from regional and local services reporting the same information. Equally important, large numbers of sites with audience-driven rankings and polls will challenge national rankings.

Rising Image of Recreational Sports

The Web is likely to boost the fortunes of many nonprofessional sports, by covering and reporting on events that traditional media don't touch.

FIGURE 11.19 Lonely Planet (http://www.lonelyplanet.com.au).

Unusual sports are likely to win new converts from casual visitors to their sites.

Wired Sports Bars

Sports bars will likely form the newest branch of the cybercafe world. With quick links to numerous sites covering virtually any sport, they will provide information to their visitors that is unavailable elsewhere, and allow fans in similar locations to meet and even compete online.

Travel

The fast worldwide access to information makes the Internet a natural for the travel industry, which has gone online in a large way since early 1995. Beginning with Phillip Greenspun's acclaimed travelogue Travels with Samantha (http://www.swiss.ai.mit.edu/samantha/table-of-contents.html), travel has steadily grown through the efforts of local tourism boards, travel agents, and sites linking the information into a virtual brochure which lists nearly every major country in the world.

Virtual Travel

The current Yahoo! travel directory, as well as sites like eGO (http://www.ego.net), list information concerning U.S. and international travel. Local tourist boards have created thousands of travel-related sites, which are easily searched using directories like CheckIn (http://www.checkin.com/database.html) and The Virtual Tourist (http://www.vtourist.com). Worldwide Brochures (http://www.wwb.com) provides a searchable database of travel brochures online. For the stay-at-home, these sites afford the luxury of virtual travel to almost any major city in the world. Sites specifically offering virtual travel include TerraQuest (http://www.terraquest.com), Virtual Jerusalem Tour (http://www6.huji.ac.il/md/vjt), and Lonely Planet (Figure 11.19).

The Travel Channel (http://travelchannel.com) is planning a virtual circumnavigation of the globe to be presented in cyberspace. Virtual travel also provides the chance to visit interesting countries, including exotic islands such as Aruba (http://www.setarnet.aw) and Sri Lanka (http://www.is.lk/is). For those who question the wisdom of virtual travel, consider the advantages of exploring Virtual Antarctica (Figure 11.20) or

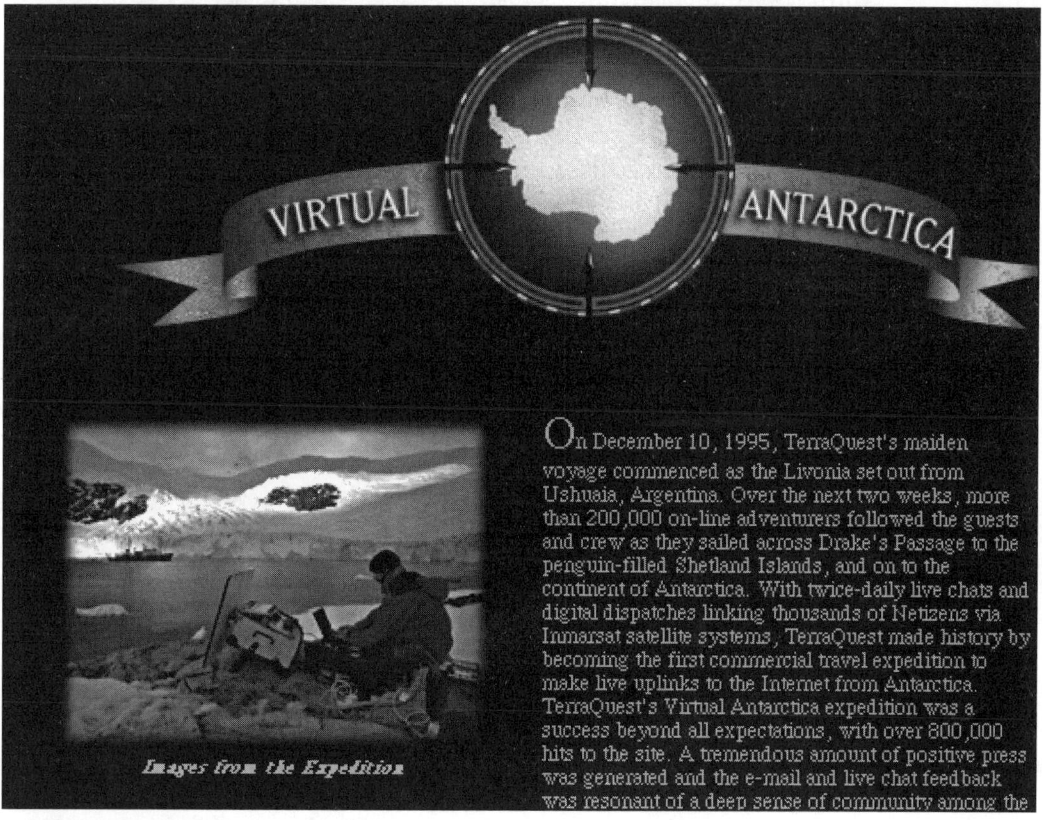

VIRTUAL
ANTARCTICA
On December 10, 1995, TerraQuest's maiden voyage commenced as the Livonia set out from Ushuaia, Argentina. Over the next two weeks, more than 200,000 on-line adventurers followed the guests and crew as they sailed across Drake's Passage to the penguin-filled Shetland Islands, and on to the continent of Antarctica. With twice-daily live chats and digital dispatches linking thousands of Netizens via Inmarsat satellite systems, TerraQuest made history by becoming the first commercial travel expedition to make live uplinks to the Internet from Antarctica. TerraQuest's Virtual Antarctica expedition was a success beyond all expectations, with over 800,000 hits to the site. A tremendous amount of positive press was generated and the e-mail and live chat feedback was resonant of a deep sense of community among the
Images from the Expedition

FIGURE 11.20 Virtual Antartica (http://www.terraquest.com/antarctica/).

deep space as seen by the Hubble Deep Field Project (http://www.stsci.edu/ftp/observer/hdf/hdf.html) from your home. For experiences closer to home, the ResortCam Web site (http://www.rsn.com/cam.html) provides random connections to a large number of vacation resorts throughout the United States. Recent advances include the use of virtual reality through QuickTime VR at sites like The Armchair Travel Company Ltd (http://www.armchair-travel.com) and Preview Vacations (http://www.vacations.com). The QuickTime VR panoramas are only a short step away from true virtual navigation in remote environments.

Travelogues

The cyberspace equivalent of the slide show is found on Web sites containing personal accounts of travel. Travelogues range from leisurely around-the-world trips like Russell Gilbert's Around The World Journal (http://home.city.net/travel/atwj) to ongoing reports from Road Trip America (http://www.roadtripamerica.com) to Solo Antarctica (http://www.theplanet.net/soloantarctica)—which details a harrowing personal journey across the frozen continent by a lone unassisted mountain climber. Other good sites include Philip Greenspun's Costa Rica (http://webtravel.org/cr) and NBC's Everest Assault (http://www.nbc.com/everest). These sites illustrate a trend developing in travelogues in which the Web site is used for publicity before the event, a reporting service during it, and as an archive after it is completed.

> ***One day, the Internet will be the most convenient and accepted way of doing research on upcoming trips and travel information. We may already be there. I love traveling too much to believe that we can simulate the experience of travel through HTML, VRML and their immediate successors. Virtual travel is a cerebral experience. But what about our senses? How do they get their kicks?***
>
> — Jean Noel Frydman, Owner, France Online
> http://www.france.com

Agencies

There are thousands of travel agencies online, whose sites range from simple ads to full-featured services like Travelocity (http://www.travelocity.com) and the Internet Travel Network (Figure 11.21), which both provide services including airline tickets, travel reservations, hotel reservations, and car rentals. Other sites providing travel agent services can be found in directories such as the European Travel Network

FIGURE 11.21 Internet Travel Network (http://www.itn.net).

(http://www.adlatjes.com) and Travelhub (http://travelhub.com); the latter provides a searchable database for specialty travel agencies. The Bucket Shop (http://www.etn.nl/bucketshops) provides links to a worldwide list of agents selling discount airline tickets.

Tourist Attractions

Theme parks and other tourist attractions could be viewed as a set of large-scale, participatory travel adventures with an artificial rather than a natural environment. Tourist spots run the gamut from more traditional theme parks such as Six Flags (http://www.sixflags.com) and Disneyland (http://www.disneyland.com) to unusual specialty attractions such as Medieval Times Dinner & Tournament (http://www.primenet.com/~proclaim/medieval.htm). Despite the obvious possibilities for virtual travel, the majority of these sites are strictly promotional. An exception is found at Universal Studios (http://www.mca.com/unicity), where a number of interactive games straddle the line between information and virtual travel.

For real-world travelers, sites such as FunGuide (http://www.funguide.com) provide international listings of theme parks; an international listing of water parks is available through The World Waterpark Association (http://www.waterparks.com). Several zoos, such as the Santa Ana Zoo (Figure 11.22), have created virtual tours of some of their outstanding exhibits. In addition to present-day attractions, historical societies such as the Palisades Amusement Park Historical Society (http://members.aol.com/palisades1/index.html) preserve the memory of the golden era of theme parks during the first part of the twentieth century. Fan sites have also been constructed for popular rides such as Rollercoaster! (Figure 11.23) and Carousel! (http://www.

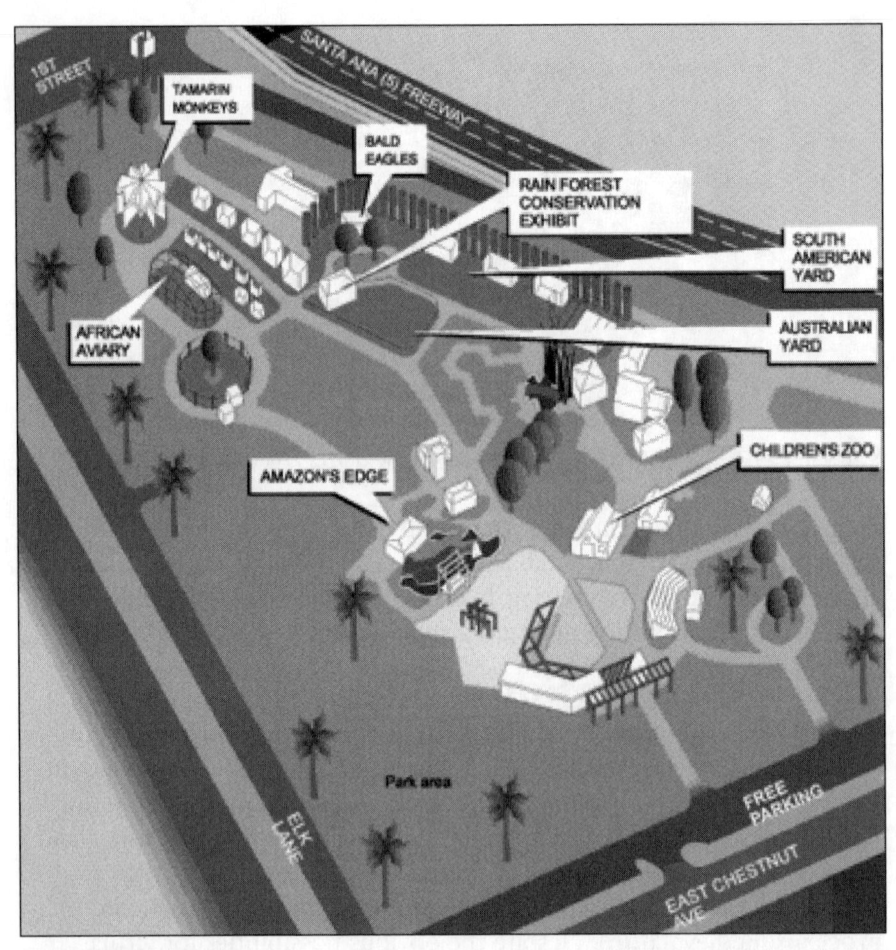

FIGURE 11.22 Santa Ana Zoo (http://www.santaanazoo.org).

access.digex.net/~rburgess/). For park developers, ITEC Productions (http://www.itecprod.com) and BRC Imagination Arts (http://www.brcweb.com) design theme park attractions; park engineering services are available at the Alcorn-McBride Theme Park Engineering (http://www.magicnet.net/alcorn) site.

Future Trends

Virtual travel seems more and more certain as developers work to bring immersive-style three-dimensional worlds to the Web. With the steady advance of virtual reality technology, it is likely in a few years that it will be possible to arrange spectacular virtual trips. The chief barrier to this is the slow speed of the Internet which restricts the delivery of real-time visual and auditory data from travel sites. As the production values on travel sites rise, their entertainment value may converge with fictional storytelling sites—providing a fictionalized reality of a personal travel experience. Travel sites, particularly those associated with tourist agencies, have exclusive access to compelling content. When virtual travel becomes established, travel sites will compete directly with the traditional entertainment industry. One possible form for these sites is virtual theme parks which mix real and fantasy travel. Another challenge will be to link the thousands of travel sites into a consistent whole. One possibility is to use the Global Positioning System (GPS) (http://galaxy.einet.net/editors/john-beadles/introgps.htm) to locate Web sites on a world map. Other possiblities include *web ring* software systems (see Chapter 15). In the near future, navigation through some parts of cyberspace may take the same route as the real world.

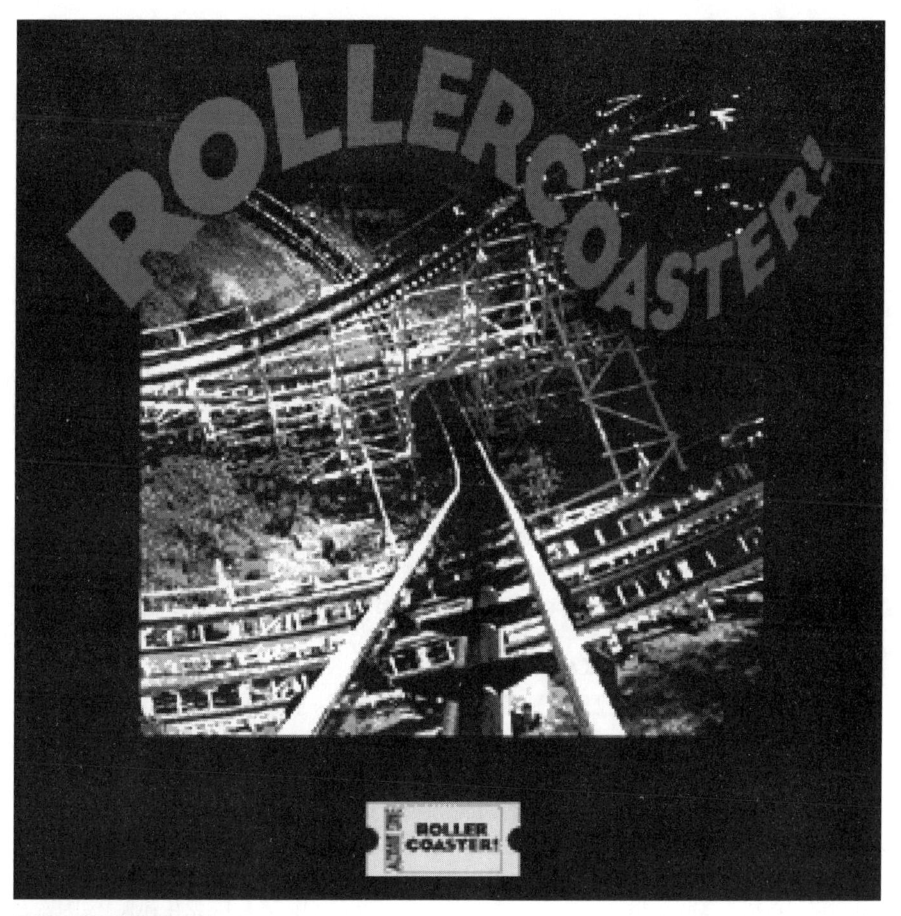

FIGURE 11.23 Rollercoaster! (http://mosaic.echonyc.com/~dne/Rollercoaster!).

FIGURE 11.24 Cupid's Network (http://www.cupidnet.com).

Personals

With the Internet's built-in support for communication at the individual and small group level, dating, matchmaking, and personals services are obvious candidates for Web development. While the traditional personals industry is currently just discovering the Web, a set of innovative startups is setting the pace for creating commercial services online. Significantly, these sites are moving beyond traditional matchmaking to embrace the ideal of electronic community (Chapter 14).

Directories

A good starting point for matchmaking and personals services is Cupid's Network (Figure 11.24), which contains listings of regional and global sites, singles events, matchmaking consultants and services, dating, travel, and even a woman and man of the month feature. Cupid's Network has become the major organizational system for personals sites; its seal appears on most of the other dating and personals sites currently on the Internet.

Online Personals

Match.com (Figure 11.25), the largest personals site on the Internet, currently passes more than 100,000 members. Each person pays a monthly subscription fee of $5.00 on average, making the site one of the most successful subscription-based services on the Internet. The site's main service (besides an online magazine for singles), is to create personality profiles which may then be matched against the Match.com database for compatibility. Members conduct their own searches through the Match.com database, instead of passively receiving the results of an old-style computer dating service. Besides this basic service, matchmaking sites frequently include other services their members are likely to use. Other new sites such as One-and-Only Internet Personals (http://www.one-and-only.com), webpersonals.com (http://www.webpersonals.com), Webmatch (http://www.webmatch.com), Cyberpark (http://www.cyberpark.com) and Flirt On-Line (http://www.flirt.com) integrate their matching databases with online chat, astrological counseling, and product sales. Unlike Match.com, these are (currently) free services. Some of these sites allow their members to submit pictures; in the near future they will include graphics, audio, and even video clips—all searchable by the appropriate program.

FIGURE 11.25 Match.com (http://www.match.com).

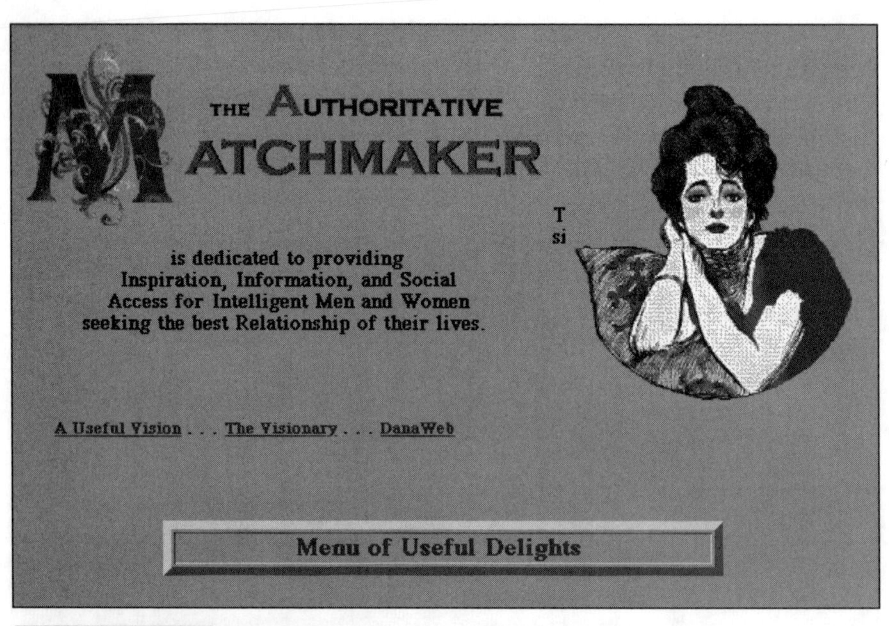

FIGURE 11.26 The Authoritative Matchmaker (http://on-demand.com/dnd).

> ***Community-building services are extremely important to the Web as it transitions from a business marketing communications and technical suppport vehicle to a place where communities are created. At the same time there is a risk of extreme societal fragmentation into microcommunities where together, consensus is impossible. Entertainment sites are one place where broader communities can form.***
>
> — GARY KREMEN, CHAIRMAN, BOARD OF DIRECTORS, ELECTRIC CLASSIFIEDS, INC. AND MATCH.COM
> http://www.match.com

Counseling Services

In addition to automated services, some services advertise direct one-on-one interaction with a counselor. The Authoritative Matchmaker (Figure 11.26) provides an advice column and a chance to talk directly to the site operator in its chat room. The Dear Kim (http://www.ny.com/nyc/kim) Web site and Dr. Tracy Cabot's Ask Dr. Tracy (http://www.loveadvice.com) sites provide an advice column as well as links to resources useful in relationships. A somewhat more satirical look at dating is available at The Definitive Guide to Relationships (http://www.odyssee.net/~jlevy).

Future Trends

Surprisingly slow in developing, increasing numbers of personal and matchmaking services are moving to the Web. With guaranteed audience interest, the role of dating and personals in Web entertainment can only rise, if those involved are successful in creating the social environment needed for these services to be successful. Community-building sites such as Firefly (http://www.firefly.com) are forms of personals, but have included additional features necessary to support a complete virtual community (discussed further in Chapter 14). With community-building services playing an increasing role in the evolution of the Web, matchmaking, and personals sites will have to expand their own boundaries and person-to-person contact will have a major role in the experience of Intertainment.

Web-wide Parties

The beginnings of a new era were heralded in the Three Worlds Party Mixer (http://www.ccon.org/events/mixup1.html), held on July 13, 1996. In this event, a virtual mixer ran across three software "worlds"—the two-dimensional chat world of The Palace (http://www.thepalace.com), and virtual-reality chat rooms from Worlds, Inc. (http://www.worlds.net) and Black Sun Interactive (http://www.blacksun.com). Hosted by Match.com (http://www.match.com) and The Contact Consortium (http://www.ccon.org), it is likely to be the first of many Web-wide singles parties.

Personal Counseling

Remarkably, given the enormous amount of spontaneous flirtation taking place online (Chapter 12), none of the matchmaking or personals services devote themselves specifically to cyber-style counseling. In the near future, it is likely that sites will be created that arrange and manage wholly virtual relationships.

Flirting Avatars and Agents

As Internet audience members create increasingly sophisticated models of their personalities in computer databases, the software itself may possibly extend the matchmaking process by contacting other models. Such avatars and agents may have the equivalent of brief electronic dates in order to screen encounters made by real individuals. Sites which provide software which can reliably do this are likely to become highly popular.

Homepages as Mini-personals

Already, individual Web pages bear many of the attributes of personals. In the near future, matchmaking services will likely develop meta-systems for linking and organizing home pages into their services. Since home pages frequently provide graphics, audio, and video not available in current sites, the latter will be force to upgrade their personals.

Links to Real-world Events

With the appearance of virtual parties on the Internet, it will become common to link them to real-world events. In many cases, the Internet may host a single giant virtual party, with its real-world components scattered over the globe.

Merging with Traditional Entertainment

Like many other areas of recreational Intertainment, rising standards may render dating and personals service sites almost indistingushible from those created by traditional entertainment. As personals provide gaming and entertainment sites provide chat, the trend towards a common form is already evident.

In the next chapter, the remaining areas of Internet-based entertainment are discussed. The new forms fuse the appeal of traditional narrative, artist-driven entertainment with the shared, social aspects of recreational entertainment, and are a new class of entertainment.

CHAPTER 12

NEW INTERTAINMENT:

Exploratory Fiction, Collaborative Arts, Tele-Operation, Chat Rooms, Multiplayer Games, Virtual Worlds, and Advertainment

While most traditional entertainment organizations and individuals are repurposing existing content for the Web, a few forward-thinking groups are developing standards for tomorrow's Intertainment. These efforts at original content development require the global interactivity of the Internet and frequently turn existing ideas of performance, marketing, and distribution on their collective heads. Currently found on a minority of entertainment sites, new Intertainment is nevertheless the future of the Web. This is a point that many industry professionals are just realizing. While traditional entertainment is not going away, it is no longer alone.

While some groups await the first success of a Web "broadcast" or "sitcom," the truth of the matter is that these hits—if and when they occur—will be almost unrecognizable. By its very definition, new Intertainment creates a conceptual hurdle that individual entertainers, companies, and the public have to overcome. The following discussion addresses this necessary mental switch by analyzing current examples of new Intertainment and predicting their long-term fortunes.

Features of New Intertainment

Is new Intertainment really so different from traditional material? After all, episodic Web "soaps" bear at least a distant relationship to television and multiplayer games appear to be merely an extension of the gaming industry (and have been used on local BBS networks for years prior to the rise of the Internet). New Intertainment distinguishes itself in the following areas.

Interactivity

The most important feature of new Intertainment is interactivity; only a small percentage of the millions of Web pages online have it. In the context of this discussion, interactivity is not defined by the ability to *select content*, but by the ability to *modify and add to content*. By this definition, standard Web pages, as well as non-Web systems such as interactive TV, are not truly interactive. Traditional entertainment assumes that content creation may be separated from its enjoyment, while new Intertainment requires that you can influence it in some way. By allowing the audience to participate in the content, new Intertainment lessens the distinctions between the entertainer and the entertained.

Exploration

Unlike linear media, new Intertainment actually works better when its content is chopped up and left in small pieces for the audience to sample at will. In traditional entertainment, the point of view—whether it is a movie scene, audience seat, or third-person perspective in a novel—is assigned by the creator. In new Intertainment, the audience can control its own point of view.

Social Contact

Earlier forms of electronic media (such as CD-ROM and computer games) traditionally pit an audience of one against a machine's software. This has contributed to a perception of electronic entertainment as exclusive and isolationist. By contrast, the new Intertainment uses the Internet to link groups of individuals. Instead of multimedia software tricks, the entertainment experience depends on the existence of *people* on the other end of the Net connection. In its focus on individuals instead of algorithms, new Intertainment returns electronics to its rightful role as *conduit* instead of *narrator*.

A key concept in social interaction on the Internet is the representation of the person by an *agent* and/or *avatar*. These software constructs allow visitors to dissolve the "fourth wall" separating them from a story or event, and interact as a character. Agents represent the mental aspect of the audience member's presence in the world and consist of information describing the person's personality, desires, interests, and so on. Avatars represent the appearance of the visitor. Taken together, these aspects represent the visitor in cyberspace. Current virtual worlds support agents and avatars to varying degrees, with community-oriented sites like Firefly (http://www.firefly.com) making strong use of agents, and multiuser games focusing almost exclusively on avatars.

Each type of new Intertainment considered in the rest of this chapter embodies one or more of these features. A discussion of the sociopolitical consequences of the public experiencing new Intertainment is in Chapter 14.

Exploratory Fiction

Much excitement in the traditional industry has been focused on Web sites that have transferred traditional narrative storytelling stories common in film and television to the Web. Often referred to as *episodic Web fiction*, the latter type of site was pioneered by The Spot (Figure 12.1). After The Spot became one of the most popular sites on the Web, its creators developed a new "network" called American Cybercast (http://www.amcy.com) in partnership with the Creative Artists Agency (http://caa.com) to continue to explore the concept. As a group, these sites differ from other interactive fiction in having distinct episodes and relying heavily on high-quality graphics and short blocks of text to tell their message. Many episodic sites also distinguish themselves in their high-quality writing, which uses strong plot and character development familiar in movies and television. With money and the traditional industry putting its weight behind the approach, episodic Web sites will be increasingly popular forms of new Intertainment.

Like traditional broadcast programs or novels, exploratory Web fiction has a well-developed, preconceived plot with a regular cast of characters. To maintain audience interest, the story is serialized, with installments appearing at regular intervals. However, certain characteristics of storytelling and graphic design distinguish themselves from books and television programs. Audience members visiting episodic sites do not watch a linear narrative like a movie. Instead, interactive Web fiction allows access to content at random to find phone transcripts, letters, and even short videos describing events in the story—which may be viewed or examined in any order. In this way, the audience member is less like an

FIGURE 12.1 The Spot (http://www.thespot.com).

observer and more like an invisible detective trying to reconstruct a plot. While some of the immediacy of a novel or movie is lost, the audience is, in fact, free to view the story from a variety of angles instead of a single point of view imposed by the author. Most episodic sites are not strongly interactive, despite the presence of posting boards and chat rooms. While readers are encouraged to send fan mail, they do not directly affect the story and cannot become characters themselves.

> ***A lot of people in the interactive media world, after witnessing many admirable but failed attempts, felt that outside of computer games and MUs, "interactive narrative" was an oxymoron. The Spot's creators really did get it about using the Net to create community; they stayed true to the principle and proved that it was***

possible to do so — with a soap opera of all things! Concept-wise, it's old hat now — The Spot was the first, but won't likely go down in history as the best — but it was quite significant in the evolution of the medium.

— JEANNINE PARKER, DIRECTOR, NATIONAL INFORMATION INFRASTRUCTURE AWARDS, PRINCIPAL, MAGNITUDE ASSOCIATES; EXECUTIVE BOARD, INTERNATIONAL INTERACTIVE COMMUNICATIONS SOCIETY (IICS); BOARD OF DIRECTORS, INTERNET DEVELOPERS ASSOCIATION (IDA)
http://www.gii-awards.com

Interactive fiction distinguishes itself from an ordinary narrative in having to support multiple story threads. In narrative fiction, the audience follows a single line through the story and the authors do not have to pay attention to areas immediately outside the narrative. Thus, for example, if characters leave the room in a film narrative, the author does not necessarily need to plot the details of their movement until they return to the thread of the story. In interactive storytelling, the opposite is true. After the main story line is developed, the authors must fill in details for *every character* involved in the story, whether each one participated in the main plot. Nonlinear plotting on the Web (as well as CD-ROM stories) dramatically changes authoring requirements for Web-based storytelling. For example, consider a character who is not present in a scene critical to the main plot. In Web-based storytelling, the character's behavior must still be completely worked out, even though that person doesn't take part in the main action.

Technology

While interactive fiction sites normally boast cutting-edge graphics and advanced multimedia extensions, their basic form can be implemented in HTML. Typically, the site is simply a series of linked Web pages that are updated for each episode. Each page contains elements of the plot, embodied in letters, notes, pictures, and short audio and video clips. While many sites create scenes using actors, settings, and support personnel common in film and television, they normally do not broadcast this information in real time.

Episodic Sites Online

High-profile sites include Marinex Multimedia's East Village (http://pathfinder.com/eastvillage), Internet Broadcasting Company's Richard III Interactive (http://www.ashakespeare.com), and American

FIGURE 12.2 Ferndale (http://www.ferndale.com).

Cybercast's new science fiction adventure, Eon 4 (http://www.eon4.com). Moving closer to planet Earth, Ferndale (Figure 12.2) follows four people exploring their problems by allowing the audience to eavesdrop on their therapy sessions. The Ferndale site is interactive and audience participation is encouraged by asking readers to submit their own personal secrets. Stories like Gay Daze (http://www.gaydaze.com) deal with topics censored from network television.

A recent trend is to mix the episodic material provided on the Web site with live action. The location of the event is normally provided on the Web site and must be unlocked using a puzzle. Both KAPOW (http://www.kapow.com) and Dreadnot (Figure 12.3) have taken this approach and run live-action parallels to the Web story in their respective cities.

Future Trends

With big-name sponsors and traditional Hollywood talent pouring into Web fiction, the trend toward episodic fiction and Web-based networks such as American Cybercast will likely continue. At present, the greatest challenge to the medium is finding a way to incorporate more true interactivity into the content, as opposed to providing simple content exploration. Already some steps are being taken along this line with Grapejam, The Spot creator Scott Zakarin's new episodic site which is modeled after a famous Saturday Night Live sketch. By increasing interactivity between performers and audience, the site seeks to create the intimate environment of a comedy club. As the medium matures, episodic fiction will begin to show the interactivity characteristic of other new Intertainment and let the visitor through the "fourth wall" to join the characters.

Collaborative Arts

One area of interactive expression that the Web specifically enables is in the area of collaborative arts and entertainment. These systems create a visual, verbal, or auditory canvas to which artists from all over the Internet can contribute. This form of Intertainment is two-phased: It supports interactivity during its creation and it is passively viewed or experienced after completion. By relying on the audience to submit content, they differ dramatically from exploratory sites such as the episodic Web sites.

Technology

The technology behind individual collaborative art projects was developed specifically for the sites it is implemented on; Web developers seeking to provide multiuser art have to do considerable custom programming to make it work. With rapid developments in Java programming technology, commercial programs for implementing collaborative art should be available in the near future.

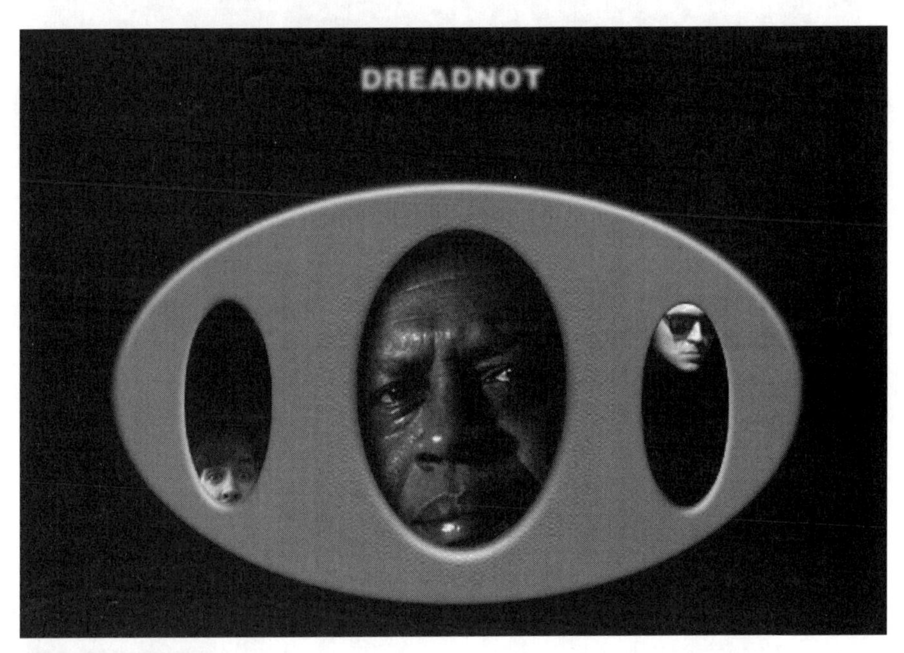

FIGURE 12.3 Dreadnot (http://www.sfgate.com/dreadnot).

FIGURE 12.4 HypArt (http://rzsun01.rrz/uni-hamburg.de).

Collaborative Art Mosaics

Another form of collaborative art is being pursued at HypArt (Figure 12.4), where each artist contributes a small panel that forms a part of a work of art. Such *mosaic* sites are becoming increasingly popular and reached their climax in the first Internet-wide event on the Web, 24 Hours in Cyberspace (http://www.cyber24.com). Part art, part journalistic reporting, this project integrated the individual pictures of thousands of photographers on February 24, 1996. Judged a huge success by its developers and the Internet audience, it is likely to be followed by other, more ambitious collaborative projects.

I think some new style of art will be born via the Web soon. Some artists think about collaborating with artists overseas; some are thinking about how to have their home page more artistic. The Japanese art scene is going to the next stage after the collapse of Japan's overheated stock and real estate markets. Large companies do not use money for artists any more. So independent artists are looking for another way to show their art works and keep creating them. It is true that independent artists don't have much money and not as many artists have computers. But they are very interested in the Internet for their opportunities.

— Minori Watanabe, Founder, Japanese art server, UMMIT. Ink
http://www.ummit.co.jp

Collaborative Music

While less common than collaborative visual art, a few experiments are underway which integrate music submitted over the Internet into a single work. Currently, the best example is honoria in ciberspazio (http://www.en.utexas.edu/~slatin/opera), a collaborative musical work whose genesis is being moderated by Sandy Stone at the University of Texas' Advanced Communication Technologies Laboratory or ACT (http://www.actlab.utexas.edu). The home page of the project invites Internet surfers to the site to examine the opera's lyrics and provide their own arias. Described as a romantic comedy, the libretto relates the adventures of several people discovering each other in cyberspace. The show has received submissions from close to 100 musicians and is scheduled for performance in October 1996 using Apple Computer's WebCast (http://www.live.apple.com) system.

While creating the opera is a participatory event, the actual performance will follow standard operatic format, with a conventional venue. Information on other collaborative music projects (particularly those using *MIDI*) is available by joining the Make-Music email list (http://www.mailbase.ac.uk/lists-k-o/make-music).

More recently, several real-time collaborative music projects have appeared on the Web by exploiting the low bandwidth of MIDI files. These projects allow several musicians at different locations on the Internet to jam together. The most sophisticated site is found at Res Rocket Surfer (http://www.resrocket.com). This site organizes collaborative music sessions and provides specialized MIDI software to support collaborative music. Another collaborative music site is the Internet JAM Session (http://www.infopark.de/gmh/jame.html).

Virtual Graffiti Walls

To date, this art has precisely mimicked that other example of collaborative art in a public environment—graffiti. Unlike collaborative mosaics, graffiti walls allow each audience member access to the entire canvas, with the added ability to alter previous material left by others. Graffiti walls exist on a variety of Web sites, including Real Graffiti (http://militzer.me.tuns.ca/graffiti) and The Virtual Graffiti Wall (Figure 12.5). An especially interesting site is available from Singapore at The BOG (http://www.technet.sg/BOG/), which allows visitors to leave printed messages on a variety of wall textures. Since graffiti of *any* sort is strictly forbidden in Singapore, this site is the only place in the country where collaborative art can be expressed.

Collaborative Novels

A large number of authors have used the Web as a way to extend writing beyond the confines of the basic novel. In form, these sites rely almost entirely on text to tell their story; anyone who can type can contribute. The author's own Kaleidospace site was a pioneer in this area; during 1994 and 1995 it featured collaborative stories contributed by high-profile writers David Brin and Clive Barker. Some sites, such as Death Has a

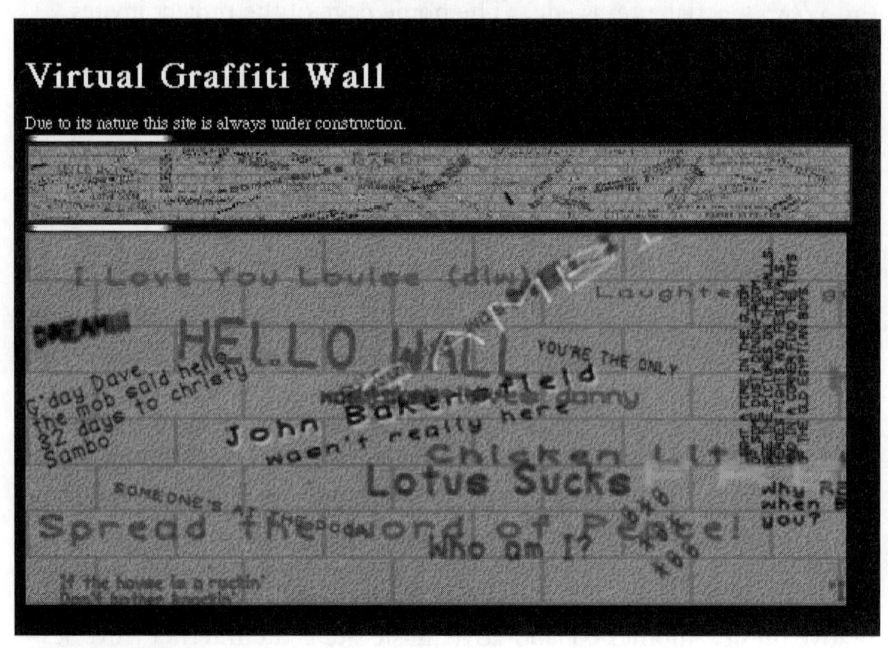

FIGURE 12.5 The Virtual Graffiti Wall (http://www.sorceror.com/thewall.html).

Home Page (http://www.avenuepark.com/novel.html), provide prewritten chapters; at the end of each, readers vote on possible courses of action the story can take next. More complex stories have multiple authorship and are the verbal equivalent of collaborative graffiti walls and art mosaics. Some extreme sites, such as Storyline (http://members.gnn.com/kwosepka/storyline.htm), build up a long narrative, a single sentence at a time—each contributed by a different visitor. In contrast, editorial control is applied to the "raw" Internet collaboration at Gav and Peloso's Interactive Story (http://www.nuc.berkeley.edu/neutronics/gav/wayfarence/welcome.html). Despite the intriguing concepts, the difficulties of reading long text documents onscreen may have prevented collaborative novels from achieving greater popularity.

Future Trends

While the application of collaborative art to date has had elements of an academic pursuit, it also has very strong potential for entertainment sites, particularly with part of their appeal coming from one or more celebrities. One possibility is for the content provider to provide a sketch of a scene from a story and allow visitors to fill in the details. In the long term, content providers may consider allowing audience members to control the appearance of the site itself (such as graphical headers) in a letters or fan support area. Collaborative music offers even more interesting potential. For example, a popular band on an entertainment site could provide basic music tracks as MIDI files and encourage visitors to provide additional tracks, or even allow group jams online. Individual bands might use this system to review potential new members, and lyricists and composers could also collaborate on a work-in-progress in this way.

Tele-operation

Remote control of devices through the Internet is a completely new form of Intertainment with no real precedent in other media. Until the recent growth of the Web, remote device control or *tele-operation* existed in highly specialized environments such as nuclear reactors and research robots. Now, literally thousands of cameras, faxes, speakers, pagers, and even robot arms are available for use by the Internet audience. Unlike classical tele-operation, dozens and sometimes hundreds of Internet surfers may try to control the equipment at the same time, with unpredictable results. Useful indices of Internet-controlled devices are available from bsy's List of Internet Accessible Machines (http://www-cse.ucsd.edu/users/bsy/iam.html) and Anthony's List of Internet-Accessible Machines (http://www.dsu.edu/~anderbea/machines.html).

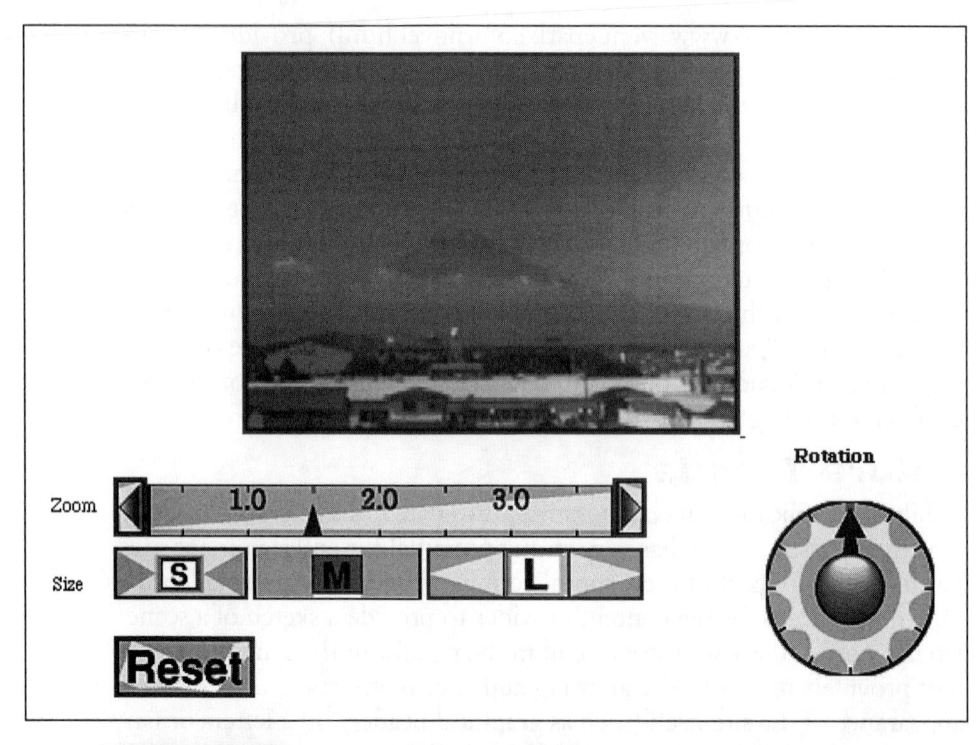

FIGURE 12.6 Internet Advanced Communications' Mt. Fuji Camera (http://www.city.fujiyoshida.yamanashi.jp/mtfuji/tonbo/index-e.html).

Technology

Internet-based device control is still very new and only a handful of products are available for Web site developers to use with their own system. Perceptual Robotics, Inc. (http://www.nethomes.com/InterCam/prinews.html) sells the LabCam hardware and software spy camera which allows Internet control of tilt, pan, and the zoom lens. Currently, other systems controlling robot arms or sensors are built with custom software. Web developers interested in adding these systems to their sites will need to hire someone familiar with the technology; start by contacting the developers of devices already online.

Spy Cameras

Beginning in early 1994—at Cambridge University's Trojan Room Coffee Machine (http://www.cl.cam.ac.uk/coffee/coffee.html)—thousands of cameras have been connected to the Internet; comprehensive lists are available at places like Cameras, Cameras and More Cameras! (http://www.intertain.net/~cameras), which also provides a searchable database.

Most of these devices provide simple passive viewing; however, in a few cases the cameras go beyond simply providing a view and allow the visitor to interactively point and zoom in on certain areas of a larger scene. Steerable cameras are maintained at NYU's LabCam (http://found.cs.nyu.edu/cgi-bin/rsw/labcam), Internet Advanced Communications' Mt. Fuji Camera (Figure 12.6), and a system using different technology is available at VTV Webcam (http://www.warp.com/vtvwebcam/howitworks.html).

Sensors

These sites allow visitors from the Internet to examine the state of objects connected to the Internet. The original, and in some ways the best, is Paul Haas' home page (http://www.hamjudo.com) which allows visitors to eavesdrop on the temperatures of various items in Paul's refrigerator and even check and see if the hot tub is running. Similarly bizarre statistics may be found at The Buzbee Bat House Temperature Plot (http://www.nyx.net/~jbuzbee/bat_house.html) and Crasher 3 (http://puck.nether.net/crasher3), which records the odometer reading of a 1986 Chevrolet.

Robotic Arms and Effectors

Some Web sites actually allow visitors to control devices that influence the physical environment. Hardware and software needed to create these systems is largely ad hoc and is usually pieced together by tinkerers. One of the first experiments was USC's The Mercury Project (http://www.usc.edu/dept/raiders)—the precursor to the new Tele-Garden (http://www.usc.edu/dept/garden) which allows visitors to tend and water plants near a robotic arm. Another outstanding site is available at the iNTERFACE (http://www.quadrant.net/interface) robotic arm site. This project was activated on September 7, 1996, allows the visitor to paint on a warehouse floor and view the results from a vertically mounted spy camera. A less serious device is available at the University of Ulm's Interactive Model Railroad (Figure 12.7). This site provides controls to drive a model train between platforms—unless another visitor gets to it first.

A slightly more artistic, and threatening, situation is found at The Telematic Sculpture (http://iis.joanneum.ac.at/kriesche/biennale95.html). At this site, a huge mobile sculpture (length 21.8 meters; weight 1800 kg) called T.S.4 is physically positioned in the Austrian pavilion during the biennale of Venice. A computer program compares the number of art discussions occurring on the Web and Usenet to computer discussions—and, if the former is too small, it smashes the sculpture into the wall of the Austrian pavilion.

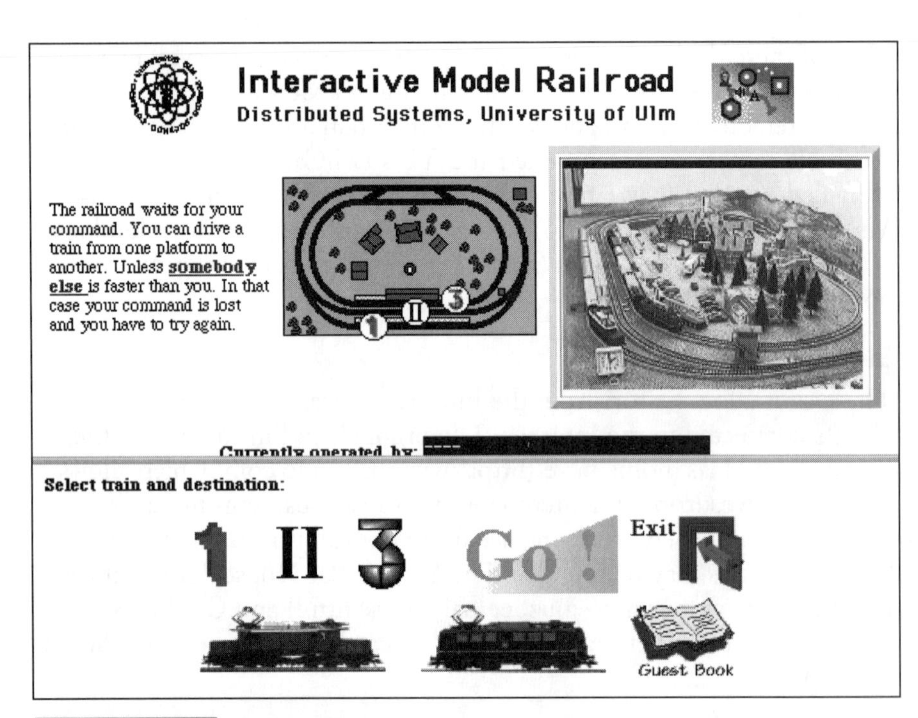

FIGURE 12.7 University of Ulm's Interactive Model Railroad (http://rr-vs.informatik.uni-ulm.de/rr/).

Future Trends

While Internet-controlled devices may seem something of a joke, they may have a serious future in Intertainment. After all, celebrities routinely chat with members of the Internet audience; why not arm-wrestle them? Remote devices and sensors could also be used to take the Internet audience behind the scenes for TV and film production. Considering the interest of fans in the personal lives of celebrities, providing temperature readouts from a refrigerator may not be out of order. This is a completely unexplored area that could result in high-visibility for entertainment sites that use it correctly. Remote device monitoring may also become useful as entertainment companies increasingly decentralize their operations and rely on telecommuting. Remote sensing and control of such devices as mixing consoles, nonlinear editors, and even stage lighting could play a major role in the future of behind-the-scenes entertainment.

Another step in the use of Internet-connected devices was taken recently by the developers of Rob's Digital Cast (Figure 12.8). By supplying appropriate instructions on the Web site, Internet visitors could trigger a vibrating beeper encased in a leg cast. It is left to the reader's imagination as to how such devices will be used in the future.

Chat Rooms

Chat is one of the jewels in the crown of the Internet. Far more sophisticated than phone "party lines," chat allows a few to thousands of people to socialize in environments ranging from printed text to elaborate fantasy worlds. Chat-based Intertainment shows extreme interactivity and exploration, and contributes to a leveling between content providers and consumers. Large numbers of entertainment sites run chat servers to increase their audience and demonstrate a commitment to their audience.

Technology

Text-only discussions mediated through the Internet Relay Chat (ftp://ds.internic.net/rfc/rfc1459.txt) system have been available for some time. While gates to the IRC system are available through the Web at sites like Alamak's Web IRC Gateway (http://www.alamak.com/chat/index.html), the primary chat system on the Web is a text-based program called WebChat (http://www.IRsociety.com/wbs.html). Written entirely using pure HTML-style programming, it creates a text chat environment with the option of adding user-specific pictures. Its main virtue is compatibility with almost all Web browsers in current use and variants are available of thousands of sites all over the Internet. Other text-only chat systems based off of IRC include Prospero's GlobalChat (http://www.

FIGURE 12.8 Rob's Digital Cast (http://ttt.media.mit.edu/cgi-bin/r).

qdeck.com/chat) system. Another chat system called PowWow (http://www.tribal.com/powwow) allows small numbers of chatters to cruise the Web as a group. Chat systems incorporating audio, video, and three-dimensional objects are actually examples of virtual worlds and are discussed in detail later in the chapter.

Indices

The WebChat-based WBN (http://www.irsociety.com/wbs/events.html) is the current center of the Internet chat world; it provides links to chat rooms and a schedule of events. Another excellent directory is available at WebChat Navigator (http://www.goodnet.com/~roberte/webchatnavigator.html). This site provides direct links to a variety of chat rooms and indicates topics being discussed. Other useful indices are available at the Ultimate Chat List (Figure 12.9), Internet Chat Guide (http://arachnid.qdeck.com/chat/schedule.html), and Celebrity Chat Schedule (http://pathfinder.com/vibe/theroom/docs/chat.html) posted at Vibe Online on a regular basis.

Using Chat on Web Sites

One of the simplest ways to increase interest in a Web site is to leave a chat room open and unattended 24 hours a day. As individuals discover the room, they will rapidly build a list of regular visitors who use it as a meeting place. While the majority of visitors tend to respect each other and the room, a few "potty mouths" (see Chapter 8) are likely to appear with time. If the room is not occasionally checked, their actions can frighten regular visitors or even damage the room itself. To avoid this, the Internet addresses of all visitors should be visible to the chat moderator (or to the entire room if no moderator is present).

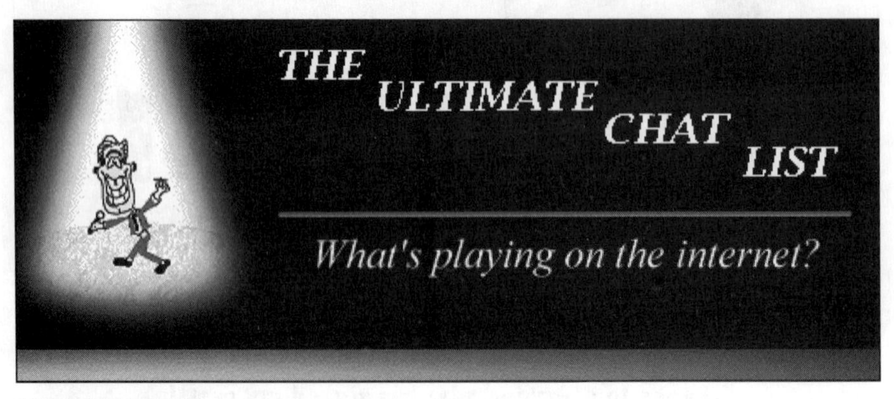

FIGURE 12.9 Ultimate Chat List (http://american.recordings.com/WWWoM/chat/).

FIGURE 12.10 Chat Soup (http://www.chatsoup.com).

An alternate strategy is to stage the chat sessions following the normal pattern of event programming—with advance publicity, a set time for operation, and archives and transcripts of the events available afterward. Such moderated events are useful for more formal situations such as interviews with individual entertainers. Examples of such use include celebrity chats on major sites such as Vibe Online (http://pathfinder.com/vibe/theroom/docs/chat.html) and moderated chat with independent artists and musicians in our Kaleidospeak (http://kspace.com/chat) chat room. To create a moderated room, it is necessary to assign individuals to act as MC/interviewers, chat police, and to open and close for specific events. After the chats are complete, most sites archive them as a source of additional content—and services like Chat Soup (Figure 12.10) comb them for interesting gossip.

Future Trends

With the continual development of graphical chat systems, the appeal of the system becomes greater, along with the opportunity to design a unique chat environment. The most likely trend in chat is professionalization, the creating of sophisticated chat environments that audience members will be willing to pay for on a subscription or micropayment basis. This change will be aided by introducing chat into sophisticated virtual worlds environments (see later discussion). Another possibility is to use the chat area to break down the "fourth wall" of an interactive play or story. Instead of asides to live audiences, characters in an ongoing story could send messages to the chat room to reveal their character's private thoughts. Entertainment of this type will run anywhere from narrative storylines to a virtual date with the performer.

Multiplayer Games

In Chapter 11, we discussed traditional computer games—whose limited interactivity consists of a visitor paired with a software program. The features of the Internet allow this model to be extended to multiple users playing the same game. Interactive Internet gaming in many senses represents the simplest example of new Intertainment. While the rigid rules of most games exclude some forms of interactivity, multiple players can create a social environment where part of the overall entertainment depends upon the participants themselves. Traditional play-by-mail companies such as Midnight Games (http://www.mgames.com) have branched out to create email and Web-based games. While the interface remains simple, these are true interactive games run through a mixture of interactive postal and electronic networks. Games supported by this system include versions of sports, board games like chess, and shared fantasies.

Commercial multiplayer games running over proprietary modem-based networks have existed for several years. While these games have reduced interactivity and social features relative to the role-playing games previously mentioned (due to rigid rules of play), they partly compensate by containing rich graphical environments and the fast response necessary for *twitch* combat games. Multiuser games are adapted for the online medium by *gaming networks* that do not create content but modify existing games for use online. While many game networks have been popular, the industry's $30 million intake in 1995 is a far cry from the $8 billion of the video game industry. Several forces (such as lack of email) have hindered their growth, but the primary problem—the requirement for long-distance dialing by most of their customers—is removed by running the network over the Internet.

Technology

At present, software enabling online gaming is a proprietary, and jealously guarded, secret of the companies involved. Individual Web site operators may incorporate multiplayer gaming into their own sites using

FIGURE 12.11 Total Entertainment Network [TEN] (http://www.ten.net).

software packages like the Web Games Online Entertainment System (http://www.eden.com/~springer/). This system provides Windows-based software for the game client and server, as well as a set of sample games.

Companies

Industry pioneer, The ImagiNation Network (http://www.inngames.com), has gone to the Internet along with networks specializing in low-latency twitch games which include the Total Entertainment Network or TEN (Figure 12.11), The Concentric Network (http://www.concentric.net)—which is also an Internet service provider—MPath (http://www.mpath.com), and Mac-only network Outland Games (Figure 12.12). Most companies require use of their proprietary programs to connect to the games, though a few like Virtual Worlds (http://www.vwnet.com) have created Netscape plug-ins allowing direct play through the Web. To replace their own proprietary network, gaming companies have contracted with Internet service providers (ISPs) to ensure fast response times and collect fees from audience members using the services.

FIGURE 12.12 Outland Games (http://www.outland.com).

Recently, some larger gaming companies have disclosed plans for multiplayer gaming over the Internet using existing cartridge game systems as a starting point. Sega America (http://www.sega.com) began selling an Internet link and Web browser add-on to its Saturn game system, and Apple Computer (http://www.apple.com) has been selling an Internet-ready version of its Pippin CD-ROM multimedia player. In both cases, players will pay standard (about $20) monthly fees for access to the Internet and shared multiuser games. While many Web sites offer electronic versions of traditional board games, only a few such as The Internet Gaming Zone (http://www.zone.com) allow interactive multiuser contests similar to the action games previously listed.

Increasing Interactivity

Online gaming companies have begun to realize that most of their game systems—even when multiplayer capabilities are present—still reduce to individual-computer play if they cannot interact with other players. While several individuals may participate in traditional game networks, their interactions are extremely limited and the normal conversational "give and take" in real-world games is absent. The ImagiNation Network has attempted to increase the community aspects of network games by extensive use of avatars. Out of the remaining game networks, MPath has gone the furthest in realizing the need for forming a community and plans to turn its games into an environment supporting general interactivity between its players. MPath's current MPlayer (http://www.mplayer.com) system provides for conferencing between game players via voice or text-based chat. In addition, the system provides a shared canvas on which players on the same team may map out their strategies.

Future Trends

Due to the limitations of standard Web-based programming and text-based multiuser games, several companies have developed custom Internet software designed to support a few to thousands of players at the same time in a rich graphical environment. Recently, software company RTime (http://www.rtimeinc.com) announced a set of software tools that will allow online game developers to support simultaneous play by hundreds of thousands of users scattered over the Internet. Existing games were never designed for such massive playing audiences; therefore, their design, rules, and interactivity will need to be re-thought to make their use by large audiences a relevant experience. A good online publication covering trends in online gaming is Hyper@ctive Online (http://hyperactive.com).

 Virtual Worlds

The most advanced forms of Web-based Intertainment simultaneously support the narrative adventures of episodic Web fiction and the conversational intimacy of gaming and chat. These models for new Intertainment, referred to collectively as online communities or *virtual worlds*, are the cutting edge of the Internet. Virtual worlds are not new and form a long tradition beginning with Lucasfilm's Habitat (http://www.digitalcentury.com/encyclo/update/lucas.html) project in the mid-1980s. However, it is only in the last few years that hardware and software networks combined to create the global structure capable of supporting first-generation virtual reality. A good place to begin looking at virtual worlds is Electric Communities Habitat (http://www.communities.com/habitat.html), which lists a variety of environments currently in testing or in use.

MUDS and MOOs

MultiUser Domains (MUDs) and MultiUser Domains Object-Oriented (MOOs) are components of Internet-specific, multiuser text-based games providing for exploration of interactive, social fantasy worlds (see the MUD FAQ at http://math.okstate.edu/~jds/mudfaqs.html for a definitive discussion). As such, they are perfect examples of new Intertainment. Working without graphics, MUDs nevertheless succeed in creating complex virtual worlds whose nature can be altered by their participants. With this potential, it is somewhat surprising that there has been little movement to transfer them to the Web. One approach has been to add a small software *gateway* which allows the Web server to query the MUD/MOO server database for information. A site available to the Web through this means is at CardiffMOO (http://www.ccs.neu.edu/home/nop/mudwww.html). While the gateway works with any browser, the resulting MOO is strictly text-based and does not use any of the multimedia capabilities of the Web.

An alternate means for entering the MUD world is provided by Hot Mudslide (http://www.drscc.com/mudslide/index.htm), a Java applet that

FIGURE 12.13 Avalon Mud (http://www.avalon.co.uk).

allows Web visitors to access any of the hundreds of MUDs in operation. A complete database of all the MUD worlds currently running is maintained at MUD Collector (http://www.absi.com/mud). From this list, the Avalon MUD (Figure 12.13) provides a good point of departure and contains one of the more detailed worlds available. MUDs represent one of the "best kept secrets" of new, Internet-specific entertainment. Despite their text-based orientation, they embody all the new features of Internet-based entertainment. Unfortunately, the limited interface of MUDs has prevented most Internet audience members from ever experiencing them. A few commercial groups, such as Virtual Destiny Interactive (http://www.VirtDest.com), are running pay-for play services.

One additional role-playing game recently converted to the Web that is worth exploring is the *definitive* port of the original Colossal Cave (http://tjwww.stanford.edu/adventure.html) adventure, which occupied many a college student in the 1970s and 1980s. Like the MUD/MOO world, this program uses pure text to create "twisty little tunnels" that form the core of the game. Despite its primitive interface, over 60,000 people explored the site during the first half of 1996—and it is a model for interactive gaming.

HTML-based Worlds

In order to ensure that all visitors to the site may explore the virtual world, some systems—such as Pathfinder's S. P. Q. R.—The Quest Begins (Figure 12.14)—use nothing but standard HTML coding. S. P. Q. R. is realized through a large number of images of the virtual city that are accessed by selecting with the mouse. A similar type of world/game is provided at FrameZero (http://www.framezero.com), which also provides more sophisticated QuickTime VR versions of the game for download. In form and structure, these worlds are virtually identical to the pioneering MYST (http://www.cyan.com) CD-ROM game: no avatars are present and the visitor occupies an abstract point of view. While the game can be quite engaging, download times for individual pictures are fairly slow (10-20 seconds) for the majority of audience members accessing the site via modem.

Multimedia-based

Some groups familiar with storytelling in the CD-ROM format have used *Director* and similar multimedia tools to create interactive stories. Each episode is actually a collection of multimedia modules. Since the graphical and animation features of multimedia programs are used, there is less need for live performers and support personnel. A current example of this form of fiction is Digital Planet's Madeline's Mind (Figure 12.15),

FIGURE 12.14 S.P.Q.R. — The Quest Begins (http://www.pathfinder.com/twep/rome).

a "pilot" interactive story available through the Web developer's main site. Though frequently lumped with other episodic Web sites, Madeline's Mind has several features which set it apart and make it similar to interactive stories created for CD-ROMs. By using multimedia development principles, Madeline's Mind achieves a high degree of interactivity. Unlike episodic Web sites, the visitor is quickly co-opted into the story and required to solve puzzles in order to bring it to completion. While they are difficult to effectively plot and create, multimedia-based systems are more effective at using the interactive potential of the Internet.

FIGURE 12.15 Madeleine's Mind (http://www.madmind.com).

Two-dimensional Worlds

Both The Palace (http://www.thepalace.com) and Ubique (http://www.ubique.com) function in two-dimensional environments and allow visitors to move their avatars over fantasy backgrounds. Ubique has the additional feature in that chatters can use real-time audio to communicate. These environments have the advantage of requiring less sophisticated software to run than VRML worlds; therefore, they are accessible to a greater number of the Internet audience. Other two-dimensional worlds are available through Sierra Online's The Realm (http://www.therealm.com), ImagiNation Network's Cyber Park (Figure 12.16), CompuServe's Worlds Away (http://www.ossi.com/Worldsaway/away.html), and Microsoft Network's V-Chat (http://www.msn.com/v-chat/index.htm). Admission to these worlds requires membership in these proprietary online services, which are not available from the general Web. Worlds Away and V-Chat allow emotions to be expressed by varying the facial expressions of avatars and The Realm allows the creation of highly customized male and female characters. Worlds Away also has the distinction of hosting the first wedding in a virtual world.

FIGURE 12.16 ImagiNation Network's CyberPark (http://www.inngames.com).

VMRL-based Worlds

Virtual Reality Markup Language or VRML (http://www.vrml.org) is the current favorite of Web-based virtual-world developers. Originally developed to create a stronger "sense of place" on the Web, VRML creates extremely compact virtual worlds that are well-suited to the slow transmission speeds of the Web. Cutting-edge VRML combines the interactivity of chat rooms with the three-dimensional environments of advanced multimedia and, as such, seems to be the direction all media on the Web is heading.

The first version of VRML (1.0) allowed visitors to explore static, unmodifiable worlds using relatively simple HTML-type commands. Unlike text-based MUD/MOO worlds, the environment cannot be modified by the audience member. Since the utility of static worlds is limited to the display of objects and navigation tools, the new VRML 2.0 standard was designed to introduce true interactivity into virtual reality. This update provides for an environment that changes automatically with respect to the visitor (e.g., sounds originate from a distinct location in space that may be heard with stereo speakers) and allows the visitor to interactively manipulate and modify objects in the VRML world. More importantly, VRML 2.0 allows multiple visitors to the world to meet and interact with each other.

VRML is at a very early stage of development and a variety of companies are currently competing to create the industry standard. Due to the demands of VRML and the need to develop an economic model, most companies distribute VRML viewers for free and charge content providers for authoring environments and VRML servers which can be integrated with existing Web sites. Examples include Chaco Communications (http://www.chaco.com), which integrates games, MUDS, and MIDI sound into its environments; Black Sun Interactive (http://www.blacksun.com), which emphasizes avatars in its Pointworld (http://www2.blacksun.com/pointworld/index.html) environment; the IDS VRML Server (http://www.ids-net.com); and Worlds Inc.'s Alphaworld (http://www.worlds.net/alphaworld). The latter is currently the most advanced of these services and it also offers a local newspaper, The New World Times Gazette (http://www.worlds.net/alphaworld/docs/nwt). Educational software manufacturer Knowledge Adventure (http://www.adventure.com) has been active in developing a specialized, "kid-safe" VRML world.

Future Trends

During the latter half of 1996, VRML 2.0 viewers and programs should begin to make an impact on the Web. Like HTML before it, VRML will probably replace proprietary formats and emerge as a common standard for all virtual worlds on the Internet. The long-term success of VRML will be determined by several factors, some of which are discussed in the following sections.

Hardware Performance

The speed and memory of the typical Windows or Macintosh computer owned by most of the Internet audience is barely capable of displaying simple VRML worlds. More complex VRML worlds enabling true multiuser entertainment cannot become standard until the performance of consumer equipment increases significantly. In 1998, when the average home computer is several times more powerful than it is now, complete VRML worlds will become commonplace for multiuser Intertainment.

Content Creation

With the introduction of VRML 2.0, the biggest challenge facing this form of entertainment is in content. The early VRML worlds were simply objects which could be examined from different angles; this can be interesting but is not competitive with the rich entertainment afforded by the highly interactive game worlds previously described. In the future, VRML developers are likely to borrow wholesale from these text-based worlds, particularly the MUD/MOO text-based worlds which inspired them in the first place.

Competition with Broadcast Models

Compared to broadcasting, virtual worlds offer fast downloads and true interactivity—allowing the audience to enter into and participate in the entertainment content. These features will contribute to a competition between virtual reality and broadcast as the Web continues to grow (see Chapter 15). It is likely that hybrid broadcast-VRML solutions will become widespread. For example, a broadcast of a performance might be set in a custom VRML environment whose dimensions and color could be controlled by the audience members.

Avatars and Digital Organisms

Avatars are currently the only "living" things in virtual worlds, but this state of affairs will change in the near future. Currently, researchers in *artificial life* such as those at the Santa Fe Institute (http://www.santafe.org) are developing software programs which can grow, reproduce, and evolve within a digital environment. A proposal to include digital organisms called NERVES (Figure 12.17) was recently introduced. When NERVES or a similar protocol becomes practical, virtual worlds will begin teeming with autonomous digital life, and content development will be less a matter of total creation than *gardening*. The novelty of these worlds will pose a major challenge for the ways in which entertainment is distributed.

Advertainment: From Ragu's Soap Opera to the Mentos Cult

Nowhere is the distinction between Internet and other media more apparent than in the entertainment value of companies not considered part of the industry. Instead of sponsoring Web sites through billboard-style advertising, many companies are building entertainment into their online presence. Sites creating entertainment include income tax sites,

FIGURE 12.17 Nerves Project (http://www.digitalspace.com/nerves/index.html).

electronics distributors, marketing firms, and the food and beverage industry. Such sites are clear examples of new Intertainment, since they fuse information and entertainment into a unique package.

> ***Advertising? Uh-uh! I want* information *about a product. That info has to be* easy *to find I don't want* old, useless *information. And I want you to entertain me while you do it!***
>
> — Pat Ortman, Creative Director, Empty Street Productions, Inc.
> http://www.generationx.com and http://www.emptystreet.com

Traditional wisdom has it that, while current content provided by these groups is interesting, ultimately they will return to outsourcing all their entertainment development to traditional production. On the Web, this appears unlikely for a number of reasons. While the cost of Internet entertainment development may seem high (see Part II), it is far less than providing entertainment in the real world. Web sites can afford to create a year's worth of entertainment for the cost of a single television commercial. Once the site is built, the way the audience uses the site means that the

FIGURE 12.18 Ragu's Mama's Cucina (http://www.eat.com).

company does not so much sell to a crowd but develop a committed community. Finally, since the Internet audience perceives exploration of any site as a form of entertainment (see Chapter 2), nonentertainment companies will still find themselves ranked on entertainment value. Therefore, it pays to have an entertainment concept in mind while developing any site. The following considers three nonentertainment sites which are entertainment in themselves and discusses the reasons for their success.

Ragu's Soap Opera

Instead of a corporate "presence" site, Van den Bergh Foods, Inc.'s Mama's Cucina (Figure 12.18) is a personality-based Web site with a variety of entertainment centered on pasta themes. Examples of entertainment include a lengthy, text-based soap opera, an extensive cookbook integrated into suggested Italian films, a slowly expanding suite of rooms, and—last but not least—an extensive questionnaire asking the audience to grade different portions of the site. While there is a little corn tucked into the Web pages, the overall effect is of an interesting place that is worth a visit. Visitors to the site, even if they chuckle, will remember it as an attempt at relatively honest contact and will contrast it with comparable *Web-silent* brands on the their next shopping trip. The chief challenge with the site will be to keep the original concept updated, so that its difference from commercials in other media becomes more noticeable over time.

Joe Boxer's Sense of Place

The first, and still champion, site of the nonentertainment world is Joe Boxer (Figure 12.19). The site uses a variety of design features to make it primarily an entertainment experience, instead of a corporate site, mall, or billboard for products. One of the main achievements of the design is creating a sense of place. In order to enter the site, the visitor must navigate through a series of humorous screens leading to the main site. By allowing the visitor to control movement—yet be required to go through each screen—the site conveys the impression of entering a place. More obscure references, such as suggesting how to stand in front of the monitor, make the visit an intrinsically spatial experience.

Once inside the site, visitors are presented with a variety of options for exploration, including games, chat, and product expositions. In order to continue maintaining the illusion of movement, links on the site often refer to directions in space (e.g., "look behind you"). Customers are invited to learn more about the company itself as well as the product—

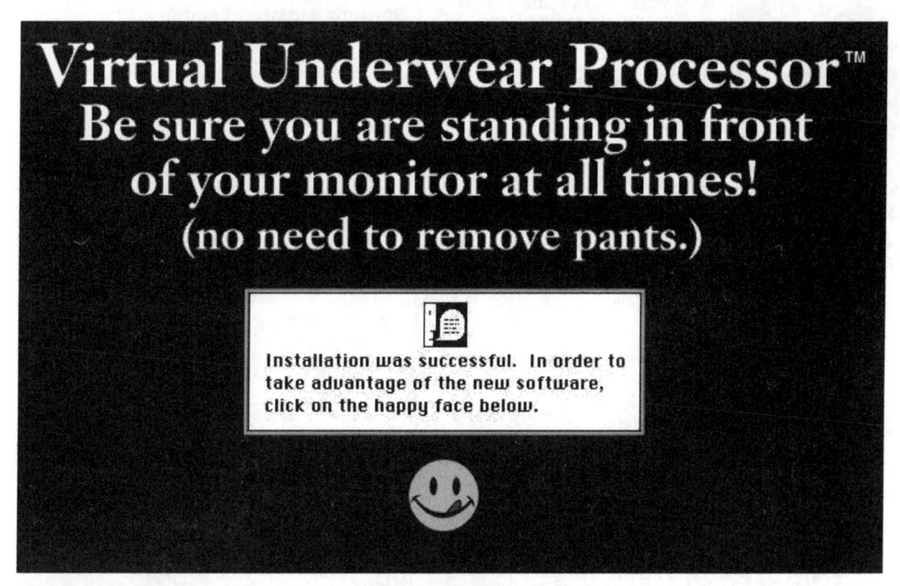

FIGURE 12.19 Joe Boxer (http://www.joeboxer.com).

ENQUIRER

Volume One
Issue Two

AS THE WEB SPINS

Part 2 of the TERRIFYING 4 Part Series
HTML HORROR STORIES
They Came From
Outerspace

Scientists have uncovered shocking proof of an insidious plot by alien beings to take over the minds of earthlings by infiltrating the World Wide Web. The aliens' evil plan, dubbed "Operation Demoralization," is based on widespread distribution of **infuriating and incomprehensible HTML editing tools** to innocent humans who simply want to publish Web pages for their businesses, work groups, schools, or personal interests.

N.E.A.T.O. member
Dr. E.T. Grep

"It's 'orrible, just'orrible!" says Dr. E.T. **Grep**, a high-ranking member of the elite Netwide Extraterrestrial Anti-Terror Organization **(NEATO)**, who encountered some of the alien software. "There's just no way that stuff was made by humans for humane use by other humans. Real living, breathing, decent *people* would have created a program like **Claris Home Page.** There must be a plot."

NEXT ISSUE...
Tune In July 29th
for Issue #3

Check out all of the AWARD WINNING Back Issues

- Issue 1
- Issue 2
- Issue 3
- Issue 4

BREAKING STORIES

- Mind meld with aliens? No way! Download Claris Home Page today
- Some guaranteed E.T.-free Web resources you should check out.

New Software

SAVES THE WORLD

Net-savvy alien spacecraft

Seeking nothing less than world domination, a race of **Net-savvy aliens** have unleashed a collection of terrifying HTML tools capable of turning anyone attempting to build a Web site into a gibbering **pod-person.**

However, the space beings' plans may yet be thwarted by a group of quick-witted software specialists in **Santa Clara, Ca.**, who have invented a new tool for Web page creation.

"Well, we just thought heck, maybe we could try giving people an **HTML editor that's *easy*** to use," explains Claire S. Wysiwyg. "We didn't realize it could, like, save the world."

FIGURE 12.20 The Claris Enquirer (http://www.claris.com/products/homepage/enquirer).

which reinforces the direct connection between producer and consumer. In the company area, the site provides a slide show of its employees to remind visitors that real people create a product. Conversation between visitors is encouraged by chat rooms, which have been highly effective at converting the site to a hangout. The most recent addition was a Net-controlled device—a billboard in Times Square that flashed email messages directed from the Joe Boxer site.

Claris Tabloid

Claris Software runs new product announcements on its Web site through a pseudo-tabloid format. Drawing on the frequently irritating experience new developers have with creating Web pages, the site provides The Claris Enquirer: As The Web Spins (Figure 12.20), a lurid exposé of the difficulties of coding in HTML. In a recent issue, the site showed creative use of outlinks in a story tracing culprits responsible for programming problems back to teenager home pages at Nerd World Media (http://www.nerdworld.com/nw1123.html). The Claris site also features some of the most sophisticated Web-based animation to date, making movement more lifelike by using blurring. By casting information in a tabloid—a form considered by many to be the very embodiment of half-truth—the Claris site implicitly acknowledges its visitors' ingrained skepticism of corporate blurbs and by default wins their support.

Mentos Cult

Currently, the "official" site for Mentos Mints (http://www.mentos.com) is merely a placeholder leading to several fact sheets, fans, and shrines dedicated to the soft mint. Dan Wood's Mentos Art Gallery (Figure 12.21) accepts submissions for *fresh artist* works, usually consisting of classic art which has been *fractured* by the addition of the product. In addition to the gallery, a huge fact sheet is maintained by several individuals at The Mentos FAQ (http://www3.gse.ucla.edu/~cjones/mentos-faq.html). Even stronger product commitment is revealed at Mentos—The Church (http://www.btf.com/mentos), which provides a belief system for members of the mint cult. Additional sites such as The Cult of Mentos (Figure 12.22) and The Day Mentos Ruled the Earth (http://pilot.msu.edu/user/sebenic2/play.html) serve to reinforce the basic principle of the value of fan sites. In a few months of operation, these sites have received numerous "best of the Web" awards and continue to draw huge audiences (despite a frequently reported irritation with TV commercials created for the product). Due to the fan base, the appeal of the product on the Net far exceeds any paid ad placement. Thus, it is surprising that a company representative quoted in Internet Underground

mint
from Dali's "Soft Construction with Boiled Beans:Premonition of Civil War" editing by Michal Migurski

FIGURE 12.21 Mentos Art Gallery (http://zocalo.net/~danwood/mentos/).

Magazine (http://www.underground-online.com) says simply, "It's set up by the consumers. . . . it's not used at all by us." Other companies with nascent followings on the Web should consider how to support, rather than suppress, such quirky publicity.

The trends in traditional, recreational, and new Internet-based entertainment demonstrate the extraordinary potential of the medium. One of the key issues raised by the discussion of current Intertainment is whether its enormous diversity will last. Some within the traditional industry see the Internet as ripe for "shakeout" and subsequent consolidation of content providers into a few networks. Others, while not discounting the impact of traditional entertainment on the Web, see long-term diversity as a continuing feature of interactive entertainment. In the next chapter, Internet entertainment is considered in larger legal, social, technological perspectives which will help determine Intertainment's future possibilities.

FIGURE 12.22 Cult of Mentos (http://www.mhv.net/%7Enute/mentos.htm).

PART V

CASTING THE FUTURE NET

Entertainment Is Transformed

http://kspace.com/intertainment

CHAPTER 13

CYBERLAW

The unprecedented growth of the Internet and other electronic networks has created a new, virtual territory for the legal profession. Cyberlaw includes cases, statutes, and constitutional provisions that impact the world of global interactive computer networks, particularly the Internet. In practice, Internet cyberlaw affects the availability of content to the Internet audience; the distribution of Internet entertainment; and the creation of hardware, software, and services that enable Internet access.

Features of Cyberlaw

Cyberlaw, especially as it addresses Internet-based entertainment and electronic distribution, is already representing itself as distinct from telecommunications and multimedia law. Despite the superficial similarity of a page on the Internet's World Wide Web to a television or CD-ROM screen, the Internet is a unique medium that requires additional new rules for its use.

Lack of Central Control

The Internet is not "owned" or controlled by anyone. The core software necessary for its operation is in the public domain and many of its key programs (such as email and the World Wide Web) are the results of collaborative efforts over many years by thousands of people worldwide. Anyone can connect to the Internet, as long as basic hardware and software is used. Due to its extreme decentralization, laws affecting the Internet as a whole directly impact large numbers of access and content providers.

Rapid Growth

The fundamentally decentralized nature of the Internet has fueled its enormous growth relative to other "new" media, such as interactive television, and the law has been hard-pressed to keep up. The Internet has doubled in size every nine months since its inception almost 20 years ago, and the number of content providers on the Web has increased by a factor of 10,000 in only two years (see Chapter 3). Regulation has run well behind this growth. Content providers on the Internet frequently find themselves in situations for which there are no firm legal guidelines and they must make decisions based on incomplete information.

Open Exchange of Information

The Internet was designed and nurtured by individuals who believed that "information wants to be free." To this end, they created one of the most open systems for communication ever designed which, in effect, interprets efforts at control as network "damage." Many features of the World Wide Web demonstrate this bias. For example, Web browsers enable surfers to read the HTML source code behind virtually any Web page on the Internet and also allow the copying of any displayed text, graphics, audio, or video files directly to their hard disk.

Audience Control

Despite widespread interest in Internet broadcasting, people generally do not watch or listen to Internet programs in the sense that they exist in the mass media. Instead, entertainment programming such as episodic Web sites and virtual worlds require site visitors to actively select what they want to see and hear. The high degree of user control calls into question whether regulations designed for passive viewing of broadcast media can be effectively applied to the Internet, since the burden of choosing content is partly shifted to the consumer.

Prosumer Effect

As discussed in Chapter 2, a substantial portion of Internet entertainment is generated by the audience itself—resulting in a *prosumer* effect or the integration of producer and consumer. Email between individuals is the most common form of Internet communication, and discussion groups, bulletin boards, and online chat form the mainstay of many entertainment sites. Mass content creation extends into the Web as well; while there may be millions of viewers for a single television program, the current ratio of Web sites to users on the Internet is only 200:1—and dropping! If one takes into account the *personal home pages* many individuals maintain on the Internet, a substantial fraction of all individuals online may be considered content providers of some sort. Effective cyberlaw must address an environment where most members of the Internet "audience" are also content producers and distributors.

No Boundaries

Just as the distinction between the producer and consumer is blurred, so are geographical boundaries. The Internet is truly global: Over 130 countries had Web-capable links at the beginning of 1996 and one-third of the total Internet population is outside the United States. The structure of the Web makes it just as easy to visit a computer on the other side of the world as one across the hallway. Individuals exploring the Internet have no preferred order of *movement* through cyberspace; they may cross dozens of national boundaries in a matter of minutes, with no regard to the country's physical location or laws. Considerable legal effort is now underway to define exactly *where* events in cyberspace occur. This is of particular interest to the gambling industry (see Chapter 11). For example, a surfer in Kansas—where gambling is heavily restricted—could potentially participate in the Liechtenstein Government's InterLotto (http://www.interlotto.li). The actual connection between Kansas and Liechtenstein may easily run through a dozen countries, each of which may or may not permit gambling.

New Modes of Communication

The most common mode of Internet communication is many-to-many in groups that exchange information as part of a virtual community. Examples of this new form of communication (see Chapter 12) include online chat rooms, multiplayer games, virtual worlds, and discussion groups on the Web and Usenet. The versatility of the Internet has blurred the boundaries between private communication and mass broadcasting by enabling a variety of intermediates between these two extremes. In such an environment, issues of censorship and privacy will require redefinition in order to be effective.

Cyberlaw Resources

The Internet is already responsible for a new body of law that emphasizes the unique features of content distribution through global interactive networks. In its short history, cyberlaw has already accumulated a body of opinion, which is available online at resources like Jonathan Rosenoer's Cyberlaw Worldwide (http://www.cyberlaw.com), UCLA's Cyberspace Law (http://www.gse.ucla.edu/iclp/prac.html), and the Netwatcher's Cyberzine (http://www.ionet.net/~mdyer/front.shtml). Individuals interested specifically in entertainment law should check Steve Schiffman's Global Law Resource Center (http://pages.nyu.edu/~schiffmn), which provides resources for real-world and online courses in entertainment law, media law, and Internet law. Additional commentary and articles are available at the Hollywood Law Cybercenter (http://www.hollywoodnetwork.com/Law/). Useful online electronic magazines include Michael Leventhal's Wiredlaw (http://www.primenet.com/wiredlaw/) and the Multimedia and Entertainment Law Online News (http://www.degrees.com/melon).

Issues for Entertainment Cyberlaw

Due to the unique nature of the Internet, many traditional areas of entertainment law require fresh examination. The fluid, multinational exchange of information—coupled with near universal access for content distribution—recast many problems in a new light.

Intellectual Property

Due to the rapid, anonymous exchange of information over the Internet—and the fact that much of this exchange resembles private conversation—there is considerable controversy over the roles of copyright protection versus the *fair use* doctrine applied in other media. Recently, a group of major copyright holders introduced the NII Copyright Act of 1995 (http://www.ari.net/dfc/legislat/legislat.html). In the form favored by its proponents, fair use is severely restricted relative to other media. The current act would prevent anyone who purchased a copy of a protected work from lending, selling, or even speaking about it to anyone on the Internet, without express permission of the copyright holder. If an equivalent law was in place in the real world, such institutions as libraries and video stores would not exist. The law is opposed by a diverse group of educators, libraries, copyright holders, and civil liberties organizations united under the Digital Future Coalition or DFC (Figure 13.1). A good resource for understanding copyright in a multimedia project is provided by J. Dianne Brinson and Mark F. Radcliffe in the Intellectual Property Law Primer for Multimedia Developers (http://www2.eff.org/pub/CAF/law/ip-primer). Another set of valuable articles explaining the features of fair use (and many other aspects of copyright law) are available at the Copyright and Wrong (http://planetnews.sfsu.edu/planetnews/copyright/index2.html) site maintained at the Journalism Department at San Francisco State University.

> ***Intellectual property rights are man's greatest and unique assets which are plundered by those with lesser abilities and character for profit.***
>
> —DENNIS POST, FUTURISTIC KEYBOARDIST
> http://kspace.com/post

Whatever the outcome of the NII Copyright Act, Web developers need to ensure that they have appropriate releases for copyrighted material. For example, on Kaleidospace, individual artists and musicians promoting their work sign contracts which release selected clips of their work for downloads by the Internet audience. Copyrighted material should be clearly marked on the Web site itself so that the Internet audience is aware of its status. Newer audio formats like that available from RealAudio (http://www.realaudio.com) allow the copyright notice to be attached directly to the sound clips.

> ***[Intellectual property rights on the Internet are] complex: If I ask to get money from downloads, the server will not show my pages or will raise rates . . . unless the user accepts [the idea of paying] for download property rights—which I doubt, since in France local telephone communications are already very expensive.***
>
> —KAPRISS, HEAVY POP MUSICIAN
> http://kspace.com/kapriss

Trademarks

One feature of the "Internet boom" of 1995 was widespread appropriation of corporate names by speculators. While wholesale *name grabs* by speculators have largely ceased, the use of trademarked material remains an issue. Already, Datalytics, Inc.'s (http://www.datalytics.com) Mark-Watch software patrols the Internet for illegal use of trademarks. Interestingly, most reported infringements consist of "friendly fire" trademark use, and involve unofficial fan sites for popular media icons such as Star Trek. To date, most companies have used knowledge of the infringement to promote—rather than suppress—these fan sites.

FIGURE 13.1 Digital Future Coalition or DFC (http://www.ari.net/dfc).

FIGURE 13.2 ASCAP (http://www.ascap.com).

One area which entertainment cyberlaw in particular will have to address is the use of trademarked symbols and iconic characters. A trip to any of the graphically based chat rooms reveals dozens of trademarked characters being used to identify individuals. While such use is against the law, the enforcement problem is of a magnitude never experienced and it ultimately may be unworkable without compromising individual privacy rights.

> ***I would like to be paid for the use of my music. I think that the current system of licensing performing rights favors the large record companies. I know that my music has gotten airplay for which I have received no royalties. I hope that any system of licensing of performing rights on the Internet will be more equitable.***
>
> —John McGill, Reflective Instrumental Guitarist
> http://kspace.com/mcgill

Performance Rights

This area is of particular interest to artists, musicians and entertainers creating content for the Internet. In other media, organizations such as ASCAP (Figure 13.2) and BMI (Figure 13.3) provide for centralized collection of royalties from broadcast distributors. At present, no similar system exists for the Internet—and a significant body of opinion believes that transmission through the Internet does not amount to a performance (especially if the transmission is an excerpt of the copyrighted work and is used as a promotion in order to achieve the sale of the complete work). Currently, most Internet-based content providers have sidestepped the issue by providing free material specifically to promote an artist or encourage sales of the product. As the Internet continues its evolution and content providers begin using artists' work to enhance the value of their sites, compensation mechanisms will need to be developed.

> ***From an intellectual property standpoint (software and content), creators need a way to track, protect and be paid for their creations or they won't have an incentive to release them via the Internet. No creative content, no interest. That's a long-term problem.***
>
> —John Braheny, Executive V.P., Wynnward Music Enterprises; Co-Founder of the Los Angeles Songwriters Showcase

While performance rights organizations are steadily becoming more "Internet-aware," many content providers on the Web have already developed their own schemes. For example, software developer Chaco Communications (http://www.chaco.com) has developed a royalty system

FIGURE 13.3 BMI (http://www.bmi.com).

FIGURE 13.4 Electronic Frontier Foundation or EFF (http://www.eff.org).

for anyone who creates a virtual world using its Pueblo software. Under Chaco's system, customers pay for time spent in the virtual world and a portion of the proceeds go back to the world's creator. As micropayments (the ability to charge tiny fractions of a cent for use of Web sites and other content) become practical, Chaco will be able to pay artists. This is a reversal of the current Internet model where artists usually pay to display their material.

Censorship on the Internet

Control of "indecent" or "obscene" content on the Internet is one of the most widely discussed issues in cyberlaw. With the ratification of the Telecommunications Act in early 1996, the Communications Decency Act or CDA (http://www.epic.org/free_speech/censorship/) also became law. Opponents, led by the Electronic Frontier Foundation or EFF (Figure 13.4), quickly got a restraining order while the law's constitutionality was debated. Largely considered a victory for religious rights activists, this highly restrictive legislation prohibits transfer of material termed "indecent" over the Internet, and makes both the individuals involved and the operators of *any* subnetwork over which the information is transferred liable for the violation. Currently, the law stands in limbo—declared unconstitutional at the federal appeals level (a transcript is available at the American Civil Liberties Union's site at http://www.aclu.org/court/cdadec.html) and awaiting review by the Supreme Court.

> ***I don't want the Internet to be polluted by perversity promoters. I see it as a potentially wonderful tool to elevate the public—not reduce it to the lower levels of obscenity. Maybe I'm an idealist. . . ?***
>
> —Steven Lavaggi, Visionary Painter and Muralist
> http://kspace.com/lavaggi

The activity surrounding the CDA led to Internet-wide activism designed to let Washington know how the majority of individuals on the Internet felt about the law. Overnight, thousands of Web sites turned their pages black in protest and participated in the Blue Ribbon Campaign (Figure 13.5) provided through the Electronic Frontier Foundation. The Internet community has also responded with resource archives like HotWired's 24 Hours in Democracy (http://www.hotwired.com/staff/userland/24), archives of censored material such as poetry in Freedom of Expression and America Online (http://www.motley-focus.com/~timber/aol.html), and investigative reports of procensorship *net.nannies*. On the opposite side, the rise of vigilante patrols like the CyberAngels (http://www.safesurf.com/cyberangels) indicates continuing interest in censorship issues.

While CDA's vagueness and extreme position make a strong case for its eventual overturn, censorship will continue to be a major issue on the Internet. This is hardly a new issue. In a recent online essay entitled The Unstamped Press and the 'Net (http://www.hevanet.com/demarest/marc/unstamped.html), author Marc Demarest argued that the current Internet censorship controversy almost perfectly echoes the legal battles which surrounded the introduction of advanced printing presses during the first half of the nineteenth century. Individuals concerned with the future course of cyberlaw may therefore be able to learn by studying historical revolutions in the media.

With most online users agreeing that centralized control of content is inherently unworkable, solutions are appearing in the form of software which allows end-users to selectively block access to individual Web sites and Usenet discussion groups. These systems will most likely incorporate the Platform for Internet Content Standard or PICS

FIGURE 13.5 Blue Ribbon Campaign (http://www.eff.org/blueribbon.html).

(http://www.w3.org/pub/WWW/PICS/), a voluntary ratings system being developed by the World Wide Web Consortium. PICS does not establish ratings, but allows content developers to rate themselves on a potentially infinite number of content scales. While its initial use will be for sexual content, PICS will ultimately incorporate ratings on religious or business value. Until PICS is widely implemented, software tools such as SafeSurf (http://www.safesurf.com) and Surfwatch (http://www.surfwatch.com) may be used by members of the Internet audience to block access to controversial sites.

> ***[Internet censorship is] an ignorant knee-jerk reaction to 'save the kids'. . . whatever happened to good 'ole parental upbringing?***
>
> —JOHN A. HOBSON, PRESIDENT, E-DISTRIBUTORS CORPORATION; DBA: THE LONEZONE
> http://lonezone.com or http://wickedweb.com

Privacy

The average Internet surfer faces considerable challenges to personal privacy while exploring Web sites and communicating with others via email, chat, and other means. In their daily interaction with the Internet community, entertainment providers need to address these legal and political issues.

Involuntary Demographics

Many Web sites routinely monitor the movements of each visitor in their site and store this information for later use in targeted advertising. While this information has been kept anonymous to date, it is only a matter of time until a site sells its information to direct marketers on and off the Internet. The most common method of collecting anonymous demographics is through the *cookie* system developed by Netscape. Despite publicity describing cookies, many visitors are never aware that a site they've visited collected information about their movements.

Private Communications

Currently, individuals in the United States are restricted from using *strong crypto*, meaning that it is impossible for them to send and receive messages that the government cannot eavesdrop on. This policy has been pushed aggressively by the Clinton Adminstration, which is trying to force the adoption of Clipper and Clipper II government key *escrow* systems. Under Clipper, all encoded messages may be read by government agencies, opening the doors to a variety of privacy abuse. Widespread implementation of these systems will have a profound effect on

FIGURE 13.6 Golden Key Campaign (http://www2.eff.org/goldkey.html).

entertainment providers. Under Clipper, the government could eavesdrop on a message containing a controversial work of art or fiction and take action against the artist. To counter this, EFF and other organizations have announced the Golden Key Campaign (Figure 13.6). The key and envelope symbols allow the Internet community to show support for the ability to send the digital equivalent of a love letter or credit card number with confidence that the message won't be read by a government bureaucrat. These issues form the primary interest of the Internet Privacy Coalition (http://www.privacy.org/ipc), which is an advocate of strong cryptography.

Unsolicited Advertising

A related privacy issue concerns the right not to be bombarded with unsolicited advertising. Many groups are already discussing "killing the virtual remote"—and forcing audience members visiting Web sites to sit through ads before they can regain control of their computer. To counter these attacks by advertisers, companies like PrivNet (http://www.privnet.com) are actively developing countermeasures that block individual ad banners on Web sites (see Chapter 9) and prevent the automatic collection of demographic data through software cookies. Web sites that rely on advertising are faced with a major challenge: They either must design their advertising so that it is informative and unobtrusive (thereby removing the motivation to block it), confront their audience and lock out visitors that won't look at the ads, or refrain from using obtrusive and irritating advertising techniques. Entertainment providers will need to make sure they clearly state their position in these issues to their audience.

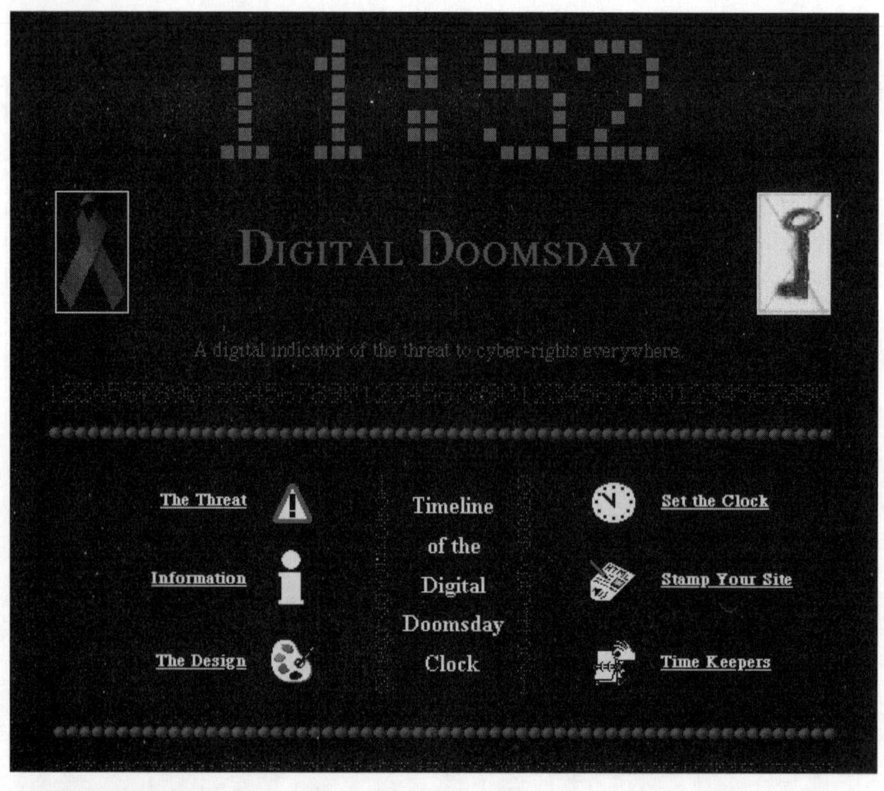

FIGURE 13.7 Digital Doomsday Clock (http://www.io.org/~sherlock/doom/doom.html).

With pressure rising from many groups to somehow control behavior on the Internet, the community is increasingly turning to political motivation. An example of this trend is found at an information site for the Electronic Freedom March on Washington (http://march.tico.com), scheduled for the Fall of 1996. The purpose of the march is to lobby for the legal and political issues important to cyberspace, including privacy rights and anti-censorship protection for the Internet. The widespread concern of the Internet community is also evident at the Digital Doomsday Clock (Figure 13.7). This site takes its cue from the original doomsday clock used on the cover of The Bulletin of Atomic Scientists (Figure 13.8) to heighten concern about nuclear weapons. At present, the digital version stands eight minutes away from midnight.

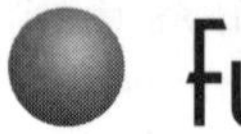

Future Trends

While current decisions in cyberlaw have produced widely different results, the medium as a whole appears to be converging on the publishing—rather than broadcasting—model for content distribution and censorship. If this trend continues, it will have a major impact on Internet-based entertainment. Lines are appearing between those who embrace the coming of the Internet and the potential it affords and those who see it primarily as a threat to their existing business, property, and even way of life. In addition, current legal issues involving cyberlaw frequently pit the *unwired* against the *wired.* For example, while opponents of the CDA are readily accessible through the Internet, most of its supporters have publicly indicated that they have never been online. This pattern is typical of much of cyberlaw: Those attempting to restrict the Internet typically do not use it. The following suggests some possible future legal trends affecting Internet entertainment.

Content-blocking Software

Since centralized control of Internet content seems certain to fail, members of the Internet audience will increasingly rely on blocking programs

FIGURE 13.8 Bulletin of Atomic Scientists Doomsday Clock (http://neog.com/atomic).

to screen part or all of the content of a Web site. Conflict is sure to arise over the ability to selectively screen content versus damage to the artistic integrity of the work. There is also likely to be controversy over audience members slectively blocking ads on Web sites while continuing to receive the content (see Chapter 9).

Internet-specific Royalties and Copyrights

Current royalty arrangements for artistic performance presuppose a relatively small number of broadcasters distributing content and reporting to well-established centralized collection agencies. As with other areas, the Internet's basic structure is likely to encourage more decentralized systems and possibly a wider variety of schemes for artist protection and compensation.

Hyperlink Content Liability

At present, most moves to censor the Internet are aimed at the access providers who supply the infrastructure for content delivery. If most of these attempts end in failure, the burden is likely to shift to the content providers themselves. Unlike broadcast media where a small group of companies is involved, liability on the Internet will affect the millions of individuals who currently provide Internet content. The problem is also greater because the hyperlink system on the Web automatically ties every piece of content to every other piece. Considerable work will be needed to settle the status of a site that has links to a site *which has links* to censored content. Furthermore, Web sites may create links to any other site without the latter's consent or knowledge. A site operator who took great pains to mark the content as adult or controverseal might be thwarted by another site that linked to the content through a misleading message.

Legal Status for Avatars

As virtural worlds continue to proliferate on the Internet, there will be an increasing need to develop standards for the use of avatars and agents. The issues go beyond the use of copyrighted icons in chat rooms: Is a celebrity "visit" in cyberspace more real if it is a recorded broadcast of the celebrity or the celebrity manipulating a virtual body in real time?

Within a few short years, the Internet will be a major force shaping the personal lives of everyone worldwide. It is also clear that it will become a major form of entertainment. The challenge of cyberlaw is to protect the ability of the Internet to empower citizens, artists, and entertainers while safeguarding rights to free speech, intellectual property, and privacy.

CHAPTER 14

CYBERCULTURE

People now feel obligated to at least having an email address and possibly a website. It's a trendy thing.

—Bernard Yin of the salt-water damaged alternative rock band Brazil 2001
http://kspace.com/brazil

Early in 1996, thousands of photographers over the entire world combined to post pictures to a Web archive designed to capture a day in the evolution of the Internet. This event—24 Hours in Cyberspace (http://www.cyber24.com)—was a watershed in the new medium's history and is seen as one of the first major Net-specific cultural events of the Web era. As an Internet-specific media event, it demonstrates that the Internet is rapidly developing its own social, political, and cultural voice. This chapter considers the effect of the Internet's cyberculture and the steps needed to ensure that your own entertainment successfully integrates into this community.

Despite its intense interest in the Internet and Web, much of the traditional entertainment industry has not "caught on" to what is happening. A common mindset is typified by the home page of American Cybercast (Figure 14.1), a leading network for episodic Web-based programming. (While this group has been responsible for some highly progressive sites such as The Spot (http://www.thespot.com), the image is a distinct throwback to pre-Web entertainment.) The ad depicts a family staring at a set of computer monitors disconnected from their keyboards and mouses, both of which are symbols of user control. Information (represented by lightning bolts) flows without interruption from the monitors into the waiting eyes of the family. The image tries very hard to make the Web look "just like television," echoing the beliefs of some individuals in the traditional entertainment community.

FIGURE 14.1 American Cybercast (http://www.amcy.com).

While such comparisons to traditional media may aid in proving the value of the Internet, they are also profoundly misleading. The fundamental lesson that entertainment providers need to learn about this new medium is that it is not a blank slate in the way that the radio spectrum was in 1920. Far more than the wires and computers creating it, or even the millions of people who sit in front of their computer screens, the Internet is a well-established culture that is doing a surprisingly good job of retaining its identity while welcoming huge influxes of new citizens. Furthermore, the features of the medium have helped to create a culture fundamentally different from the culture created by traditional mass media.

Understanding the Internet's Cyberculture

Paying attention to cyberculture will ensure that the content provider's entertainment fits within the larger community—and it may even help to suggest new content ideas specific to cyberspace. Archives covering the issues of cyberculture can be found at independent sites like Net Tribes (Figure 14.2) or Cyberpunk Culture (http://www.dwave.net/~rery/CPCulture.html). Additional resources are available in a searchable database at alt.culture (http://www.altculture.com) or in the large curated libraries at The Electronic Frontier Foundation (http://www2.eff.org/pub/Net_culture/) (see Chapter 13) and Cyberlit (http://omni.cc.purdue.edu/~stein/stein.htm). Following is a summary of the main features of cyberculture and its impact on entertainment created for the Web.

Cyberpunk Influence

The dominant cultural "tilt" of the Internet is Cyberpunk, a hip and anti-authoritarian mindset deriving from a small group of works produced or rediscovered in the 1980s. Cyberpunk originated in William Gibson's novel, *Neuromancer* (Figure 14.3), which was the first to illustrate the notion of a worldwide network that acted as an alternate reality. His work continued a tradition of fiction begun by renegade science fiction author Phillip K. Dick (http://www.users.interport.net/~regulus/pkd/pkd-int.html), whose book, *Do Androids Dream of Electric Sheep* was the inspiration for another classic cyberpunk work, director Ridley Scott's *Bladerunner* (http://kzsu.stanford.edu/uwi/br/off-world.html). Key notions embodied in these works include a universally wired world, a strong anti-authoritarian streak, a desire to take power by tinkering (e.g., hacking) into the system, and profound skepticism of the motives of consumer culture.

FIGURE 14.2 Net Tribes (http://www.eerie.fr/~alquier/cyber.html).

Neuromancer

Comments By: Michaela Drapes

Neuromancer was the second 'cyberpunk' book that I ever read. (The first was *Snow Crash*.) I already dug Stephenson's "second-generation" cyberpunk writing, and wanted to see what all the fuss about *Neuromancer* was about. And I wasn't dissapointed. Gibson's style was dizzyingly quick paced, and unlike anything I had ever read. I remember at one point where several plot lines collided, I was reading on the bus. The action had accelerated to a breakneck pace, and I was caught up in the Sprawl, in Case's hack, in Molly's progress through the Tessier-Ashpool universe. And I remember looking up, and looking at the rush-hour traffic on I-35 and shuddering. It was at that point when I looked out at the sea of cars that I realized that Gibson's fiction is such a believeable future, that it's both frightening and exhilerating at the same time.

And, I have to admit that Molly is my favorite character in any Science Fiction book I have ever read. I am amazed at the way Gibson broke down so many barriers that encapsulated female characters in SF. She's tough and sexy and smart; and definitely not someone to mess with.

Count Zero | Mona Lisa Overdrive | Virtual Light

biography | books | the gibson hotlist

FIGURE 14.3 William Gibson's Neuromancer (http://www-user.cibola.net/~michaela/gibson).

A more recent key work, Neal Stephenson's *Snow Crash* (http://www-user.cibola.net/~michaela/diamondage/stephen.htm), provides cyberpunk's current manifesto. *Snow Crash* introduced the notion of cyberspace as a visual environment in which virtual reality (referred to as the Metaverse) has quite literally replaced the real world for most activities. Many common slang words, concepts, and political positions derive from this basic ethic.

Cyberzines

Despite its short history, hundreds of electronic magazines are available on the Internet which address its cyberculture. While magazines representing a more mainstream literary establishment such as Microsoft's

Slate Magazine (http://www.slate.com) are coming online, they compete with popular cyberzines like HotWired (http://www.hotwired.com), Stim (http://www.stim.com), Suck (http://www.suck.com), and Crash Site (Figure 14.4).

In general, these cyberzines reflect cyberpunk tempered to varying degrees with an independent, cooperative, and anti-authoritarian outlook. Unlike extreme cyberpunk, this mindset embraces many aspects of popular culture while rejecting much of its corporate and political underpinnings. Not limited by reproduction on "dead trees," these magazines frequently contain Internet-specific features like chat rooms and interactive games. Content providers should look to this group of cyberzines to feel the pulse of the majority of their audience.

Cybercults

The Internet already has a fantastic number of ceremonies, pseudoreligions, and cult behavior that help to define its unique culture. An example of a cyberculture-style ceremony that took place in the "real world" is found at the Burning Man (Figure 14.5) festival, a three-day

FIGURE 14.4 Crash Site (http://www.crashsite.com/Crash).

FIGURE 14.5 Burning Man (http://www.well.com/user/tcircus/Burnman/index.html).

artistic celebration which culminates with the destruction of a giant human form. Net cults include Kibo (http://www4.ncsu.edu/~asdamick/kibo); Usenet Notables (http://www4.ncsu.edu/~asdamick/www/news/notables.html) lists gods and demigods of the Internet. Knowledge and participation in these adventures further helps to distinguish cyberculture from mainstream.

Cybergrrls

The clearest tip-off that the Internet is not another techie toy is the enormous number of women who have become involved—not as viewers or as "shoppers" but as content creators. The overall number of women online is estimated to be between 30 to 40 percent of the total (see Chapter 2), and women are playing a far greater role in cyberspace than they did in the evolution of the personal computer. The best known cyberculture-specific organization for women is Webgrrls (Figure 14.6). This group provides a real-world, face-to-face networking group for women interested in new media. Created by Aliza Sherman (Cybergrrl at http://www.cybergrrl.com) in New York City, it now has branches in several dozen cities across the United States and provides mentoring, training, and support for women joining the internet revolution. Other women's resources include Femina (http://www.femina.com), a general directory aimed at women, Womenspace (http://www.womenspace.com), an online magazine addressing grrl culture, and Women's Wire (http://www.womenswire.com) a large online service recently moved to the Web.

Cybercafes

The newest components of cyberculture are coffeehouses and other institutions which combine a local "live" meeting place with Internet connectivity (see Chapter 11). As a trend, this phenomenon is sure to grow and significantly change the audience dynamic from at-home to social surfing. With increasing support for performances by artists and musicians, many cybercafes are likely to form a second type of Net-specific cultural center supporting independently produced entertainment. Already, some cybercafes like Cafe No No (http://www.cafenono.com) in Vermont have artist-in-residence programs.

> ***[The Internet will humanize media stars] because the Internet is basically minds chatting with other minds. Ideas flow freely without the constraints of body language, tone of voice, bashfulness.***
>
> —David Bluefield, The Clazzax, contemporary jazz musician
> http://kspace.com/clazzax

FIGURE 14.6 Webgrrls (http://www.webgrrls.com).

FIGURE 14.7 Echo (http://www.echonyc.com).

Cybercommunities

Despite the commercial influx, the essence of cyberspace continues to be the enabling of new forms of interactive communication between people. Throughout the 1980s, the dynamics of interactive networks led to the formation of virtual communities which still exert a strong effect on the Internet's overall culture. Chief among these is The Well (http://www.well.com), which pioneered the development of interactive conferencing in a close-knit, supportive virtual neighborhood. Similar communities at New York's Echo (Figure 14.7) also have a strong influence. With the rise of the Web, sites like Firefly (http://www.firefly.com) and RARE (http://www.surf.com/rare/home.html) are adding multimedia and software agents to the virtual community model, and groups like Real Time Groove Network (RTGN) (http://ctdnet/acns.nwu.edu/hugo/drgn.html) are uniting scattered artists and musicians into communities through collaborative art creation and performance. Despite the commercialization of the Internet and the arrival of companies from outside cyberspace, the community model formed by these organizations continues to guide attitudes to privacy, censorship, and politics on the Internet.

> ***The Internet is far enough removed from the flesh and blood presence of the person that some mystique will still remain.***

—John Burnett, surrealist painter
http://kspace.com/burnett

Cyberactivists

Groups such as the Electronic Frontier Foundation (http://www.eff.org) and The Voter's Telecommunications Watch or VTW (http://www.vtw.org) represent the beginnings of a distinct political community on the Internet, as do the new block of pro-cyberspace members of the U.S. Congress. The Internet community is already highly active in censorship and copyright issues (see Chapter 13), as well as problems like email spamming. Indeed, as documented by political commentary e-zines like David Rothman's Networld! (http://www.clark.net/pub/rothman/networld.html), 1995 and 1996 saw a siege mentality in many parts of cyberspace. During this time, Netizens were challenged by as legislators and moralists among the "great unwired" who repeatedly tried to stop something they didn't understand.

In a recent study conducted by the Georgia Institute of Technology's Fifth World Wide Web User Survey (http://www.cc.gatech.edu/gvu/user_surveys), 34 percent of the respondents identified themselves as independents, 25 percent as Democrats, and 21 percent as Republicans. This confirms many other studies that find cyberculture's politics to be individualistic, libertarian, and cutting across traditional party lines. Astonishingly, 91 percent of Internet users polled indicated they were registered to vote and 63 percent of them had voted in a recent election. With organizations like the Voter's Telecommunication Watch already organizing a political platform for cyberspace, the community is well on its way to organizing a distinct political as well as cultural agenda.

Clueless Newbies

If you're new to cyberspace, you or your group will be providing your entertainment within the larger context of the group culture previously described. One of your top priorities is to make sure that you have joined the Internet culture. Everyone in cyberspace enjoys a few laughs now and then over a large, real-world company that stumbles badly when it gets on the Web. Content providers should work to ensure that they and their entertainment aren't the next object of Net humor.

Get Online

It has been said many times in the course of the book, but it deserves one more mention: *Nobody*—individual actor, rock band, or mega-mogul—can build effective Internet entertainment unless the key decisionmakers for the content are online themselves. Since the Internet is interactive, looking over someone's shoulder or attending a seminar won't be enough to truly understand the medium.

Avoid Hubris

Your site may attract a huge initial audience if it features the latest in multimedia programming techniques, but some visitors may hesitate to return if your cutting-edge technology tends to crash their computer. Creating sites designed for 21" monitors and $50,000 workstations may challenge your competition—but is a sure way to announce a lack of concern for your audience. If you provide high-bandwidth material, ensure that visitors can choose to view it—and consider creating low-bandwidth versions of the same content.

Use Advertising Appropriately

Frustrated with the difficulties of Internet advertising, providers have turned to expensive, high-end multimedia product showcases to sell their content. While this method may work for other media without the Internet's download problems, it will likely only irritate visitors on slow modems who wait an hour to view a spinning diet drink. At the very least, make sure that the audience can choose to see such extravaganzas and consider providing low-bandwidth versions of the same material. It is also important to provide appropriate advertising, For example, a site devoted to surf videos may advertise surf boards, wet suits, surf shops, other water sports, and travel sites that showcase regions where surfing is popular.

Keep It Interactive

Interactive media encourage audience members to explore past entertainment to the providers themselves. Content providers must be ready to reveal themselves and provide information on their interests and goals. For example, in the Georgia Tech study (http://www.cc.gatech.edu/gvu/user_surveys), 79 percent of the respondents said they would submit their personal information at sites if told how it would be used. In contrast, only 6 percent said they would not give out information under any circumstances. Content providers who fail to establish an open, direct relationship are treated with great suspicion by the Internet community and their material is unlikely to be accepted.

Show Community Interest

While companies struggle to enable one-way Internet broadcasting for the Web, it is simultaneously being converted to handle inline chat, voice messages, videoconferencing, and virtual world systems. The most successful media forms on the Internet today are those which use the two-way nature of the medium such as bulletin boards, postings, personal home pages, and chat rooms. Your site should promote contact within the audience, as well as contact between the audience and provider.

 Cybercultural Feedback

While most people in entertainment are worried about how their Web sites will affect the Internet audience, it is also important to be aware of how the Internet can change you, the content provider. Since the Internet is a dramatically interactive medium, it has an effect on producers and consumers alike. Content providers may find, in learning to use the Internet effectively, that they can improve their own business as well.

Disintermediation

A long word for a simple concept, *disintermediation* refers to the removal of the "middleman" between producer and consumer enabled by the Internet. In a typical broadcast system, content distribution flows from a relatively small number of sources to a large number of people. Since the equipment and production values required for content creation and distribution are traditionally quite expensive, access to distribution is controlled by *gatekeepers*—licensers, legal support, management, agents—who decide what gets to the mass audience. This system nearly vanishes on Internet. With access to global promotion and distribution (for hundreds rather than millions of dollars), small entertainment providers may reach their audience directly.

The long-term consequence for a company that invests heavily in Intertainment will be an increase in content production and a reduction in the number of gatekeepers. Performers and artists will always be essential, but fewer individuals will be necessary to provide "middle management" on entertainment projects. The effects of this on the current industry, particularly the largest organizations, will be dramatic. While disintermediation is already a reality on the Internet, there is still a place for mediators (as opposed to distributors) in the interactive age. Producers, agents, and managers whose job is to promote entertainment will find the state of affairs vastly improved for their clients—while those holding their position on the basis of exclusivity and nothing else will be severely challenged.

Fan Sites

Virtually any popular movie or television show will attract a large collection of independently produced sites, which serve as a nucleus for organizing fans. By tapping into this area, producers may learn a great deal about how their show is being received by the public and often receive suggestions for improvement. However, if a show moves in a direction that the community doesn't like, its communication can rapidly turn into attacks on the show and the people involved. Since Internet communication is relatively anonymous, many attacks reach a level that would never be tolerated in the real world. All fans have their own opinions; it is up to content providers to encourage feedback from fans without being controlled by it.

One of the most vexing issues for providers of traditional entertainment concerns fan sites which display copyrighted or trademarked material or use characters in original fiction (see Chapter 13). While theses cases are clear examples of intellectual property infringement, in practice a major crackdown on fans severely damages the credibility of the program. To date, problems between fans and media companies have been relatively minor, except in cases where the fan sites have altered original content in a negative way or used the Web site to sell products. In some cases, studios have resolved the problem by working with fans or supplying specific material for their use. The situation is complicated by the international nature of Internet communications. If fans are forced to remove local pages, they could conceivably post them on Web servers where a comparable local trademark law does apply. Dealing with the new ability of fans to act as content providers on the Web will continue to be a major challenge for media professionals entering cyberculture.

Virtual Corporations

With increasing levels of telecommuting and virtual collaboration, the Internet allows companies to decentralize their own operations. As discussed in landmark books like Davidow and Malone's *The Virtual Corporation*, companies are increasingly adopting a less hierarchial, distributed model for their business. The Internet, with low-cost universal access, can enable these new ways of management for companies of any size. Individual entertainers can benefit as well; by replacing long-distance calls with email and chat rooms, much of the overhead of telecommuting can be eliminated. Individual entertainers may also benefit directly from the Web by organizing tours and bookings online, avoiding the need for travel.

Larger companies can also build internal organization structure by posting company information on internal Web servers running on an *Intranet*, a private corporate network that uses the software of the Web to organize information. Intranets may be enormously effective at in-house company organizations; instead of mailing material or sending out reports, the information may simply be posted on the company's internal Web site for organization-wide access. Production text, memos, and graphics may be reasonably distributed via postings to a Web site. Since the Web runs under public-domain software protocols, it is possible to cut through the complexity of incompatible software products that MIS and computing managers have traditionally had to use to maintain their internal networks. Intranet information is readily available in online. Archives such as The Complete Intranet Resource (http://www.lochnet.com/client/smart/intranet.htm) and e-zines such as Intranet Design Magazine (http://www.innergy.com) and The Intranet Journal (http://www.brill.com/intranet) can help a group begin the move to Web-based company information networks.

International Cyberculture

The Internet does not distingush international boundaries; people from countries throughout the world are increasingly putting their own visions into the matrix of cyberspace. With the continuing development of remote collaboration software, international production of art and entertainment will become increasingly simple and barriers to entertainment currently maintained by geographic isolation will dissappear. Currently, the Internet still reflects its origins in the United States, but by the year 2000, 70 percent of the audience will be outside the United States. Well before this point, cyberculture will have altered to accommodate an increasing variety of religions, customs, and political beliefs. Such an environment can be a great asset to content developers. While the uniformity of the Internet audience will decrease, ethnic and indigenous entertainment currently unable to attract an audience may find support in the vastly expanded environment.

> ***With the former Soviet block countries, their ability to control the dissemination of information has been severely crippled by the Internet. This is why most people I have spoken to indicate that the greatest weapon of peace has been the Internet—which has allowed them access to uncensored information, political and humanistic.***
>
> —ALEXANDER LEHR, WRITER AND PRODUCER, PRESIDENT, IMAGINATION INTERNATIONAL PRODUCTIONS

Will the Internet be the "new television?" Despite the record numbers of former couch potatoes joining the interactive Internet community, it is unlikely that the unique features of cyberculture will disappear. While some have anticipated a loss of coummunity, the Internet-specific vision appears to be strengthening rather than diminishing. The true test of cyberculture will come when it gets its vision—a high-speed network capable of carrying all the sensory experience of an alternate reality. The next and final chapter explores how the coming changes in hardware, software, and infrastructure will contribute to the evolution of Internet-based entertainment.

CHAPTER 15

CYBERMEDIA

If the last few years since the introduction of the Web are any indication, the future for Internet-based entertainment promises to be an exciting and challenging environment. Rapid change is occurring at the hardware, software, and content level—all of which will take the Internet in unpredictable directions in the years ahead. This final chapter examines various aspects of these changes to see where they are taking the Internet and how they will affect the type of entertainment content developers will create for the Web.

Hardware Trends

The most obvious changes in the Internet during the next few years will occur in the equipment used to form the Internet itself. Changes in computer technology and network hardware will provide faster and cheaper access for the majority of the Internet audience. Integration of network and local media storage will help to reduce Net traffic as production standards increase.

Network Computers

Over the next few years, the average consumer systems will split into two forms: one is a faster version of today's personal computer (PC) and the other is a cheap ($500) "network" computer (NC) whose primary use will be for Web-surfing. Network computers lack expensive processors, hard disks, and monitors; they require an Internet connection in order to function. Many in the industry have high hopes for NC computing as a way to draw in the 90 percent of the United States population who do not have Internet connections and who are expected to have a strong interest in entertainment. Current devices fitting the NC designation include Apple's Pippin (http://product.info.apple.com/pr/press.releases) and NC devices promoted by companies like Oracle (http://www.oracle.com/products/nc/). Along with Apple, IBM, Netscape, and Sun

Microsystems, Oracle recently announced a set of standards for developing NC hardware and software; about 30 hardware manufacturers have already adopted the guidelines for creating NCs.

> ***The biggest problem is that it is a pain to 'get online'. Even after all the software is set, it takes too long, for example, to connect the computer, dial the number, login, etc. Using the Net must become as simple as pressing the 'ON' button on the TV remote control. I hope cable-modems and other Net appliances help.***
>
> —ARIEL POLER, CHAIRMAN AND FOUNDER, I/PRO
> http://www.ipro.com

If NC devices fulfill the hopes of their creators and enter the mainstream in a big way, they will present significant challenges for Internet entertainment providers. Their limited performance relative to a personal computer will make it difficult for them to properly display Web sites using advanced multimedia like Java and Shockwave. Because these technologies are dependent on the user's local computing power, it is possible that the first generation of NCs will not handle advanced Web-based multimedia at all. Even when they correctly display Web contents, current designs make little or no provision for visitor feedback through email and order forms, and they cannot be used for PC applications such as word processing.

ISDN Modems

Integrated Services Digital Network (ISDN) appears to finally be happening for real, almost 20 years after it was initially developed. Running up to five times faster than a 28.8 modem over ordinary phone lines, it promises to eliminate the long waits currently needed to access multimedia Web sites. Costs for ISDN modems have fallen dramatically from around $1,000 to as low as $200 for systems produced by Cardinal and other companies (Figure 15.1).

The main barrier to widespread use of ISDN does not occur at the hardware level, but at installation. Though over half of all American homes potentially had access to ISDN in mid-1996, the difficult setup process is complicated by equipment incompatibilities and poorly trained personnel, in many cases. The problem has been serious enough that manufacturers like Motorola have created an ISDN LifeGUARDs (http://www.mot.com) service which provides help in hardware selection and line setup with a compatible Internet service provider. As the Internet's popularity continues to increase, phone companies are paying more attention to their ISDN service and a significant fraction of the Internet

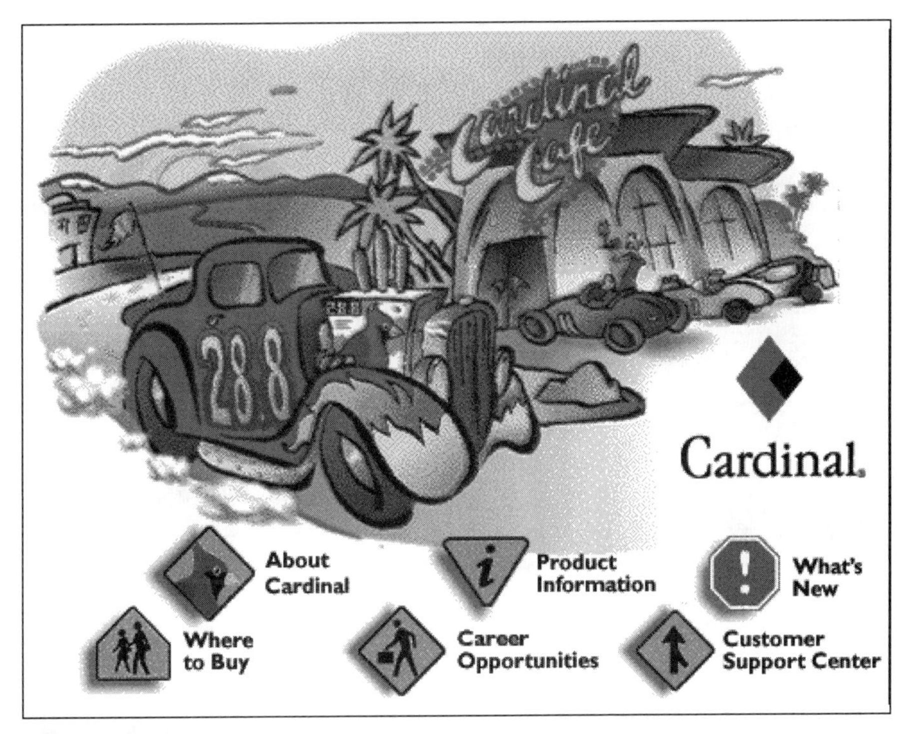

FIGURE 15.1 Cardinal (http://www.cardtech.com).

audience is expected to be using ISDN by the end of 1997. ISDN's biggest near-term impact on Internet entertainment may be to give large numbers of industry professionals high-speed, inexpensive access to the Internet for their work.

Cable Modems

With low bandwidth standing between the reality of the Web and its potential, many groups are aggressively seeking the fastest speeds possible for media delivery. Cable modems, which connect to existing networks to provide high-speed Internet access, offer one of the best chances to bring *broadband* access to the Internet and other services into the home. A good discussion of the pros and cons of cable modems can be found at Cablemodems.com (http://www.cablemodems.com), and at the Cable Modem FAQ (http://www.cox.com/modemfaq.html). Compared to phone lines, cable has the potential of handling connections up to 1,000 times faster than a state-of-the-art 28.8 modems, though current trials have used systems providing about 10 times the bandwidth. Even at these speeds, long waits for Web pages to download virtually vanish. Current costs for cable modem are in the $500 range.

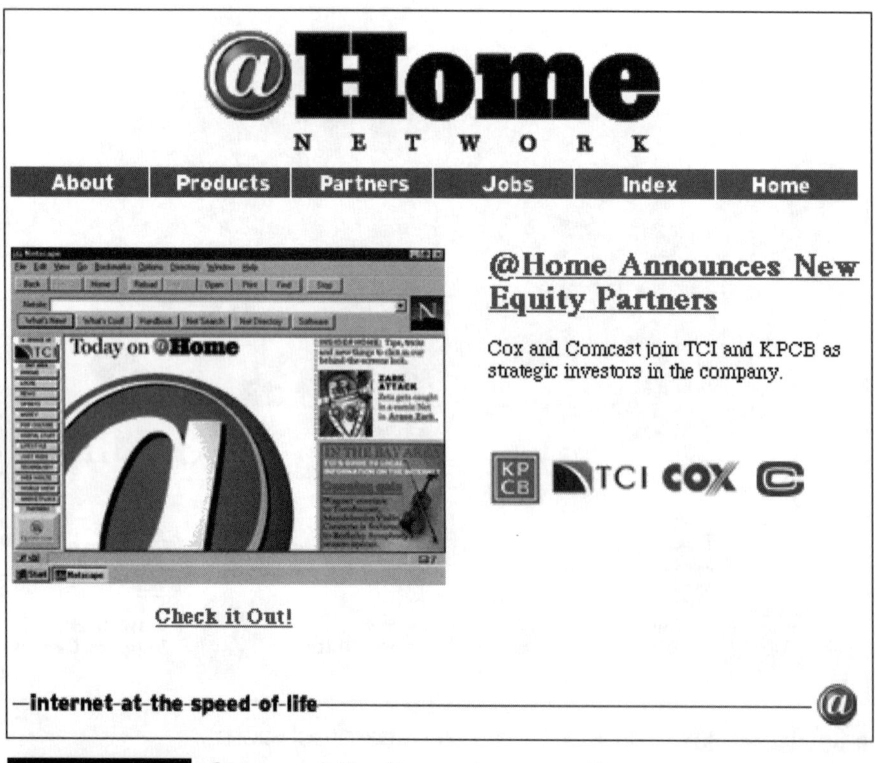

FIGURE 15.2 @Home (http://www.home.net).

> ***Computers are too complex for the average American, but as Internet connect speeds increase and computers come down in price as well as get simpler to use, then the Net will have its own niche for maybe 40 percent of the American population by the end of the next 10 years. But NOTHING will REPLACE the beloved 'idiot box'!***
>
> —JOHN A. HOBSON, PRESIDENT, E-DISTRIBUTORS CORPORATION; DBA: THE LONEZONE
> http://lonezone.com and http://wickedweb.com

Despite the interest of the entertainment community in this technology, several major hurdles stand in the way of widespread use of cable modems. In practice, the infrastructure of the cable network is frequently inadequate to handle high data rates, and modem setup and configuration is too difficult for many consumers. An indication of the problems can be seen in the slow implementation of @Home (Figure 15.2) network. Originally, @Home offered cable companies a way to deliver high-speed Internet access for consumers in the Sunnyvale, California region—but during the first half of 1996, it repeatedly revised its

FIGURE 15.3 Westell's FlexCAP ADSL section (http://www.westell.com): ADSL versus ISDN download speeds.

estimate for the start of service. In contrast, Canadian cable companies such as Rogers Cable (http://www.rogers.com) successfully brought cable access to thousands of customers in the Ontario area during 1996.

Other problems exist with cable modems, particularly in their use by content providers and business networks. Unlike standard modems, cable modems have widely differing rates of upstream versus downstream transmission. In fact, if highways acted like cable modems, one lane would run at 100 mph and the other would either be closed entirely or allow 1.5 mph speeds. This makes cable modems useless for content providers who need to send as well as receive information. While this may work for digital broadcasting, Internet use requires two-way traffic. Fortunately, new standards put forth by Terayon Corp. (http://www.terayon.com) may enable faster upstream speeds over cable networks and make them competitive with other technologies.

Even after problems with the cable networks are resolved, high-speed access will be inhibited by the Internet itself. Currently, the major data backbones of the Internet cannot accommodate an influx of new customers with extremely fast access. One possibility under exploration by @Home and others is local caching of Web pages on individual cable networks.

ADSL Technology

With the rise of the Web, the phone companies have dusted off a technology originally designed to deliver video through phone lines.

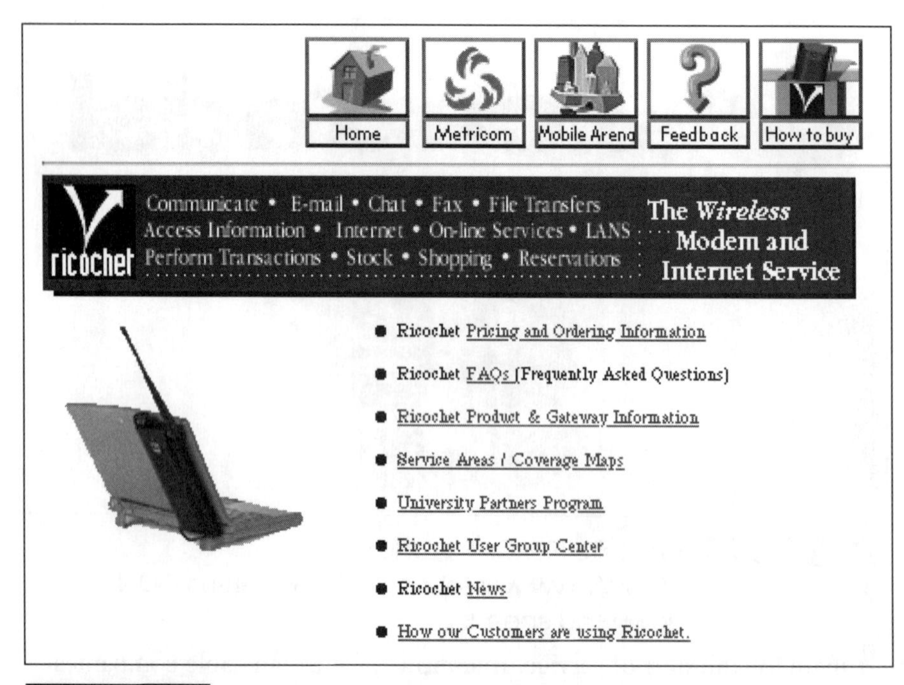

FIGURE 15.4 Ricochet (http://www.ricochet.net/ricochet).

The Asymmetric Digital Subscriber Line (ADSL) protocol allows speeds between 25 and 100 times faster than ordinary modems over existing telephone lines. While this is slower than speeds quoted for cable modems, its ability to use standard phone lines and enable high data rates will make it highly competitive. Current costs per unit are comparable to cable modems. If ADSL takes off, the biggest loser may be ISDN technology. Unlike ISDN, ADSL does not require special line setups by the phone company. A few providers such as PairGain (http://www.pairgain.com) and Westell (Figure 15.3) already offer megabit ADSL *supermodems* for trial use. Widespread introduction is expected at the end of 1996.

Wireless Computing

The hottest thing in Internet access is wireless. Systems designed to adapt existing digital cellular networks provide high-speed connections to wireless modems, allowing individuals to access the Internet simply by attaching their systems. Infocom, Inc. (http://www.om-net.com/infocom/) provides products that transfer data at 25.6 mps, or almost 1,000 times faster than a 28.8 modem. While the system provides high speeds, upstream data must be sent through slow modem connections. Two-way personal wireless access to the Internet is already offered by Ricochet

FIGURE 15.5 Sony's DVD section (http://www.sel.sony.com/SEL/consumer/dvd).

(Figure 15.4). Individuals using the service may instantly access the Internet from any location at 28.8 modem speeds.

DVD Technology

The Digital Versatile Disk (DVD) (http://www.sel.sony.com/SEL/consumer/dvd/index.html) combines audio, video, and computer data into a single common format. Despite their superficial similarity to audio CD and CD-ROM disks, DVDs have capacities up to 20 times greater—enough to store complete feature films at extremely high resolution. Unlike earlier formats such as the CD-ROM, the DVD standard is identical for computers and consumer electronics—eliminating the problems found with existing mixed media formats such as CD+. DVD players will cost about as much as audio CD players and will be able to play audio CDs as well. Figure 15.5 introduces Sony's DVD section.

With widespread introduction during 1997, DVD technology will be particularly attractive for hybrid entertainment products mixing Internet access with local material. For example, a hybrid DVD disk could provide Internet access to Web pages for a classic movie, while simultaneously displaying the film itself from data stored on the disk. Individual hyperlinks on the Web page would trigger access to specific portions of the film. This system sidesteps the long download times necessary to transfer video over the Internet and may be ideal for creating multiuser

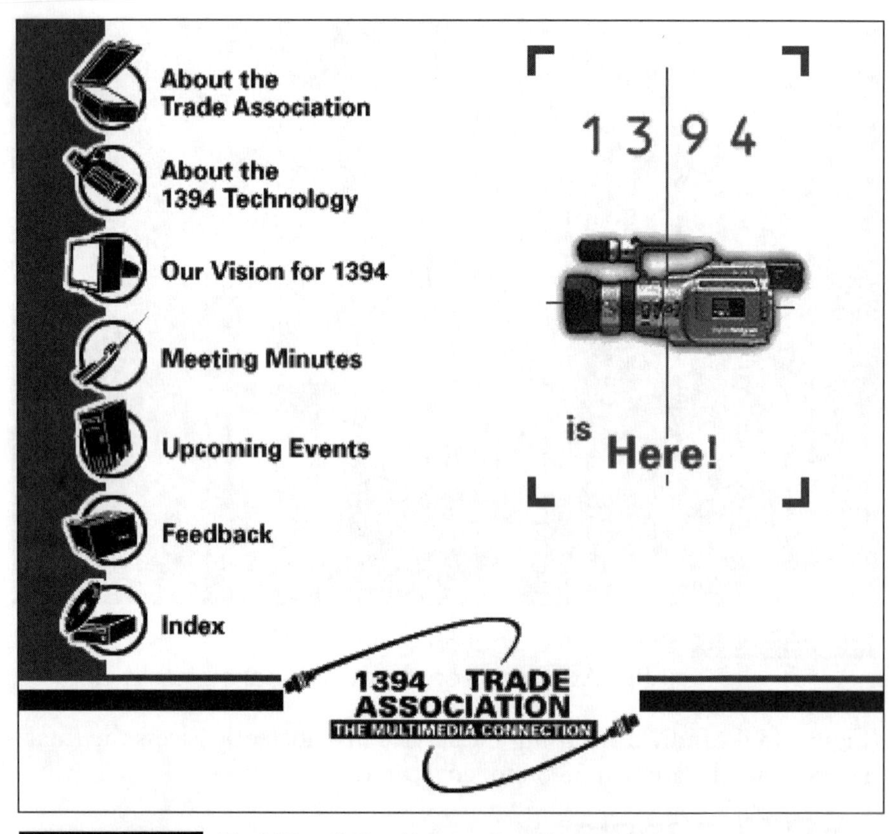

FIGURE 15.6 FireWire (http://www.firewire.org).

games played over the Internet (see Chapter 12) which use large, high-resolution graphics. Production companies which have been producing enhanced CDs such as Circumstance (http://www.circumstance.com/enter/) are already advertising DVD products to companies which currently use CD+ technology.

Internet and TV Hybrids

> ***Television, radio, and Internet boundaries will blur—resulting in an amalgam, with unlimited variations.***
>
> —Chuck Wild of Liquid Mind, ambient keyboardist
> http://kspace.com/mind

Many groups are developing consumer products which integrate the functions of a computer and TV. In some cases, the systems will resemble the NC computers previously mentioned, while in others they will combine high-end computer modules with the large-screen television formats. Zenith Electronics is expected to be first on the market with a Web-enabled TV sometime in 1997. Interest in hybrid technology was also demonstrated in recent announcements by Compaq Computer Corp and Thomson Consumer Electronics.

While much interest surrounds TV and computer hybrids, the concept has been tried before; witness the failed TV and computer released by Apple a few years ago. An alternate possibility now being explored is to connect TVs and computers to a common network in the home via Microsoft's Simply Interactive (http://www.microsoft.com) PC specification. Under the scheme, a network system called FireWire, currently referred to as "1394" (Figure 15.6), integrates computers with keyboards, scanners, printers, and DVD players. The major advantage of FireWire is that devices connected to it will automatically self-configure when connected. FireWire will be particularly useful for families using PCs who will welcome a way to convert their television to a second, low-cost computer.

Software Trends

As hardware continues to improve, Internet software will continue its headlong pace of upgrades and acquisition of new features. With time, the Web browser as a distinct program may simply disappear and Web access will become part of everything from word processors to tax preparation.

Robust Internet Broadcasting

Since the Internet's original protocol, TCP/IP, was not designed to handle large multimedia files, efforts are underway to upgrade it to handle the expected boom in Internet broadcasting. Currently, the emerging standard most likely to succeed is the Resource Reservation Protocol (RSVP). RSVP sends "warnings" to computers along a broadcast route on the Internet and allows them to clear traffic for more efficient audio and video digital transmission. While RSVP will *not* enable mass television-style broadcasting over the Internet, it will allow higher quality, non-jerky video to be delivered for promotion and video-conferencing.

Ubiquity of Java

Developed by Sun Microsystems (http://www.sun.com), Java is one of the first major Web-specific innovations. Java enlarges the possibilities for software development beyond Microsoft Windows applications. With the integration of Java into Web browsers, virtually any software developer can ship an application into a Windows platform without working with Microsoft. Since Java programs are designed to download over the

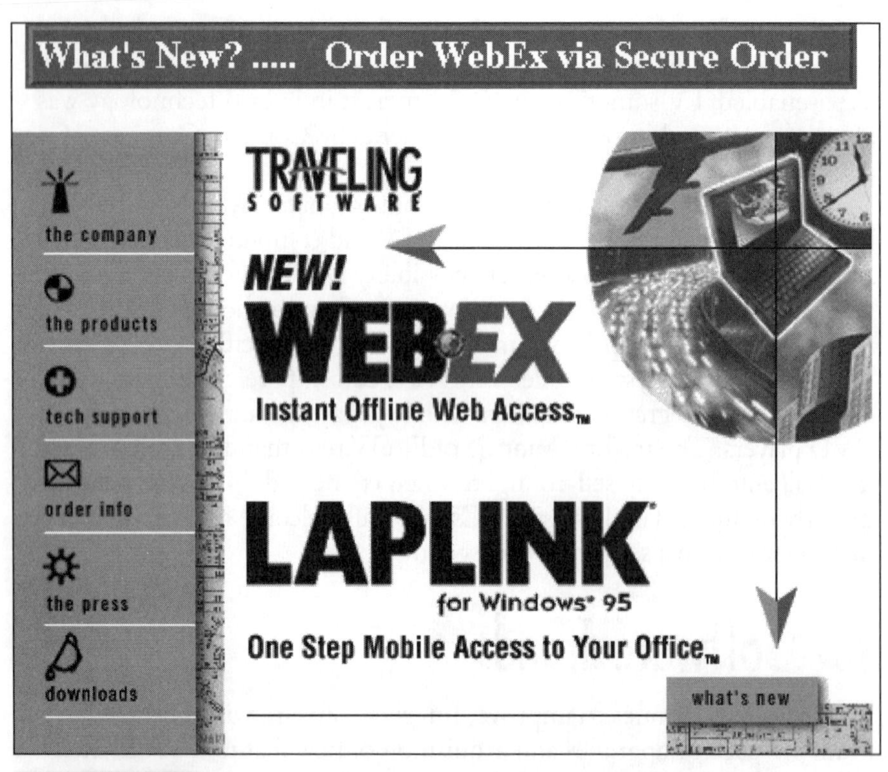

What's New? ..... Order WebEx via Secure Order
the company
the products
tech support
order info
the press
downloads
TRAVELING SOFTWARE
NEW!
WEBEX
Instant Offline Web Access™
LAPLINK
for Windows® 95
One Step Mobile Access to Your Office™
what's new

FIGURE 15.7 Traveling Software (http://www.travsoft.com).

Internet, it is not even necessary to have a distributor, which will precipitate major changes in the software industry. These advantages will attract great numbers of programmers to Java, who will likely make it the "next thing" after the Web. For content providers, the message is clear: Program in Java to remain at the cutting edge of Web development.

Full Document Style Support

Using software standards like The World Wide Web Consortium's Web Style Sheets (http://www.w3.org/pub/WWW/Style) documentation, it will be possible to apply standard type styles and colors across large numbers of documents. This may contribute to the ongoing trend seen at many Web sites, which lay out their pages in magazine or book format.

Offline Browsing

Groups such as Freeloader Software (http://www.freeloader.net) and Traveling Software (Figure 15.7) have developed software that allows all or part of a Web site to be downloaded for later viewing. In practice, individuals using the software could choose a Web site before going to bed and have all or part of the site downloaded to their hard disk by morning for later use. This will make Web surfing faster and more efficient, but will also raise intellectual property issues for consumers who create a working copy of an entertainment Web site on their computer. Another problem particularly affecting content providers is updates; in order to save time, the audience may continue to use outdated local information instead of downloading new material. Offline browsing also could have major effects on Web design; sites that store their content several layers beneath the home page will not work well with offline browsers.

Free Internet Access

A variety of companies are developing products that allow free access to the Internet—as long as you watch their ads. Juno Online (http://www.juno.com) offers free email accounts by allowing individuals to view ads while sending and receiving email. While most feel that ad-supported Web surfing is too expensive for current advertisers, Hyper Net, Inc.'s Hyper System (Figure 15.8) plans to introduce target ads in a window next to the Web browser. HyperNet feels that by microtargeting ads to individuals, it can raise rates enough to charge for the service. Since access will be free, the companies expect consumers who are unwilling to pay subscription charges to sign up for their service. While

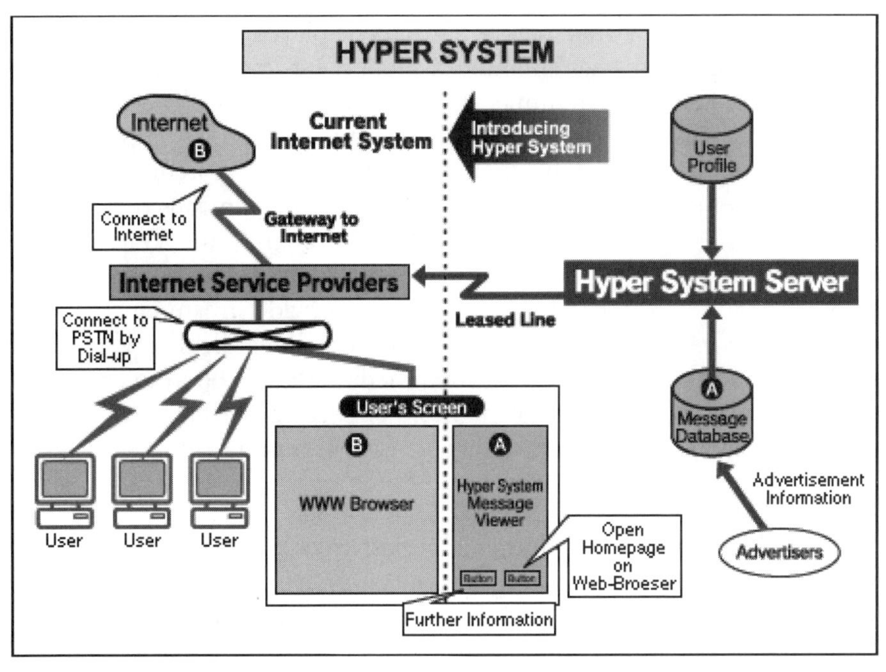

FIGURE 15.8 Hyper Net, Inc.'s Hyper System Flow chart (http://www.hypernet.co.jp).

some expect free access to drive an advertising model for Internet content delivery, others argue that consumers will continue to pay for ad-free access to their favorite Web sites.

> ***Television is a passive medium, forcing both entertainment and subject matter down the viewers' throats. This passive entertainment, however popular, lacks the ability of choice and pace—the two factors which have given magazines and print such a long life-span. By combining the instant gratification factor of television with the choice and pace of a magazine, the Internet, along with new technologies such as DVD, promises to redefine entertainment and entertainment value.***
>
> —Zack Zalon, designer of The Troubadour, KSCA Radio, and LA Live sites, President, The Factory Network
> http://www.factorynet.com

Streaming Media Support

Currently, content delivered by Web-based multimedia platforms like Macromedia's Shockwave (http://www.macromedia.com) still follows the CD-ROM model—which means that multimedia presentations have to be completely downloaded before they can be played. To overcome this problem, Macromedia has announced support for *streaming* animation in which components of a multimedia presentation are downloaded only when needed, instead of all at once. Macromedia is also developing *look-ahead* streaming, a system in which the program tries to predict which multimedia objects will be needed in advance and downloads them first. Animation is also getting streaming support through FutureWave Software's CelAnimator (Figure 15.9) authoring program. Developed specifically for the Web, the system may be able to provide streaming animation more efficiently than its competitors. Regardless of which system becomes standard, streaming multimedia will be a boon to entertainment providers who will be able to more efficiently provide cutting-edge content to audience members with slow Internet connections.

Internet Phones

Since Web surfers only pay local connect charges to use the Internet, any system transferring voice messages is the equivalent of a flat-rate, worldwide long-distance service. Such Internet telephones and videophones have become one of the hottest software products on the market and products like QuarterDeck's VocalTec (http://webtalk.qdeck.com) integrate Internet telephony directly into Web browsing. Significantly, most

FIGURE 15.9 Cel Animator Demo (http://www.futurewave.com).

Internet telephone systems allow conversations between several site visitors and use the existing metaphor of chat rooms. Using such a system, content providers will be able to deliver entertainment such as music broadcasts—and allow the virtual audience to talk between themselves as well. Internet videophone systems are also being developed by larger companies like Lucent Technologies (http:/www.lucent.com) and Intel (http://www.intel.com). With time, these systems will include more than voice; plans exist to provide shared virtual graffiti *blackboards* which can be drawn on by anyone using the phones.

Virtual Reality

It is likely that the introduction of the VRML 2.0 standard will precipitate a shakeout in the currently chaotic VRML world, after which virtually all hardware and software will come to support for three-dimensional, participatory worlds. Currently, the biggest limitation of VRML is that it is really two-dimensional; instead of immersing the viewer in the simulation, it is viewed on flat monitors. New technology such as Virtual i-O headsets (Figure 15.10), and The Virtual Retinal Display Project (http://www.hitl.washington.edu/projects/vrd/) send images that fill the viewer's field of vision, and dramatically change the experience of VRML. While hardware advances, implementation of new features in

FIGURE 15.10 Virtual i-O's Virtual i-Glasses (http://www.vio.com).

VRML 2.0 will support directional sound and allow for incorporating other tasks (e. g., word processing) in the VR environment.

As time passes, it is likely that pure VRML—or a mixture of VRML and broadcasting—will supersede current Internet video broadcasts. With its small file sizes and data rates, VRML will always be easier to transmit than broadcast video, particularly to a large number of audience members. In addition, the participatory nature of VRML can provide greater involvement for the Internet audience. Competition will probably emerge between the two technologies, but ultimately a hybrid system is likely. In order to do this, technology needs to be developed which opens up virtual windows in VRML worlds allowing the introduction of broadcast data. With these additions, the VRML environment will consist of virtual objects, audience avatars, images of well-known celebrities, and autonomous digital organisms using artificial intelligence. These worlds may become so rich that they may spawn new forms of entertainment beyond any current conceptions.

New Programming

Several other exciting technologies promise to extend the experience of Internet entertainment. One such system is *web rings*, available through the Web Ring (http://www.webring.org) site. Web rings link a set of participating sites in a circular pattern and form an alternative to reciprocal links. Another new technology is hyperlinked video, as typified by Ephyx's Hypervideo (http://www.ephyx.co.il). The Ephyx VideoActiv authoring system allows characters and objects in the video to carry along hyperlinks to other parts of the video or external destinations on the Web. By introducing interactivity into video streams, Hypervideo opens up the possibility of converting one-way broadcast-type data into interactive entertainment.

 Media and Content Convergence

Rapid advancements in hardware and software add up to overall changes in the Internet as an entertainment medium. As the entertainment industry learns to create content for the Web, the Internet's ability to mimic media will progressively erase the difference between print, broadcasting, and telephone-based communication. When this happens, the Web site created by a print media company may be very similar to that created by a movie studio—which may in turn look very similar to a site developed by a fan club. Thus, media convergence will drive content convergence within the industry, resulting in direct competition between existing entertainment providers, as well the emergence of new ones. Traditional entertainment will face increasing challenges from these groups as the Internet develops and may have to re-evaluate its offerings in order to stay competitive. The following lists some of the new content providers likely to be enabled by media convergence.

Fans

Traditionally, fans have been the greatest asset that entertainers have to promote and support their work. On the Web, however, media convergence has allowed fans to create Web sites with content which is often the equal of the "official" Web site. As fan sites become major entertainment resources, it will be necessary to create standards governing their relationship with the primary content providers. Large media companies which simply "crack down" on fan groups risk having them branch out to create their own original entertainment content.

Venues and Cybercafes

Both traditional clubs and performance spaces, as well as cybercafes have the potential for providing unique entertainment to the Internet. As broadcast technology advances, clubs sites will increasingly be seen as entertainment programming. Cybercafes will be able to provide content in another way: by providing for downloads of art and music from the Web. With the falling costs of CD-ROM mastering systems, in the near future it may be possible for cybercafe patrons to "cut their own" custom CDs using material downloaded from the Web. Cybercafes will mediate payment for the artists and musicians on the Web providing the content and collect fees for using their mastering service. If this becomes practical, cybercafes have the potential for directly competing with standardized products sold through music retail outlets.

ISPs

Internet service providers providing dialup access to consumers are actively looking for ways to convert their access service into value-added access. By accumulating content through hosting Web sites ISPs have the potential of replicating the model of online services and charging for access to their content. To ground their services, many ISPs may also become cybercafes as an additional point of sale for their services and as an alternate distribution outlet as previously described.

Advertising Agencies

Major entertainment milestones on the Web, such as The Spot (http://www.thespot.com) were created as original content by advertising agencies who have frequently developed entertaining sites for non-entertainment companies (see Chapter 12). In such an environment, it is only a matter of time before some agencies decide to develop original entertainment themselves, either to support their clients or to expand their services. It is not improbable that the entertainment on some of these sites will be fully competitive with that created by traditional entertainment companies.

Independent Web Developers

Many medium to large Web developers are already beginning to develop plans for original content sites. An example of this is Digital Planet (http://www.digiplanet.com), whose original multimedia interactive adventure Madeleine's Mind (http://www.madmind.com; see Chapter 12) foreshadows similar future efforts by content developers. Virtual world developers such as Worlds, Inc. (http://www.alphaworld.com) and Chaco Communications Corp. (http://www.chaco.com) are actively soliciting content developers for long-term relationships in world-building. These groups will have the advantage of producing interactive, immersive entertainment for their audiences from the start and will lack many of the constraints applying to broadcast companies entering the Web. A long-term trend may find individual artists deriving royalties from a *look and feel* of a particularly interesting world, with the virtual worlds software developer replacing organizations which provide artist compensation in broadcast media.

"Old" Cyberspace Communities

Cyberspace had active, strongly motivated communities long before the current Web explosion. Currently, many of these groups are realigning around the Web's new multimedia paradigm and have a relatively low profile. Once the Web's software enables full interactivity, old cyberspace is likely to return with a vengeance and form a competing source of entertainment for the huge numbers of individuals joining the Internet. The competitive advantage of these communities will be simple—instead of just a movie ticket, their entertainment will offer cyberspace citizenship in their community as well.

Meta-sites

Meta-sites hosting a variety of art and entertainment under their home page are also candidates for original content development. Frequently working with large numbers of unsigned artists and musicians, they have the potential of tapping these resources for original content development.

Travel Agencies and Tourist Boards

As mentioned in Chapter 11, travel organizations are creating highly entertaining sites that are becoming increasingly difficult to distinguish from pure entertainment. Based on its vision of the Internet as a autonomous world, cyberculture will quickly accept the validity of virtual travel and increasingly make it similar to other Web-based entertainment. The convergence of travel and entertainment sites is already happening at Terraquest (Figure 15.11), whose virtual expeditions to Antarctica and the Galapagos have garnered widespread media attention and a large Internet audience. In all probability, travel agencies and national tourist boards are destined to aggressively compete with traditional entertainment by offering sites that mix regional information with original entertainment content. Travel-related entertainment on the Web will also offer a springboard to the development of indigenous entertainment in each country it visits. Within the United States, efforts at state and county levels to create virtual communities are likely to provide support for local entertainment providers at the expense of traditional mass media.

FIGURE 15.11 Terraquest's virtual Galapagos section (http://www.terraquest.com).

Merging of Entertainment and Information

Chapter 12 provided examples of several companies that have successfully combined information and entertainment on their Web sites. With this growth in Internet-based entertainment, there is a real question of whether the Internet will continue to provide "real" information to its audience. Basing their ideas on the history of broadcast media, some industry watchers have predicted a shift away from information resources toward entertainment more similar to television. In the authors' view, this position misrepresents the interdependence of information and entertainment in an interactive—as opposed to passive—viewing environment. Intertainment will not "go mindless"; instead, it will exist in a matrix of information which serves to continually inform the audience. Similarly, organizations who have not defined themselves as entertainment providers—including most businesses—will find that their Web sites will increasingly incorporate entertainment features.

> ***My personal hope is that the Internet kills television and its lousy ads, talk radio, and hype music programming—most of which is geared to getting consumers to keep their minds on 'buying.' Passive media is exactly that: It makes sonambulists of all of us. What it does to a child's attention span is criminal.***
>
> —Diane Rapaport, Author (*How to Make and Sell Your Own Recording*); Producer and Co-Publisher (*The Musician's Business and Legal Guide, The Visual Artist's Business and Legal Guide*, and *Sound Advice for the Acoustic Musician* [forthcoming in early 1997]), Jerome Headlands Press
> http://kspace.com/jhp

Online users today view the Web as a resource for discovering more about favorite recordings, performers, or "behind-the-scenes" technical information. As such, the Web provides information unavailable in current broadcast media due to their centrally-controlled, one-way nature. In broadcast media, competition for "time slots" and "audience share" promotes the creation of short-term amusement and there is simply less time to create and distribute information-rich entertainment. In contrast to the broadcast audience, online users can actively explore interactive entertainment products at their own time and place—and frequently expect them to be imbedded in a meaningful context of knowledge, history, and purpose.

It can be argued further that this integration of entertainment with information will exert subtle long-term pressure to raise the quality of entertainment itself. Since the Internet does not restrict distribution, the same Web browser displaying a high-profile site can effortlessly jump to a site created by independent filmmakers with a fraction of the budget. This will allow the audience to make direct comparisons between mainstream and "artistic" entertainment, to the betterment of both.

As corporate Web sites have matured, they have increasingly blended their informational content with entertainment. A spectacular example of this is provided by Intel's site (http://www.intel.com), which created cutting-edge, virtual-reality objects and environments specifically designed to promote its product line. When virtual worlds were introduced, vast numbers of the Internet audience went to the Intel site—treating it as a source of entertainment and frequently learning something in the process. Other non-entertainment groups on the Internet have created sites that have include interactive adventures, quizzes, puzzles, and contests. An early example of this trend is found at TaxWizard (http://taxwixard.com), in which the dry information provided by an accounting firm is given pleasing treatment as a wizard's oracle. One of the largest examples of this trend is the Yahoo! (http://www.yahoo.com) search engine. Recognizing the audience's interest in entertainment, Yahoo! made itself look like an entertainment site and even publishes a slick magazine *(Yahoo! Internet Life)* whose purpose is clearly less business than pleasure.

Intranets are prime candidates for the fusion of information and entertainment. With much higher bandwidth than the global Internet, Intranets can support real-time audio, video, and multimedia impossible elsewhere. Originally bare-bones information resources, during the first half of 1996 Intranets have acquired an increasingly rich, multimedia feel.

The merging of information and entertainment on the Internet will lead to a new media classification that may greatly impact the current relationship between business, education, and entertainment. The Internet facilitates integrating these separate areas by breaking down barriers of time, location, and economics. The long-term integration of information and entertainment may also have a great impact on all entertainment—by allowing the convergence of work and play in daily life.

The Future of Intertainment

Despite tremendous progress, there is a general consensus that the Internet is still in its infancy. By the year 2000, the 1996 audience of 30 to 40 million may have expanded to up to a billion—while hardware, software, and infrastructure continues to change rapidly. As a group, the entertainment community will feel these changes as much or more than any other group. Entertainment providers must learn to create content on the Web, promote it effectively, and find their place in the larger personal, educational, and business community.

> ***Again, while waiting for "a major entertainment medium" to emerge on the Web, many so-called entertainment outfits are missing the boat. In fact, the boat is already under full sail and there's a major "party" going down on deck. If you don't know this by now, then maybe you have a great future ahead of you in shoe sales. Businesses that do not understand the celebration are doomed.***
>
> —CHRISTOPHER LOCKE, CHAIRMAN AND CHIEF EXECUTIVE OFFICER, ENTROPY GRADIENT REVERSALS
> http://www.panix.com/~clocke/EGR/index.html and
> PROGRAM DIRECTOR, ONLINE COMMUNITY DEVELOPMENT, IBM
> http://www.panix.com/~clocke/

As a medium, the two-way interactivity of the Internet poses particular challenges to individual artists and entertainers. While musicians, performers, and other entertainers traditionally have welcomed interaction with their audience, the evaporation of the "fourth wall" on the Internet will require some adjustment. Artists will need to learn to incorporate interactivity into their work without violating their personal artistic vision in favor of a collective homogenization. Entertainers who have enjoyed nearly exclusive access to large audiences will find challenges from others, as well as from their fans! Many artists will need to lose their fear of the technology and see the Internet for what it is—a network of people that only incidentally uses computers for communication. Individual artists and entertainers are being offered an unprecedented chance to reach their audience directly and develop careers outside the structure of the current industry. This is an opportunity which should not be ignored, particularly from those groups that traditionally have had difficulty getting promotion and distribution for their work.

In larger entertainment groups, the change from one-way broadcasting to two-way interaction will have a tremendous effect on entertainment and will require providers to literally relearn the rules of their profession. With the rise of the Internet, the era of exclusive control of content is giving way to an era of widespread, personal expression. The traditional industry will see increasing fragmentation of the traditional mass audience into diverse groups with specialized interests, along with the emergence of an array of new content providers to service them. Like individual artists and entertainers, the professional community will need to overcome resistance to new technology or face increasing irrelevancy in the digital age.

> ***I definitely see the Internet rivaling mass media entertainment. Uncensored-perpetual-simultaneous-mass-exposure? What can rival radio and television better than that?***
>
> —THOMAS FROOD OF INDUSTRIAL PUNK BAND AnA BLACK
> http://kspace.com/anablack

For groups at all levels, the Internet represents empowerment and a chance to try out new forms of entertainment unavailable today. In order to safeguard their right to create material unafraid of exploring provocative social and political themes, the entertainment community will need to become part of cyberculture (see Chapter 14) and support its agenda of free expression. Despite the primitive state of the Internet, the time to begin developing an agenda for entertainment is today. Entertainment providers who do not begin to learn how to use the medium run the risk of being left out of the coming digital world.

APPENDIX

About the CD-ROM

The software on the CD-ROM with this book provides "one-step" Internet access for Macintosh and Windows computers. In addition to the basic Internet connectivity program, it includes a copy of Microsoft's Internet Explorer (http://www.microsoft.com) web browser and third-party "plug-ins" which add real-time audio, video, and multimedia capabilities. Demos of additional products, including web authoring tools are also available. Internet connectivity is provided by Leonardo Internet, an Internet Service Provider (ISP). The Leonardo account provides five free hours of surfing with full access to the Internet and Web. Further documentation for the software and accessory programs is available on the Internet at the Web sites of each vendor.

Web Site

By default, your first stop will be the Intertainment site (http://kspace.com/intertainment) created by Kaleidospace for the book. The site contains updates and new information related to the material in this book, links to Intertainment resources and companies described in the book, and forms for ordering additional copies of the book online. You can easily cruise all Web sites mentioned in this book by consulting the URL index on this Intertainment site.

Freeware and Shareware

Some of the software is provided as *freeware*. There is no charge for using freeware, and it can be distributed freely as long as its use follows the license agreement included with it. Other items are provided as *shareware*. The authors of shareware retain all rights to the software under the copyright laws while still allowing free distribution. This gives the user a chance to freely obtain and try out the software. Shareware should not be confused with Public Domain software even though they are often obtained from the same sources. If you continue to use shareware after trying it out, you are expected to register your use with the author and pay a registration fee. What you get in return depends on the author, but it may include a printed manual, free updates, telephone support, access to updates through the Internet, etc.

Hardware Requirements

The software provided supports computers with the following configuration:

Windows:	**Macintosh:**
486 or Pentium system	Quadra or PowerMac
at least 8 megabytes RAM	at least 8 megabytes RAM
14.4 or 28.8 modem	14.4 or 28.8 modem
Windows 3.x or Windows 95	System 7.1 or greater
256+ color monitor	256+ color monitor
15 megs disk space	10 megs disk space

In general, you can improve performance, particularly for multimedia, by adding more RAM to your system. In particular, if you plan to explore advanced multimedia on the Internet you should consider increasing your RAM to 16 or 32 megabytes. Increasing your monitor colors beyond the required 256 will also improve the appearance of many Web pages.

Installing the Software

To install the Internet Connectivity Software on a Windows system, follow these steps:

1. Start Windows on your computer.
2. Place the CD-ROM into your CD-ROM drive.
3. From Program Manager, Select File, Run, and type **X:\SETUP** (where **X** is the correct letter of your CD-ROM drive).

To install the software on a Macintosh system, follow these steps:

1. Start your computer.
2. Place the CD-ROM into your CD-ROM drive.
3. Double-click on the Installer icon.

On both systems, complete the installation by following the screen prompts. Note that you must have a modem connected to your computer and to an open phone line to complete the installation.

Additional Software

Some programs and utilities on the CD-ROM are not installed by default due to their large size or restricted application. To install these,

Windows users should open the CD-ROM and select individual packages to "drag and drop" onto the hard disk. Mac users can select from a similar set of programs in the "Mac" directory on the CD-ROM. While the Explorer Web browser is an excellent Inwternet surfing tool, you may also want to download Netscape Navigator (http://www.netscape.com) to take full advantage of these additional programs. A listing of this software is provided in the "contents.htm" file on the CD-ROM, which is best read by opening it with the Web browser.

Contents of the CD-ROM

The following programs are provided for the platforms noted.

- CDLink for the Mac and Windows allows Web pages to access content stored on audio CDs
- CoolFusion for the Mac and Windows is a MPEG movie viewer
- Crescendo for Mac and Windows is an Internet MIDI music player
- Eudora for Mac and Windows provides support for Internet email
- Fractal Imager provides ultra-high compression of complex graphics using fractal technology
- FutureSplash for the Mac and Windows is an animation player and authoring system for the Web
- HTML Transit for Windows automates the production of Web page from standard word processing document
- Internet Fast Forward for the Mac and Windows filters ads from Web pages
- Leonardo Internet connectivity package contains programs, utilities and automated scripts needed to set up Internet access for Mac, Windows 3.x and Windows 95
- Microsoft Internet Explorer is an industry-standard web browser. Mac and Windows 3.x versions provide support for standard Internet audio and video. The Windows 95 version also includes Shockwave for Windows 95, a multimedia extension for playing Macromedia Director movies
- The Palace for the Mac and Windows is a 2D virtual world chat software package
- Projector for Windows is a graphics and video viewer handling virtually any file format
- Pueblo for Windows 95 provides an authoring systems for virtual worlds
- Rapid Transit Player for Windows is an audio compressor and player for the Web
- Sizzler for the Mac is a streaming animation viewer for the Web
- The TOOB for the Mac and Windows is an MPEG video and audio multimedia player

- VDOLive for the Mac and Windows is streaming video viewer for the Web
- V-Realm for Windows is a 3D virtual world VRML viewer technology
- VR Scout for Windows is a 3D viewer for virtual worlds created with Pueblo word processor documents

User Assistance and Information

The software accompanying this book is being provided as is without warranty or support of any kind. Should you require basic installation assistance, or have difficulty making your Internet connection work, you should contact the EarthLink Network at (800) 876-3151. If your CD-ROM is physically defective, please call Wiley's product support number at (212) 850-6194 weekdays between 9 A.M. and 4 P.M. Eastern Standard Time. Or, we can be reached via e-mail at: wprtusw@wiley.com.

To place additional orders or to request information about other Wiley products, please call (800) 879-4539.

Visit the Intertainment site (http://kspace.com/intertainment) created by Kaleidospace for the book. The site contains updates and new information related to the material in this book, as well as forms for ordering additional copies of the book online.

GLOSSARY

Access Log — File written by *Web servers* that records each request for information made by visitors to a Web site.

ActiveX — Windows-specific, proprietary technology created by Microsoft that allows Web developers to create sophisticated onscreen controls such as sliders and switches using existing Microsoft tools.

Ad Server — Specialized Web server that dynamically adds advertising (such as graphic banners) onto Web pages scattered through a large number of Web sites and tracks how many times ads are selected by visitors to each site.

Affinity Targeting — Sending advertising and other promotional material only to people who—based on demographics or behavior—are likely to be interested in it.

Agent — Software program that records an individual's interests, likes, dislikes, and opinions, and uses this information to construct a model of that person's personality. This model is then used to conduct information searches, screen email and news for items likely to be of interest, and even "stand in" for the real person.

Agent Log — Record written by many Web servers that lists the type of software being used by visitors to the Web site.

ALT — Command in *HTML* which allows text to be displayed in place of a given graphic on a Web page. It provides an alternative display for visitors that cannot display graphics on their system or who have deliberately turned graphics off to speed up downloads of the Web pages.

Applet — Computer programs that *download* and immediately execute on individual computers, supported by computer programming systems such as *Java* and *ActiveX.*

Artificial Life — Programs which can copy themselves, mutate and evolve, and provide "living" agents in virtual worlds. They are similar to—but frequently far more sophisticated—than computer viruses.

A&R — Music industry professionals whose major job is scouting new talent for record labels. Originated as Artists & Repertoire.

Asymmetric Digital Subscriber Line (ADSL) — High-speed protocol originally developed by the phone companies to deliver video over phone lines; it is rapidly being adapted as a method of enabling extremely fast Internet connections. Unlike for *ISDN* connections, the phone company does not have to create a special circuit.

Asynchronous — Data forming a two-way interaction which is sent and received at different times; answering machines and email are good examples of this method of communication.

Avatar — Software entity which graphically represents an individual in *virtual worlds* on the Internet and other systems. If the *agent* represents the individual's mind, the avatar represents his or her body.

Bandwidth — A measure of the speed with which data can be transmitted between two digital devices over a network. Internet bandwidth (measured in bits per second) ranges from a few thousand to several hundred million.

Bookmark — Saved reference to the address of a Web site that an individual can add into a customized list of favorite or useful Web sites (hotlinks).

Broadband — Generic term for high-speed digital communication, generally considered to be in the range which allows high-quality, real-time audio and video.

Browser — Software used for accessing the Web that interprets *HTML* commands to display text, graphic, audio, video, and multimedia content.

Bulletin Board System (BBS) — Non-Internet computer network consisting of a single server computer and individual client computers, which usually connect to it via phone lines. BBS systems often provide local information, games, and *chat* areas where individuals can talk to each other. Many, but not all BBS systems, now provide an Internet connection for their members.

Channel Service Unit/Digital Service Unit (CSU/DSU) — Specialized, *modem*-like device which enables extremely high-speed transmissions over *leased-lines.*

Chat Room — Multiuser programs that allow several individuals on the Internet to converse in real-time. Originally, chat rooms were text-only; more recent versions allow the chat to take place in a graphical environment and may even allow voice communication.

Click-through — Measurement of the number of times a visitor to a Web site viewing an ad actually selects it and visits the vendor's Web site.

Common Gateway Interface (CGI) — Programming system used on the Web to extend the capability of *Web servers* to store and process information provided by visitors to the site. CGI programs typically take information provided by a site visitor and use it to search databases, create *posting* boards, opinion polls, and construct new Web pages.

Cookie — Files maintained by Web browsers and servers that allow the Web site operators to identify and track access by repeat visitors.

Coopetition — Arrangements made between normally competitive groups for a common end. Its original appearance was in the computer industry, which created universal standards for certain hardware and software in the 1980s. The most common example of coopetition on the Web is the exchange of *reciprocal links* to mutually enhance visitor traffic.

Cost Per Thousand (CPM) — A standard fee which Web sites (and other media outlets) charge advertisers for a thousand "looks" at their promotional material.

Digital Organism — Generic name for a software program that manifests lifelike or intelligent behavior; a probable candidate for residency in *virtual worlds.*

Digital Signature — Any of a variety of methods for uniquely identifying a single document, image, or other file on a computer.

Digital Versatile Disc (DVD) — New format for data storage which puts audio, video, and computer data into a common digital format, on a disc similar in size and appearance to current audio CDs but with much greater capacity. DVDs are anticipated to replace audio CDs, CD-ROMs and laserdisks. With low costs for production and distribution, DVDs are ideal for film and multimedia distribution, and for creating hybrid systems with local and Web-based information.

Director — Popular authoring system for multimedia produced by Macromedia, Inc. It is widely used for CD-

ROM development and can be adapted for Web-based multimedia using *Shockwave* programming tools.

Disintermediation — A change in the social structure of businesses and other organizations that allows top management to communicate directly with consumers or workers, making middle management and administration redundant. The Internet, with its strong support for two-way communication between producer and consumer, is considered a prime enabler for disintermediation.

Domain Name — Symbolic shorthand for the location of a Web site or other Internet service, it must be assigned by the *InterNIC* (http://www.internic.com). A domain name also provides information characterizing the organization using the site (e.g., commercial .com or educational .edu) and the country in which the site is located.

Download — The process of receiving a block of information from a *server* computer. In the case of audio and video, the download may proceed at a rate too slow to see or hear the information in real time. In this case, the receiver must wait until the download is complete to use the file.

EMBED — Command in *HTML* that allows controls, readouts, and media displays from third-party programs to be displayed in the window of a *Web browser.*

Extensions — Programs referred to variously as *helpers* or *plug-ins* that expand the basic text and graphic displays of Web browsing software to include audio, video, and multimedia. Unless the *EMBED* command is available, the extensions run in a separate window.

Firewall — Specialized hardware and software that restricts and monitors traffic between the local computer and the general Internet, preventing *hackers* from gaining access to sensitive information.

Flames — Long-winded, opinionated attacks on a person's point of view, usually *posted* to Internet resources like *Usenet* and mailing lists.

Free-for-All — Specialized Web sites that allow visitors to *post* the addresses of their favorite Web sites automatically, without editorial intervention.

Graphics Interchange Format (GIF) — File format used for storing compressed graphical information, supported by virtually all Web *browsers.*

Hackers — In the current usage, individuals who break into electronic networks and computers—sometimes for economic gain—but often for no other reason than to prove they can do it. In the more general and original sense, hackers are those who can use limited computer resources to create elegant and efficient solutions to problems.

Hit — Information registered by a *Web server* each time a visitor to the site requests a block of text, graphic image, audio, or video clip. Since Web pages frequently combine these elements, and most visitors to a Web site look at several pages, the number of hits is usually much greater than the number of unique visitors to a Web site.

Home Page — The first (and sometimes only) Web page a visitor to a site encounters after entering its address into the *Web browser.* On large Web sites, it occupies the informational position of a magazine cover.

Hotlist — A series of personal, *bookmarked* Web site addresses, stored by individuals on their local computer for easy access and recall.

Htaccess — A common password system available on *Web servers* restricting access to all or part of the contents of a Web site.

Hunter-gatherer — In this text, referring to societies who hunt and/or forage for food and other resources, and travel through a large "home range." In contrast, agricultural societies remain in the same location and actively cultivate and harvest resources.

Hyperlink — A key feature distinguishing the Web from other forms of Internet communication, a hyperlink allows any text or graphic on a Web page to be connected to another Web page, graphic, audio, or video file anywhere on the Internet.

Hypertext Markup Language (HTML) — The programming system of the Web. HTML is a mixture of document formatting commands, *hyperlinks* to other Web content, and calls to external programs. Currently, HTML 3.0 provides a near-universal standard—but companies such as Netscape and Microsoft have created proprietary additions to the language to support their own systems.

Impression — Used to determine advertising rates, an impression refers to the moment that an individual views an ad, whether he or she responds to its message. On the Web, this is roughly equivalent to the number of times a Web page containing the ad is viewed by a visitor to the site.

Integrated Services Digital Network (ISDN) — Digital system developed 20 years ago by the phone companies but only now being put into widespread service. ISDN allows Internet users to send and receive information at up to 128,000 bits per second—five times faster than the best *modems*. While increasingly popular, ISDN is sometimes difficult to set up and is more expensive to use than modem connections.

Internet — Global network of computers running *TCP/IP* protocol and supporting services such as email, *Usenet* and the *World Wide Web.*

Internet Presence Provider (IPP) — A company that hosts Web sites created by other organizations on large, fast computers with high-speed connections to the Internet. IPPs may also provide programming and design services to their clients.

Internet Relay Chat (IRC) — Specialized, Internet-specific, text-only *chat* system that forms the basis for more sophisticated communication on the Web.

Internet Service Provider (ISP) — A company that provides Internet access, either through phone lines, *ISDN*, *leased-lines*, or other methods. Several thousand local, regional and national ISPs exist in the United States alone. ISPs may allow their customers to create basic Web sites in their access accounts and many also function as *Internet Presence Providers.*

InterNIC — The closest name to a centralized organization for the Internet, the InterNIC (http://www.internic.com) serves as an authority assigning *domain names* to individuals and groups.

Intranet — Specialized internal company network, that uses the Internet/Web model for sharing information. For a variety of reasons, Intranets are currently replacing older, proprietary networks used for similar purposes.

Java — Full-featured, advanced programming language developed by Sun Microsystems (http://www.sun.com). Java shifts the computing load from the central *server* to the user's local computer by downloading small, hardware-independent *applet* programs. By using the Internet for distribution Java promises to bypass traditional means for selling software.

JavaScript — Simplified form of the **Java** programming language that Web *browsers* such as Netscape can interpret. JavaScript allows developers to add useful functions to their Web pages without committing major programming efforts required for Java itself.

Key Escrow — Digital coding system used to ensure secure transmission of sensitive data over the Internet or other electronic networks.

Leased-Lines — Specialized, all-digital connections provided by phone companies that carry Internet traffic at much higher speeds than ordinary phone lines. *T1s* (about 1.4 megabit per second) and *T3s* (about 10 megabit per second) are the most common examples of leased lines.

Lingo — Name for a *Director*-specific programming language used to develop multimedia presentations.

Listserv — An electronic system enabling email exchange between a closed group, otherwise referred to as a *mailing list.* Listserv is also the name for a specific software package commonly used to support mailing lists.

Lynx — Text-only Web browser used on older computers which cannot display graphics or multimedia. Lynx is confined to university environments.

Mailing List — Electronic system enabling email exchange between a closed group of subscribers, frequently used to support specialized discussions.

Management Information Systems (MIS) — Department in many companies responsible for administration of computer hardware and software.

META — An *HTML* programming command that can be used by some *search engines* to record formatted information about the contents of a Web document.

Micropayments — One of several schemes being developed by online banking and financial institutions, enabling small ($1 or less) transactions over the Internet.

Mirror — Web site that stores and delivers a copy of another Web site's contents to a local or regional audience.

Modem — Electronic device that sends digital signals over phone lines. The current industry standard can send 28,800 bits per second, which is adequate for text and small graphics but too slow for high-fidelity audio and video.

Motion Picture Expert Group (MPEG) — Standard for reducing the size of large data files, usually containing audio and video content. MPEG-compressed audio and video files are several times smaller than the original, with some loss of fidelity and resolution. Popular in film and television, MPEG is not as efficient as competing technologies (such as *wavelet*) at providing the extreme compression required for delivering data over the Web.

Multicast — Generic term for Internet broadcasts that split the primary broadcast among a large number of computers for efficient delivery.

Multiuser Domain (MUD) — An Internet-specific game program providing text-only, multiuser fantasy adventures. MUD-style environments form the starting point for many graphical *virtual worlds* being developed.

Multiuser Domain/Object-Oriented (MOO) — Similar to a *MUD*, an Internet-specific game program that allows multiple users to interact in text-only, but complex, *virtual worlds*.

Multipurpose Internet Mail Extensions (MIME) — Data coding instructions that tell a computer how to interpret files after they are downloaded. For example, a computer receiving a graphical MIME-typed file can immediately select the appropriate graphics program for viewing it.

Musical Instrument Digital Interface (MIDI) — Music coding system which records features of a sound, including instrument and pitch, without actually sending an audio signal. MIDI commands are frequently used by computers to automatically operate synthesizers. On the Web, MIDI files provide an extremely fast, efficient way of delivering music to an audience—with the loss of real-time audio ambience.

Netpublicity — The process of promoting a Web site online, including *postings* to lists of Web addresses, email messages, and solicitation of awards and seals of approval from relevant organizations.

Netscape — Web *browser* software created by Netscape Communications Corp. (http://www.netscape.com) and the current standard for Web page visualization.

Network Access Points (NAPs) — Points of data interchange between phone companies or *ISPs* carrying Internet data.

Niche — In Internet terms, a small audience with highly specific interests that can be reached by highly targeted promotion and marketing techniques.

Outlink — A *hyperlink* on a Web site that points to other Web sites, making the Web a real "Web" of interconnections between content providers.

Packet — An individual piece of information created by splitting up a larger file. On the Internet, individual packets are sent separately through the network and reassembled into the original file at the receiving end. Using packets makes Internet transmissions extremely fault-tolerant and efficient at using available network *bandwidth*.

Point-to-Point Protocol (PPP) — Protocol used by many Internet communication devices to exchange digital data.

Posting — Information uploaded to Web sites or other Internet services by visitors. Postings allow a Web site's audience to modify the site's content; Web address postings are a common form of *netpublicity*.

Potty-mouth — Term for individual who uses email and other Internet communication primarily as a place to post foul and/or abusive language.

Practical Extraction and Report Language (Perl) — Simple, flexible and powerful programming language that allows rapid development of useful behind-the-scenes programs, frequently called by *Web servers* using *CGI* protocol.

Private Key — Used in many Internet security systems, it is an encrypted number stored by a Web browser that must be matched by a *public key* to initiate confidential communications.

Prosumer — A term popularized by futurist Alvin Toffler, it describes an individual who produces as much as he or she consumes—thereby going beyond the current producer-consumer divisions in society.

Proxy Server — Specialized Web server that regulates traffic between an individual's *Web browser* and another Web server. Most commonly used to enable Web communication through a *firewall*.

Public Key — Used in many Internet security systems, it is an encrypted number which must be sent to the holder of a *private key* to initiate confidential communications.

QuickTime — Digital movie standard developed by Apple Computer (http://www.quicktime.com). Its main advantage over other digital formats is its support for synchronizing audio and video tracks and for a wide variety of digital compression schemes.

QuickTime VR — An extension of QuickTime, it is a specialized movie which records a complete 360° view of an area.

Random-Access Memory (RAM) — Electronic memory on all computers. Different software requires varying amounts of RAM for its operation.

RealAudio — Sound delivery standard developed by Progressive Networks (http://www.realaudio.com), which makes it practical to deliver real-time music and voice over 14.4 and 28.8 *modems.*

Reciprocal Links — Hyperlinks on two Web sites that create a two-way path between them. Often created when sites decide to mutually share their visitor traffic.

Referer Log — File created by *Web servers* that records the last Web site a visitor was on before coming to the local site. Referer logs show which sites are delivering visitors to the local site.

Reservation Resource Protocol (RSVP) — Proposed standard that could improve audio and video delivery over the Internet by assigning priorities to individual data *packets.*

Router — Specialized computer whose sole purpose is to direct Internet traffic. Routers are essential for the functioning of the Internet.

Search Engine — A program that maintains a large database listing content on the Internet, that may be searched by keywords. Search engines have become a major tool for Internet navigation.

Serial Line Internet Protocol (SLIP) — A method enabling digital communications over phone and other lines, similar to *PPP* connections.

Server — A computer that responds to requests over a network by sending stored information. In the case of Web servers, this information consists of files with text, graphics, audio and video data. Servers designed specifically for particular media types (e.g., real-time audio and video) are also common on the Internet.

Server-push — Method for animating or updating Web pages in which a *Web server* periodically re-downloads information to a Web browser.

Server-Side Programs — Programs that execute behind-the-scenes on a *server* computer in conjunction with a Web server; they are distinguished by programs written in Java or ActiveX that execute on a client or user's computers after downloading. On the Web, *CGI* is the most common method used to call server-side programs.

Shell — Term for an old-style, text-only environment available to Internet users. Different types of shells are distinguished by the type and number of commands available for use.

Shockwave — Addition to Macromedia's Director multimedia authoring system that allows completed Director files to be used over the Web.

Shopping Cart — A type of ordering system common on Web sites where the *Web server* maintains a list of items selected by a visitor for possible purchase. Items in the virtual shopping cart can be examined, added to, deleted, or ordered at any time. Also referred to as a *shopping bag* system.

Snail Mail — Internet term for mail delivered by real-world postal services.

Spam — Mass email messages directed to unwilling recipients; an electronic form of direct postal mail. Widely disliked on the Internet, spammers frequently receive "back-talk" in the form of returned mail messages.

Spider — Program that automatically searches through all the Web sites on the Internet and catalogs their content in a database that may be used by a *search engine*.

Streaming — Method for transmitting audio, video, or multimedia program that breaks down the information and sends only those portions needed at a given time. For example, when audio and video is streamed, only the portions being listened to or viewed by the audience at any one time are sent. Streaming requires complex programming to run effectively over the Internet.

Strong Crypto — Slang term for information put into *unbreakable* code for secure transmission over electronic networks. Used on the Internet to protect sensitive information.

Structured Query Language (SQL) — Commonly used database programming language. Many programs exist that convert data between the Web and SQL databases.

Synchronous — Two-way data streams in which the sender and receiver communicate at the same time. Phone conversations are usually synchronous, as opposed to answering machines, which are *asynchronous.*

T1 — Common term for high-speed, digital *leased-line* which sends and receives data at 1.44 million bits per second. T1 speeds are required to support Web sites that receive thousands of visitors daily.

T3 — Common term for very high-speed digital *leased-line* that sends and receives data at 45 million bits per second. T3 lines are typically used to support thousands of *ISP* accounts or dozens to hundreds of Web sites.

Technologically Advanced First-Adopters (TAFs) — Term frequently used for consumers who are first to buy advanced electronic and computer equipment. Most of the Internet audience to date consists of this demographic subgroup of the general population.

Tele-Operation — The act of controlling a physical device, such as a camera, telescope, or robot arm remotely over a network. Many Web pages now allow access to shared devices that can be tele-operated.

Telnet — Internet protocol for sending and receiving text-only information, often used to access or directly control remote computers over a network.

Threaded Discussion Group — Specialized form of *posting* that puts comments and responses in a sequential list, allowing visitors to follow the train of thought in a discussion over time. The largest area with threaded groups on the Internet is *Usenet*.

Thumbnail — Generic term for small copy of a graphic, audio, or video clip which is preloaded. By allowing a site visitor to examine the thumbnails, Web sites can give their visitors a choice whether to take the time to *download* a larger file.

Transmission Communication Protocol/Internet Protocol (TCP/IP) — Basic, nonproprietary method used by all computers on the Internet for digital communication. To increase efficiency, TCP/IP breaks down information into small chunks, or *packets*, that are individually received and reassembled into the original file.

Uniform Resource Locator (URL) — Standard method for specifying the address of a Web site on the Internet.

UNIX To UNIX Copy Protocol (UUCP) — Older, pre-Internet method for computers to share data and thereby form a network. Primarily used to transmit *Usenet* information.

Upload — The process of sending digital data from a local computer to a recipient. Normally used to describe data sent by an Internet user to a centralized archive or *server.*

Usenet — A huge, text-only, *threaded discussion group* system on the Internet. Running independently of the Web, Usenet supports tens of thousands of discussions covering virtually any topic.

Virtual Reality Markup Language (VRML) — Language for creating *virtual worlds,* it shares simplicity and other features with the Web's *HTML*—and it is increasingly supported by many Web browsers. The current 2.0 version supports users interacting with and modifying a virtual world.

Virtual World — Software that creates the illusion that its users occupy a shared space, which may have attributes of the real world including time, light, motion, and even *digital organisms.*

Wavelet Compression — Developed by Houston Center for Advanced Technology (http://www.harc.edu), this technology is used to compress large audio and video files. Due to the method used to compress the information, it is better suited to delivering real-time audio and video through the Internet than competing technologies such as *MPEG.*

Web Rings — Developed as an alternate way of grouping Web sites with similar content, Web rings (http://www.webring.org) create a circle of *reciprocal links* that visitors can follow to reach each participating site.

Workstation — High-speed computer, typically tens to hundreds of times faster than personal computers but only costing a few times as much. Workstations are frequently used as Web *servers*, as well as for computer-hungry applications such as animation.

World Wide Web — Originally a system for sharing research documents, the Web has become a protocol for integrated multimedia delivery over the Internet using the *HTML* programming language.

INDEX

B

C

I

J

K

N

O

P

Q

R

S

T

U

What's on the CD-ROM

The following programs are included on the CD-ROM:

- CDLink
- CoolFusion
- Crescendo
- Eudora
- Fractal Imager
- FutureSplash
- HTML Transit
- Internet Fast Forward
- Leonardo Internet
- Microsoft Internet Exporer
- The Palace
- Projector
- Pueblo
- Rapid Transit Player
- Sizzler
- The TOOB
- VDOLive
- V-Realm
- VR Scout

What's on the Web Site

Visit the Web site (http://kspace.com/intertainment) for updates and new information related to the material in this book, links to Intertainment resources and companies described in the book, as well as forms for ordering additional copies of the book online.